**Fodor's 2003**

# Vancouver and British Columbia

The Guide
for All Budgets

Completely
Updated

Where to Stay, Eat,
and Explore

On and Off
the Beaten Path

When to Go,
What to Pack

Maps, Travel Tips,
and Web Sites

Fodor's Travel Publications • New York, Toronto, London, Sydney, Auckland
**www.fodors.com**

# Vancouver and British Columbia 2003

**EDITOR:** William Travis

**Editorial Contributor:** Sue Kernaghan
**Maps:** David Lindroth, *cartographer;* Rebecca Baer and Robert Blake, *map editors*
**Design:** Fabrizio La Rocca, *creative director;* Guido Caroti, *art director;* Jolie Novak, *senior picture editor;* Melanie Marin, *photo editor*
**Cover Design:** Pentagram
**Production/Manufacturing:** Colleen Ziemba
**Cover Photo** (Butchart Gardens): Paul A. Souders/Corbis

## Copyright

ISBN 1–4000–1100–0

ISSN 1531–3425

## Important Tip

Although all prices, opening times, and other details in this book are based on information supplied to us at press time, changes occur all the time in the travel world, and Fodor's cannot accept responsibility for facts that become outdated or for inadvertent errors or omissions. So **always confirm information when it matters,** especially if you're making a detour to visit a specific place.

## Special Sales

Fodor's Travel Publications are available at special discounts for bulk purchases for sales promotions or premiums. Special editions, including personalized covers, excerpts of existing guides, and corporate imprints, can be created in large quantities for special needs. For more information, contact your local bookseller or write to Special Markets, Fodor's Travel Publications, 1745 Broadway, New York, NY 10019. Inquiries from Canada should be directed to your local Canadian bookseller or sent to Random House of Canada, Ltd., Marketing Department, 2775 Matheson Boulevard East, Mississauga, Ontario L4W 4P7. Inquiries from the United Kingdom should be sent to Fodor's Travel Publications, 20 Vauxhall Bridge Road, London SW1V 2SA, England.

PRINTED IN THE UNITED STATES OF AMERICA

10 9 8 7 6 5 4 3 2 1

# CONTENTS

# ON THE ROAD WITH FODOR'S

A trip takes you out of yourself. Concerns of life at home completely disappear, driven away by more immediate thoughts—about, say, what marvels will beguile the next day, or where you'll have dinner. That's where Fodor's comes in. We make sure that you know all your options, so that you don't miss something that's around the next bend just because you didn't know it was there. Mindful that the best memories of your trip might have nothing to do with what you came to Vancouver and British Columbia to see, we guide you to sights large and small all over town. You might set out for dinner in Vancouver, but back at home you find yourself unable to forget the whales you saw off the coast of Tofino or strolling through Butchart Gardens. With Fodor's at your side, serendipitous discoveries are never far away.

## About Our Writers

Our success in showing you every corner of Vancouver and British Columbia is a credit to our extraordinary writers. Although there's no substitute for travel advice from a good friend who knows your style, our contributors are the next best thing—the kind of people you would poll for travel advice if you knew them.

Vancouver-born freelance writer **Sue Kernaghan,** now a resident of Salt Spring Island, enjoyed getting reacquainted with her hometown for this book. A fourth-generation British Columbian, Sue has gathered historical insights and covered a lot of dirt roads, open water, and country pubs while researching the places covered in this book.

## How to Use This Book

Up front is **Smart Travel Tips A to Z,** arranged alphabetically by topic and loaded with tips, Web sites, and contact information. **Destination: Vancouver and British Columbia** helps get you in the mood for your trip. Subsequent chapters in Vancouver and British Columbia are arranged regionally. All city chapters begin with exploring information, with a section for each neighborhood

(each recommending a good tour and listing sights alphabetically). All regional chapters are divided geographically; within each area, towns are covered in logical geographical order, and attractive stretches of road between them are indicated by the designation En Route. To help you decide what you'll have time to visit, all chapters begin with our writers' favorite itineraries. (Mix itineraries from several chapters, and you can put together a really exceptional trip.) The A to Z section that ends every chapter lists additional resources.

## Icons and Symbols

★  Our special recommendations
✕  Restaurant
🏠  Lodging establishment
⚠  Campgrounds
☺  Good for kids (rubber duck)
☞  Sends you to another section of the guide for more information
✉  Address
☎  Telephone number
☉  Opening and closing times
💲  Admission prices (those we give apply to adults; substantially reduced fees are almost always available for children, students, and senior citizens)

Numbers in white and black circles ③ ❸ that appear on the maps, in the margins, and within the tours correspond to one another.

## Don't Forget to Write

Your experiences—positive and negative—matter to us. If we have missed or misstated something, we want to hear about it. We follow up on all suggestions. Contact the Vancouver and British Columbia editor at editors@fodors.com or c/o Fodor's at 1745 Broadway, New York, NY 10019. And have a fabulous trip!

Karen Cure
*Editorial Director*

# ESSENTIAL INFORMATION

## AIR TRAVEL

### BOOKING

When you book **look for nonstop flights** and **remember that "direct" flights stop at least once.** Try to avoid connecting flights, which require a change of plane. Two airlines may operate a connecting flight jointly, so ask if your airline operates every segment of the trip; you may find that the carrier you prefer flies you only part of the way. To find more booking tips and to check prices and make on-line flight reservations, log on to www.fodors.com.

### CARRIERS

When flying internationally, you must usually choose between a domestic carrier, the national flag carrier of the country you are visiting, and a foreign carrier from a third country. National flag carriers have the greatest number of nonstops. Domestic carriers may have better connections to your hometown and serve a greater number of gateway cities. Third-party carriers may have a price advantage.

Of the U.S. airlines, American, Continental, Delta, Northwest, and United fly to Vancouver. Among smaller carriers, Horizon Air (an affiliate of Alaska Airlines) flies to Vancouver and Victoria from many western U.S. cities. From the United Kingdom, Air Canada and British Airways fly to Vancouver. Canadian charter line Air Transat flies to Montréal and Toronto, with connections to Vancouver, usually at lower rates than the other airlines offer.

Within Canada, regularly scheduled flights to every major city and to most smaller cities are available on Air Canada and its regional feeder airlines. Air Canada Tango provides discounted service to most Canadian cities. Air Canada's regional carrier, Air Canada Jazz, flies to most major towns in B.C. WestJet is a regional carrier serving western Canada, Ontario, and New Brunswick. Within B.C., WestJet flies to Vancouver, Victoria, Abbotsford, Comox, Kelowna, and Prince George.

For more information on flights within British Columbia, *see* the A to Z sections in each chapter.

For regulations and for the locations of air bases that allow private flights, check with regional tourist agencies for carriers and with the Transport Canada Centre in Vancouver. Private pilots should obtain information from the Canada Map Office, which has the "Canada Flight Supplement" (lists of airports with Canada Customs services) as well as aeronautical charts.

➤ MAJOR AIRLINES: **Air Canada** (☎ 888/422–7533, WEB www.aircanada. ca). **American** (☎ 800/433–7300, WEB www.aa.com). **Continental** (☎ 800/525–0280, WEB www.continental. com). **Delta** (☎ 800/241–4141, WEB www.delta.com). **Northwest** (☎ 800/ 225–2525, WEB www.nwa.com). **United** (☎ 800/241–6522, WEB www. ual.com).

➤ SMALLER AIRLINES: **Horizon Air** (☎ 800/547–9308, WEB www. horizonair.com).

➤ FROM AUSTRALIA AND NEW ZEALAND: **Air Canada** (☎ 612/9286–8900 in Sydney; 649/379–3371 in Auckland; WEB www.aircanada.ca). **Air New Zealand** (☎ 800/663–5494 in Vancouver; 0800/737–767 in Auckland; WEB www.airnz.com). **Qantas** (☎ 800/227–4500; 612/13–13–13 in Sydney; WEB www.qantas.com.au).

➤ FROM THE U.K.: **Air Canada** (☎ 0870/524–7226, WEB www.aircanada. ca). **Air Transat** (☎ 877/872–6728; 8457/125–478 in the U.K.; WEB www. airtransat.com). **British Airways** (☎ 0845/773–3377 or 800/247–9297, WEB www.britishairways.com).

➤ WITHIN CANADA: **Air Canada** (☎ 888/247–2262, WEB www.aircanada. ca). **Air Canada Tango** (✉ ☎ 800/ 315–1390, WEB www.flytango.com). **WestJet Airlines** (☎ 800/538–5696, WEB www.westjet.com).

➤ CONTACTS FOR PRIVATE PILOTS: **Canada Map Office** (✉ 130 Bentley Ave., Nepean, Ontario K1A 0E9, ☎ 800/465–6277, WEB aero.nrcan.gc.ca).

## CHECK-IN AND BOARDING

Always **ask your carrier about its check-in policy.** Plan to arrive at the airport about 2 hours before your scheduled departure time for domestic flights and 2½ to 3 hours before international flights. Assuming that not everyone with a ticket will show up, airlines routinely overbook planes. When everyone does, airlines ask for volunteers to give up their seats. In return, these volunteers usually get a certificate for a free flight and are rebooked on the next flight out. If there are not enough volunteers, the airline must choose who will be denied boarding. The first to get bumped are passengers who checked in late and those flying on discounted tickets, so **get to the gate and check in as early as possible,** especially during peak periods.

Always **bring a government-issued photo ID to the airport;** even when it's not required, a passport is best. You will be asked to show it before you are allowed to check in. U.S. Customs and Immigration maintains offices at the airports in Montréal, Toronto, and Vancouver; U.S.-bound passengers should arrive early enough to clear customs before their flight.

Security measures at Canadian airports are similar to those in the United States. Be sure you're not carrying anything that could be construed as a weapon: a letter opener, Swiss Army knife, or a toy weapon, for example. Flights departing from Canadian airports are assessed a $12 security fee, to help pay for increased airport security measures. Some airlines include this fee in the price of the ticket.

Passengers departing from Vancouver must pay an airport-improvement fee before they can board their plane.

The fee is C$5 for flights within British Columbia, C$10 for flights within North America, and C$15 for overseas flights. Cash and credit cards are accepted.

## CUTTING COSTS

The least expensive airfares to Canada are priced for round-trip travel and must usually be purchased in advance. Airlines generally allow you to change your return date for a fee; most low-fare tickets, however, are nonrefundable. It's smart to **call a number of airlines,** and when you are quoted a good price, **book it on the spot**—the same fare may not be available the next day. Always **check different routings** and look into using alternate airports. Also, price off-peak flights, which may be significantly less expensive than others. Travel agents, especially low-fare specialists (☞ Discounts and Deals), are helpful.

Consolidators are another good source. They buy tickets for scheduled international flights at reduced rates from the airlines, then sell them at prices that beat the best fare available directly from the airlines. Sometimes you can even get your money back if you need to return the ticket. Carefully read the fine print detailing penalties for changes and cancellations, purchase the ticket with a credit card, and **confirm your consolidator reservation with the airline.**

➤ CONSOLIDATORS: **Cheap Tickets** (☎ 800/377–1000 or 888/922–8849, WEB www.cheaptickets.com). **Discount Travel Network** (☎ 800/409–6753, WEB www.bestfares.com).

## ENJOYING THE FLIGHT

**State your seat preference** when purchasing your ticket, and then repeat it when you confirm and when you check in. For more legroom, you can request one of the few emergency-aisle seats at check-in, if you are capable of lifting at least 50 pounds—a Federal Aviation Administration requirement of passengers in these seats. Seats behind a bulkhead also offer more legroom, but they don't have under-seat storage. Don't sit in the row in front of the emergency aisle or in front of a bulkhead, where seats may not recline.

If you have dietary concerns, **ask for special meals when booking.** These can be vegetarian, low-cholesterol, or kosher, for example. It's a good idea to pack some healthy snacks and a small (plastic) bottle of water in your carry-on bag. On long flights, try to maintain a normal routine, to help fight jet lag. At night, **get some sleep.** By day, **eat light meals, drink water** (not alcohol), and **move around the cabin** to stretch your legs. For additional jet-lag tips consult *Fodor's FYI: Travel Fit & Healthy* (available at bookstores everywhere).

Smoking policies vary from carrier to carrier. Many airlines prohibit smoking on all of their international flights; others allow smoking only on certain routes or certain departures. Ask your carrier about its policy. None of the major airlines or charter lines permit smoking, and all Canadian carriers ban smoking.

### FLYING TIMES

Flying time to Vancouver is 5½ hours from New York, 6½ hours from Montréal, 4 hours from Chicago, and 2½ hours from Los Angeles.

### HOW TO COMPLAIN

If your baggage goes astray or your flight goes awry, complain right away. Most carriers require that you **file a claim immediately.** The Aviation Consumer Protection Division of the Department of Transportation publishes *Fly-Rights,* which discusses airlines and consumer issues and is available on-line. At PassengerRights. com, a Web site, you can compose a letter of complaint and distribute it electronically.

➤ AIRLINE COMPLAINTS: **Aviation Consumer Protection Division** (✉ U.S. Department of Transportation, Room 4107, C-75, Washington, DC 20590, ☎ 202/366–2220, WEB www. dot.gov/airconsumer). **Federal Aviation Administration Consumer Hotline** (☎ 800/322–7873).

### RECONFIRMING

Check the status of your flight before you leave for the airport. You can do this on your carrier's Web site, by linking to a flight-status checker (many Web booking services offer these), or by calling your carrier or travel agent. Always confirm international flights at least 72 hours ahead of the scheduled departure time.

### AIRPORTS

The major airport is Vancouver International Airport (YVR). For information on regional airports, *see* the A to Z sections in each chapter.

➤ AIRPORT INFORMATION: **Vancouver International Airport** (✉ Grant McConachie Way, Richmond, ☎ 604/ 207–7077, WEB www.yvr.ca).

### BIKE TRAVEL

Despite British Columbia's demanding landscape, bicycle travel is very popular. One of the most spectacular routes follows the abandoned 600-km-long (370-mi-long) Kettle Valley Railway through the mountains of the B.C. interior. The Kelowna Visitors Bureau has details. Gentler options include the 100-km (62-mi) Galloping Goose Regional Trail near Victoria and the rolling hills of the Gulf Islands. The Cycling Victoria Web site has information about bike touring on Vancouver Island and the Gulf Islands.

➤ BIKE MAPS: **Cycling Victoria** (☎ no phone, WEB www.cyclingvictoria.com). **Galloping Goose Regional Trail** (☎ 250/478–3344, WEB www.crd.bc.ca/ parks). **Kelowna Visitors Bureau** (☎ 250/861–1515).

### BIKES IN FLIGHT

Most airlines accommodate bikes as luggage, provided they are dismantled and boxed; check with individual airlines about packing requirements. Airlines sell bike boxes, which are often free at bike shops, for about $15 (bike bags start at $100). International travelers often can substitute a bike for a piece of checked luggage at no charge; otherwise, the cost is about $100. Domestic and Canadian airlines charge $40–$80 each way.

### BOAT AND FERRY TRAVEL

Ferries play a central role in British Columbia's transportation network. In some areas, ferries provide the only access (besides floatplanes) into and out of communities. For visitors, ferries are one of the best ways to get a feel for the region and its ties to the sea. The British Columbia (BC) Ferry Corporation operates one of the largest ferry fleets in the world, serving about 40 ports of call on the west coast. The ferries carry all vehicles as well as bicycles and foot passengers.

Reservations are required for vehicles on BC Ferries' Inside Passage services; they are optional on services between Vancouver and Vancouver Island and between Vancouver and the Southern Gulf Islands. Most other services do not accept reservations and load vehicles on a first-come, first-served basis.

Ferries operate between the state of Washington and British Columbia's Vancouver Island, and coastal freighters take passengers and supplies to remote Vancouver Island outports. For additional information about regional ferry service, *see* individual chapters.

### FARES AND SCHEDULES

Payments and reservations are accepted in advance via phone or the Internet on reservable routes; for other routes, you must purchase tickets at the terminal before sailing time. BC Ferries accepts cash and traveler's checks in Canadian and U.S. funds at all of its terminals; American Express, MasterCard, and Visa are accepted at all but the smallest terminals. Direct debit or Interac payments are not accepted. Always check with BC Ferries before traveling; check-in times vary by route and season.

➤ BOAT AND FERRY INFORMATION: **British Columbia (BC) Ferry Corporation** (✉ 1112 Fort St., Victoria, BC V8V 4V2, ☎ 250/386–3431; 888/ 223–3779 in British Columbia outside Victoria; WEB www.bcferries.com).

### BUS TRAVEL

Greyhound serves most towns in the province and provides frequent service on popular runs. Laidlaw Coach Lines serves most towns on Vancouver Island, Malaspina Coach Lines provides service from Vancouver to towns on the Sunshine Coast, and Pacific Coach Lines operates frequent service between Victoria and Vancouver on BC Ferries. All bus companies

ban smoking, and most long-distance buses have washrooms on board. Some long-haul buses even play videos.

### CUTTING COSTS

Greyhound's Canada Coach Pass provides unlimited bus travel for 7, 10, 15, 21, 30, 45, or 60 days between points from Halifax to the west coast. You must purchase these passes in Canada, at any Greyhound terminal. Greyhound also has passes that allow unlimited travel throughout North America, or travel throughout the western or eastern half of the continent. All these passes are an excellent value for travelers who want to wander the highways and byways of the country, packing a lot of miles into a relatively short period of time. However, for occasional, short daytrips, they're hardly worth it.

➤ DISCOUNT PASSES: **Greyhound Lines** (✉ 877 Greyhound Way SW, Calgary, AB T3C 3V8, ☎ 800/661–8747 in Canada; 800/231–2222 in the U.S.; WEB www.greyhound.ca).

### FARES AND SCHEDULES

Bus terminals in major cities and even in many smaller ones are usually efficient operations with service all week and plenty of agents on hand to handle ticket sales. In villages and some smaller towns, the bus station is simply a counter in a local convenience store, gas station, or snack bar. Getting information on schedules beyond the local ones is sometimes difficult in these places. For information on specific destinations within British Columbia, *see* the A to Z sections at the end of each chapter.

### PAYING

In major bus terminals, most bus lines accept at least some of the major credit cards. Some smaller lines require cash or take only Visa or MasterCard. All accept traveler's checks in U.S. or Canadian currency with suitable identification, but it's advisable to exchange foreign currency (including U.S. currency) at a bank or exchange office. To buy a ticket in really small centers, it's best to use cash.

## RESERVATIONS

Most bus lines do not accept reservations. You should plan on picking up your tickets at least 45 minutes before the bus's scheduled departure time.

➤ BUS INFORMATION: **Greyhound Lines** (✉ 877 Greyhound Way SW, Calgary, AB T3C 3V8, ☎ 800/661–8747 in Canada; 800/231–2222 in the U.S.; WEB www.greyhound.ca). In the United Kingdom: **Greyhound International** (✉ Sussex House, London Rd., E. Grinstead, East Sussex RHI9 1LD, ☎ 01342/317317). **Laidlaw Coach Lines** (☎ 250/385–4411 or 800/663–8390; 800/318–0818 in British Columbia). **Malaspina Coach Lines** (☎ 877/227–8287). **Pacific Coach Lines** (☎ 604/662–8074 or 800/661–1725, WEB www.pacificcoach.com).

## BUSINESS HOURS

### BANKS AND OFFICES

Most banks in British Columbia are open Monday–Thursday 10–3 and Friday 10–5 or 6. Some banks are open longer hours and also on Saturday morning. All banks are closed on national holidays. Most banks (and some gas stations and convenience stores) have automatic teller machines (ATMs) that are accessible around the clock. Many small islands and rural areas, however, do not have ATMs.

### GAS STATIONS

Most highway and city gas stations in Canada are open daily (although there's rarely a mechanic on duty Sunday), and some are open around the clock. In small towns, gas stations are often closed on Sunday, although they may take turns staying open.

### MUSEUMS AND SIGHTS

Hours at museums vary, but most open at 10 or 11 and close in the evening. Some smaller museums close for lunch. Many museums are closed on Monday; some make up for it by staying open late on Wednesday or Thursday, often waiving admission.

### PHARMACIES

Pharmacies are usually open daily 9–6, though some small-town outlets may close on Sunday. (*See* individual chapter A to Z sections for locations of late-night pharmacies.)

## SHOPS

Stores in B.C. are usually open Monday–Saturday 9–6. Shops in the major cities and in areas frequented by tourists are usually open Sunday as well. Stores often stay open Thursday and Friday evenings, most shopping malls until 9 PM. Many supermarkets are open 7:30 AM–9 PM, and some food and convenience stores in Vancouver are open 24 hours. B.C.'s government-run liquor stores are closed on Sunday, but most towns also have a private beer and wine store that stays open evenings and on Sunday.

## CAMERAS
## AND PHOTOGRAPHY

Canada is one of the world's most scenic countries, and the misty light of the West Coast is particularly intriguing for photographers. The natural splendor of British Columbia vies for the attention of your camera lens.

The *Kodak Guide to Shooting Great Travel Pictures* (available at bookstores everywhere) is loaded with tips.

➤ PHOTO HELP: **Kodak Information Center** (☎ 800/242–2424, WEB www.kodak.com).

### EQUIPMENT PRECAUTIONS

Water, whether from rain, atmospheric humidity, sea, or river spray, is the camera's biggest enemy in British Columbia. Local photographers tuck silica gel packs into their camera cases to absorb moisture and take a small hand towel to wipe off raindrops. On rafting or whale-watching trips (where salt spray is especially damaging to equipment), consider taking a waterproof or a disposable camera instead of your usual equipment. Light conditions can change rapidly in B.C., so you may want to pack a variety of film speeds. Be sure to stock up on slide and high-speed film in cities; both are hard to find in the backcountry. Also, consider packing something red for your traveling companion to wear: it makes a nice contrast to the province's pervasive greens and blues.

**Don't pack film and equipment in checked luggage,** where it is much more susceptible to damage. X-ray machines used to view checked luggage are becoming much more powerful and therefore are much more likely to ruin your film. Try to **ask for hand inspection of film,** which becomes clouded after repeated exposure to airport X-ray machines, and **keep videotapes and computer disks away from metal detectors.** Always keep film, tape, and computer disks **out of the sun.** Carry an extra supply of batteries, and **be prepared to turn on your camera, camcorder, or laptop** to prove to airport security personnel that the device is real.

## CAR RENTAL

Rates in Vancouver begin at about $40 a day or $230 a week. Car rentals in B.C. also incur a 14.5% sales tax, a $1.50-per-day social services tax, and a vehicle licensing fee of 91¢ per day. An additional 15.44% Concession Recovery Fee, an extra fee charged by the airport authority for retail space in the terminal, is levied at airport locations. If you prefer a manual-transmission car, check whether the rental agency of your choice offers stick shifts; some companies, such as Avis, don't in Canada.

➤ MAJOR AGENCIES: **Alamo** (☎ 800/522–9696; 099/0999–4000 in the U.K.; WEB www.alamo.com). **Avis** (☎ 800/331–1084; 800/879–2847 in Canada; 02/9353–9000 in Australia; 09/526–2847 in New Zealand; 0870/606–0100 in the U.K.; WEB www.avis.com). **Budget** (☎ 800/527–0700; 0870/156–5656 in the U.K.; WEB www.budget.com). **Dollar** (☎ 800/800–6000; 0124/622–0111 in the U.K., where it's affiliated with Sixt; 02/9223–1444 in Australia; WEB www.dollar.com). **Hertz** (☎ 800/654–3001; 800/263–0600 in Canada; 020/8897–2072 in the U.K.; 02/9669–2444 in Australia; 09/256–8690 in New Zealand; WEB www.hertz.com). **National Car Rental** (☎ 800/227–7368; 020/8680–4800 in the U.K.; WEB www.nationalcar.com).

### CUTTING COSTS

Car rental rates vary by supply and demand, so it pays to shop around and to reserve well in advance. Vancouver's airport and downtown locations usually have the best selection. Some car rental agencies itemize fees, and some roll it into their rental rates. When comparing costs, take into account any mileage charges: an arrangement with unlimited mileage is usually the best deal if you plan to tour the province.

For a good deal, **book through a travel agent, who will shop around.** Also, **price local car-rental companies**— whose prices may be lower still, although their service and maintenance may not be as good as those of major rental agencies—and **research rates on-line.** Remember to ask about required deposits, cancellation penalties, and drop-off charges if you're planning to pick up the car in one city and leave it in another. If you're traveling during a holiday period, also make sure that a confirmed reservation guarantees you a car.

### INSURANCE

When driving a rented car you are generally responsible for any damage to or loss of the vehicle. You may also be liable for any property damage or personal injury that you may cause while driving. Before you rent, see what coverage you already have under the terms of your personal auto-insurance policy and credit cards.

### REQUIREMENTS AND RESTRICTIONS

In Canada your own driver's license is acceptable. In B.C., children up to 40 pounds or 18 kilos in weight must use a child seat. Car seats cost about C$8 per day; fees vary, however, by agency. Additional drivers are charged about C$5 per day. Some agencies put a cap on these fees for longer rentals.

### SURCHARGES

Before you pick up a car in one city and leave it in another, **ask about drop-off charges or one-way service fees,** which can be substantial. Note, too, that some rental agencies charge extra if you return the car before the time specified in your contract. To avoid a hefty refueling fee, **fill the tank just before you turn in the car,** but be aware that gas stations near the rental outlet may overcharge. It's almost never a deal to buy the tank of gas in the car when you rent it; the understanding is that you'll return it empty, but some fuel usually remains.

## CAR TRAVEL

Canada's highway system is excellent. It includes the Trans-Canada Highway, which uses several numbers and is the longest highway in the world—running about 8,000 km (5,000 mi) from Victoria, British Columbia, to St. John's, Newfoundland, using ferries to bridge coastal waters at each end. The second-longest Canadian highway, the Yellowhead Highway (Highway 16), follows a route from the Pacific Coast and over the Rockies to the prairies. North of the population centers, roads become fewer and less developed.

Your driver's license may not be recognized outside your home country. International driving permits (IDPs) are available from the American and Canadian automobile associations and, in the United Kingdom, from the Automobile Association and Royal Automobile Club. These international permits, valid only in conjunction with your regular driver's license, are universally recognized; having one may save you a problem with local authorities.

### FROM THE U.S.

Drivers must carry owner registration and proof of insurance coverage, which is compulsory in Canada. The Canadian Non-Resident Inter-Provincial Motor Vehicle Liability Insurance Card, available from any U.S. insurance company, is accepted as evidence of financial responsibility in Canada. If you are driving a car that is not registered in your name, carry a letter from the owner that authorizes your use of the vehicle.

The main entry point into British Columbia from the United States by car is on I–5 at Blaine, Washington, 48 km (30 mi) south of Vancouver. Three highways enter British Columbia from the east: Highway 1, or the Trans-Canada Highway; Highway 3, or the Crowsnest Highway, which crosses southern British Columbia; and Highway 16, the Yellowhead Highway, which runs through northern British Columbia from the Rocky Mountains to Prince Rupert. From Alaska and the Yukon, take the Alaska Highway (from Fairbanks) or the Klondike Highway (from Skagway or Dawson City).

Border-crossing procedures are usually quick and simple (☞ Passports and Visas). Every British Columbia border crossing (except the one at Aldergrove, which closes at midnight) is open 24 hours. The I–5 border crossing at Blaine, Washington (also known as the Douglas, or Peace Arch, border crossing), is one of the busiest border crossings between the United States and Canada. Weekend and holiday traffic tends to be heaviest; listen to local radio traffic reports for information about wait times.

➤ INSURANCE INFORMATION: **Insurance Corporation of British Columbia** (ICBC; ☎ 604/661–2800 or 800/663–1466, WEB www.icbc.com).

### EMERGENCY SERVICES

In case of emergency anywhere in B.C., call **911**; if you are not connected immediately, dial "0" and ask for the operator. The British Columbia Automobile Association (BCAA) provides 24-hour roadside assistance to AAA and CAA members.

➤ ROADSIDE ASSISTANCE: **BCAA** (☎ 604/268–5555 or 800/663–1956; nonemergencies; 604/293–2222 or 800/222–4357 emergencies; WEB www.bcaa.com).

### RULES OF THE ROAD

By law, you are required to wear seat belts (and to use infant seats). Motorcycle and bicycle helmets are mandatory. Right turns are permitted on red signals. Speed limits, given in kilometers, are usually within the 50–110 kph (30–66 mph) range outside the cities.

### WINTER DRIVING

In coastal areas, the mild, damp climate contributes to roadways that are frequently wet. Winter snowfalls are not common (generally only once or twice a year), but when snow does fall, traffic grinds to a halt and the roadways become treacherous and stay that way until the snow melts.

Tire chains, studs, or snow tires are essential equipment for winter travel in mountain areas such as Whistler, British Columbia. If you're planning to drive into high elevations, be sure to check the weather forecast beforehand. Even the main-highway mountain passes can be forced to close because of snow conditions. During the winter months, provincial highway departments operate snow-advisory telephone lines that give pass conditions.

## CHILDREN
## IN BRITISH COLUMBIA

Travelers crossing the border with children should **carry identification for them** similar to that required by adults (i.e., passport or birth certificate). Children traveling with one parent or other adult should **bring a letter of permission** from the other parent, parents, or legal guardian. Divorced parents with shared custody rights should **carry legal documents establishing their status.**

If you are renting a car, don't forget to **arrange for a car seat** when you reserve. For general advice about traveling with children, consult *Fodor's FYI: Travel with Your Baby* (available in bookstores everywhere).

➤ LOCAL INFORMATION: **Tourism Vancouver**'s free *Kids Guide Vancouver* is available on its Web site or at brochure racks around town.

### FLYING

If your children are two or older, **ask about children's airfares.** As a general rule, infants under two not occupying a seat fly at greatly reduced fares or even for free. When booking, **confirm carry-on allowances** if you're traveling with infants. In general, for babies charged 10% of the adult fare you are allowed one carry-on bag and a collapsible stroller; if the flight is full, the stroller may have to be checked or you may be limited to less.

Experts agree that it's a good idea to use safety seats aloft for children weighing less than 40 pounds. Airlines set their own policies: U.S. carriers usually require that the child be ticketed, even if he or she is young enough to ride free, since the seats must be strapped into regular seats.

Do **check your airline's policy about using safety seats during takeoff and landing.** Safety seats are not allowed everywhere in the plane, so get your seat assignments as early as possible.

When reserving, **request children's meals or a freestanding bassinet** (not available at all airlines) if you need them. But note that bulkhead seats, where you must sit to use the bassinet, may lack an overhead bin or storage space on the floor.

### LODGING

Most hotels in British Columbia allow children under a certain age to stay in their parents' room at no extra charge, but others charge for them as extra adults; be sure to **find out the cutoff age for children's discounts.**

➤ BEST CHOICES: **Lake Okanagan Resort** (✉ ☎ 250/769–3511 or 800/663–3273). **Manteo Resort Waterfront Hotel and Villas** (✉ ☎ 250/860–1031 or 800/445–5255). **Tigh-na-Mara Resort** (✉ ☎ 250/248–2072 or 800/663–7373).

### SIGHTS AND ATTRACTIONS

Places that are especially appealing to children are indicated by a rubber-duckie icon (🐥) in the margin. In Vancouver, Granville Island has both a children's water park and the toy-and-games-filled Kids' Market. Stanley Park, with its aquarium, miniature train, petting zoo, and beaches, is also a must-see for kids, as are the science-oriented exhibits at Science World and the H. R. MacMillan Space Centre. In Victoria, must-sees are the Bug Zoo and the lifelike exhibits (including a simulated submarine ride) at the Royal British Columbia Museum. Farther afield, the sandy beaches and warm waters of Okanagan Lake and the eastern shore of Vancouver island make these two top family destinations. Whistler Resort is justifiably famous for its year-round family activities, but the smaller, less expensive ski resorts in the High Country and the Okanagan are good value for money and have plenty of kid-oriented activities.

## CONSUMER PROTECTION

Whether you're shopping for gifts or purchasing travel services, **pay with a major credit card** whenever possible, so you can cancel payment or get reimbursed if there's a problem (and you can provide documentation) This also ensures that you receive a fair exchange rate on your currency. If you're doing business with a particular company for the first time, **contact your local Better Business Bureau and the attorney general's offices** in your state and (for U.S. businesses) the company's home state as well. Have any complaints been filed? Finally, if you're buying a package or tour, always **consider travel insurance** that includes default coverage (☞ Insurance, *below*).

➤ BBBs: **Council of Better Business Bureaus** (✉ 4200 Wilson Blvd., Suite 800, Arlington, VA 22203, ☎ 703/276–0100, FAX 703/525–8277, WEB www.bbb.org).

## CRUISE TRAVEL

Vancouver is the major embarkation point for Alaska cruises, and virtually all Alaska-bound cruise ships call there; some also call at Victoria and Prince Rupert. Once leaving Vancouver, however, most luxury liners make straight for Alaska, leaving the fjords and islands of B.C. to smaller vessels and expedition ships. Some operators lead sailing trips around B.C.'s islands; independent travelers can explore the coast on BC Ferries or on one of the coastal freighters serving remote outposts. (*See* individual chapters for more information about ferry and freighter travel.)

To learn how to plan, choose, and book a cruise-ship voyage, consult *Fodor's FYI: Plan & Enjoy Your Cruise* (available in bookstores everywhere).

➤ CRUISE LINES: **Carnival Cruise Lines** (☎ 800/327–9501, WEB www.carnival.com). **Crystal Cruises** (☎ 310/785–9300 or 800/446–6620, WEB www.crystalcruises.com). **Celebrity Cruises** (☎ 800/437–3111, WEB www.celebritycruises.com). **Holland America** (☎ 206/281–3535 or 877/724–5425, WEB www.hollandamerica.com). **Norwegian Cruise Lines** (☎ 305/436–4000 or 800/327–7030, WEB www.ncl.com). **Princess Cruises** (☎ 661/753–0000 or 800/568–3262, WEB www.princess.com). **Radisson Seven Seas Cruises**

(☎ 800/285–1835, WEB www.rssc.com). **Royal Caribbean** (☎ 800/327–6700, WEB www.royalcaribbean.com). **World Explorer Cruises** (☎ 415/820–9200 or 800/854–3835, WEB www.wecruise.com).

The small, expedition-style ships operated by American Safari Cruises, Clipper Cruise Lines, and Cruise West explore the British Columbia coast on their way to Alaska. Bluewater Adventures has 8- to 10-day sailing cruises of the B.C. coastline, including the Queen Charlotte Islands.

➤ LOCAL CRUISE LINES: **American Safari Cruises** (✉ 19101 36th Ave. W, Suite 201, Lynnwood, WA 98036, ☎ 425/776–4700 or 888/862–8881, WEB www.amsafari.com). **Bluewater Adventures** (✉ 3–252 E. 1st St., North Vancouver V7L 1B3, ☎ 604/980–3800 or 888/877–1770, WEB www.bluewateradventures.ca). **Clipper Cruise Lines** (✉ 11969 Westline Industrial Dr., St. Louis, MO 63146–3220, ☎ 314/727–2929 or 800/325–0010, WEB www.clippercruise.com). **Cruise West** (✉ 2401 4th Ave., Suite 700, Seattle, WA 98121-1438, ☎ 206/441–8687 or 800/580–0072, WEB www.cruisewest.com).

## CUSTOMS AND DUTIES

When shopping abroad, **keep receipts** for all purchases. Upon reentering the country, **be ready to show customs officials what you've bought.** If you feel a duty is incorrect, appeal the assessment. If you object to the way your clearance was handled, note the inspector's badge number. In either case, first ask to see a supervisor. If the problem isn't resolved, write to the appropriate authorities, beginning with the port director at your point of entry.

### IN AUSTRALIA

Australian residents who are 18 or older may bring home A\$400 worth of souvenirs and gifts (including jewelry), 250 cigarettes or 250 grams of tobacco, and 1,125 ml of alcohol (including wine, beer, and spirits). Residents under 18 may bring back A\$200 worth of goods. Prohibited items include meat products. Seeds, plants, and fruits need to be declared upon arrival.

➤ INFORMATION: **Australian Customs Service** (Regional Director, ✉ Box 8, Sydney, NSW 2001, ☎ 02/9213–2000, FAX 02/9213–4000, WEB www.customs.gov.au).

## IN CANADA

American and British visitors may bring in the following items duty-free: 200 cigarettes, 50 cigars, and 7 ounces of tobacco; 1 bottle (1.1 liters or 40 imperial ounces) of liquor or wine, or 24 355-ml (12-ounce) bottles or cans of beer for personal consumption. Any alcohol and tobacco products in excess of these amounts is subject to duty, provincial fees, and taxes. You can also bring in gifts up to a total value of C$60.

A deposit is sometimes required for trailers (refunded upon return). Cats and dogs must have a certificate issued by a licensed veterinarian that clearly identifies the animal and certifies that it has been vaccinated against rabies during the preceding 36 months. Seeing Eye and other assistance dogs are allowed into Canada without restriction. Plant material must be declared and inspected. There may be restrictions on some live plants, bulbs, and seeds. With certain restrictions or prohibitions on some fruits and vegetables, visitors may bring food with them for their own use, providing the quantity is consistent with the duration of the visit.

Canada's firearms laws are significantly stricter than those in the United States, and it is strongly advised that, if you do plan to bring a gun into Canada, you contact the Canadian Firearms Centre for up-to-date information before leaving home. All handguns and semiautomatic and fully automatic weapons are prohibited and cannot be brought into the country. Sporting rifles and shotguns may be imported provided they are to be used for sporting, hunting, protection from wildlife in remote areas, or competition while in Canada. All firearms must be declared to Canada Customs at the first point of entry. Failure to declare firearms will result in their seizure, and criminal charges may be made. Regulations require visitors to have a confirmed "Firearms Declaration" to bring any guns into Canada; a fee of $C50 applies, good for one year.

➤ INFORMATION: **Travellers' Division, Operational Policy and Coordination Directorate, Canada Customs and Revenue Agency** (✉ Sir Richard Scott Building, 191 Laurier Ave. W, Ottawa, ON K1A 0L5, ☎ 204/983–3500; 800/461–9999 in Canada; FAX 613/954–4570; WEB www.ccra-adrc.gc.ca/customs/individuals/visitors-e.html). **Canadian Firearms Centre** (☎ 800/731–4000, WEB www.cfc.gc.ca).

## IN NEW ZEALAND

All homeward-bound residents may bring back NZ$700 worth of souvenirs and gifts; passengers may not pool their allowances, and children can claim only the concession on goods intended for their own use. For those 17 or older, the duty-free allowance also includes 4.5 liters of wine or beer; one 1,125-ml bottle of spirits; and either 200 cigarettes, 250 grams of tobacco, 50 cigars, *or* a combination of the three up to 250 grams. Meat products, seeds, plants, and fruits must be declared upon arrival to the Agricultural Services Department.

➤ INFORMATION: **New Zealand Customs** (✉ Head Office, The Customhouse, 17–21 Whitmore St. [Box 2218, Wellington], ☎ 09/300–5399, WEB www.customs.govt.nz).

## IN THE U.K.

From countries outside the European Union, including British Columbia, you may bring home, duty-free, 200 cigarettes or 50 cigars; 1 liter of spirits or 2 liters of fortified or sparkling wine or liqueurs; 2 liters of still table wine; 60 ml of perfume; 250 ml of toilet water; plus £145 worth of other goods, including gifts and souvenirs. Prohibited items include meat products, seeds, plants, and fruits.

➤ INFORMATION: **HM Customs and Excise** (✉ St. Christopher House, Southwark, London SE1 OTE, ☎ 020/7928–3344, WEB www.hmce.gov.uk).

## IN THE U.S.

U.S. residents who have been out of the country for at least 48 hours (and who have not used the $400 allowance or any part of it in the past 30 days) may bring home $400 worth of foreign goods duty-free; the duty-free allowance drops to $200 for fewer than 48 hours.

U.S. residents 21 and older may bring back 1 liter of alcohol duty-free. In addition, regardless of your age, you are allowed 200 cigarettes and 100 non-Cuban cigars. Antiques, which the U.S. Customs Service defines as objects more than 100 years old, enter duty-free, as do original works of art done entirely by hand, including paintings, drawings, and sculptures. You may also send packages home duty-free, with a limit of one parcel per addressee per day (except alcohol or tobacco products or perfume worth more than $5). You can mail up to $200 worth of goods for personal use; label the package PERSONAL USE and attach a list of its contents and their retail value. If the package contains your used personal belongings, mark it PERSONAL GOODS RETURNED to avoid paying duties. You may send up to $100 worth of goods as a gift; mark the package UNSOLICITED GIFT. Mailed items do not affect your duty-free allowance on your return.

➤ INFORMATION: **U.S. Customs Service** (for inquiries, ✉ 1300 Pennsylvania Ave. NW, Washington, DC 20229, 🌐 www.customs.gov, ☎ 202/354–1000; for complaints, ✉ Customer Satisfaction Unit, 1300 Pennsylvania Ave. NW, Room 5.5A, Washington, DC 20229; for registration of equipment, ✉ Office of Passenger Programs, 1300 Pennsylvania Ave. NW, Room 5.4D, Washington, DC 20229, ☎ 202/927–0530).

### DINING

The restaurants we list are the cream of the crop in each price category. Properties indicated by a ✕🏠 are lodging establishments whose restaurant warrants a special trip. For information about regional dining, including a price chart, *see* Dining *in* Pleasures and Pastimes at the beginning of each chapter.

### RESERVATIONS AND DRESS

Reservations are always a good idea; we mention them only when they're essential or not accepted. Book as far ahead as you can, and reconfirm as soon as you arrive. (Large parties should always call ahead to check the reservations policy.) We mention dress only when men are required to wear a jacket or a jacket and tie.

### SPECIALTIES

Despite dwindling stocks, wild Pacific Salmon—fresh, smoked, dried, candied, barbecued, or grilled on an alderwood plank in the First Nations fashion—remains British Columbia's signature dish. Other local delicacies served at B.C.'s upmarket restaurants include Fanny Bay or Long Beach oysters and Salt Spring Island lamb. Another homegrown treat is the Nanaimo Bar. Once a Christmas bake-sale standard, this chocolate-and-icing concoction has made its way to trendy city cafés.

### WINE, BEER, AND SPIRITS

Though little known and virtually unobtainable outside the province, British Columbia wines have beat many more established regions in international competitions. A tasting tour of B.C's Okanagan wine region is a scenic way to experience some of these vintages. British Columbians are also choosy about their beer, brewing and drinking (per capita) more micro-brewed ales and lagers than anyone else in the country. The liquor stores sell a daunting selection of oddly named brews, but many cottage breweries produce only enough for their local pubs, so its always worth asking what's on draft.

### DISABILITIES
### AND ACCESSIBILITY

Canadian legislation with respect to access and provision of services for people with disabilities is similar to that in the United States. Transportation facilities are largely accessible, and accessible restaurants and hotels are relatively easy to find, especially in the Vancouver area. Most major attractions—museums, churches, theaters—are equipped with ramps and lifts to handle wheelchairs. National and provincial institutions—parks, public monuments, and government buildings—almost always are accessible.

The British Columbia Paraplegic Association has information about touring in the province. The Government of Canada's Access to Travel Web site has information about travel in Canada for people with all manner of disabilities. You can also use this site to file a complaint about transportation obstacles in Canada.

➤ LOCAL RESOURCES: **Access to Travel** (WEB www.accesstotravel.gc.ca). **British Columbia Paraplegic Association** (✉ 780 S.W. Marine Dr., Vancouver V6P 5Y7, ☎ 604/324–3611 or 877/324–3611, WEB www.canparaplegic.org).

## RESERVATIONS

When discussing accessibility with an operator or reservations agent, **ask hard questions.** Are there any stairs, inside *or* out? Are there grab bars next to the toilet *and* in the shower/tub? How wide is the doorway to the room? To the bathroom? For the most extensive facilities meeting the latest legal specifications, **opt for newer accommodations.** If you reserve through a toll-free number, consider also calling the hotel's local number to confirm the information from the central reservations office. Get confirmation in writing when you can.

The Access Canada program rates accommodations by accessibility. The ratings are published in the British Columbia Accommodations Guide, available from Tourism B.C. Note that grab bars are common in B.C. hotels, but wheel-in showers are rare and bath benches are not normally provided.

➤ ACCOMMODATION INFORMATION: **Hello B.C. (Tourism B.C.)** (☎ 800/435–5622, WEB www.hellobc.com).

## SIGHTS AND ATTRACTIONS

Most city attractions, such as museums and galleries, and including the Grouse Mountain Skyride, are wheelchair accessible. During the summer, you can tour Stanley Park on the free, wheelchair-accessible Stanley Park Shuttle.

## TRANSPORTATION

About one in three of Vancouver's TransLink buses is equipped with wheelchair lifts. The SeaBus ferry is wheelchair accessible, as is the Sky-Train system, with the exception of the Granville Street Station. BC Ferries' larger vessels, including those sailing between Vancouver and Vancouver Island and through the Inside Passage, are equipped with elevators. Tell the ticket agent before boarding that you would like to be parked near the elevator. Some smaller vessels on shorter routes do not have accessible washrooms or passengers lounges. Greyhound Bus lines have lift-equipped service to most towns on the B.C. mainland and Nanaimo; reservations are essential. Pacific Coach Lines provides accessible service between Vancouver and Victoria. Rocky Mountain Railtours offers accessible two-day trips from Vancouver to Jasper with a stop at an accessible hotel en route. Budget Rent a Car and Enterprise Rent a Car (☞ Car Rental) rent hand-controlled cars. To rent a lift-equipped van, contact Freedom Accessible Van Rentals or Sidewinder Conversions. Most Vancouver cab companies have some vans with ramps or lifts. Disabled-parking stickers (windshield cards) from anywhere in North America are recognized in B.C.

➤ WHEELCHAIR ACCESSIBLE TRANS-PORTATION: **Freedom Accessible Van Rentals** (☎ 604/952–4490, WEB www.wheelchairvanrentals.com). **Sidewinder Conversions** (☎ 888/266–2299, WEB www.sidewinderconversions.com).

➤ COMPLAINTS: **Aviation Consumer Protection Division** (☞ Air Travel) for airline-related problems. **Departmental Office of Civil Rights** (for general inquiries, ✉ U.S. Department of Transportation, S-30, 400 7th St. SW, Room 10215, Washington, DC 20590, ☎ 202/366–4648, FAX 202/366–9371, WEB www.dot.gov/ost/docr/index.htm). **Disability Rights Section** (✉ U.S. Department of Justice, Civil Rights Division, Box 66738, Washington, DC 20035-6738, ☎ 202/514–0301; 800/514–0301 for ADA inquiries; WEB www.usdoj.gov/crt/ada/adahom1.htm).

## TRAVEL AGENCIES

In the United States, the Americans with Disabilities Act requires that travel firms serve the needs of all travelers. Some agencies specialize in working with people with disabilities.

➤ Travelers with Mobility Problems: **Access Adventures** (✉ 206 Chestnut Ridge Rd., Scottsville, NY 14624, ☎ 716/889–9096, dltravel@ prodigy.net), run by a former physical-rehabilitation counselor. **Accessible Vans of America** (✉ 9 Spielman Rd., Fairfield, NJ 07004, ☎ 877/282–8267; 888/282–8267 reservations; FAX 973/808–9713; WEB www. accessiblevans.com). **CareVacations** (✉ No. 5, 5110–50 Ave., Leduc, Alberta T9E 6V4, Canada, ☎ 780/986–6404 or 877/478–7827, FAX 780/986–8332, WEB www.carevacations. com), for group tours and cruise vacations. **Flying Wheels Travel** (✉ 143 W. Bridge St. [Box 382, Owatonna, MN 55060], ☎ 507/451–5005 or 800/535–6790, FAX 507/451–1685, WEB www.flyingwheelstravel.com).

➤ Travelers with Developmental Disabilities: **New Directions** (✉ 5276 Hollister Ave., Suite 207, Santa Barbara, CA 93111, ☎ 805/967–2841 or 888/967–2841, FAX 805/964–7344, WEB www.newdirectionstravel.com).

## DISCOUNTS AND DEALS

Be a smart shopper and **compare all your options** before making decisions. A plane ticket bought with a promotional coupon from travel clubs, coupon books, and direct-mail offers or purchased on the Internet may not be cheaper than the least expensive fare from a discount ticket agency. And always keep in mind that what you get is just as important as what you save.

## DISCOUNT RESERVATIONS

To save money, **look into discount reservations services** with Web sites and toll-free numbers, which use their buying power to get a better price on hotels, airline tickets, even car rentals. When booking a room, always **call the hotel's local toll-free number** (if one is available) rather than the central reservations number—you'll often get a better price. Always ask about special packages or corporate rates.

When shopping for the best deal on hotels and car rentals, **look for guaranteed exchange rates,** which protect you against a falling dollar. With your rate locked in, you won't pay more, even if the price goes up in the local currency.

➤ Airline Tickets: ☎ **800/AIR-4LESS.**

➤ Hotel Rooms: **Accommodations Express** (☎ 800/444–7666, WEB www. accommodationsexpress.com). **Hotel Reservations Network** (☎ 800/964–6835, WEB www.hoteldiscount.com). **Quikbook** (☎ 800/789–9887, WEB www.quikbook.com). **RMC Travel** (☎ 800/245–5738, WEB www. rmcwebtravel.com). **Steigenberger Reservation Service** (☎ 800/223–5652, WEB www.srs-worldhotels.com). **Turbotrip.com** (☎ 800/473–7829, WEB www.turbotrip.com).

## PACKAGE DEALS

Don't confuse packages and guided tours. When you buy a package, you travel on your own, just as though you had planned the trip yourself. Fly-drive packages, which combine airfare and car rental, are often a good deal.

## EMBASSIES AND CONSULATES

➤ Australia: **Australian Consulate** (✉ 888 Dunsmuir St., Suite 1225, Vancouver V6C 3K4, ☎ 604/684–1177).

➤ New Zealand: **New Zealand Consulate** (✉ 888 Dunsmuir St., Suite 1200, Vancouver V6C 3K4, ☎ 604/684–7388).

➤ United Kingdom: **British Consulate General** (✉ 1111 Melville St., 8th floor, Vancouver V6E 3V6, ☎ 604/683–4421).

➤ United States: **U.S. Consulate General** (✉ 1095 W. Pender St., 21st floor, Vancouver V6E 2M6, ☎ 604/685–4311).

## GAY AND LESBIAN TRAVEL

Canada is a tolerant country, and same-sex couples should face few problems in Vancouver, where there's a large, visible, and very active gay and lesbian community.

The epicenter of Vancouver's gay scene is the stretch of Davie Street between Burrard and Jervis streets—a cluster of cafés, casual eating places, and shops offering designer T-shirts and sleek housewares. The city's lesbian community centers on Commercial Drive, a neighborhood shared with the Italian and Latin American community. Vancouver Pride Week, held in early late July and early August, features parties, tea dances, and cruises and culminates in a parade on Sunday.

Much of the British Columbia interior harbors more conservative views, although Whistler, the Gulf Islands, and Victoria are all gay-friendly destinations. The Web site www.gay-vancouver.net has the latest on gay events, nightlife, and travel in B.C.

For details about the gay and lesbian scene, consult *Fodor's Gay Guide to the USA* (available in bookstores everywhere).

➤ GAY- AND LESBIAN-FRIENDLY TRAVEL AGENCIES: **Different Roads Travel** (✉ 8383 Wilshire Blvd., Suite 902, Beverly Hills, CA 90211, ☎ 323/651–5557 or 800/429–8747, FAX 323/651–3678, lgernert@tzell. com). **Kennedy Travel** (✉ 314 Jericho Turnpike, Floral Park, NY 11001, ☎ 516/352–4888 or 800/ 237–7433, FAX 516/354–8849, WEB www.kennedytravel.com). **Now, Voyager** (✉ 4406 18th St., San Francisco, CA 94114, ☎ 415/626–1169 or 800/255–6951, FAX 415/626–8626, WEB www.nowvoyager.com). **Skylink Travel and Tour** (✉ 1006 Mendocino Ave., Santa Rosa, CA 95401, ☎ 707/546–9888 or 800/ 225–5759, FAX 707/546–9891, WEB www.skylinktravel.com), serving lesbian travelers.

## HOLIDAYS

Canadian national holidays for 2003 are as follows: New Year's Day, Good Friday (March 29), Easter Monday (April 21), Victoria Day (May 19), Canada Day (July 1), Labour Day (September 1), Thanksgiving (October 13), Remembrance Day (November 11), Christmas, and Boxing Day (December 26). British Columbia Day (August 4) is a provincial holiday.

## INSURANCE

The most useful travel-insurance plan is a comprehensive policy that includes coverage for trip cancellation and interruption, default, trip delay, and medical expenses (with a waiver for preexisting conditions).

Without insurance you will lose all or most of your money if you cancel your trip, regardless of the reason. Default insurance covers you if your tour operator, airline, or cruise line goes out of business. Trip-delay covers expenses that arise because of bad weather or mechanical delays. Study the fine print when comparing policies.

U.K. residents can buy a travel-insurance policy valid for most vacations taken during the year in which it's purchased (but check preexisting-condition coverage). British and Australian citizens need extra medical coverage when traveling overseas.

Always **buy travel policies directly from the insurance company**; if you buy them from a cruise line, airline, or tour operator that goes out of business you probably will not be covered for the agency or operator's default, a major risk. Before making any purchase, **review your existing health and home-owner's policies** to find what they cover away from home.

➤ TRAVEL INSURERS: In the United States: **Access America** (✉ 6600 W. Broad St., Richmond, VA 23230, ☎ 800/284–8300, FAX 804/673–1491 or 800/346–9265, WEB www.etravelprotection.com). **Travel Guard International** (✉ 1145 Clark St., Stevens Point, WI 54481, ☎ 800/826–1300; 715/345–0505 international callers; FAX 800/955–8785; WEB www.travelguard. com).

➤ INSURANCE INFORMATION: In the United Kingdom: **Association of British Insurers** (✉ 51 Gresham St., London EC2V 7HQ, ☎ 020/7600–3333, FAX 020/7696–8999, WEB www. abi.org.uk). In Canada: **RBC Travel Insurance** (✉ 6880 Financial Dr., Mississauga, Ontario L5N 7Y5, ☎ 905/791–8700 or 800/668–4342,

FAX 905/813–4704, WEB www. rbcinsurance.com). In Australia: **Insurance Council of Australia** (✉ Level 3, 56 Pitt St., Sydney, NSW 2000, ☎ 02/9253–5100, FAX 02/ 9253–5111, WEB www.ica.com.au). In New Zealand: **Insurance Council of New Zealand** (✉ Level 7, 111–115 Customhouse Quay [Box 474, Wellington], ☎ 04/472–5230, FAX 04/ 473–3011, WEB www.icnz.org.nz).

## LODGING

In Vancouver and Victoria you have a choice of luxury hotels, moderately priced modern properties; bed-and-breakfasts, both simple and luxurious; and smaller, older hotels with perhaps fewer conveniences but more charm. Options in smaller towns and in the country include large, full-service resorts; remote wilderness lodges; small, privately owned hotels; roadside motels; and bed-and-breakfasts. Even here you need to make reservations at least on the day on which you plan to pull into town.

Canada doesn't have a national government rating system for hotels, but in British Columbia, a blue Approved Accommodation decal on the window or door of a hotel or motel indicates that it has met provincial hotel-association standards for courtesy, comfort, and cleanliness.

Expect accommodations to cost more in summer than in the off-season (except for places such as ski resorts, where winter is high season). When making reservations, **ask about special deals and packages.** Big-city hotels that cater to business travelers often offer weekend packages, and many city hotels offer rooms at up to 50% off in winter. If you're planning to visit a major city or resort area in high season, **book well in advance.** Also be aware of any special events or festivals that may coincide with your visit and fill every room for miles around. For resorts and lodges, consider the winter ski-season high as well and plan accordingly. Note also that many out-of-the-way lodgings are closed during the winter.

The lodgings we list are the cream of the crop in each price category. We always list the facilities that are available—but we don't specify whether they cost extra; when pricing accommodations, always ask what's included and what costs extra. Properties indicated by a ✗☵ are lodging establishments whose restaurant warrants a special trip. For price charts, *see* Lodging *in* Pleasures and Pastimes at the beginning of each chapter.

Assume that hotels operate on the European Plan (EP, with no meals) unless it's otherwise specified that they use the Continental Plan (CP, with a Continental breakfast daily), Breakfast Plan (BP, with a full breakfast), Modified American Plan (MAP, with breakfast and dinner daily), or the American Plan (AP, with all meals).

### APARTMENT AND HOUSE RENTALS

If you want a home base that's roomy enough for a family and comes with cooking facilities, **consider a furnished rental.** These can save you money, especially if you're traveling with a group. Home-exchange directories sometimes list rentals as well as exchanges.

Rental houses, apartments, and cottages are popular in B.C., particularly on the coast, the islands, and in Whistler. Whistler condos are usually time-share or consortium arrangements and can be booked directly through Tourism Whistler. Vacation rentals elsewhere are usually privately owned and range from simple summer cottages to luxurious waterfront homes. Rates range from $C800 per week to several thousand; popular places book up as much as a year in advance.

➤ INTERNATIONAL AGENTS: **Hideaways International** (✉ 767 Islington St., Portsmouth, NH 03801, ☎ 603/ 430–4433 or 800/843–4433, FAX 603/ 430–4444, WEB www.hideaways.com; membership $129).

➤ LOCAL AGENTS: **Chalet Select** (✉ 135 Wildwood Ave., Victoria V8S 3V8, ☎ 250/382–9363 or 888/468–0329, WEB www.chaletselect.com).**5 Star Accommodation** (✉ 1821 Cook St., 2nd floor, Victoria V8T 3P5, ☎ 250/479–8600 or 888/479–8600, WEB www.bcacc.com). **Tourism Whistler** (✉ 4010 Whistler Way,

Whistler V0N 1B4, ☎ 604/664–5625 or 800/944–7853, WEB www.tourismwhistler.com).

### BED-AND-BREAKFASTS

Bed-and-breakfasts can be found in both the country and the cities. For assistance in booking these, **contact Tourism British Columbia.** Be sure to **check out the B&B's Web site,** which may have useful information, although you should also find out how up-to-date it is. Room quality varies from house to house as well, so you should **ask to see a room before making a choice.**

➤ RESERVATION SERVICES: **Garden City B&B Reservation Service** (✉ 660 Jones Terr., Victoria V8Z 2L7, ☎ 250/479–1986, FAX 250/479–9999, WEB www.bc-bed-breakfast.com). **Hello B.C. (Tourism B.C.)** (☎ 800/435–5622, WEB www.hellobc.com). **Town & Country Bed and Breakfast Reservation Service** (✉ 2803 W. 4th Ave. [Box 74542, Vancouver V6K 1K2], ☎ FAX 604/731–5942, WEB www.townandcountrybedandbreakfast.com).

### CAMPING

Campgrounds in British Columbia range from rustic woodland settings far from the nearest paved road to facility-packed open fields full of sleek motor homes next to major highways. Some of the best sites are in national and provincial parks—well cared for, well equipped, and close to plenty of nature and activity programs for both children and adults. The campgrounds in the mountains of British Columbia are particularly beautiful. Wilderness camping for hikers and canoeists is available in national and provincial parks. You can reserve a site in any of 67 provincial parks, or at the Pacific Rim National Park Reserve, through B.C. Parks' Discover Camping service.

➤ CAMPSITE RESERVATIONS: **Discover Camping** (☎ 604/689–9025 or 800/689–9025, WEB www.discovercamping.ca).

### HOSTELS

No matter what your age, you can **save on lodging costs by staying at hostels.** In some 4,500 locations in more than 70 countries around the world, Hostelling International (HI), the umbrella group for a number of national youth-hostel associations, offers single-sex, dorm-style beds and, at many hostels, rooms for couples and family accommodations. British Columbia's 20 Hostelling International locations are clean, well equipped, and, for the most part, set in prime resort, island, and city-center locations. Most have kitchen facilities, family and private accommodations, and low-cost tours and outdoor activities. Chores are not required (as they are in some European hostels), and nonmembers are welcome at (slightly higher rates). B.C. also has a number of unofficial, or non-HI, hostels. Most are similar to HI hostels, though the quality varies and some of Vancouver's non-HI hostels are in rough neighborhoods.

Membership in any HI national hostel association, open to travelers of all ages, allows you to stay in HI-affiliated hostels at member rates; one-year membership is about $25 for adults (C$35 for a two-year minimum membership in Canada, £12.50 in the United Kingdom, A$52 in Australia, and NZ$40 in New Zealand); hostels run about $10–$25 per night. Members have priority if the hostel is full; they're also eligible for discounts around the world, even on rail and bus travel in some countries.

➤ ORGANIZATIONS: **Hostelling International—American Youth Hostels** (✉ 733 15th St. NW, Suite 840, Washington, DC 20005, ☎ 202/783–6161, FAX 202/783–6171, WEB www.hiayh.org). **Hostelling International—Canada** (✉ 400–205 Catherine St., Ottawa, Ontario K2P 1C3, ☎ 613/237–7884; 800/663–5777 in Canada; FAX 613/237–7868; WEB www.hihostels.ca). **Youth Hostel Association of England and Wales** (✉ Trevelyan House, 8 St. Stephen's Hill, St. Albans, Hertfordshire AL1 2DY, U.K., ☎ 0870/870–8808, FAX 01727/844126, WEB www.yha.org.uk). **Youth Hostel Association Australia** (✉ 10 Mallett St., Camperdown, NSW 2050, ☎ 02/9565–1699, FAX 02/9565–1325, WEB www.yha.com.au). **Youth Hostels Association of New Zealand** (✉ Level 3, 193 Cashel St. [Box 436, Christchurch], ☎ 03/379–9970, FAX 03/365–4476, WEB www.yha.org.nz).

## HOTELS

Because of British Columbia's cool climate, air-conditioning is usually only found in climate-controlled modern hotels or in the Okanagan, where summers do get hot. All hotels listed have no air-conditioning unless otherwise noted. All hotels listed have private bath unless otherwise noted. Bathrooms almost always have a shower but don't necessarily have a bathtub. Queen beds are the norm, and many chain hotels have two queen beds in each room to cover all the accommodation options. Fishing and hunting lodges·are the exception: they typically have twin beds, though this is changing as these lodges increasingly cater to families rather than to just anglers. Most hotels can provide your choice of queen or twin beds if you book ahead. Rooms can be difficult to find throughout British Columbia during July and August, except in ski areas, where the peak season is December–April.

➤ TOLL-FREE NUMBERS: **Best Western** (☎ 800/528–1234, WEB www. bestwestern.com). **Choice** (☎ 800/ 221–2222, WEB www.choicehotels. com). **Clarion** (☎ 800/252–7466, WEB www.clarionhotel.com). **Coast Hotels and resorts** (☎ 800/663–1144, WEB www.coasthotels.com). **Comfort Inn** (☎ 800/228–5150, WEB www. comfortinn.com). **Delta Hotels & Resorts** (☎ 888/663–8811 or 800/ 441–1414). **Fairmont Hotels & Resorts** (☎ 800/866–5577). **Four Seasons** (☎ 800/332–3442, WEB www. fourseasons.com). **Hilton** (☎ 800/ 445–8667, WEB www.hilton.com). **Holiday Inn** (☎ 800/465–4329, WEB www.basshotels.com). **Howard Johnson** (☎ 800/654–4656, WEB www. hojo.com). **Hyatt Hotels & Resorts** (☎ 800/233–1234, WEB www.hyatt. com). **Inter-Continental** (☎ 800/327– 0200, WEB www.interconti.com). **Marriott** (☎ 800/228–9290, WEB www. marriott.com). **Omni** (☎ 800/843– 6664, WEB www.omnihotels.com). **Quality Inn** (☎ 800/228–5151, WEB www.qualityinn.com). **Radisson** (☎ 800/333–3333, WEB www.radisson. com). **Ramada** (☎ 800/228–2828; 800/854–7854 international reservations; WEB www.ramada.com or www.ramadahotels.com). **Relais & Châteaux** (☎ 800/735–2478, WEB www.relaischateaux.com). **Renaissance Hotels & Resorts** (☎ 800/ 468–3571, WEB www.renaissancehotels. com). **Ritz-Carlton** (☎ 800/241– 3333, WEB www.ritzcarlton.com). **Sheraton** (☎ 800/325–3535, WEB www.starwood.com/sheraton). **Sleep Inn** (☎ 800/753–3746, WEB www. sleepinn.com). **Westin Hotels & Resorts** (☎ 800/228–3000, WEB www. starwood.com/westin). **Wyndham Hotels & Resorts** (☎ 800/822–4200, WEB www.wyndham.com).

## MAIL AND SHIPPING

In British Columbia you can buy stamps at the post office or from many retail outlets and some newsstands. If you're sending mail to or within Canada, **be sure to include the postal code** (six digits and letters). Note that the suite number often appears before the street number in an address, followed by a hyphen. The postal abbreviation for British Columbia is BC.

### POSTAL RATES

Within Canada, postcards and letters up to 30 grams cost 48¢; between 31 grams and 50 grams, the cost is 77¢; and between 51 grams and 200 grams, the cost is 96¢. Letters and postcards to the United States cost 65¢ for up to 30 grams, 90¢ for between 31 and 50 grams, and $1.40 for up to 200 grams. Prices do not include GST (Goods and Services Tax).

International mail and postcards run $1.25 for up to 30 grams, $1.75 for 21 to 50 grams, and $3 for up to 200 grams.

### RECEIVING MAIL

Visitors may have mail sent to them c/o General Delivery in the town they are visiting, for pickup in person within 15 days, after which it will be returned to the sender.

## MEDIA

### NEWSPAPERS AND MAGAZINES

*Maclean's* is Canada's main general-interest magazine. It covers arts and culture as well as politics. Canada has two national newspapers, the *National Post* and the *Globe and Mail*—both are published in Toronto and both are available at newsstands in major foreign cities. Both have Web sites with limited information on cultural events. For more-detailed information, consult the two major daily newspapers in British Columbia, the *Vancouver Sun* and the *Province*.

## RADIO AND TELEVISION

U.S. television dominates Canada's airwaves. In border areas—where most people live—Fox, PBS, NBC, CBS, and ABC are readily available. Canada's two major networks, the state-owned Canadian Broadcasting Corporation (CBC) and the private CTV, and the smaller Global Network broadcast a steady diet of U.S. sitcoms and dramas in prime time with only a scattering of Canadian-produced dramas and comedies. The selection of Canadian-produced current-affairs programs, however, is much wider. Cable subscribers in British Columbia have the usual vast menu of specialty channels to choose from, including the all-news outlets operated by CTV and CBC.

The CBC operates the country's only truly national radio network. In fact, it operates four of them, two in English and two in French. Its Radio 1 network, usually broadcast on the AM band, has a daily schedule rich in news, current affairs, and discussion programs. One of the most popular shows, "As It Happens," takes a quirky and highly entertaining look at national, world, and weird events every evening at 6:30. Radio 2, usually broadcast on FM, emphasizes music and often features live classical concerts by some of Canada's best orchestras, opera companies, and choral groups.

## MONEY MATTERS

Throughout this book, unless otherwise stated, all prices, including dining and lodging, are given in Canadian dollars.

Prices throughout this guide are given for adults. Substantially reduced fees are almost always available for children, students, and senior citizens. For information on taxes, *see* Taxes, *below*.

## ATMS

ATMs are available in most bank and credit-union branches across the country, as well as in many convenience stores, malls, and gas stations.

## CREDIT CARDS

Visa and MasterCard are widely accepted throughout British Columbia. Diners Club, also known as En Route, is less widely accepted. Discover is little known in Canada outside the major hotel chains. Many small retailers are reluctant to accept American Express cards because of the high fees charged.

Throughout this guide, the following abbreviations are used: **AE**, American Express; **D**, Discover; **DC**, Diners Club; **MC**, MasterCard; and **V**, Visa.

➤ REPORTING LOST CARDS: **American Express** (☎ 800/528–4800). **Diners Club** (☎ 800/234–6377). **Discover** (☎ 800/347–2683). **MasterCard** (☎ 800/307–7309). **Visa** (☎ 800/336–8472).

## CURRENCY

U.S. dollars are accepted in much of Canada (especially in communities near the border). However, to get the most favorable exchange rate, **exchange at least some of your money into Canadian funds at a bank or other financial institution.** Traveler's checks (some are available in Canadian dollars) and major U.S. credit cards are accepted in most areas.

The units of currency in Canada are the Canadian dollar (C$) and the cent, in almost the same denominations as U.S. currency ($5, $10, $20, 1¢, 5¢, 10¢, 25¢, etc.). The $1 and $2 bill are no longer used; they have been replaced by $1 and $2 coins (known as a "loonie," because of the loon that appears on the coin, and a "toonie," respectively).

## CURRENCY EXCHANGE

For the most favorable rates, **change money through banks.** Although ATM transaction fees may be higher abroad than at home, ATM rates are excellent because they are based on wholesale rates offered only by major banks. You won't do as well at exchange booths in airports or rail and bus stations, in hotels, in restaurants, or in stores. To avoid lines at airport exchange booths, **get a bit of local currency before you leave home.**

➤ EXCHANGE SERVICES: **International Currency Express** (☎ 888/278–6628 orders, WEB www.foreignmoney.com). **Thomas Cook Currency Services** (☎ 800/287–7362 orders and retail locations, WEB www.us.thomascook.com).

## NATIONAL PARKS

If you plan to visit several national parks in Canada, you may be able to **save money on park fees by buying a multipark pass.** Parks Canada sells a National Parks of Canada pass, good for 12 months at most Canadian national parks, for $38. You can buy passes at the parks covered by the pass. Contact the park you plan to visit for information. Most parks in B.C. are provincial parks that did not, at press time, charge day-use fees, though this may change. A National Historic Sites of Canada pass, offered by Parks Canada for $30, includes a year's admission to National Historic Sites. A Discovery package, which includes admission to national parks and national historic sites, is $48 per year.

➤ PARK PASSES: **Parks Canada** (national office: ✉ 25 Eddy St., Hull, QC K1A 0M5, ☎ 888/773–8888, WEB www.parkscanada.pch gc.ca).

## OUTDOORS AND SPORTS

### BICYCLING

➤ ASSOCIATION: **Canadian Cycling Association** (✉ 702–2197 Riverside Dr., Ottawa, ON K1H 7X3, ☎ 613/248–1353, FAX 613/248–9311, WEB www.canadian-cycling.com).

### CANOEING AND KAYAKING

➤ ASSOCIATION: **Canadian Recreational Canoeing Association** (✉ Box 398, 446 Main St. W, Merrickville, ON K0G 1N0, ☎ 613/269–2910 or 888/252–6292, FAX 613/269–2908, WEB www.paddlingcanada.ca).

### CLIMBING/MOUNTAINEERING

➤ ASSOCIATION: **Alpine Club of Canada** (✉ Indian Flats Rd., Box 8040, Canmore, AB T1W 2T8, ☎ 403/678–3200, FAX 403/678–3224, WEB www.alpineclubofcanada.ca).

### GOLF

➤ ASSOCIATION: **Royal Canadian Golf Association** (✉ 2070 Hadwen Rd., Mississauga, Ontario L5K 2T3, ☎ 905/849–9700, FAX 905/845–7040, WEB www.rcga.org).

## PACKING

Weather in British Columbia is changeable and varied; you can expect cool evenings and some chance of rain even in summer. If you plan on camping or hiking in the deep woods in summer, particularly in northern British Columbia, **always carry insect repellent.** It's also a good idea to carry bear spray and/or wear bells to warn bears of your presence. Both are available in camping and hardware stores in B.C.

In your carry-on luggage, **pack an extra pair of eyeglasses or contact lenses and enough of any medication** you take to last the entire trip. You may also ask your doctor to write a spare prescription using the drug's generic name, since brand names may vary from country to country. In luggage to be checked, **never pack prescription drugs or valuables.** And don't forget to carry with you the addresses of offices that handle refunds of lost traveler's checks. Check *Fodor's How to Pack* (available in bookstores everywhere) for more tips.

To avoid customs and security delays, carry medications in their original packaging. Don't pack any sharp objects in your carry-on luggage, including knives of any size or material, scissors, manicure tools, and corkscrews, or anything else that might arouse suspicion.

### CHECKING LUGGAGE

You are allowed one carry-on bag and one personal article, such as a purse or a laptop computer. Make sure that everything you carry aboard will fit under your seat or in the overhead bin. Get to the gate early, so you can board as soon as possible, before the overhead bins fill up.

If you are flying internationally, note that baggage allowances may be determined not by piece but by weight—generally 88 pounds (40 kilograms) in first class, 66 pounds

(30 kilograms) in business class, and 44 pounds (20 kilograms) in economy.

Airline liability for baggage is limited to $2,500 per person on flights within the United States. On international flights it amounts to $9.07 per pound or $20 per kilogram for checked baggage (roughly $640 per 70-pound bag) and $400 per passenger for unchecked baggage. You can buy additional coverage at check-in for about $10 per $1,000 of coverage, but it excludes a rather extensive list of items, shown on your airline ticket.

Before departure, **itemize your bags' contents** and their worth, and label the bags with your name, address, and phone number. (If you use your home address, cover it so potential thieves can't see it readily.) Inside each bag, **pack a copy of your itinerary.** At check-in, **make sure that each bag is correctly tagged** with the destination airport's three-letter code. If your bags arrive damaged or fail to arrive at all, file a written report with the airline before leaving the airport.

## PASSPORTS AND VISAS

When traveling internationally, **carry your passport** even if you don't need one (it's always the best form of ID) and **make two photocopies of the data page** (one for someone at home and another for you, carried separately from your passport). If you lose your passport, promptly call the nearest embassy or consulate and the local police.

U.S. passport applications for children under age 14 require consent from both parents or legal guardians; both parents must appear together to sign the application. If only one parent appears, he or she must submit a written statement from the other parent authorizing passport issuance for the child. A parent with sole authority must present evidence of it when applying; acceptable documentation includes the child's certified birth certificate listing only the applying parent, a court order specifically permitting this parent's travel with the child, or a death certificate for the nonapplying parent. Application forms and instructions are available on the Web site of the U.S. State Department's Bureau of Consular Affairs (www.travel.state.gov).

### ENTERING CANADA

Citizens and legal residents of the United States do not need a passport or a visa to enter Canada, but proof of citizenship (a birth certificate or valid passport) and some form of photo identification will be requested. Naturalized U.S. residents should carry their naturalization certificate. Permanent residents who are not citizens should carry their "green card." U.S. residents entering Canada from a third country must have a valid passport, naturalization certificate, or "green card."

Citizens of the United Kingdom need only a valid passport to enter Canada for stays of up to six months.

### PASSPORT OFFICES

The best time to apply for a passport or to renew is in fall and winter. Before any trip, check your passport's expiration date, and, if necessary, renew it as soon as possible.

➤ AUSTRALIAN CITIZENS: **Australian State Passport Office** (☎ 131–232, WEB www.dfat.gov.au/passports).

➤ NEW ZEALAND CITIZENS: **New Zealand Passport Office** (☎ 04/494–0700 or 04/474–8100 application procedures, WEB www.passports. govt.nz).

➤ U.K. CITIZENS: **London Passport Office** (☎ 0870/521–0410, WEB www.ukpa.gov.uk) for application procedures and emergency passports.

## SENIOR-CITIZEN TRAVEL

To qualify for age-related discounts, **mention your senior-citizen status up front** when booking hotel reservations (not when checking out) and before you're seated in restaurants (not when paying the bill). Be sure to have identification on hand. When renting a car, ask about promotional car-rental discounts, which can be cheaper than senior-citizen rates.

➤ EDUCATIONAL PROGRAMS: **Elderhostel** (✉ 11 Ave. de Lafayette, Boston, MA 02111-1746, ☎ 877/426–8056, FAX 877/426–2166, WEB www.elderhostel.org). **Interhostel** (✉ University of New Hampshire, 6 Garrison Ave., Durham, NH 03824,

☎ 603/862–1147 or 800/733–9753, FAX 603/862–1113, WEB www.learn. unh.edu).

## SHOPPING

The low Canadian dollar has made B.C. a favorite shopping destination. Although the selection of manufactured goods isn't as wide as it is in the United States, B.C. towns have a wide range of independent shops selling handmade and imported goods. Popular souvenirs include handcrafted items made by First Nations and other local artists.

### KEY DESTINATIONS

Victoria's British heritage has left a legacy of import shops selling sweets, tea, tweeds, and linens from the British Isles. Salt Spring Island is known for its wealth of handcrafted items sold through artists' studios or at the island's Saturday market. At Okanagan wineries, you can pick up bottles of hard-to-find B.C. wines. Vancouver has the greatest selection of shops: Pacific Centre Mall in downtown Vancouver and Metrotown Mall in Burnaby are among the largest area malls.

### SMART SOUVENIRS

Frozen fish may seem an odd souvenir, but given the price of salmon elsewhere in the world, Pacific salmon, at $3 to $5 a pound, is one of the more popular items to take home from B.C. Most fishmongers in areas frequented by tourists will pack your salmon for travel, as will your fishing outfitter if you've caught your own. First Nations (particularly Haida) art and handcrafted items are available at galleries, shops, and artists' studios throughout the province. Look for cedar boxes or silver jewelry with traditional designs, or items carved from argillite, a black slate unique to the Queen Charlotte Islands. Items can range from under $100 to several thousand. Heavy sweaters knit with traditional designs are made by the Cowichan people near Duncan; they start at about $200.

### WATCH OUT

Cuban cigars are sold legally in Canada, but it's still illegal to take them back to the United States.

## STUDENTS IN CANADA

Persons under 18 years of age who are not accompanied by their parents should **bring a letter from a parent or guardian** giving them permission to travel to Canada.

➤ IDs AND SERVICES: **Council Travel** (CIEE; ✉ 205 E. 42nd St., 15th floor, New York, NY 10017, ☎ 212/822–2700 or 888/268–6245, FAX 212/822–2699, WEB www.counciltravel. com). **Travel Cuts** (✉ 187 College St., Toronto, Ontario M5T 1P7, ☎ 416/979–2406; 800/667–2887 in Canada; FAX 416/979–0956; WEB www.travelcuts.com).

## TAXES

A Goods and Services Tax (GST) of 7% applies on virtually every transaction in Canada except for the purchase of basic groceries.

In addition to the GST, British Columbia levies a sales tax of 7.5% on most items (although services, accommodation, groceries, children's clothes, and restaurant meals are exempt). Hotel rooms are subject to an 8% tax (in addition to the GST), and some municipalities levy an additional 2%. Wine, beer, and spirits purchased in bars and restaurants are subject to a 10% tax. Some restaurants build this into the price of the beverage, but others add it to the bill.

### GST REFUNDS

You can **get a GST refund** on purchases taken out of the country and on short-term accommodations of less than one month, but not on food, drink, tobacco, car or motor-home rentals, or transportation; rebate forms, which must be submitted within 60 days of leaving Canada, may be obtained from certain retailers, duty-free shops, customs officials, or from the Canada Customs and Revenue Agency. Instant cash rebates up to a maximum of $500 are provided by some duty-free shops when you leave Canada, and most provinces do not tax goods that are shipped directly by the vendor to the purchaser's home. Always **save your original receipts** from stores and hotels (not just credit-card receipts), and **be sure the name and address of the establishment are shown on the**

**receipt.** Original receipts are not returned. To be eligible for a refund, receipts must total at least $200, and each individual receipt for goods must show a minimum purchase of $50.

➤ INFORMATION: **Canada Customs and Revenue Agency** (✉ Visitor Rebate Program, Summerside Tax Centre, 275 Pope Rd., Suite 104, Summerside, PE C1N 6C6, ☎ 902/432–5608; 800/668–4748 in Canada; WEB www.ccra-adrc.gc.ca).

## TIME

Most of British Columbia lies within the Pacific time zone and is on the same time as Los Angeles and Seattle. It's 19 hours behind Sydney, 8 hours behind London, 3 hours behind New York City and Toronto, 2 hours behind Chicago, and 1 hour ahead of Alaska. B.C.'s Rocky Mountain region is on Mountain time, which is one hour ahead of Pacific time.

## TIPPING

Tips and service charges are not usually added to a bill in Canada. In general, tip 15% of the total bill. This goes for waiters, waitresses, barbers and hairdressers, and taxi drivers. Porters and doormen should get about $2 a bag. For maid service, leave at least $2 per person a day ($3 in luxury hotels).

## TOURS AND PACKAGES

Because everything is prearranged on a prepackaged tour or independent vacation, you spend less time planning—and often get it all at a good price.

### BOOKING WITH AN AGENT

Travel agents are excellent resources. But it's a good idea to collect brochures from several agencies, as some agents' suggestions may be influenced by relationships with tour and package firms that reward them for volume sales. If you have a special interest, **find an agent with expertise in that area**; the American Society of Travel Agents (ASTA; ☞ Travel Agencies) has a database of specialists worldwide.

Make sure your travel agent knows the accommodations and other services of the place being recommended. Ask about the hotel's location, room size, beds, and whether it has a pool, room service, or programs for children, if you care about these. Has your agent been there in person or sent others whom you can contact?

Do some homework on your own, too: local tourism boards can provide information about lesser-known and small-niche operators, some of which may sell only direct.

### BUYER BEWARE

Each year consumers are stranded or lose their money when tour operators—even large ones with excellent reputations—go out of business. So **check out the operator.** Ask several travel agents about its reputation, and try to **book with a company that has a consumer-protection program.** (Look for information in the company's brochure.) In the United States, members of the National Tour Association and the United States Tour Operators Association are required to set aside funds to cover your payments and travel arrangements in the event that the company defaults. It's also a good idea to choose a company that participates in the American Society of Travel Agents' Tour Operator Program (TOP); ASTA will act as mediator in any disputes between you and your tour operator.

Remember that the more your package or tour includes the better you can predict the ultimate cost of your vacation. Make sure you know exactly what is covered, and **beware of hidden costs.** Are taxes, tips, and transfers included? Entertainment and excursions? These can add up.

➤ TOUR-OPERATOR RECOMMENDATIONS: **American Society of Travel Agents** (☞ Travel Agencies, *below*). **National Tour Association** (NTA; ✉ 546 E. Main St., Lexington, KY 40508, ☎ 859/226–4444 or 800/682–8886, WEB www.ntaonline.com). **United States Tour Operators Association** (USTOA; ✉ 275 Madison Ave., Suite 2014, New York, NY 10016, ☎ 212/599–6599 or 800/468–7862, FAX 212/599–6744, WEB www.ustoa.com).

## TRAIN TRAVEL

Amtrak has service from Seattle to Vancouver, providing connections between Amtrak's U.S.-wide network and VIA Rail's Canadian routes. VIA Rail Canada provides transcontinental rail service. In B.C. VIA Rail has two routes: Vancouver to Jasper, and Jasper to Prince Rupert with an overnight stop in Prince George. Rocky Mountaineer Railtours operates a variety of spectacular all-daylight rail trips through the Canadian Rockies from the west coast. B.C. Rail's *Whistler Northwind* conducts luxury catered trips from Vancouver through B.C.'s interior.

### CUTTING COSTS

If you're planning to travel a lot by train, **look into the Canrail pass.** It allows 12 days of coach-class travel within a 30-day period; sleeping cars are available, but they sell out very early and must be reserved at least a month in advance during the high season (June to mid-October), when the pass is $C678 (discounts for youths and senior citizens). Low-season rates (October 16 to May) are $C423. For more information and reservations, contact VIA Rail, or a travel agent in the United States or Canada. In the United Kingdom, Leisurail represents both VIA Rail and Rocky Mountaineer Railtours.

Train travelers can **check out the 30-day North American RailPass** offered by Amtrak and VIA Rail. It allows unlimited coach–economy travel in the United States and Canada. You must indicate at least one leg of your journey in each country when purchasing the pass. The cost is C$1,029 from June to October 15, C$725 at other times.

➤ TRAIN INFORMATION: **Amtrak** (☎ 800/872–7245, WEB www.amtrak. com). **BC Rail** (☎ 604/984–5246 or 800/663–8238, WEB www.bcrail.com). In the United Kingdom: **Leisurail** (✉ 12 Coningsby Rd. [Box 5, Peterborough PE3 8XP], ☎ (44)0870/750–0222, WEB www.leisurail.co.uk). **Rocky Mountaineer Railtours** (☎ 800/665–7245, WEB www.

rockymountaineer.com). **VIA Rail Canada** (☎ 800/561–8630 in Canada; 800/561–3949 in the U.S.; WEB www.viarail.ca).

### PAYING

All the train services accept major credit cards, traveler's checks, and cash. VIA and BC Rail will accept U.S. and Canadian currency.

### RESERVATIONS

Reservations are essential on BC Rail's Whistler Northwind and on the Rocky Mountaineer and highly recommended on Amtrak and VIA routes. There is no extra charge for reservations on any of the train services listed.

## TRANSPORTATION AROUND
## BRITISH COLUMBIA

Although cars and motor homes give the most freedom to tour B.C.'s byways, a combination of train tours, long-distance buses, internal flights, and coastal ferries makes it possible to see this huge region car-free. Among the roadless fjords and islands of the coast, ferries, private boats, and floatplanes provide the only access to many communities. In pedestrian-friendly Vancouver and Victoria, simply strolling is the best way to see the sights.

## TRAVEL AGENCIES

A good travel agent puts your needs first. Look for an agency that has been in business at least five years, emphasizes customer service, and has someone on staff who specializes in your destination. In addition, **make sure the agency belongs to a professional trade organization.** The American Society of Travel Agents (ASTA)—the largest and most influential in the field with more than 24,000 members in some 140 countries—maintains and enforces a strict code of ethics and will step in to help mediate any agent-client disputes involving ASTA members if necessary. ASTA (whose motto is "Without a travel agent, you're on your own") also maintains a Web site that includes a directory of agents. (If a travel agency is also acting as your tour operator, *see* Buyer Beware *in* Tours and Packages)

➤ LOCAL AGENT REFERRALS: **American Society of Travel Agents** (ASTA; ✉ 1101 King St., Suite 200, Alexandria, VA 22314, ☎ 800/965–2782 24-hr hot line, FAX 703/739–3268, WEB www.astanet.com). **Association of British Travel Agents** (✉ 68–71 Newman St., London W1T 3AH, ☎ 020/7637–2444, FAX 020/7637–0713, WEB www.abtanet.com). **Association of Canadian Travel Agents** (✉ 130 Albert St., Suite 1705, Ottawa, Ontario K1P 5G4, ☎ 613/237–3657, FAX 613/237–7052, WEB www.acta.net). **Australian Federation of Travel Agents** (✉ Level 3, 309 Pitt St., Sydney, NSW 2000, ☎ 02/9264–3299, FAX 02/9264–1085, WEB www.afta.com.au). **Travel Agents' Association of New Zealand** (✉ Level 5, Tourism and Travel House, 79 Boulcott St. [Box 1888, Wellington 10033], ☎ 04/499–0104, FAX 04/499–0827, WEB www.taanz.org.nz).

### VISITOR INFORMATION

➤ TOURIST INFORMATION: **Canadian Tourism Commission** (☎ 613/946–1000, WEB www.canadatourism.com). **Hello B.C. (Tourism B.C.)** (☎ 800/435–5622, WEB www.hellobc.com). **Vancouver Tourist InfoCentre** (✉ Plaza Level, 200 Burrard St., Vancouver V6C 3L6, ☎ 604/683–2000, WEB www.tourismvancouver.com).

➤ IN THE U.K.: **Visit Canada Center** (✉ 62–65 Trafalgar Sq., London WC2 5DY, ☎ 0891/715–000 for 50p per minute peak rate and 45p per minute cheap rate).

### WEB SITES

Do check out the World Wide Web when planning your trip. You'll find everything from weather forecasts to virtual tours of famous cities. Be sure to **visit Fodors.com** (www.fodors.com), a complete travel-planning site. You can research prices and book plane tickets, hotel rooms, rental cars, vacation packages, and more. In addition, you can post your pressing questions in the "Travel Talk" section. Other planning tools include a currency converter and weather reports, and there are loads of links to travel resources.

For festivals in British Columbia, check out www.festivalseeker.com.

### WHEN TO GO

Most travelers visit British Columbia between June and September, when the sun shines and the wilderness is at its most accessible. The cities—Vancouver and Victoria—are perhaps most enjoyable in the shoulder seasons: May and June, September and October, when the weather is still mild and the crowds thin. December to April brings snow to the interior ski resorts, but on the coast, the winter months mean rain and dramatic winter storms. Spring brings the wine festival in the Okanagan and the Whale Festival on the West Coast of Vancouver Island.

#### CLIMATE

The following are average daily maximum and minimum temperatures Vancouver.

➤ FORECASTS: **Weather Channel Connection** (☎ 900/932–8437), 95¢ per minute from a Touch-Tone phone.

**VANCOUVER**

| Jan. | 42F | 6C | May | 60F | 16C | Sept. | 65F | 18C |
|------|-----|-----|------|-----|-----|-------|-----|-----|
|      | 33  | 1   |      | 47  | 8   |       | 52  | 11  |
| Feb. | 45F | 7C  | June | 65F | 18C | Oct.  | 56F | 13C |
|      | 36  | 2   |      | 52  | 11  |       | 45  | 7   |
| Mar. | 48F | 9C  | July | 70F | 21C | Nov.  | 48F | 9C  |
|      | 37  | 3   |      | 55  | 13  |       | 39  | 4   |
| Apr. | 54F | 12C | Aug. | 70F | 21C | Dec. 4 | 3F | 6C  |
|      | 41  | 5   |      | 55  | 13  |       | 35  | 2   |

## FESTIVALS AND SEASONAL EVENTS

➤ JANUARY: The annual **Icewine Festival at Sun Peaks** (☎ 250/861–6654, WEB www.thewinefestivals.com) is held in alpine Sun Peaks Village, in Okanagan Valley. The event showcases British Columbian ice wine, a sweet wine made from grapes frozen on the vine. At the **Polar Bear Swims** on New Year's Day in Vancouver, Victoria, and many smaller communities throughout the province, locals mark the new year by plunging into the icy ocean waters.

➤ MARCH: The **Pacific Rim Whale Festival** (☎ 250/726–4641 or 250/725–3414) on Vancouver Island celebrates the spring migration of gray whales with guided tours by whale experts and music and dancing.

➤ APRIL: Sip the best vintages at the **Vancouver Playhouse International Wine Festival** (☎ 604/872–6622, WEB www.playhousewinefest.com), which attracts wineries from around the world. Victoria's **TerrifVic Jazz Party** (WEB www.terrifvic.com), held in mid-April, hosts top international bands.

➤ MAY: The **Vancouver International Children's Festival**, said to be the largest event of its kind in the world, presents dozens of free open-air stage performances in mime, puppetry, music, and theater. **Swiftsure International** draws more than 200 competitors to Victoria's harbor for an international yachting event.

➤ LATE MAY: **Victoria Day**, on the second-to-last weekend in May, is a holiday throughout Canada, but Victoria celebrates in earnest, with picnics and a parade.

➤ JUNE: Vancouver's **Alcan Dragon Boat Festival** (☎ 604/688–2382, WEB www.canadadragonboat.com) in late June hosts races between long, slender boats decorated with huge dragon heads, an event based on a Chinese "awakening the dragons" ritual. The festival also includes community and children's activities, dance performances, and arts exhibits. The **Vancouver International Jazz Festival**, in late June, celebrates a broad spectrum of jazz, blues, and related improvised music, with more than 200 performances in venues around Vancouver.

➤ JUNE–SEPT.: **Bard on the Beach** is a series of Shakespearean plays performed under a huge seaside tent at Vancouver's Vanier Park. **Whistler Summer Festivals** present street entertainment and a variety of music at Whistler Resort.

➤ JULY 1: **Canada Day** inspires celebrations around the province in honor of Canada's birthday. In Vancouver, **Canada Place** hosts an entire day of free outdoor concerts followed by a fireworks display in the harbor. Victoria's daylong **Great Canadian Family Picnic** is hosted in Beacon Hill Park. The event usually includes children's entertainment, bands, and a huge Canada Day cake.

➤ JULY: People travel from all over Canada to attend the **Folk Music Festival,** held in Vancouver on the third weekend in July. The **Steamworks Tour de Gastown** brings elite cycle racers to the cobblestone streets of Vancouver's Gastown.

➤ LATE JULY–EARLY AUGUST: In Vancouver, the **Celebration of Light,** an international musical fireworks competition, blasts off over four evenings from a barge in English Bay. The **Vancouver International Comedy Festival** presents all manner of silliness (much of it free) on Granville Island.

➤ AUGUST: **Festival Vancouver,** the city's largest musical event, stages orchestral, chamber, choral, world music, early music, opera, and jazz performances. The **Squamish Days Loggers' Sports** (☎ 604/892–9244, WEB www.squamishdays.org) is a four-day event that draws loggers from around the world to compete in tree climbing, ax throwing, speed chopping, and birling (log rolling).

➤ SEPTEMBER: The **Vancouver Fringe Festival** attracts cutting-edge theater to the city's smaller stages.

➤ LATE SEPTEMBER–EARLY OCTOBER: The **Vancouver International Film Festival** showcases lesser-known international filmmakers.

➤ OCTOBER: The Annual **Okanagan Fall Wine Festival** (☎ 250/861–6654, WEB www.TheWineFestivals.com) takes place over 10 days, with more than 110 events. There is also an annual wine festival in the spring and summer. In the third week in October, pop and highbrow authors read, sign books, and speak at the **Vancouver International Writers Festival.**

➤ NOVEMBER: Wine makers, restaurateurs, and food-lovers gather for tastings and seminars at **Cornucopia** (☎ 800/944–7853, WEB www. tourismwhistler.com/cornucopi),

Whistler's annual Food and Wine Celebration

➤ DECEMBER: **Skiing competitions** take place at most alpine ski resorts throughout British Columbia (through February). The **Carol Ships,** sailboats full of carolers and decorated with colored lights, ply Vancouver harbor from November 30 to December 23.

# 1 DESTINATION: VANCOUVER AND BRITISH COLUMBIA

The Beauty and the Buzz

What's Where

Pleasures and Pastimes

Fodor's Choice

Great Itineraries

# THE BEAUTY AND THE BUZZ

**I**T'S FAIR TO SAY that British Columbia, from the fjord-cut coast to the forests, lakes, and mountains inland to the wilderness of the north, is one of the most beautiful places on earth. Even the metropolis of Vancouver, with 2 million people and counting, enjoys a dramatic natural setting, with the sea at its toes and the mountains as a backdrop.

The scenery, of course, has always been here (and much of the environmentally conscious population is working hard to keep it that way), but what's new is the buzz. Every time you turn around, a new fashionable restaurant opens in Yaletown, another Rodeo Drive transplant pops up on Robson Street, a music festival is inaugurated, and even a new downtown neighborhood is designated. Vancouver isn't getting bigger exactly (there's not much room left on the downtown peninsula), but it is becoming more interesting, with the fusty, the provincial, and the dull being replaced with the trendy, the urban, and the vibrant.

It wasn't always like this. In 1886, when a small town site on Burrard Inlet was incorporated as the City of Vancouver, it amounted to little more than a sawmill, a few saloons, and enough shacks for about 400 frontier types. Vancouver was a rough town in those days. Saloons outnumbered churches, and city fathers, unwilling to tax one another, filled their coffers by fining the local prostitutes. It was a good place to make money, though, especially if you turned your hand to lumber, whiskey sales, or land speculation.

The next 100 years or so were a bit, well, dull. For most of the 20th century Vancouver was a staid, provincial little place, its multiculturalism buried under a cloak of British colonial propriety. Vancouverites looked to the old country (be that England or Ontario) for new fashions and ideas; turned some of their best waterfront property over to warehouses, industry, and rail yards; and had so little regard for their early history that at one point there were plans (happily scuttled) to build a freeway through the oldest part of the city.

Things lightened up a bit in the 1960s, when thousands of young Canadians—and Americans—flocked to the West Coast under the misguided notion that it was an easygoing place. It wasn't, but by sheer weight of numbers they made it so. Vancouver's hippie legacy is manifest in funky shops along 4th Avenue and Commercial Drive, a popular nude beach, the Vancouver Folk Music Festival and other long-running events, and a deep-seated reputation for flakiness.

The biggest change happened in the mid-1980s, when the city cleaned up a section of its old industrial waterfront and invited the planet to Expo '86, the World's Fair. The event was uncommonly profitable and a lot of fun, but few envisioned the watershed in Vancouver's history that it would become. To this day people define Vancouver as two different cities: pre- and post-'86. "Expo changed everything," they'll say, often with mixed emotions.

What happened? The fair opened up a good stretch of waterfront to public use and left the city a number of other people-friendly legacies, including the cruise-ship terminal and convention center at Canada Place, and the SkyTrain, a rapid-transit link. It also showed millions of visitors something that they, and many locals, had overlooked: that Vancouver is one of the most beautifully situated cities anywhere.

As growing numbers of tourists were discovering Vancouver during the 1980s and '90s, so were thousands of newcomers from Asia. The wave of immigration, led by relatively well-off people from Hong Kong and Taiwan, boosted property values, dramatically improved the culinary scene, and added an element of urban sophistication that was new to Canada's west coast. The Vancouver of 2003 is a modern metropolis, with one foot in Asia, the other in the Pacific Northwest, and better access than ever before to the surrounding wilderness—nothing like the sleepy backwater it used to be.

Of course one can pine for the pre-1986 days, when traffic was lighter and that famous laid-back West Coast attitude more evident. For that, though, there's Victoria, British Columbia's capital, at the tip of Vancouver Island. Worth the trip for the ferry ride alone, Victoria, a virtually industry-free government town, has always been a looker. Its Inner Harbour, bobbing with sailboats, lined with hanging flower baskets and stately Victorian brick edifices, and backed with the mountain peaks of the mainland, has impressed visitors from the early days.

When James Douglas, British Columbia's first governor, arrived in 1842, he wrote: "The place appears a perfect Eden in the midst of the dreary wilderness of the Northwest Coast, and so different is its general aspect . . . that one might be pardoned for supposing it had dropped from the clouds." Yes, Victoria is a pretty town; however, the surrounding wilds have been occupied for at least 10,000 years by native peoples who, thanks in part to the wealth of forest and sea, were able to create one of the richest cultures in North America. Their legacy is in evidence in British Columbia's two leading museums—the Royal British Columbia Museum in Victoria and the Museum of Anthropology in Vancouver—as well as in villages and museums throughout the province.

Fortunately, much of British Columbia's hinterland is intact, in provincial and national parks and in areas such as the roadless fjords of the northern coast and the forests of the far north, which have never had much population. You'll find some of the last remaining true wilderness in North America here, and, despite the pleasures of the cities, a chance to experience this wild, from a kayak, sailboat, floatplane, or hiking path—while lodging at a luxury resort or a simple campsite—is the main attraction for many visitors to the province.

The sheer size of the province means that even long-term residents find they have to pick and choose their experiences: the old-growth rain forest and Pacific surf of Vancouver Island, the hiking trails and ski resorts of the interior mountains, the Okanagan wine country and Cariboo guest ranches, the pure wilderness of the northern coast. Chances are no one has ever seen it all.

— Sue Kernaghan

# WHAT'S WHERE

The combination of water, mountains, ancient woods, and a deep, restorative stillness foreign to all but a lucky few is at the heart of the British Columbia experience. The particular outdoor pleasure you choose—whether it be fishing, hiking, skiing, sailing, or golfing, among others—may mean less at day's end than the setting in which you do it. This is a land that heals the nicks and scrapes of the soul. You can combine your wilderness holiday with a stay in a lovely city—vibrant Vancouver, easygoing Victoria, or both—and enjoy the culture, dining, shopping, and views they provide. But the great outdoors is always close at hand; you can steal away from the cities within minutes, to Pacific beaches, rugged peaks, forested islands, to ride the trails, kayak, whale-watch, or ski. Or simply sit and watch the play of shadows in a secluded cove or glade and let the peace sink in.

## Vancouver

One of the most beautifully sited cities in the world, Vancouver is much more than a pretty layover for Alaskan cruises. The Pacific Ocean and the mountains of the North Shore form a dramatic backdrop to the gleaming towers of commerce downtown. Vancouver is a new city when compared to others but one that's rich in culture and diversity. Indeed, it's become a hot destination. The arts scene bubbles in summer, when the city stages most of its film, music, and theater festivals. You'll also find first-class opera, ballet, and symphony, as well as plenty of bars and nightclubs. The cuisine scene is equally vibrant and diverse. Superb Chinese food and creative Pacific Northwest cooking, long on seafood, are special treats, but other fine ethnic menus also dazzle. For all its culinary and cultural temptations, Vancouver also provides great strolls. One obligatory amble is through **Gastown,** the oldest quarter, now brimming with cafés, shops, and lofts. Adjacent is **Chinatown**—the third largest in North America—site of the Ming Dynasty–style Dr. Sun Yat-Sen Classical Chinese Garden. On **Granville Island,** buskers, bright colors, and outdoor eateries delight the senses. Don't miss the Granville Island Public Market, a charming antidote to mall culture. Half an hour's drive west, on the University of British

Columbia campus, the Museum of Anthropology serves as a window on civilizations that flourished here long before the British sailed in. A celebrated aquarium and other attractions punctuate nature's work in the trail-laced wilderness of **Stanley Park,** just blocks from the city center. **Kitsilano Beach,** a short hop across English Bay, is as trendy as the neighborhood around it but is graced by hidden coves where you can contemplate, among other things, how clever you were to vacation in this splendid place.

## Victoria and Vancouver Island

Worth the trip for the ferry ride alone, **Victoria** is a stunner. The capital of British Columbia, it is full of stately Victorian structures such as the Parliament Buildings, outlined at night with small, starry lights. Victoria grew up Anglophile but has been reinventing itself as a city of the Pacific Rim, with due regard for its Asian and native heritage. You can still find a proper afternoon tea, but you'll also find the country's oldest and most intact Chinatown and, at the Royal British Columbia Museum, the definitive First Peoples exhibit. Don't miss Beacon Hill Park; it provides spectacular views of the Olympic Mountains and the Strait of Juan de Fuca, as well as a slim chance for baseball fans to get hooked on cricket. North of town, **Butchart Gardens'** 50 glorious acres are a celebration of flowers and garden styles—Japanese, Italian, rose—with summer fireworks and live music. Farther north, the rest of **Vancouver Island** stretches 483 km (300 mi) end to end—the largest Pacific coastal island. At **Strathcona Provincial Park,** in the middle of the island, stargazers escape the haze of city lights, as do hikers, canoeists, and campers. Whales and seals are among the sights at the **Pacific Rim National Park Reserve,** but winter storms, symphonic in their grandeur, are the draw for tempest lovers. At the park's northern edge are funky, charming **Tofino** and island-dotted **Clayoquot Sound,** where lodging options include high-end retreats. What you can't put a price on is the experience, spiritual for many, of the stillness, the clarity of light, the beauty all around.

## British Columbia

British Columbia is clearly a world apart. This sprawling province includes some of the last true wilderness in North America—and the chance to enjoy it from a kayak, sailboat, floatplane, or hiking path before bedding down at a high-style lodge or a back-to-nature campsite. In the Lower Mainland, in and around Vancouver, it appears a brash young province with a population that sees its future on the Pacific Rim. Paradoxically, in the north are ancient rain forests, untamed wilderness, and First Nations peoples who have lived on the land for more than 10,000 years. A short drive from Vancouver is Brackendale Eagles Park, where thousands of bald eagles gather in winter, and the superb runs at Blackcomb and Whistler mountains, where great numbers of skiers do the same. At the massive Garibaldi Provincial Park, hiking is just one of a slew of options for outdoors enthusiasts. Eastward lie the vineyards and orchards of the Okanagan Valley, where the tastings can be many and a driver should be designated at breakfast. In the lovely Haida Gwaii, or Queen Charlotte Islands, native Haida culture is undergoing a renaissance. Kayakers love these waterways. If you'd rather not paddle, let a ferry take you through the enchanted Inside Passage to the funky seaport of Prince Rupert. Explore a few of the Gulf Islands (there are hundreds, each with its own personality), or head north to the Cariboo for living history and a Wild West flavor. Those with the time and a taste for adventure could head even farther north, to the wildlife-rich wilderness that stretches to the Yukon border and on to Alaska. Plan well: this is big country. You can't do it all in one go, which gives you a fine reason to return.

# PLEASURES AND PASTIMES

## First Nations Culture

Before the arrival of Europeans, the lush landscapes of the Pacific Northwest gave rise to one of the continent's richest and most artistically prolific cultures. Along with numerous archaeological sites and museums, attractions and cultural centers—such as the re-created villages at 'Ksan, near Hazelton, at Secwepemc in Kamloops, and the Quw'utsun Cultural Centre on Vancouver Island—share this living culture through music, dance, and food. Although the Museum of Anthropology in Vancouver and the Royal British Columbia Museum in Victoria have renowned collections of Northwest Coast First Nations art, smaller museums in northern and coastal communities are also building world-class collections as artifacts are gradually repatriated to their communities of origin.

## Food and Wine

Although British Columbian cuisine in not easily definable, all the ingredients are there: A rich bounty from the land and sea (oysters, salmon, organic produce, game, lamb, and forest foraged mushrooms); a multicultural population bringing culinary influences from every corner of the world; and such a passion for fresh, local, organic foods that small-scale farming is actually on the increase here. A food and wine tour of B.C. could start in Vancouver, with its vast selection of excellent restaurants and refreshingly low prices. Then take in a visit to some small-scale producers and country inns on southern Vancouver Island and the Gulf Islands, and finish up with a tour of the Okanagan Wine Country, where 50 small wineries produce chardonnay, riesling, and gewürztraminer wines in a scenic lakeside setting.

## Skiing

British Columbia has some of the best, and least expensive, skiing in the world. Whistler Resort, now bidding with Vancouver to be the site of the 2010 Winter Olympics, is known internationally for its long runs, wealth of activities, and high-end après scene. Inland, though, such smaller resorts as Big White, Silver Star, and Sun Peaks, have all the facilities, with fluffier powder and a more family-friendly, laid-back ambience.

## Outdoor Activities

Whether it's kayaking among the transparent waters of the Broken Group Islands, hiking through the old growth forest of the West Coast Trail, or paddling across a northern lake, British Columbia has plenty of opportunity for outdoor adventure. For a gentler introduction to the wilds, deserted beaches, forest trails, and mountain lakes are easily reached from the cities, and a network of campsites, wilderness lodges, floatplanes, and outdoor outfitters provide access to the untouched corners of the province.

# FODOR'S CHOICE

## Dining

**C Restaurant, Vancouver.** The name and decor are minimalist, but the innovative seafood and the stunning location overlooking False Creek make this one of Vancouver's most exciting restaurants. *$$$–$$$$*

**Imperial Chinese Seafood, Vancouver.** This Cantonese restaurant in the Art Deco Marine Building has two-story floor-to-ceiling windows with stupendous views of Stanley Park and the North Shore mountains across Burrard Inlet. *$$–$$$$*

**Il Giardino di Umberto, Vancouver.** A vine-draped courtyard with a wood-burning oven is a romantic place to enjoy the Tuscan favorites served here. *$$–$$$*

**Liliget Feast House, Vancouver.** Near English Bay is one of the few restaurants in the world where you can have original Northwest Coast First Nations cuisine. The longhouse setting is intimate. *$$–$$$*

**Tojo's, Vancouver.** Sushi master Hidekazu Tojo has more than 2,000 preparations tucked away in his creative mind. For the best view of the action, take a ringside seat at the sushi bar. *$$–$$$*

**Vij's, Vancouver.** Vikram Vij, who calls his elegant South Granville restaurant a "curry art gallery," brings together the best of the subcontinent and the Pacific Northwest for a new take on Indian fare. *$$*

## Lodging

**Fairmont Hotel Vancouver.** The copper roof of this château-style hotel dominates the skyline. Opened in 1939 by the Canadian National Railway, the Fairmont commands a regal position in the city center. *$$$$*

**Pan Pacific Hotel, Vancouver.** A centerpiece of the Canada Place complex, the luxurious Pan Pacific has a dramatic three-story atrium lobby and expansive views of the harbor and mountains. *$$$$*

**Sooke Harbour House, Vancouver Island.**
West of Victoria, this airy oceanfront inn looks like the home of a discerning but casual art collector. The restaurant is one of Canada's finest. *$$$$*

**Sutton Place, Vancouver.** With its gracious service and rich, dark-wood furnishings, this large, modern hotel has the feeling of an exclusive European guest house. *$$$$*

**English Bay Inn, Vancouver.** Antiques fill a 1930s Tudor-style house a block from the ocean and Stanley Park. The more lavish rooms have sleigh or four-poster beds. *$$$–$$$$*

**River Run Cottages, Ladner.** The accommodations at this unique bed-and-breakfast 30 minutes south of Vancouver include a floating house, a loft, and two river's-edge cottages. *$$$–$$$$*

**West End Guest House, Vancouver.** From its elegant front parlor, cozy fireplace, and period furniture to its bright-pink exterior, this lovely 1906 Victorian house is a true "painted lady." *$$–$$$$*

## Parks and Gardens

**Butchart Gardens, Victoria.** There stunning gardens exhibit more than 700 varieties of flowers.

**Pacific Rim National Park Reserve, Vancouver Island.** This park on Canada's far west coast has a hard-packed white-sand beach, a group of islands, and a demanding hiking trail with panoramic views of the sea and the rain forest.

**Stanley Park, Vancouver.** An afternoon in this 1,000-acre wilderness park blocks from downtown can include beaches, the ocean, the harbor, Douglas fir and cedar forests, children's attractions and sculptures, and a good look at the North Shore mountains.

## Sights and Attractions

**Chesterman Beach, Tofino.** The open Pacific Ocean meets old-growth forest at Canada's western edge.

**Dr. Sun Yat-Sen Classical Chinese Garden, Vancouver.** The first authentic Ming Dynasty–style garden outside of China was built in 1986 by 52 artisans from Suzhou, the Garden City of the People's Republic.

**Granville Island, Vancouver.** This small sandbar was a derelict factory district, but its industrial buildings and tin sheds, painted in primary colors, now house restaurants, a public market, marine activities, and artists' studios.

**Museum of Anthropology, Vancouver.** The city's most spectacular museum displays aboriginal art from the Pacific Northwest and around the world—dramatic totem poles and canoes; exquisite carvings of gold, silver, and argillite; and masks, tools, and textiles from many cultures.

# GREAT ITINERARIES

## Highlights of British Columbia

*7 to 11 days.* Larger than many countries, British Columbia can be daunting for its size alone. Fortunately, some of its best mountain, ocean, and island scenery lies within easy driving—and sailing—distance of Vancouver. After a few days of exploring the city, head north into the mountains.

**Whistler** *1 or 2 days.* The Sea to Sky Highway hugs fjordlike Howe Sound before veering into the Coast Mountains toward Whistler, arguably the best ski resort on the continent. In warm weather you can golf, raft, bike, or hike in the surrounding wilds or shop, dine, and celebrity-spot in the pedestrian-only alpine village. ☞ *Coast Mountain Circle in Chapter 4.*

**Pacific Rim National Park Reserve** *2 or 3 days.* You need a full day to get here from Whistler, including the ferry crossing from Horseshoe Bay to Vancouver Island (arrive at the ferry terminal an hour before sailing time for Nanaimo, even if you have a reservation). It's worth it, though, to see the crashing Pacific surf and old-growth forest on British Columbia's wild west coast. Stay a day or two to go whale-watching, visit Hot Springs Cove, hike in the temperate rain forest, or beachcomb along the 16-km (10-mi) stretch of sand at Long Beach. The villages of Tofino and Ucluelet, which bracket the park, have several of the province's best oceanfront lodges. ☞ *Vancouver Island in Chapter 3.*

**Victoria** *2 or 3 days*. The British Empire may not have tamed the wilderness, but it certainly made its mark on Victoria, British Columbia's flower-draped 19th-century capital. You can stop in for a formal afternoon tea at the ivy-covered Fairmont Empress Hotel and stroll through Butchart Gardens. Don't miss the excellent historical and First Nations artifacts at the Royal British Columbia Museum. ☞ *Victoria in Chapter 3*.

**Southern Gulf Islands** *2 or 3 days*. From Swartz Bay, the bucolic islands of Salt Spring, Mayne, and Galiano are a ferry ride away (35 minutes to Salt Spring, one to three hours to the other two). Salt Spring is known for its galleries, Saturday crafts market, and artisans' studios, though rustic country inns, seaside pubs, and white-shell beaches are common to all. ☞ *The Gulf Islands in Chapter 4*.

*By Public Transportation*. Though it takes some planning, this tour can be done by public transportation. Buses link all the towns and ferry terminals, and floatplanes serve the coastal and island villages. The Gulf Islands don't have public transportation, though Salt Spring has a taxi service.

---

## The Gold Rush Trail and Inside Passage

*7 to 15 days*. In the mid-19th century, rumors of gold in the province tempted thousands of men and women to risk their lives on an arduous journey north. These days, though the traveling is easier, much of the landscape is unchanged. You also have the option of a return trip by sea along the fjord-cut wilderness of the north coast.

**Fraser Canyon** *1 day*. From Vancouver the Trans-Canada Highway follows the route tracked by the early prospectors along the Fraser River and into the deep gorge of the Fraser Canyon. At Hell's Gate, the river's narrowest and deepest point, you can cross the churning waters by cable car. ☞ *Coast Mountain Circle in Chapter 4*.

**The Cariboo** *1 to 3 days*. From the town of Cache Creek, Highway 97 heads north through the ranchland of the Cariboo region, where more than a few Hollywood westerns have been filmed. You can stop at a dude ranch or spa for a break. ☞ *The Cariboo-Chilcotin in Chapter 4*.

**Barkerville** *1 or 2 days*. Once the largest town north of San Francisco and west of Chicago, Barkerville was the hub of B.C.'s gold rush. It's now a living museum where stagecoaches roll through town and actors play the townsfolk. ☞ *The Cariboo-Chilcotin in Chapter 4*.

**Yellowhead Highway** *2 to 5 days*. You can spot eagles, deer, and possibly bears as you follow Highway 16 north of Barkerville, through the forest to the coast. Several historic sites make worthwhile detours, including the restored Hudson's Bay trading post at Fort St. James National Historic Site; the 'Ksan Historical Village, a First Nations site near Hazelton; the North Pacific Historic Fishing Village, south of Prince Rupert; and the excellent collection of First Nations artifacts at Prince Rupert's Museum of Northern British Columbia. ☞ *Northern British Columbia in Chapter 4*.

**Inside Passage** *1 day*. The roadless fjord-cut coast of B.C.'s northwest is among the last true wilderness areas in North America. One of the easiest ways to see it is from the deck of BC Ferries' *Queen of the North*, which hugs the misty coastline from Prince Rupert to Port Hardy, on the northern tip of Vancouver Island. ☞ *North Coast in Chapter 4*.

**Vancouver Island** *1 to 3 days*. Explore the northern reaches of this forested island, visit the stilt village of Telegraph Cove, see the whales in Johnstone Strait, fish for salmon in Campbell River, or hike or canoe in Strathcona Provincial Park. A ferry from Nanaimo or Victoria gets you back to the mainland. ☞ *Vancouver Island in Chapter 3*.

*By Public Transportation*. B.C.'s rail lines and ferry routes link up to make public transportation for this tour an easy option. BC Rail's Whistler Northwind, a luxury train tour, connects North Vancouver to Prince George. VIA Rail's Skeena line continues to Prince Rupert, where you can catch the ferry that travels along the Inside Passage (it's a 15-hour trip to Port Hardy). From Port Hardy you can get a bus to Nanaimo or Victoria and another ferry back to Vancouver. BC Rail can arrange the journey.

# 2 VANCOUVER

People from every corner of the world create a vibrant atmosphere in Canada's gateway to the Pacific. A city of paradoxes, Vancouver is fashionable, unpretentious, cosmopolitan, and surrounded by wilderness. Asian, British, and native cultures have had a hand in its making. This unique metropolis has something for everyone, with world-class restaurants, rich history, bustling nightlife, outdoor pleasures, and—when you have a moment to rest—a breathtaking natural backdrop.

By Sue
Kernaghan

V ANCOUVER IS A YOUNG CITY, even by North American standards. It was not yet a town when British Columbia became part of the Canadian confederation in 1871. The city's history, such as it is, remains visible to the naked eye: eras are stacked east to west along the waterfront, from cobblestone late-Victorian Gastown to shiny postmodern glass cathedrals of commerce.

The Chinese, among the first to recognize the possibilities of Vancouver's setting, came to British Columbia during the 1850s seeking the gold that inspired them to name the province Gum-shan, or Gold Mountain. As laborers they built the Canadian Pacific Railway, giving Vancouver a purpose, one beyond the natural splendor that Royal Navy captain George Vancouver admired during his cruise around its harbor on June 13, 1792. The Canadian transcontinental railway, along with Canadian Pacific's fleet of clipper ships, gave Vancouver a full week's edge over the California ports in shipping tea and silk to New York at the end of the 19th century.

These days, Vancouver has a cosmopolitan population of about 2 million. Many Asians have migrated here, mainly from Hong Kong, but other regions are represented as well. The mild climate, exquisite natural scenery, and relaxed, outdoor lifestyle continually attract new residents to British Columbia's business center, and the number of visitors is increasing for the same reasons. People often get their first glimpse of Vancouver when catching an Alaskan cruise, and many return at some point to spend more time here.

## Pleasures and Pastimes

### Dining
Vancouver has a diverse array of gastronomical options, including downtown bistros, waterfront seafood palaces, and upscale Asian restaurants. Several cutting-edge establishments are perfecting and defining Pacific Northwest fare, which incorporates regional seafood, notably salmon, and locally grown produce, often accompanied by British Columbian wines.

### The Great Outdoors
Nature has truly blessed this city, surrounding it with verdant forests, towering mountains, coves, inlets, rivers, and the wide sea. Biking, hiking, skiing, snowboarding, and sailing are among the many outdoor activities possible in or near the city. Whether you prefer to relax on a beach by yourself or join a kayaking tour with an outfitter, Vancouver has plenty to offer.

### Nightlife and the Arts
Vancouver residents support the arts enthusiastically, especially during the city's film, jazz, folk, and theater festivals, most of which take place between June and October. The city also covers the spectrum of arts and nightlife, from opera, ballet, and symphonies to live music venues, pubs, and nightclubs. A bylaw bans smoking indoors in all public places in Vancouver, including pubs and bars, though observance is uneven.

# EXPLORING VANCOUVER

The heart of Vancouver, which includes downtown, Stanley Park, Yaletown, and the West End, sits on a peninsula bordered by English Bay and the Pacific Ocean to the west; by False Creek, the inlet home to Granville Island, to the south; and by Burrard Inlet, the city's work-

**10**

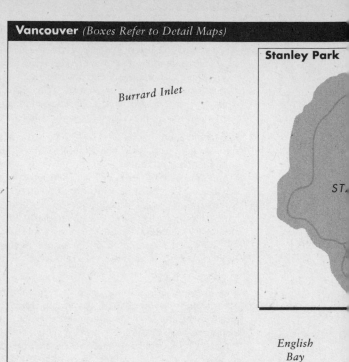

Vancouver *(Boxes Refer to Detail Maps)*

Stanley Park

Burrard Inlet

ST.

English
Bay

Vancouver

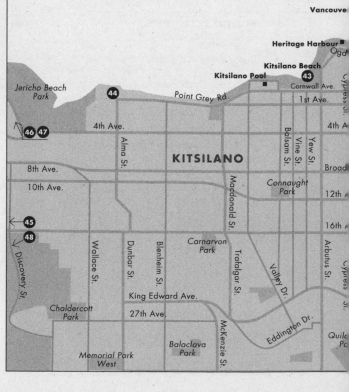

Heritage Harbour

Ogd

Kitsilano Beach

Kitsilano Pool

Cornwall Ave.

**43**

1st Ave.

Jericho Beach
Park

**44**

Point Grey Rd.

Balsam St.

Vine St.

Yew St.

4th Ave.

4th A

**46** **47**

Alma St.

**KITSILANO**

Broad

8th Ave.

Macdonald St.

Connaught
Park

12th

10th Ave.

16th

**45**

**48**

Wallace St.

Dunbar St.

Blenheim St.

Carnarvon
Park

Trafalgar St.

Valley Dr.

Arbutus St.

Cypress

Discovery St.

King Edward Ave.

McKenzie St.

Eddington Dr.

Chaldercott
Park

27th Ave.

Balaclava
Park

Quil
Po

Memorial Park
West

51
52
53

1A
99A

NORTH
VANCOUVER

Lions Gate Br.

NLEY PARK

Burrard Inlet

N

Denman St.

Davie St.

0            1 mile
0            1 km

**Downtown Vancouver**

W. Pender St.
W. Georgia St.
W. Hastings St.
W. Pender St.
Robson St.
Haro St.
Thurlow St.
Burrard St.
Howe St.
Hornby St.
Dunsmuir St.
Granville St.
Seymour St.
Richards St.
Homer St.
Combie St.

Cordova St.

Centennial

Powell St.

Hastings St.

7A

Powell St.

Dunlevy Ave.

Clark

Strathcona
Park

Aquatic Centre

30

2

41  40

Davie St.

Burrard
Br.

Pacific Blvd.

32

Plaza of Nations

Ave.

Vanier
Park

Chestnut St.

Burrard St.

33

Terminal Ave.

Granville St.

Granville
Island

31

**Granville
Island**

False Creek

Cambie Br.

2nd Ave.

Quebec St.

Broadway

7

Cedar
Cottage
Park

ay

a.

e.

Granville St.

Hemlock St.

Oak St.

Heather St.

12th Ave.

16th Ave.

Manitoba St.

Main St.

Fraser St.

Windsor St.

Shaughnessy
Park

Matthews    Ave.

99

28th Ave.

Cambie St.

King Edward

1A

na

49

50

33rd Ave.

ing port, to the north, where the North Shore Mountains loom. The oldest parts of the city, Gastown and Chinatown, lie at the edge of Burrard Inlet, around Main Street, which runs north–south and is roughly the dividing line between the east and west sides. All the avenues, which are numbered, have east and west designations. One note about printed Vancouver street addresses: suite numbers often appear *before* the street number, followed by a hyphen.

Other places of interest exist elsewhere in the city as well, such as the North Shore across Burrard Inlet, south of downtown across English Bay, and on Granville Island.

## Great Itineraries

### IF YOU HAVE 1 OR 2 DAYS

If you have only one day in Vancouver, start with an early morning walk, bike, or shuttle ride through Stanley Park to see the Vancouver Aquarium Marine Science Centre, enjoy the views from Prospect Point, and take a stroll along the seawall. Head northeast from the park on Denman Street to Robson Street for lunch, meander on foot through the trendy shops between Denman and Burrard streets, and then walk northeast on Burrard to view the many buildings of architectural interest. Stop along the way at the Vancouver Art Gallery, the Canadian Craft and Design Museum, and the Pacific Mineral Museum. On Day 2 take a leisurely walking tour of the shops, eateries, and cobblestone streets of Gastown, Chinatown, and Yaletown.

### IF YOU HAVE 3 OR 4 DAYS

If you have another day to tour Vancouver and have followed the itinerary above, head to the south side of False Creek and English Bay on Day 3 to delve into the public market and the many boutiques, eateries, and theaters of Granville Island. Buses and ferries provide easy transit, and touring the island is best accomplished on foot. (If you drive, parking is available, but traffic to the island can be congested, especially on weekends.)

On Day 4, tour the sights beyond downtown Vancouver. Make time for the Museum of Anthropology on the campus of the University of British Columbia. Also visit the Vancouver Museum, the H. R. MacMillan Space Centre, and the Vancouver Maritime Museum, all in the Kitsilano area. If you'd rather play outside, head to the North Shore Mountains, where you can swing high above the Capilano River on a suspension bridge or take in the panoramic city views as you ride the Skyride to the top of Grouse Mountain.

## Robson to the Waterfront

*Numbers in the text correspond to numbers in the margin and on the Downtown Vancouver map.*

Museums and buildings of architectural and historical significance are the primary draw in downtown Vancouver, but there's also plenty of fine shopping.

### A Good Walk

Begin on **Robson Street** ①, at Bute or Thurlow Street. Follow Robson southeast to Hornby Street to reach landscaped **Robson Square** ②, on your right. The **Vancouver Art Gallery** ③ is on the left. Head northeast on Hornby Street to get to the **Fairmont Hotel Vancouver** ④, a city landmark.

The **HSBC Bank Building** is at Georgia and Hornby streets, catercorner to the Hotel Vancouver. Its five-story-high public lobby atrium has a café, regularly changing art exhibitions, and one of the city's more intriguing public-art installations; *Pendulum,* by B.C. artist Alan Storey, is a 90-ft-long hollow aluminum sculpture that arcs hypnotically overhead. The **Cathedral Place** office tower, on the other side of Hornby Street, is one of Vancouver's most attractive postmodern buildings. The three large sculptures of nurses at the corners of the building are replicas of the statues that adorned the Georgia Medical–Dental Building, the Art Deco structure that previously occupied this site; the faux copper roof mimics that of the Fairmont Hotel Vancouver. Step into the lobby to see another interesting sculpture, Robert Studer's *Navigational Device,* suspended from high on the north wall.

The north exit of Cathedral Place (beside the café) leads to a peaceful green courtyard. Immediately next door (to the west) is the Gothicstyle **Christ Church Cathedral** ⑤ is to the west of Cathedral Place. About three blocks north (toward the water), the Art Deco **Marine Building** ⑥ is on the left side of Burrard Street.

Facing the water, make a right onto Hastings Street and follow it east less than a half block for a look at the exterior of the exclusive Vancouver Club. The club marks the start of the old financial district, which runs southeast along Hastings. The district's older temple-style banks, investment houses, and businesspeople's clubs are the surviving legacy of the city's sophisticated pre–World War II architecture.

The **Pacific Mineral Museum** ⑦ is on the south side of Hastings past Hornby Street. Continue along Hastings to **Sinclair Centre** ⑧, between Howe and Granville streets. The magnificently restored complex of government buildings houses offices and retail shops. At 698 West Hastings Street, near Granville Street, the jewelry store Birks now occupies the Roman-influenced former headquarters of the Canadian Imperial Bank of Commerce (CIBC). The 1907 cast-iron clock that stands outside was, at its previous location at Granville and Georgia streets, a favorite rendezvous point for generations of Vancouverites. The imposing 1931 Royal Bank building stands directly across the street. The elevator to the **Lookout at Harbour Centre** ⑨ is at Hastings and Seymour streets, about a block southeast of here.

On Seymour, head toward Burrard Inlet to the **Waterfront Station** ⑩. Take a peek at the murals inside the 19th-century structure, and then continue west on West Cordova to Howe Street. Turn right to see the soaring canopies of **Canada Place** ⑪, where you can stroll around the cruise ship–style decks for great ocean and mountain views or catch a film at the IMAX theater. The **Vancouver Tourist Info Centre** ⑫ is across Canada Place Way (next door to the Fairmont Waterfront Hotel).

TIMING
This tour takes about an hour to walk, not counting stops along the way. The Canadian Craft and Design Museum, the Pacific Mineral Museum, and the Vancouver Art Gallery each warrant an hour or more, depending on the exhibits.

## Sights to See

⑪　**Canada Place.** When Vancouver hosted the Expo '86 world's fair, a former cargo pier was transformed into the off-site Canadian pavilion. The complex, which now encompasses the luxurious **Pan Pacific Hotel,** the **Vancouver Convention and Exhibition Centre,** Vancouver's **World Trade Centre,** and the city's main **cruise-ship terminal,** mimics the style, and size, of a luxury ocean liner. Visitors can stroll its exterior promenade to admire views of Burrard Inlet, Stanley Park, and the North Shore Mountains. At the prow (the north end), the **CN IMAX Theatre** (☎ 604/682–4629) shows films on a five-story-tall screen. The Canada Place roof, shaped like five sails, has become a landmark of

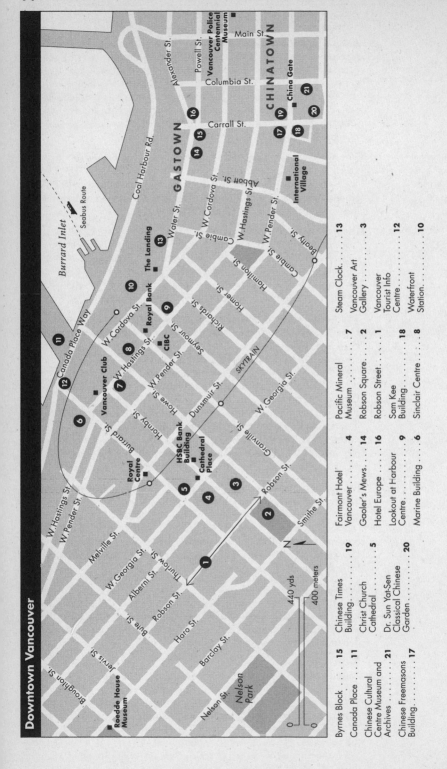

**Downtown Vancouver**

Burrard Inlet

Seabus Route

Alexander St.
Powell St.
Columbia St.
Main St.

**Vancouver Police Centennial Museum**

CHINATOWN

16
15
14

Carrall St.
**China Gate** 19
17 18 20 21

GASTOWN

Coal Harbour Rd.
Water St.
W. Cordova St.
Abbott St.
W. Hastings St.
W. Pender St.
Beatty St.

**International Village**

**The Landing** 13
**Royal Bank** 9
CIBC
10
Cambie St.
Hamilton St.
Homer St.
Richards St.
Seymour St.
SKYTRAIN

Canada Place Way
11
12
**Vancouver Club** 8
7
W. Hastings St.
W. Pender St.
Howe St.
Dunsmuir St.
W. Georgia St.

W. Hastings St.
W. Pender St.
Melville St.
6
**Royal Centre**
**HSBC Bank Building**
**Cathedral Place**
5
4
3
2
Robson St.
Granville St.
Smithe St.

N

W. Georgia St.
Alberni St.
Robson St.
Haro St.
Barclay St.
Nelson St.
Burrard St.
Hornby St.
Thurlow St.
Bute St.
Jervis St.
Broughton St.

1

**Nelson Park**

**Reedde House Museum**

440 yds
400 meters

Byrnes Block . . . . . . **15**
Canada Place . . . . **11**
Chinese Cultural Centre Museum and Archives . . . . . . . . **21**
Chinese Freemasons Building . . . . . . **17**
Chinese Times Building . . . . . . . . **19**
Christ Church Cathedral . . . . . . . **5**
Dr. Sun Yat-Sen Classical Chinese Garden . . . . . . . . **20**
Fairmont Hotel Vancouver . . . . . . . . **4**
Gaoler's Mews. . . . **14**
Hotel Europe . . . . . **16**
Lookout at Harbour Centre . . . . . . . . . . **9**
Marine Building . . . . **6**
Pacific Mineral Museum . . . . . . . . . **7**
Robson Square. . . . **2**
Robson Street . . . . . **1**
Sam Kee Building . . . . . **18**
Sinclair Centre . . . . **8**
Steam Clock . . . . . . **13**
Vancouver Art Gallery . . . . . . . . . **3**
Vancouver Tourist Info Centre . . . . . . . . **12**
Waterfront Station . . . . . . . . . **10**

Vancouver's skyline. ✉ *999 Canada Place Way, Downtown,* ☎ *604/ 775–8687,* WEB *www.canadaplace.ca.* 🎫 *IMAX $10.50.*

**⑤ Christ Church Cathedral.** The oldest church in Vancouver was built between 1889 and 1895. Constructed in the Gothic style, it looks like the parish church of an English village from the outside, though underneath its sandstone-clad exterior, it's made of Douglas fir from what is now south Vancouver. The 32 stained-glass windows depict Old and New Testament scenes, often set against Vancouver landmarks (St. Nicholas presiding over the Lions Gate Bridge, for example). The building's excellent acoustics enhance the choral evensong, carols, and Gregorian chants frequently sung here. ✉ *690 Burrard St., Downtown,* ☎ *604/682–3848.* ☉ *Weekdays 10–4. Services Sun. at 8 AM, 10:30 AM, and 9:30 PM; weekdays at 12:10 PM.*

**④ Fairmont Hotel Vancouver.** One of the last railway-built hotels in Canada, the Fairmont Hotel Vancouver was designed in the château style, its architectural details reminiscent of a medieval French castle. Construction began in 1928 and wrapped up just in time for King George VI of England's 1939 visit. The exterior of the building, one of the most recognizable in Vancouver's skyline, has carvings of malevolent-looking gargoyles at the corners, native chiefs on the Hornby Street side, and an assortment of figures from classical mythology decorating the building's facade. During the summer, the concierge runs free hour-long tours of the hotel on Saturday at 10:30 AM and 1 PM. Reservations are essential. ✉ *900 W. Georgia St., Downtown,* ☎ *604/684–3131; 604/ 662–1935 tour reservations;* WEB *www.fairmont.com.*

**🦢 ⑨ Lookout at Harbour Centre.** The lookout looks like a flying saucer stuck atop a high-rise. At 553 ft high, it affords one of the best views of Vancouver. A glass elevator whizzes you up 50 stories to the circular observation deck, where knowledgeable guides point out the sights and give a tour every hour on the hour. On a clear day you can see Vancouver Island. Tickets are good all day, so you can visit in daytime and return for another peek after dark. The top-floor restaurant makes one complete revolution per hour; the elevator ride up is free for diners. ✉ *555 W. Hastings St., Downtown,* ☎ *604/689–0421,* WEB *www. vancouverlookout.com.* 🎫 *$10.* ☉ *Mid-May–Sept., daily 8:30 AM–10:30 PM; Oct.–mid-May, daily 9–9.*

**⑥ Marine Building.** Terra-cotta bas-reliefs depicting the history of transportation, such as airships, steamships, locomotives, and submarines, as well as Maya and Egyptian motifs and images of marine life adorn this Art Deco structure erected in 1930. These motifs were considered radical at the time because most architects were still applying classical or Gothic ornamentation. Step inside for a look at the beautifully restored interior, and then walk to the corner of Hastings and Hornby streets for the best view of the building. ✉ *355 Burrard St., Downtown.*

**⑦ Pacific Mineral Museum.** Housed in a 1921 former bank building, this museum displays an impressive collection of minerals in all their guises considering its size. The regularly changing exhibits might include dinosaur bones, ice age fossils, amber, or pearls. The vault gallery, tucked behind a real bank-vault door, showcases stunning examples of gold, silver, platinum, and gems. The museum shop sells collectors' specimens, gifts, and souvenirs. ✉ *848 W. Hastings St., Downtown,* ☎ *604/ 689–8700,* WEB *www.pacificmineralmuseum.org.* 🎫 *$5.* ☉ *Mid-May– early Sept., weekdays 10–5, weekends 10–6; early Sept.–mid-May, Tues.–Fri. 10–5, weekends 10–6.*

**②  Robson Square.** Architect Arthur Erickson designed this plaza, which was completed in 1979, to be *the* gathering place of downtown Vancouver. Landscaped walkways connect the Vancouver Art Gallery, government offices, and law courts. Restaurants and a bookstore occupy the level below the street. Political protests and impromptu demonstrations take place on the gallery stairs, a tradition that dates from the days when the building was a courthouse. ⊠ *Bordered by Howe, Hornby, Robson, and Smithe Sts., Downtown.*

**①  Robson Street.** Ultrachic Robson Street is often called Vancouver's Rodeo Drive because of its many see-and-be-seen sidewalk cafés and high-end boutiques. The street, which links downtown and the West End, is particularly lively between Jervis and Burrard streets. The shops may be like those elsewhere, but the people-watching, café-lounging, window-shopping scene draws crowds day and night.

| | |
|---|---|
| OFF THE BEATEN PATH | **ROEDDE HOUSE MUSEUM** – Two short blocks south of the fast pace of Robson Street, and a century away, is the Roedde (pronounced *roh*-dee) House Museum, an 1893 mansion in the Queen Anne Revival style, set among Victorian-style gardens. Though the gardens (free) are worth a visit anytime, the only way to see the restored, antiques-furnished interior is to catch one of the guided tours. ⊠ *1415 Barclay St. between Broughton and Nicola, West End,* ☎ *604/684–7040,* WEB *www.roeddehouse.org.* ☺ *$4; $5 Sun., including tea.* ☉ *Tours year-round; call for times.* |

| | |
|---|---|
| NEED A BREAK? | The pastry chefs at **Sen5es Bakery** (⊠ 801 West Georgia St., Downtown, ☎ 604/633–0138) create some of Vancouver's most decadent treats. Stop in for a piece of champagne truffle cake, some hand-rolled chocolates, a raspberry financier tart, or whatever else suits your fancy. You can also grab coffee or a soup-and-sandwich lunch here. |

**⑧  Sinclair Centre.** The outstanding Vancouver architect Richard Henriquez knitted four government office buildings into Sinclair Centre, an office-retail complex that takes up an entire city block between Cordova and Hastings, Howe, and Granville streets. Inside are designer clothing shops, Federal Government offices, and a food fair (group of fast food outlets). The two Hastings Street buildings—the 1910 **Post Office,** which has an elegant clock tower, and the 1911 **Winch Building**—are linked with the 1937 **Post Office Extension** and the 1913 **Customs Examining Warehouse** to the north. As part of a meticulous restoration in the mid-1980s, the post-office facade was moved to the Granville Street side of the complex. The original clockwork from the old clock tower is on display inside, on the upper level of the arcade. ⊠ *757 W. Hastings St., Downtown.*

**③  Vancouver Art Gallery.** Painter Emily Carr's haunting evocations of the British Columbian hinterland are among the attractions at Western Canada's largest art gallery. Carr (1871–1945), a grocer's daughter from Victoria, fell in love with the wilderness around her and shocked middle-class Victorian society by running off to paint it. Her work accentuates the mysticism and the danger of B.C.'s wilderness—no pretty landscapes here—and records the passing of native cultures. The gallery, which also hosts touring historical and contemporary exhibitions, is housed in a 1911 courthouse that Arthur Erickson redesigned in the early 1980s. Lions guard the majestic front steps, and columns and domes are among the original classical architectural elements. The Gallery Café has a fine terrace, and the gallery's shop has a noteworthy selection of prints and cards. You can visit the café and shop without an admission ticket. ⊠ *750 Hornby St., Downtown,* ☎ *604/662–4719,* WEB *www.vanartgallery.bc.ca.* ☎ *$11 (rates may be higher for some exhibits), donation Thurs. 5–9.* ⊙ *Easter–mid-Oct., Mon.–Wed. and Fri.–Sun. 10–5:30, Thurs. 10–9; mid-Oct.–Easter, Wed. and Fri.–Sun. 10–5:30, Thurs. 10–9.*

⑫ **Vancouver Tourist Info Centre.** Here you can find brochures and personnel to answer questions, book tours, reserve accommodations, and see a nice view of the Burrard Inlet and the North Shore mountains. ⊠ *200 Burrard St., Downtown,* ☎ *604/683–2000,* WEB *www.tourismvancouver.com.* ⊙ *Sept.–mid-May, weekdays 8:30–5, Sat. 9–5; mid-May–Aug., daily 8:30–6.*

⑩ **Waterfront Station.** This former Canadian Pacific Railway passenger terminal was built between 1912 and 1914 as the western terminus for Canada's transcontinental railway. After Canada's railways merged, the station became obsolete, but a 1978 renovation turned it into an office-retail complex and depot for SkyTrain, SeaBus, and West Coast Express passengers. In the main concourse, panels near the ceiling depict the scenery travelers once saw on journeys across Canada. Here you can catch a 13-minute SeaBus trip across the harbor to the waterfront public market at Lonsdale Quay in North Vancouver. ⊠ *601 W. Cordova St., Downtown,* ☎ *604/953–3333 SeaBus and SkyTrain; 604/683–7245 West Coast Express.*

# Gastown

Gastown is where Vancouver originated after "Gassy" Jack Deighton canoed into Burrard Inlet in 1867 with his wife, some whiskey, and a few amenities. The smooth-talking Deighton convinced local mill workers into building him a saloon in exchange for a barrel of whiskey. (It didn't take much convincing. His saloon was on the edge of lumber-company land, where alcohol was forbidden.) In 1885, when the Canadian Pacific Railway announced that Burrard Inlet would be the terminus for the new transcontinental railway, the little town—called Granville Townsite at the time—saw its population grow fivefold over a few months. But on June 13, 1886, two short months after Granville's incorporation as the City of Vancouver, a clearing fire got out of control and burned down the entire town. It was rebuilt by the time the first transcontinental train arrived, in May 1887, and Vancouver became a transfer point for trade with the Far East and soon was crowded with hotels, warehouses, brothels, and saloons. The Klondike gold rush encouraged further development that lasted until 1912, when the so-called golden years ended. From the 1930s to the 1950s, hotels were converted into rooming houses, and the warehouse district shifted elsewhere. The neglected area gradually became run down. These days, Gastown, which along with Chinatown was declared a historic district in 1971, has been revitalized and is home to boutiques, cafés, loft apartments, and souvenir shops.

*Numbers in the text correspond to numbers in the margin and on the Downtown Vancouver map.*

## A Good Walk

Start at the **Landing,** a former warehouse at the corner of Water and Richards streets, downtown. Built in 1905 with gold rush money, it was renovated in 1988 to include upscale shops and a brewpub. From the window at the rear of the lobby you can see Burrard Inlet and the North Shore Mountains. A block east, at the corner of Water and Cambie streets, stands the world's first **steam clock** ⑬. **Gaoler's Mews** ⑭ is about two blocks east on the other side of the street, tucked behind

12 Water Street. **Byrnes Block** ⑮, on the corner of Water and Carrall streets, and the **Hotel Europe** ⑯, at Powell and Alexander streets, are two buildings of historical and architectural interest. A statue of Gassy Jack Deighton stands on the west side of Maple Tree Square, at the intersection of Water, Powell, Alexander, and Carrall streets, where he built his first saloon.

Vancouver's east side of downtown—the area between Gastown and Chinatown roughly bordered by West Cordova and West Hastings between Cambie and Gore—is Vancouver's roughest neighborhood and best avoided if you're on foot. If you're interested in law and order, though, consider a detour to the **Vancouver Police Centennial Museum** at Cordova and Gore streets, just east of Main Street.

TIMING

The walk itself will take less than half an hour each way; allow extra time for shopping. Although Gastown itself is quite safe during the day, you may want to avoid walking through the area after dark.

## Sights to See

⑮ **Byrnes Block.** George Byrnes constructed Vancouver's oldest brick building on the site of Gassy Jack Deighton's second saloon after the 1886 Great Fire, which wiped out most of the fledgling settlement of Vancouver. For a while this building was Vancouver's top luxury hotel, the Alhambra Hotel, charging a dollar a night. The site of Deighton's original saloon, east of the Byrnes Block where his statue now stands, is the zero point from which all Vancouver street addresses start. ⊠ *2 Water St., Gastown.*

⑭ **Gaoler's Mews.** Once the site of the city's first civic buildings—the constable's cabin and customs house, and a two-cell log jail—this atmospheric brick-paved courtyard today is home to cafés, an Irish pub, and architectural offices. ⊠ *Behind 12 Water St., Gastown.*

⑯ **Hotel Europe.** Once billed as the best hotel in the city, this 1908 flat-iron building is one of the world's best examples of this style of triangular architecture. Now used for government-subsidized housing and not open to the public, the hotel still has its original Italian tile work and lead-glass windows. The glass tiles in the sidewalk on Alexander Street once provided light for an underground saloon. ⊠ *43 Powell St., Gastown.*

⑬ **Steam clock.** An underground steam system, which also heats many local buildings, supplies the world's first steam clock—possibly Vancouver's most-photographed attraction. The whistle blows every quarter hour, and on the hour a huge cloud of steam spews from the apparatus. The original design, based on an 1875 mechanism, was built in 1977 by Ray Saunders of Landmark Clocks (at 123 Cambie Street) to commemorate the community effort that saved Gastown from demolition. ⊠ *Water and Cambie Sts., Gastown.*

OFF THE
BEATEN PATH

**VANCOUVER POLICE CENTENNIAL MUSEUM –** It's not in the best of neighborhoods, and its morgue and autopsy areas may be off-putting to some, but this museum provides an intriguing glimpse into the history of the Vancouver police. Firearms and counterfeit money are on exhibit, as are clues from some of the city's unsolved crimes. ⊠ *240 E. Cordova St., Downtown East Side,* ☎ *604/665–3346,* WEB *www.city.vancouver. bc.ca/police/museum.* ⊠ *$6.* ☼ *May–Aug., weekdays 9–3, Sat. 10– 3; Sept.–Apr., weekdays 9–3.*

## Chinatown

Vancouver's Chinatown, declared a historic district in 1971, is one of the oldest and largest such areas in North America. Chinese immigrants were among the first to recognize the possibilities of Vancouver's setting and have played an important role here since the 18th century. Many came to British Columbia during the 1850s seeking their fortunes in the Cariboo gold rush. Thousands more arrived in the 1880s, recruited as laborers to build the Canadian Pacific Railway.

Though they were performing the valuable and hazardous task of blasting the rail bed through the Rocky Mountains, the Chinese were discriminated against. The Anti-Asiatic Riots of 1907 stopped population growth in Chinatown for 50 years, and immigration from China was discouraged by increasingly restrictive policies that climaxed in a $500-per-head tax during the 1920s. In the 1960s the city council planned bulldozer urban renewal for Strathcona, the residential part of Chinatown, as well as freeway connections through the most historic blocks of the district. Fortunately the project was halted. Though much of Vancouver's Chinese community has now shifted to suburban Richmond, Chinatown is still a vital neighborhood. The style of architecture in Vancouver's Chinatown is patterned on that of Guangzhou (Canton).

Although Chinatown is only a few blocks from Gastown, it's best to get there by cab or bus to avoid walking through the city's rough skid-row neighborhood. The No. 19 Metrotown and No. 22 Knight buses travel east to Chinatown from stops along West Pender Street downtown.

### A Good Walk

The intersection of Carrall and Pender streets forms the western boundary of Chinatown, and Jackson Avenue forms the eastern boundary. The **Chinese Freemasons Building** ⑰ and the **Sam Kee Building** ⑱ are here, and directly across Carrall Street is the **Chinese Times Building** ⑲. The **Dr. Sun Yat-Sen Classical Chinese Garden** ⑳ is about a half block east and across Pender, tucked into a courtyard behind the brightly painted China Gate, a four-column entranceway originally built for the Chinese Pavilion at Expo '86. The free, public Dr. Sun Yat-Sen Park is next to the garden. A short path through the park takes you out to Columbia Street, where the entrance to the **Chinese Cultural Centre Museum and Archives** ㉑ (not to be confused with the Chinese Cultural Centre that fronts Pender Street) is on your left.

Finish your tour of Chinatown by poking around in the open-front markets, bakeries, and herbalist and import shops that line several blocks of Pender and Keefer streets running east. Ming Wo Cookware, at 23 East Pender, has a great selection of Eastern and Western culinary supplies. Ten Ren Tea and Ginseng Company, at 550 Main, and Ten Lee Hong Tea and Ginseng, at 500 Main, carry every kind of tea imaginable. For art, ceramics, and rosewood furniture, have a look at Yeu Hua Handicraft Ltd., at 173 East Pender. If you're in the area in summer on a Friday, Saturday, or Sunday, check out the bustling Night Market, for which the 200 block of East Pender is closed to traffic 6:30–11.

**TIMING**

The walk itself will take about 10 minutes. Allow about an hour each for the garden and the museum and extra time for shopping.

### Sights to See

㉑ **Chinese Cultural Centre Museum and Archives.** This Ming Dynasty–style facility is dedicated to promoting an understanding of Chinese-

Canadian history and culture. The art gallery on the first floor hosts traveling exhibits by Chinese and Canadian artists. A compelling permanent exhibit on the second floor traces British Columbia's history from a Chinese point of view. There's also a Chinese Canadian military museum on-site. ⊠ *555 Columbia St., Chinatown,* ☎ *604/658–8880,* WEB *www.cccvan.com.* ◻ *$4; free Tues.* ⊙ *Tues.–Sun. 11–5.*

**⑰ Chinese Freemasons Building.** Two completely different facades distinguish this structure on the northwest corner of Pender and Carrall streets. The side facing Pender represents a fine example of Cantonese recessed balconies. The Carrall Street side displays the standard Victorian style common throughout the British Empire. Dr. Sun Yat-Sen hid for months in this building from agents of the Manchu Dynasty while he raised funds for its overthrow, which he accomplished in 1911. ⊠ *3 W. Pender St., Chinatown.*

**⑲ Chinese Times Building.** Police officers during the early 20th century could hear the clicking sounds of clandestine mah-jongg games played after sunset on the hidden mezzanine floor of this 1902 structure. But attempts by vice squads to enforce restrictive policies against the Chinese gamblers proved fruitless because police were unable to find the players. The office building isn't open to the public. ⊠ *1 E. Pender St., Chinatown.*

**★ ⑳ Dr. Sun Yat-Sen Classical Chinese Garden.** The first authentic Ming Dynasty–style garden outside China, this garden was built in 1986 by 52 artisans from Suzhou, the Garden City of the People's Republic. It incorporates design elements and traditional materials from several of that city's centuries-old private gardens. No power tools, screws, or nails were used in the construction. Guided tours (45 minutes long), included in the ticket price, are conducted throughout the day; they are valuable in understanding the philosophy and symbolism that are central to the garden's design. (Call ahead for times.) Friday evenings in July and August, musicians perform traditional Chinese music in the garden. The free public park next door is also designed as a traditional Chinese garden. ⊠ *578 Carrall St., Chinatown,* ☎ *604/689–7133 or 604/662–3207,* WEB *www.vancouverchinesegarden.com.* ◻ *$8.* ⊙ *May–mid-June and Sept., daily 10–6; mid-June–Aug., daily 9:30–7; Oct.–Apr., Tues.–Sun. 10–4:30.*

**⑱ Sam Kee Building.** *Ripley's Believe It or Not!* recognizes this 6-ft-wide structure as the narrowest office building in the world. In 1913, after the city confiscated most of the then-owner's land to widen Pender Street, he built a store on what was left in protest. Customers had to be served through the windows. These days the building houses an insurance agency, whose employees make do within the 4-ft-10-inch-wide interior. The glass panes in the sidewalk on Pender Street once provided light for Chinatown's public baths, which, in the early 20th century, were in the basement here. The presence of this and other underground sites has fueled rumors that Chinatown and Gastown were connected by tunnels that enabled residents of the latter to anonymously enjoy the vices of the former. Tunnels haven't been found, however. ⊠ *8 W. Pender St., Chinatown.*

## Stanley Park

A 1,000-acre wilderness park only blocks from the downtown section of a major city is both a rarity and a treasure. In the 1860s, because of a threat of American invasion, the area that is now Stanley Park was designated a military reserve, though it was never needed. When the city of Vancouver was incorporated in 1886, the council's first act was to request that the land be set aside as a park. In 1888 permission was granted and the grounds were named Stanley Park after Lord Stanley, then governor general of Canada.

If you're driving to Stanley Park, head northwest on Georgia Street from downtown. If you're taking public transit, catch any bus labeled STAN-LEY PARK at the corner of Hastings and Granville streets downtown.

You can also catch North Vancouver Bus 240 or 246 from anywhere on West Georgia Street to the park entrance at Georgia and Chilco streets, or a Robson Bus 5 to Robson and Denman streets, where there are a number of bicycle-rental outlets.

To reach Stanley Park's main attractions, you can bike, walk, drive, or take the free park shuttle. The seawall path, a 9-km (5½-mi) paved shoreline route popular with walkers, cyclists, and rollerbladers, is one of several car-free zones within the park. If you have the time (about a half day) and the energy, strolling the entire seawall is an exhilarating experience. The seawall extends an additional mile east to Canada Place downtown, so you could start your walk or ride from there (bicycle rentals are available next to the Pan Pacific hotel). Cyclists must ride in a counterclockwise direction and stay on their side of the path.

Parking is available at or near all the major attractions; one ticket ($4 April through September; $3 the rest of the year) allows you to park all day and to move between lots. Another way to see the park is on one of the Stanley Park Horse Drawn Tours (☞ Orientation Tours in Vancouver A to Z).

The free **Stanley Park Shuttle** (☎ 604/257–8400) operates mid-June to mid-September, providing frequent (15-minute intervals) transportation between 14 major park sights. Pick it up on Pipeline Road, near the Georgia Street park entrance, or at any of the stops in the park. For information about guided nature walks in the park, contact the **Lost Lagoon Nature House** (☎ 604/257–8544) on the lagoon level, at the foot of Alberni Street.

*Numbers in the text correspond to numbers in the margin and on the Stanley Park map.*

## A Good Tour

If you're walking or cycling, start at the foot of Alberni Street, beside Lost Lagoon. Go through the underpass and veer right, following the cycle-path markings, to the seawall. If you're driving, enter the park at the foot of Georgia Street. Be sure to stay in the right lane, or you'll have to go over the Lions Gate Bridge. For direct access to the main parking lot and the **Miniature Railway and Children's Farmyard** ㉒ take the left fork just before the underpass. To continue the tour, keep right and go under the underpass. This puts you on scenic Stanley Park Drive, which circles the park.

Whether you're on the seawall or Stanley Park Drive, the old wooden structure that you pass on your right is the Vancouver Rowing Club, a private athletic club established in 1903. Just ahead and to your left is a parking lot, an information booth (staffed year-round, weather permitting), and the turnoff to the **Vancouver Aquarium Marine Science Centre** ㉓, and Painters' Corner, where artists sell their work. A Salmon Demonstration Stream, near the information booth, presents facts about the life cycle of this important fish.

Continue along and pass the Royal Vancouver Yacht Club. The causeway to Deadman's Island, a former burial ground for local Salish people and early settlers, is about ½ km (⅓ mi) farther. It's now a small

## Stanley Park

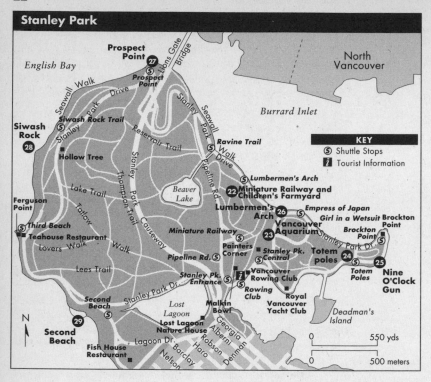

English Bay

Prospect Point ㉗

Prospect Point

North Vancouver

Seawall Walk

Stanley Park Drive

Burrard Inlet

Lions Gate Bridge

Stanley Park Walk

Siwash Rock Trail

Siwash Rock ㉘

Reservoir Trail

Ravine Trail ⓢ

Seawall Walk Drive

Stanley

Hollow Tree

KEY
ⓢ Shuttle Stops
ⓘ Tourist Information

Lake Trail

Thompson Trail

Beaver Lake

Lumbermen's Arch

Miniature Railway and Children's Farmyard ㉒

Lumbermen's Arch ㉖

Empress of Japan

Girl in a Wetsuit  Brockton Point

Ferguson Point

Tatlow

Stanley Park Causeway

Miniature Railway

Vancouver Aquarium ㉓

Brockton Point

Brockton Park Dr.

ⓢ Third Beach
■ Teahouse Restaurant

Lovers Walk

Walk

Pipeline Rd. ⓢ

Painters Corner

ⓢ Stanley Pk. Central

Totem poles ㉔

Totem Poles

Lees Trail

Stanley Pk. Entrance ⓢ

ⓘ Vancouver Rowing Club

Nine O'Clock Gun ㉕

Second Beach ⓢ

Stanley Park Dr.

Lost Lagoon

Malkin Bowl

Rowing Club

Royal Vancouver Yacht Club

Deadman's Island

N

Second Beach ㉙

Lost Lagoon Nature House

Lagoon Dr.

Georgia Alberni Robson Denman

Barclay Haro

Nelson

0          550 yds

0          500 meters

Fish House Restaurant ■

naval installation, HMCS *Discovery*, and isn't open to the public. The **totem poles** ㉔, which are a bit farther down Stanley Park Drive and on your left, are a popular photo stop. The **Nine O'Clock Gun** ㉕ is ahead at the water's edge, just past the sign for Hallelujah Point. Brockton Point and its small lighthouse and foghorn are to the north.

Brockton Oval, where you can catch a rugby game in winter or cricket in summer, is inland on your left. Next, on the water side, watch for the *Girl in a Wetsuit*, a sculpture on a rock offshore that mimics Copenhagen's *Little Mermaid*. A little farther along the seashore stands a replica of the dragon-shape figurehead from the S. S. *Empress of Japan*, which plied these waters between 1891 and 1922.

**Lumbermen's Arch** ㉖, a log archway, is at Km 3 (Mi 2) of the drive. There's a picnic area, a snack bar, and a small beach here. The Children's Water Park, across the road, is a big draw throughout the summer. Cyclists and walkers can turn off here for a shortcut back to the aquarium, the Miniature Railway and Children's Farmyard, and the park entrance.

The Lions Gate Bridge is about 2 km (1 mi) farther along the seawall or Stanley Park Drive. Here drivers and cyclists part company. Cyclists ride under the bridge and past the cormorants' nests tucked beneath **Prospect Point** ㉗. Drivers pass over the bridge and reach a viewpoint and café at the top of Prospect Point. Both routes then continue around to the English Bay side of the park and the beginning of sandy beaches. The imposing monolith offshore (though not visible from the road) is **Siwash Rock** ㉘, the focus of a native legend. If you're driving, watch for a sign for the Hollow Tree. This 56-ft-wide burnt cedar stump has shrunk over the years but still gives an idea of how large some of the old-growth trees were. Continue along to reach the swimming area and snack bar at Third Beach.

The next attraction along the seawall is the large heated pool at **Second Beach** ㉙. If you're walking or cycling, you can take a shortcut from here back to Lost Lagoon by taking the perpendicular pathway behind the pool that cuts into the park. Either of the footbridges ahead leads to a path along the south side of the lagoon that takes you back to your starting point at the foot of Alberni or Georgia Street. If you continue along the seawall from Second Beach, you will emerge from the park into a residential neighborhood of high-rises, the West End. You can walk back to Alberni Street along Denman Street, where you can stop for coffee, a drink, or ice cream at one of the many cafés. Mum's Gelati, at 855 Denman Street, serves delicious ice cream.

TIMING

The driving tour takes about an hour. Parking is available near most of the sights in the park. Biking time depends on your speed, but with stops to see the sights, expect the ride to take several hours. It takes at least two hours to see the aquarium thoroughly. If you're going to walk the park and take in most of the sights, plan on spending the day. The seawall can get crowded on summer weekends, but inside the park is a 28-km (17-mi) network of peaceful, usually deserted walking and cycling paths through old- and second-growth forest. Take a map—they're available at park concession stands—and don't go into the woods alone or after dusk.

## Sights to See

㉖ **Lumbermen's Arch.** Made of one massive log, this archway, erected in 1952, is dedicated to the workers in Vancouver's first industry. Beside the arch is an asphalt path that leads back to Lost Lagoon and the Vancouver Aquarium.

㉒ **Miniature Railway and Children's Farmyard.** A child-size steam train takes kids and adults on a ride through the woods. Next door is a farmyard full of critters, including goats, rabbits, and guinea pigs. At Christmastime, an elaborate light display illuminates the route and Halloween displays draw crowds throughout October. ✉ *Off Pipeline Rd., Stanley Park,* ☎ *604/257–8530.* ⌨ *Each site $4.* ☻ *June–Labor Day, daily 11–4; Oct., daily 6 PM–10 PM; Dec., daily 3 PM–10 PM. Labor Day–Nov. and Jan.–May, weekends 11–4 (weather permitting).*

㉕ **Nine O'Clock Gun.** This cannonlike apparatus by the water was installed in 1890 to alert fishermen to a curfew ending weekend fishing. Now it signals 9 o'clock every night.

㉗ **Prospect Point.** Cormorants build their seaweed nests along the cliff ledges here. The large black diving birds are distinguished by their long necks and beaks. When not nesting, they often perch atop floating logs or boulders. Another remarkable bird found along the park's shore is the beautiful great blue heron. The oldest heron rookery in British Columbia is in the trees near the aquarium, where the birds like to horn in during feeding time for the whales. At 211 ft, Prospect Point is the highest point in the park and provides striking views of the North Shore and Burrard Inlet. There's also a souvenir shop, a snack bar, and a restaurant here.

NEED A
BREAK?

**Prospect Point Café** (☎ 604/669–2737) is at the top of Prospect Point, with a deck overlooking the Lions Gate Bridge. It specializes in all manner of salmon dishes and makes a good lunch stop, though in the evening it's often fully booked with tour groups.

㉙ **Second Beach.** The 50-m pool, which has lifeguards and water slides, is a popular spot in summer. The sandy beach also has a playground and covered picnic areas. ☎ *604/257–8371 (summer only)*, WEB *www.city.vancouver.bc.ca/parks.* ⌦ *Beach free, pool $4.15.* ◷ *Pool mid-May–mid-June, weekdays noon–8:45, weekends 10–8:45; mid-June–Labor Day, daily 10–8:45.*

**㉘** **Siwash Rock.** According to a local First Nations legend, this 50-ft-high offshore promontory is a monument to a man who was turned into stone as a reward for his unselfishness. The rock is visible from the seawall; if you're driving, you need to park and take a short path through the woods.

**㉔** **Totem poles.** Totem poles are an important art form among native peoples along British Columbia's coast. These eight poles, all carved in the latter half of the 20th century, include replicas of poles originally brought to the park from the north coast in the 1920s, as well as poles carved specifically for the park by First Nations artists. The several styles of poles represent a cross section of B.C. native groups, including the Kwakwaka'wakw, Haida, and Nisga'a. The combination of carved animals, fish, birds, and mythological creatures represents clan history. An information center near the site has a snack bar and interpretive information about B.C.'s First Nations.

★ ☙ **㉓** **Vancouver Aquarium Marine Science Centre.** This excellent research and educational facility is a delight for children and natural-history buffs. In the Amazon rain-forest gallery you can walk through a jungle setting populated with piranhas, caimans, and tropical birds and vegetation. Other displays, many with hands-on features for kids, show the underwater life of coastal British Columbia, the Canadian Arctic, and the tropics. Huge tanks have large windows for underwater viewing of beluga whales and playful sea otters. Whale shows and dive shows (where divers swim with aquatic life, including sharks) are held daily. For an extra fee, you can help the trainers feed and train otters, seals, and sea lions. You can even hear whale sounds on radio station ORCA FM, which picks up the wild calls with an underwater microphone off Vancouver Island. A listening post is downstairs by the whale pool. There's also a café and a gift shop. Be prepared for lines on weekends and school holidays. ☎ *604/659–3474*, WEB *www.vanaqua.org.* ⌦ *$14.95.* ◷ *July–Labor Day, daily 9:30–7; Labor Day–June, daily 10–5:30.*

## Yaletown and False Creek

In 1985–86, the provincial government cleared up a derelict industrial site on the north shore of False Creek, built a world's fair, and invited the world. Twenty million people showed up at Expo '86. Now the site of the fair has become one of the largest urban-redevelopment projects in North America, creating—and, in some cases, reclaiming—a whole new downtown district.

Tucked in among the forest of green-glass, high-rise condo towers is the old warehouse district of Yaletown. First settled by railroad workers who had followed the newly laid tracks from the town of Yale in the Fraser Canyon, Yaletown in the 1880s and '90s was probably the most lawless place in Canada; the Royal Canadian Mounted Police complained it was too far through the forest for them to police it. It's now one of the city's most fashionable neighborhoods, and the Victorian brick loading docks have become terraces for cappuccino bars. The area—which also has restaurants, brewpubs, retail and wholesale fashion outlets, and shops selling upscale home decor—makes the most of its waterfront location, with a seaside walk and cycle path that runs completely around the shore of False Creek. Parking is tight in Yaletown, though there's a lot at Library Square. It's easier to walk, come by False Creek Ferry, or catch a Yaletown Bus 2 on Burrard or Pender Street.

*Numbers in the text correspond to numbers in the margin and on the Vancouver map.*

## A Good Walk

Start at **Library Square** ㉚ at Homer and Georgia streets. Leave by the Robson Street (east) exit, cross Robson, and continue south on Hamilton Street. On your right stands a row of Victorian frame houses built between 1895 and 1900, which look out of place among the surrounding high-rises. In 1995 these historic homes were plucked from the West End and moved here to protect them from the onslaught of development.

Cross Smithe Street, and continue down Mainland Street to Nelson Street; you're now in the heart of Yaletown. Stop for a coffee at one of Yaletown's loading-dock cafés or poke around the shops on Hamilton and Mainland streets.

From the foot of Mainland Street, turn left on Davie Street and cross Pacific Boulevard. This takes you to the **Roundhouse** ㉛, a former turnaround point for trains that is now a showcase for local arts groups. David Lam Park, Yaletown's waterfront green space, is behind the Roundhouse. Continue to the waterfront at the foot of Davie Street. Here, an intriguing iron-and-concrete sculpture with panels displays archival images of events around False Creek. Also at the foot of Davie Street is the Yaletown dock for Aquabus Ferries (☎ 604/689–5858), where you can catch a boat to Granville Island, Science World, Hornby Street, or Stamp's Landing.

From here you can access Vancouver's seaside path, a car-free bike, in-line skating, and pedestrian pathway that continues all the way around False Creek. You can rent a bike or in-line skates at the foot of Davie. A right turn takes you, in about 3 km (2 mi), to the West End and Stanley Park.

To continue this tour, turn left. After about 1 km (½ mi) is the Plaza of Nations, the heart of the old Expo site. Cross the plaza toward Pacific Boulevard and take the pedestrian overpass to B.C. Place Stadium. Walk around to Gate A and the **B.C. Sports Hall of Fame and Museum** ㉜. As you leave the museum, the Terry Fox Memorial is on your left. This archway at the foot of Robson Street was built in honor of Terry Fox (1958–81), a local student whose cross-Canada run raised millions of dollars for cancer research. From here, you can continue a block west to return to Library Square. To continue the tour, walk two blocks north on Beatty Street to Stadium Station and take the SkyTrain one stop east to Main Street/Science World station, or return to the waterfront and walk another 1 km (½ mi) east to **Science World** ㉝, a hands-on museum. From Science World, the SkyTrain takes you back downtown, or you can catch a ferry back to Yaletown or to other stops on False Creek. If you're here on a summer weekend, you can catch the Downtown Historic Railway to Granville Island.

TIMING

It takes about 1½ hours to walk around all the sights. Allow about an hour for the B.C. Sports Hall of Fame and museum and two hours for Science World.

## Sights to See

㉜ **B.C. Sports Hall of Fame and Museum.** Inside the B.C. Place Stadium complex, this museum celebrates the province's sports achievers in a series of historical displays. You can test your sprinting, rowing, climbing, and throwing prowess in the high-tech participation gallery. An hour-long audio tour is included with admission. ⊠ *B.C. Place, 777 Pacific Blvd. S, Gate A (at Beatty and Robson Sts.), Downtown,* ☎ *604/687–5520.* ⊠ *$6.* ⊙ *Daily 10–5.*

**㉚ Library Square.** The spiraling library building, open plazas, and shaded atriums of Library Square, completed in the mid-1990s, were built to evoke images of the Colosseum in Rome. A high-tech library is the core of the structure; the outer edge of the spiral houses cafés and boutiques. ⊠ *350 W. Georgia St., Downtown,* ☎ *604/331–3600,* WEB *www.vpl. vancouver.ca.* ⊙ *Sept.–May, Mon.–Thurs. 10–8, Fri.–Sat. 10–5, Sun. 1–5; June–Aug., Mon.–Thurs. 10–8, Fri.–Sat. 10–5.*

**Plaza of Nations.** The centerpiece of Expo '86 is one of the world's fair's least used legacies. Now home to a sports bar, a nightclub, and a comedy club, it's at its liveliest in the evening, though a pub with outdoor seating is open during the day. ⊠ *700 block of Pacific Blvd., Downtown.*

**㉛ Roundhouse.** This round brick structure was built in 1888 as the turnaround point for transcontinental trains reaching the end of the line at Vancouver. A spirited local campaign helped to create a home here (in a glass pavilion on the Davie Street side) for **Engine 374,** which pulled the first passenger train into Vancouver on May 23, 1887. Now a community center, the Roundhouse hosts festivals and exhibitions. ⊠ *181 Roundhouse Mews, Yaletown,* ☎ *604/713–1800.* ⊠ *Free; admission may be charged to some events.* ⊙ *Weekdays 9 AM– 10 PM, weekends 9–5.*

| | |
|---|---|
| NEED A BREAK? | Across from the Roundhouse, **Urban Fare** (⊠ 177 Davie St., Yaletown, ☎ 604/975–7550) supplies, among other things, truffles, foie gras, and bread air-freighted from France to Yaletown's Francophiles and foodies. It's open daily 6 AM–midnight. You can sample the wares at the café. |

**㉝ Science World.** In a gigantic, shiny dome built over an Omnimax Theater, this hands-on science center encourages children to participate in interactive exhibits and demonstrations. Exhibits change throughout the year, so there's always something new to see. ⊠ *1455 Quebec St., False Creek,* ☎ *604/443–7443 or 604/443–7440,* WEB *www.scienceworld.bc.ca.* ⊠ *Science World $12.75, Science World and Omnimax theater $15.75.* ⊙ *July–Aug., daily 10–6; Sept.–June, weekdays 10–5, weekends 10–6.*

## Granville Island

One of North America's most successful urban-redevelopment schemes was just a sandbar until World War I, when the federal government dredged False Creek for access to the sawmills that lined the shore. The sludge from the creek was heaped onto the sandbar to create the island. It was used to house much-needed industrial and logging-equipment plants, but the businesses had begun to deteriorate by the 1960s. In the early '70s, the federal government came up with a creative plan to redevelop the island with a public market, marine activities, and artisans' studios but to retain the architecture's industrial character. The refurbished Granville Island opened to the public in 1979 and was an immediate hit with locals and visitors alike.

Besides the popular public market, the island is home to a marina, an art college, several theaters, several restaurants and pubs, park space, playgrounds, and dozens of crafts shops and artisans studios. It's also

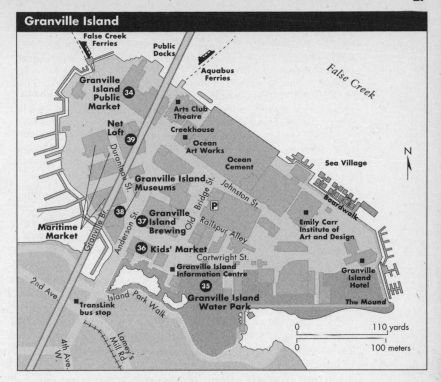

**Granville Island**

among the venues for Vancouver's comedy, jazz, writers', and fringe-theater festivals—and a great place to catch top-quality street entertainment.

Though the island is now technically a peninsula, connected years ago by landfill to the south shore of False Creek, its distinct atmosphere sets it apart from the rest of the city.

*Numbers in the text correspond to numbers in the margin and on the Granville Island map.*

## A Good Walk

To reach Granville Island on foot, make the 15-minute walk from downtown Vancouver to the south end of Hornby Street. Aquabus Ferries depart from here and deliver passengers across False Creek at the **Granville Island Public Market** ㉞, which has a slew of food and other stalls. False Creek Ferries leave every five minutes for Granville Island from a dock behind the Vancouver Aquatic Centre, on Beach Avenue, and deliver passengers between the Bridges pub and the Public Market. Still another option is to take a 20-minute ride on a TransLink bus; from Waterfront Station or stops on Granville Street, take False Creek South Bus 50 to the edge of the island. The market is a short walk from the bus, ferry, or tram stop. If you drive, parking is free for up to three hours, and paid parking is available in four garages on the island.

Another way to travel is to hop the **Downtown Historic Railway** (☎ 604/665–3903), two early 20th-century electric trams that on summer weekends and holiday afternoons run from Science World to Granville Island.

From the market, to start a clockwise tour of the island, walk south on Johnston Street or take the waterside boardwalk behind the Arts

Club Theatre and around the Creekhouse building. Either way, past the shops and studios in the Creekhouse building is Ocean Art Works, an open space where you can watch First Nations artists at work. Continue south past Ocean Cement, one of the island's last industries. Next is the Emily Carr Institute of Art and Design, the province's leading art college. Just to the right of the main entrance is the Charles H. Scott Gallery, which hosts contemporary exhibitions in various media. From the gallery, turn left and follow a covered walkway along the south side of the art school to Sea Village, one of the few houseboat communities in Vancouver. Then take the boardwalk that starts at the houseboats and continues partway around the island. Behind the Granville Island Hotel is a small hill called the Mound, a natural amphitheater for outdoor performances.

From the Granville Island Hotel, turn right onto Cartwright Street. This part of the island is home to a mix of crafts galleries, studios, and workshops and is a great place to watch artisans at work. You can see wooden boats being built at the Alder Bay Boat Company and view weavers making carpets at Ruth Jones Cartwright Studio, for example. The Federation of Canadian Artists Gallery, the Crafts Association of B.C. Crafthouse, and the Gallery of B.C. Ceramics all showcase local works. At Studio Glass, around the corner at 1440 Old Bridge Street, you can watch glassblowers at work. Railspur Alley, home to about a dozen artisans' studios, is off Old Bridge Street.

Back on Cartwright Street, you can pick up maps and find out about special events, including the festivals, outdoor concerts, and dance performances often held on the island, at the Granville Island Information Centre (open daily 9–6). The **Granville Island Water Park** ㉟, behind the information center, and the **Kids' Market** ㊱, a bit farther down the street, make any child's visit to Granville Island a thrill. Adults can head for the microbrewery tour at **Granville Island Brewing** ㊲, across the street from the Kids' Market.

Cross Anderson Street and walk north on Duranleau Street. The **Granville Island Museums** ㊳, with fishing, train, and model-boat displays, are on your left. The sea-oriented shops of the Maritime Market are next. The **Net Loft** ㊴ shopping arcade is the last place to explore. Once you have come full circle, you can either take the ferry back to downtown Vancouver or stay for dinner and catch a play at the Arts Club or the Waterfront Theatre.

TIMING

If your schedule is tight, you can tour Granville Island in three to four hours. If you like to shop, or if a festival is in progress, you'll likely need a full day.

## Sights to See

**Emily Carr Institute of Art and Design.** The institute's three main buildings—tin-plated structures formerly used for industrial purposes—were renovated in the 1970s. The **Charles H. Scott Gallery** to the right of the main entrance hosts contemporary exhibitions in various media. ✉ *1399 Johnston St., Granville Island,* ☏ *604/844–3811.* ☞ *Free.* ☉ *Weekdays noon–5, weekends 10–5.*

㊲ **Granville Island Brewing.** Tours of Canada's first modern microbrewery last about a half hour and include a souvenir glass and a taste of four brews. Kids are welcome; they get a taste of root beer. ✉ *1441 Cartwright St., Granville Island,* ☏ *604/687–2739.* ☞ *$8.75.* ☉ *July–Aug., Sun.–Wed. 10–7, Thurs.–Sat. 10–8; Sept.–June, daily 10–7 (call for tour times).*

**㊳ Granville Island Museums.** Here are three museums under one roof. The **Sport Fishing Museum** houses one of the world's leading collections of angling artifacts, including the world's biggest collection of Hardy reels and fly plates, and a mounted replica of the largest salmon ever caught with a rod and reel. The collection of the **Model Ships Museum** includes exquisitely detailed early 20th-century military and working vessels, including a 13-ft replica of the HMS *Hood,* the British Royal Navy ship that was sunk by the German warship *Bismarck* in 1941, and a model of the *Hunley,* an 1863 Confederate submarine that was the first to sink a surface vessel. The **Model Trains Museum,** the world's largest toy-train collection on public display, includes a diorama of the Fraser Canyon and the Kettle Valley that involves 1,000 ft of track and some large-scale (3-ft-high) model steam trains. Hobbyists can find goodies in the gift shop. ⊠ *1502 Duranleau St., Granville Island,* ☎ *604/683–1939,* WEB *www.granvilleislandmuseums.com.* 🖭 *All 3 museums $6.50.* ☉ *Daily 10–5:30.*

**★ ㉞ Granville Island Public Market.** Because no chain stores are allowed in this 50,000-square-ft building, each outlet here is unique. Dozens of stalls sell locally grown produce direct from the farm; others sell crafts, chocolates, cheeses, fish, meat, flowers, and exotic foods. In summer, market gardeners sell fruit and vegetables from trucks outside. At the north end of the market you can pick up a snack, espresso, or fixings for lunch on the wharf. The Market Courtyard, on the water side, is a good place to catch street entertainers. Weekends can get madly busy here. ⊠ *1689 Johnston St., Granville Island,* ☎ *604/666–6477,* WEB *www.granvilleisland.com.* ☉ *Feb.–Dec., daily 9–6; Jan., Tues.–Sun. daily 9–6.*

**㉟ Granville Island Water Park.** This kids' paradise has slides, pipes, and sprinklers for children to shower one another. ⊠ *1318 Cartwright St., Granville Island,* ☎ *604/257–8195.* 🖭 *Free.* ☉ *Late May–late June, weekends (call for hrs); July–Aug., daily 10–6.*

**㊱ Kids' Market.** A slice of kids' heaven on Granville Island, the Kids' Market has an indoor play area and two floors of small shops that sell all kinds of toys, magic gear, books, and other fun stuff. ⊠ *1496 Cartwright St., Granville Island,* ☎ *604/689–8447.* ☉ *Daily 10–6.*

**㊴ Net Loft.** This blue-and-red building includes a bookstore, a café, and a collection of high-quality boutiques selling imported and locally made crafts, exotic fabrics, handmade paper, and First Nations art. ⊠ *1666 Johnston St., across from Public Market, Granville Island,* ☎ *no phone.* ☉ *Individual shop hrs vary, but most are open daily 10–6.*

# Kitsilano

The beachfront district of Kitsilano (popularly known as Kits), south of downtown Vancouver, is among the trendiest of Canadian neighborhoods. Originally inhabited by the Squamish people, whose Chief Khahtsahlanough gave the area its name, Kitsilano began to attract daytrippers from Vancouver in the early part of the 20th century. Some stayed and built lavish waterfront mansions; others built simpler Craftsman-style houses farther up the slope. After a period of decline in the mid-20th century, Kits, which contains many restored wood-frame Craftsman houses, is once again chic.

Kitsilano is home to three museums, some fashionable shops, and popular pubs and cafés. Kits has hidden treasures, too: rare boats moored at Heritage Harbour, stately mansions on forested lots, and, all along the waterfront, quiet coves and shady paths within a stone's throw of Canada's liveliest beach.

*Numbers in the text correspond to numbers in the margin and on the Vancouver map.*

## A Good Walk

Vanier Park, the grassy beachside setting for three museums and the best kite-flying venue in Vancouver, is the logical gateway to Kits. The most enjoyable way to get here is by False Creek Ferries, from Granville Island or from behind the Vancouver Aquatic Centre, on Beach Avenue. The ferries dock at Heritage Harbour behind the Vancouver Maritime Museum. You can also walk or cycle about 1 km (½ mi) along the waterfront pathway from Granville Island (leave the island by Anderson Street and keep to your right along the waterfront). If you prefer to come by road, drive over the Burrard Street Bridge, turn right at Chestnut Street, and park in either of the museum parking lots; or take Bus 2 or 22 traveling south on Burrard Street downtown, get off at Cypress Street and Cornwall Avenue, and walk over to the park.

**Vancouver Museum** �40, which showcases the city's natural and cultural history, shares a building with the **H. R. MacMillan Space Centre** �41, a high-tech museum focusing on outer space. The **Vancouver Maritime Museum** �42, which traces the maritime history of the West Coast, is to the west and toward the water. Each museum has hands-on exhibits that appeal to kids.

Behind the Maritime Museum, where the ferries dock, is Heritage Harbour, home to a rotating series of boats of historical interest, including *BCP 45*, the picturesque fishing boat that used to appear on Canada's $5 bill. In summer the big tent, set up in Vanier Park, is the venue for the Bard on the Beach Shakespeare series.

West of the Maritime Museum is a quiet, grassy beach. A staircase leads up from the beach to a paved walkway. Take a moment to look at the 100-ft-tall replica Kwakiutl totem pole in front of the museum, and then follow the walkway west to popular **Kitsilano Beach** �43. Across the water you can see Stanley Park, and Vancouver's downtown core is behind you. Stroll along the beach about 1 km (½ mi) to the outdoor pool at the far end. Continue past the pool, along the water, and enter a shady pathway lined with blackberry bushes that runs behind the Kitsilano Yacht Club. Soon the lane opens up to a viewpoint and gives access to another sandy cove.

About ½ km (¼ mi) from the yacht club, the path ends at a staircase. This leads up to a viewpoint and a park on Point Grey Road. Across the street from the top of the staircase, at 2590 Point Grey Road, is an Edwardian-era mansion that was built by a member of Kitsilano's early elite. Double back the way you came, heading east toward Kits Beach, but this time follow Point Grey Road for a look at the front of the homes you could see from the beach path. The 1909 Logan House, at 2530 Point Grey Road, is an ivory-color Edwardian dream home with a curved balcony.

Follow Point Grey Road as it curves to the right, and cross Cornwall Avenue at Balsam Street. Turn left on either York or 1st Avenue and walk two blocks to Yew Street, where in summer you can find one of the biggest concentrations of sidewalk pubs and cafés in Greater Vancouver. Alternatively, you can hike up the hill to 4th Avenue, once the heart of the hippie district, and explore the shops between Balsam and Burrard streets. You can catch a bus back to downtown Vancouver on Cornwall or 4th Avenue, or cut across Kits Beach Park back to Vanier Park.

The walk alone takes about 1½ hours. Add two hours to see the MacMillan Space Centre and an hour for each of the other museums. With time out for shopping or swimming, a visit to Kitsilano could easily fill a whole day.

## Sights to See

**43 Kitsilano Beach.** Picnic sites, a playground, tennis courts, Vancouver's biggest outdoor pool, and some fine people-watching can all be found at Kits Beach. Inland from the pool, the **Kitsilano Showboat** hosts free performances, mostly of the children's dancing variety, in summer. ⊠ *Off Cornwall Ave., Kitsilano,* ☎ *604/738–8535 beach information; 604/731–0011 pool (both summer only);* WEB *www.city.vancouver. bc.ca/parks/2.htm.* ⊞ *Beach free, pool $4.15.* ☉ *Pool late May–mid-June, weekdays noon–8:45, weekends 10–8:45; mid-June–mid-Sept., weekdays 7 AM–9 AM (adults only) and 9 AM–8:45 PM (general public), weekends 10–8:45.*

**41 H. R. MacMillan Space Centre.** The interactive exhibits and high-tech learning systems at this museum include a Virtual Voyages ride, where visitors can take a simulated space journey (definitely not for those afraid of flying); Ground Station Canada, showcasing Canada's achievements in space; and the Cosmic Courtyard, full of hands-on space-oriented exhibits including a moon rock and a program that shows what you would look like as an alien. You can catch daytime astronomy shows or evening music and laser shows at the **H. R. MacMillan Planetarium.** When the sky is clear, the ½-m telescope at the **Gordon MacMillan Southam Observatory** (☎ 604/738–2855) is focused on whatever stars or planets are worth watching that night. Admission to the observatory is free, and it's open year-round on weekend evenings, weather permitting (call for hours). ⊠ *Vanier Park, 1100 Chestnut St., Kitsilano,* ☎ *604/738–7827,* WEB *www.hrmacmillanspacecentre.com.* ⊞ *$12.75.* ☉ *July–Aug., daily 10–5; Sept.–June, Tues.–Sun. 10–5.*

**42 Vancouver Maritime Museum.** About a third of the museum has been turned over to kids, with touchable displays that provide a chance to drive a tug, maneuver an underwater robot, or dress up as a seafarer. Toddlers and school-age children can work the hands-on displays in Pirates' Cove and the Children's Maritime Discovery Centre. The museum also has an extensive collection of model ships and is the last moorage for the *St. Roch,* the first ship to sail in both directions through the treacherous Northwest Passage. Historic boats are moored at **Heritage Harbour,** behind the museum, and a huge replica of a Kwakiutl totem pole stands out front. ⊠ *Vanier Park, 1905 Ogden Ave., north end of Cypress St., Kitsilano,* ☎ *604/257–8300,* WEB *www.vmm.bc.ca.* ⊞ *Museum $8, Heritage Harbour free.* ☉ *Mid-May–Labor Day, daily 10–5; Labor Day–mid-May, Tues.–Sat. 10–5, Sun. noon–5.*

**40 Vancouver Museum.** Life-size replicas of a trading post, the sleeping quarters of an immigrant ship, a Victorian parlor, a 1910 kitchen, and a 19th-century Canadian Pacific Railway passenger car are some of the highlights of this museum, which focuses on the city's history, from early European exploration to the present day, and histories of the Pacific Northwest Coast and the Pacific Rim. At press time, plans were in place for a number of new interactive exhibits, including a hands-on archaeology dig, a natural history lab, and a 1950s gallery, in a new wing called the Joyce Walley Learning Centre, scheduled to open in late 2002. The museum is also a major venue for national and international touring exhibitions. ⊠ *Vanier Park, 1100 Chestnut St., Kitsilano,* ☎ *604/736–4431,* WEB *www.vanmuseum.bc.ca.* ⊞ *$8.* ☉ *Fri.–Wed. 10–5, Thurs. 10–9.*

# South Vancouver and Point Grey

Some of Vancouver's best gardens, natural sights, and museums, including the renowned Museum of Anthropology, are south of downtown, on the campus of the University of British Columbia and in the city's southern residential districts. Individual attractions are easily reached by TransLink buses, but you need a car to see them all comfortably in a day.

*Numbers in the text correspond to numbers in the margin and on the Vancouver map.*

## A Good Drive

From downtown Vancouver, cross the Burrard Street Bridge and follow the marked scenic route (to the right). This takes you along Cornwall Avenue, which becomes Point Grey Road and follows the waterfront to Alma Street. The little wooden structure at the corner of Point Grey Road and Alma Street is the **Old Hastings Mill Store Museum** ㊹, Vancouver's first retail shop. If you're a golf fan, you might take a detour to the **British Columbia Golf Museum** ㊺, on Blanca Street at the edge of the University Golf Course.

The scenic route continues south on Alma Street and then west (to the right) on 4th Avenue. Take the right fork onto Northwest Marine Drive, which winds past Jericho, Locarno, and Spanish Banks beaches and up to the University of British Columbia (UBC). The **Museum of Anthropology** ㊻ is here (opposite Gate 4) and houses one of the world's best collections of Pacific Northwest First Nations artifacts. **Nitobe Memorial Garden** ㊼, a Japanese-style strolling garden, is across Marine Drive. Limited metered parking is available at the Museum of Anthropology; pay parking is available in two parkades within walking distance of the museum and the garden. To find them, turn left off Northwest Marine Drive at University Gate 4 or 6, and then follow the signs.

The **University of British Columbia Botanical Garden** ㊽, which has plenty of parking, is 3 km (2 mi) farther along Marine Drive. For more gardens, follow Marine Drive through the university grounds and take the left fork onto 41st Avenue. Turn left again onto Oak Street to reach the entrance of the **VanDusen Botanical Garden** ㊾, on your left. The complex is planted with an English-style maze, water and herb gardens, and more. Return to 41st Avenue, continue farther east (turn left), and then turn left again on Cambie Street to reach **Queen Elizabeth Park** ㊿, which overlooks the city. To get back downtown, continue north on Cambie Street and over the Cambie Street Bridge.

TIMING

Except during rush hour, it takes about 30 minutes to drive from downtown to the University of British Columbia. You should add another 30 to 45 minutes of driving time for the rest of the tour and about two hours to visit each of the main attractions.

## Sights to See

㊺ **British Columbia Golf Museum.** This offbeat museum at the edge of the University Golf Club is a treat for those who can't get enough of the game. Housed in a 1930 colonial bungalow that once served as the course clubhouse, the museum has a fine collection of historic photos, trophies, antique clubs, and other golfing memorabilia. The exhibits are arranged like a golf course in 18 sections, or holes, with a theme for each. ✉ *2545 Blanca St., Point Grey,* ☏ *604/222–4653,* WEB *www.bcgolfmuseum.org.* ☜ *Free.* ☉ *Tues.–Sun. noon–4.*

★ ㊻ **Museum of Anthropology.** Part of the University of British Columbia, the MOA has one of the world's leading collections of Northwest Coast

First Nations Art. The Great Hall displays dramatic cedar poles, bent-wood boxes, and canoes adorned with traditional Northwest Coast painted designs. On clear days, the gallery's 50-ft-tall windows provide a striking backdrop of mountains and sea. Another highlight is the work of the late Bill Reid, one of Canada's most respected Haida carvers. His *The Raven and the First Men* (1980), carved in yellow cedar, tells a Haida story of creation. Reid's gold and silver jewelry work is also on display, as are exquisite carvings of gold, silver, and argillite (a black shale found on Haida Gwaii, also known as the Queen Charlotte Islands) by other First Nations artists. The museum's visible storage section displays, in drawers and cases, thousands of examples of tools, textiles, masks, and other artifacts from around the world. The experience is a visit to the attic of a Victorian explorer. The Koerner Ceramics Gallery contains 600 pieces from 15th- to 19th-century Europe. Behind the museum are two Haida houses, set on the cliff over the water. Free guided tours—given twice daily in summer, usually at 11 and 2 (call to confirm times)—are very informative. Arthur Erickson designed the cliff-top structure that houses the MOA, which also has a good book and fine art shop and a summertime café. To reach the museum by transit, take a UBC Bus 4 or 10 from Granville Street downtown to the university loop, a 10-minute walk from the museum. ⊠ *University of British Columbia, 6393 N. W. Marine Dr., Point Grey,* ☎ *604/822–3825,* WEB *www.moa.ubc.ca.* ☒ *$7; free Tues. 5–9.* ⊙ *Memorial Day–Labor Day, Tues. 10–9, Mon. and Wed.–Sun. 10–5; Labor Day–Memorial Day, Tues. 11–9, Wed.–Sun. 11–5.*

**㊼ Nitobe Memorial Garden.** Opened in 1960 in memory of Japanese scholar and diplomat Dr. Inazo Nitobe (1862–1933), this 2½-acre walled garden, which includes a pond and a ceremonial teahouse, is considered one of the most authentic Japanese tea and strolling gardens outside Japan. Designed by Professor Kannosuke Mori of Japan's Chiba University, the garden incorporates many native British Columbia trees and shrubs, pruned and trained in the Japanese fashion and interplanted with Japanese maples and flowering shrubs. The circular path around the park symbolizes the cycle of life and provides a tranquil view from every direction. Cherry blossoms are the highlight in April and May, and in June the irises are magnificent. ⊠ *University of British Columbia, 1903 West Mall, Point Grey,* ☎ *604/822–9666,* WEB *www. ubcbotanicalgarden.org.* ☒ *Mid-Mar.–mid-Oct. $2.75, mid-Oct.–mid-Mar. by donation.* ⊙ *Mid-Mar.–mid-Oct., daily 10–6; mid-Oct.–mid-Mar., weekdays 10–2:30.*

**㊹ Old Hastings Mill Store Museum.** Vancouver's first store was built in 1865 at the foot of Dunlevy Street in Gastown and moved to this seaside spot in 1930. The only building to predate the 1886 Great Fire, the site is now a museum with displays of First Nations artifacts and pioneer household goods. ⊠ *1575 Alma St., Point Grey,* ☎ *604/734–1212.* ☒ *Donation.* ⊙ *Mid-June–mid-Sept., Tues.–Sun. 11–4; mid-Sept.–Nov. and Feb.–mid-June, weekends 1–4.*

**㊿ Queen Elizabeth Park.** Besides views of downtown, the park has lavish sunken gardens, a rose garden, and an abundance of grassy picnicking spots. Other park facilities include 20 tennis courts, pitch and putt, and a restaurant. In the **Bloedel Conservatory** you can see tropical and desert plants and 60 species of free-flying tropical birds in a glass triodetic dome. To reach the park by public transportation, take a Cambie Bus 15 from the corner of Robson and Burrard streets downtown to 33rd Avenue. ⊠ *Cambie St. and 33rd Ave., South Vancouver,* ☎ *604/ 257–8570,* WEB *www.bloedelconservatory.com.* ☒ *Conservatory $3.90.* ⊙ *Apr.–Sept., weekdays 9–8, weekends 10–9; Oct.–Mar., daily 10–5:30.*

**48** **University of British Columbia Botanical Garden.** Ten thousand trees, shrubs, and rare plants from around the world thrive on this 70-acre research site on the university campus. The complex includes an Asian garden, a garden of medicinal plants, and an alpine garden with some of the world's rarest plants. Guided tours, included in the price of admission, are given Wednesday and Saturday at 1 in summer (call to confirm). The extensive shop is a paradise for gardeners. ✉ *6804 S.W. Marine Dr., Point Grey,* ☎ *604/822–9666,* WEB *www.ubcbotanicalgarden.org.* 🎟 *Summer $4.75, winter free.* ☼ *Mid-Mar.–mid-Oct., daily 10–6; mid-Oct.–mid-Mar., daily 10–dusk.*

**49** **VanDusen Botanical Garden.** On what was a 55-acre golf course grows one of Canada's largest botanical gardens. Displays from every continent include an Elizabethan maze, five lakes, a sculpture collection and a North American aboriginal medicinal garden with a medicine wheel of standing stones, and a Sino-Himalayan garden. There's also a shop, a library, and a restaurant. In June the garden produces North America's largest (in attendance and area) outdoor flower and garden show. During the last three weeks of December, a big draw is the Festival of Lights (5–9 PM daily). The gardens are wheelchair accessible. An Oak Bus 17 gets you here from downtown. Queen Elizabeth Park is a 1-km (½-mi) walk away, on West 37th Avenue. ✉ *5251 Oak St., at W. 37th Ave., South Vancouver,* ☎ *604/878–9274 garden; 604/261–0011 restaurant;* WEB *www.vandusengarden.org.* 🎟 *$7 Apr.–Sept., $5 Oct.–Mar.* ☼ *June–mid-Aug., daily 10–9; call for off-season hrs.*

# North Vancouver

The mountains that form a stunning backdrop to Vancouver lie in the district of North Vancouver, a bridge or SeaBus ride away on the North Shore of Burrard Inlet. Although the area is part suburb, the mountainous terrain has kept large parts of North Vancouver forested. This is where Vancouverites and visitors go for easily accessible hiking, skiing, and viewing the city lights.

*Numbers in the text correspond to numbers in the margin and on the Vancouver map.*

## A Good Drive

From downtown, drive west down Georgia Street to Stanley Park and across the Lions Gate Bridge to North Vancouver. Stay in the right lane, take the North Vancouver exit, and then turn left onto Capilano Road. In about 2 km (1 mi), you come to the **Capilano Suspension Bridge and Park** ㊿. A few hundred yards up Capilano Road, on the left, is the entrance to **Capilano River Regional Park** ㊾. About 1 km (½ mi) along the park access road you'll find the Capilano Salmon Hatchery. Returning to Capilano Road and continuing north, you'll reach Cleveland Dam (also part of the park) where you can stop for great mountain views. As you continue north, Capilano Road becomes Nancy Greene Way, which ends at the base of **Grouse Mountain** ㊾. From here, a cable car to the summit gives you great city views.

Alternatively, you can take the SeaBus from Waterfront Station to Lonsdale Quay and then catch a Grouse Mountain Bus 236. This stops at the Capilano Suspension Bridge and near the Salmon Hatchery on its way to the base of Grouse Mountain.

TIMING
You need a half day to see the sights, a full day if you want to hike at Grouse Mountain or Capilano River Regional Park. To save a lot of time, avoid crossing the Lions Gate Bridge during weekday rush hours (about 7–9 AM and 3–6 PM).

## Sights to See

(S) 52 **Capilano River Regional Park.** The park contains hiking trails and foot-bridges over the Capilano River, where it cuts through a dramatic gorge. At the park's **Capilano Salmon Hatchery** (⊠ 4500 Capilano Park Rd., North Vancouver, ☎ 604/666–1790), viewing areas and exhibits illustrate the life cycle of the salmon. The best time of year to see the salmon run is between July and November. The **Cleveland Dam** (⊠ Capilano Rd., about 2 km [1 mi] past main park entrance) is at the north end of the park. Built in 1954 and named for Dr. E. A. Cleveland, a former chief commissioner of the Greater Vancouver Water District, it dams the Capilano River to create the 5½-km-long (3½-mi-long) Capilano Reservoir. A hundred yards from the parking lot, you can walk across the top of the dam to enjoy striking views of the reservoir and mountains behind it. The two sharp peaks to the west are the Lions, for which the Lions Gate Bridge is named. ⊠ *Capilano Rd., North Vancouver,* ☎ *604/224–5739.* ⊡ *Free.* ⊙ *Park daily 8 AM–dusk; hatchery June–Aug., daily 8–8 (call for off-season hrs).*

(S) 51 **Capilano Suspension Bridge and Park.** At Vancouver's oldest tourist attraction (the original bridge was built in 1889), you can get a taste of rain-forest scenery and test your mettle on the swaying, 450-ft cedar-plank suspension bridge that hangs 230 ft above the rushing Capilano River. The park also has viewing decks, nature trails, a totem park and carving center (where you can watch First Nations carvers at work), history and forestry exhibits, a massive gift shop in the original 1911 teahouse, and a restaurant. Most of the attractions are on the near side of the bridge, so you don't have to cross it to enjoy the site. May through October, guides in 19th-century costumes conduct free tours on such themes as history, nature or gardening, and fiddle bands, First Nations dancers, and other entertainers keep things lively. ⊠ *3735 Capilano Rd., North Vancouver,* ☎ *604/985–7474,* WEB *www. capbridge.com.* ⊡ *May–Oct. $13.95, Nov.–Apr. $11.95 (plus $3 for parking).* ⊙ *Apr.–Oct., daily 8:30–dusk; Nov.–Mar., daily 9–5.*

★ (S) 53 **Grouse Mountain.** North America's largest aerial tramway, the Skyride is a great way to take in the city, sea, and mountain vistas (be sure to pick a clear day or evening), and you'll have plenty to do after you arrive at the top of Grouse Mountain. The Skyride makes the 2-km (1-mi) climb up to the peak every 15 minutes. A Skyride ticket includes a half-hour video presentation at the Theatre in the Sky. Free mountaintop activities include lumberjack shows, summertime chairlift rides, walking tours, hiking, and a chance to visit grizzly cubs and other local species at the mountain's wildlife refuge. For an extra fee you can also try tandem paragliding or helicopter tours. In winter, you can snow-shoe, snowboard, downhill and cross-country ski, ice-skate, and take Sno-Cat-drawn sleigh rides. The mountaintop also has a café, a bistro, and a restaurant. The **hiwus Feast House** (☎ 604/980–9311) presents a traditional First Nations feast and entertainment in a mountaintop longhouse. It's open May through October, and reservations are essential. ⊠ *6400 Nancy Greene Way, North Vancouver,* ☎ *604/980–9311,* WEB *www.grousemountain.com.* ⊡ *Skyride and most activities $19.95.* ⊙ *Daily 9 AM–10 PM.*

OFF THE
BEATEN PATH

**LYNN CANYON PARK –** With a steep canyon landscape, a temperate rain forest complete with waterfalls, and a suspension bridge 166½ ft above raging Lynn Creek, this park provides thrills to go with its scenic views. The on-site Ecology Centre distributes maps of area hiking trails and has information about the flora and fauna. To get to the park, take the Lions Gate Bridge and Capilano Road, go east on Highway 1, take the Lynn Valley Road exit, and turn right on Peters Road. From downtown Vancouver, you can take the SeaBus to Lonsdale Quay, then Bus 228 or 229 from the quay; both stop near the park. ✉ *3663 Park Rd. (at end of Peters Rd.), North Vancouver,* ☎ *604/981–3103,* WEB *www. dnv.org/ecology.* ✉ *Ecology Centre by donation, suspension bridge free.* ☉ *Apr.–Sept., daily 10–5; Oct.–Mar., weekdays 10–5, weekends noon–4.*

# DINING

Vancouver dining is fairly informal. Casual but neat dress is appropriate everywhere. Smoking is prohibited by law in all Vancouver restaurants (indoors). A 15% tip is expected. A 7% Goods and Services Tax (GST) is levied on the food portion of restaurant bills, and a 10% liquor tax is charged on wine, beer, and spirits. Some restaurants build the liquor tax into the price of the beverage, but others add it to the bill. *See* the Downtown Vancouver Dining map to locate downtown restaurants and the Greater Vancouver Dining map to locate restaurants in Kitsilano, Granville Island, and other neighborhoods.

| CATEGORY | COST* |
| --- | --- |
| $$$$ | over $32 |
| $$$ | $22–$32 |
| $$ | $13–$21 |
| $ | under $13 |

*\*per person, in Canadian dollars, for a main course at dinner*

## Downtown Vancouver

### Casual

$–$$  ✕ **Earl's.** This locally grown chain is a favorite among Vancouverites looking for a lively place to go with a group. Big rooms, cheery decor, cozy booths, upbeat music, chipper service, and consistently good burgers, soups, sandwiches, pastas, steaks, and vegetarian options keep people coming back. Food and drink are served all day until midnight, and the Robson Street location has a big outdoor deck away from traffic. Reservations are accepted only for parties of eight or more. ✉ *1185 Robson St., Downtown,* ☎ *604/669–0020. AE, MC, V.*

### Chinese

$$–$$$$  ✕ **Imperial Chinese Seafood.** The two-story floor-to-ceiling windows
★ at this Cantonese restaurant in the Art Deco Marine Building have lovely views of Stanley Park and the North Shore Mountains across Coal Harbour. Any dish with lobster, crab, or shrimp from the live tanks is recommended, as is the dim sum, served daily 11 AM to 2:30 PM. ✉ *355 Burrard St., Downtown,* ☎ *604/688–8191. DC, MC, V.*

$$–$$$  ✕ **Kirin Mandarin Restaurant.** A striking silver mural of a *kirin,* a mythical dragonlike creature, presides over this elegant two-tiered restaurant two blocks from most of the major downtown hotels. The specialties here are northern Chinese (Mandarin and Szechuan) dishes, which tend to be richer and spicier than the Cantonese cuisine served at Kirin's other locations. Try the Peking duck, or the kung pao lobster, which is sautéed lobster meat served with a deep-fried lobster claw. Dim sum is served daily. ✉ *1166 Alberni St., Downtown,* ☎ *604/682–8833. AE, DC, MC, V.*

$–$$  ✕ **Hon's Wun-Tun House.** Mr. Hon has been keeping Vancouver residents in Chinese comfort food since the 1970s. The best bets on the 300-item menu are the pot stickers (dumplings), the wonton and noodle dishes, and anything with barbecued meat. The Robson Street outlet has a separate kitchen for vegetarians and an army of fast-moving waitresses. The original Keefer Street location is in the heart of Chi-

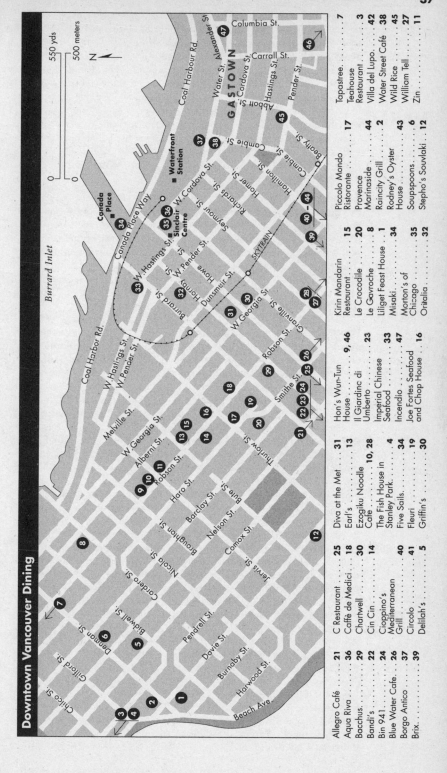

natown. ⊠ *1339 Robson St., West End,* ☎ *604/685–0871. Reservations not accepted. MC, V.* ⊠ *268 Keefer St., Chinatown,* ☎ *604/688–0871. Reservations not accepted. No credit cards.*

$–$$   ✕ **Wild Rice.** The decor is decadent postmodern (lounging couches on the mezzanine, melamine-topped tables, an underlit aquamarine bar); the food, served in tasting portions or on larger plates meant for sharing, borrows from all regions of China and beyond. Dishes include wild boar with jasmine rice and plantain, fried duck and rabbit wontons with hoi su pear sauce, and a dessert of warm rice pudding with chocolate and ginger. A short but well-chosen wine list is augmented by a wide-ranging tea and martini selection. ⊠ *117 W. Pender St., Chinatown,* ☎ *604/642–2882,* WEB *www.wildricevancouver.com. Reservations not accepted. AE, MC, V.*

## Contemporary

$$$–$$$$   ✕ **Chartwell.** Named after Sir Winston Churchill's country home (a painting of it hangs over one of this elegant restaurant's two fireplaces), the flagship dining room at the Four Seasons hotel has rich wood paneling, deep leather chairs, and a reputation for innovative contemporary cuisine. The seasonally changing menu makes the most of British Columbia's regional bounty, notably lamb and seafood, and always lists good vegetarian options. ⊠ *791 W. Georgia St., Downtown,* ☎ *604/844–6715. AE, DC, MC, V. No lunch Sat.*

$$$–$$$$   ✕ **Diva at the Met.** At this multitiered restaurant in the Metropolitan Hotel, the presentation of the innovative contemporary cuisine is as appealing as the Art Deco decor. The menu changes seasonally, but top creations from the open kitchen have included wild sockeye salmon with crab and leek gratin, and organic cinnamon-smoked Fraser Valley duck breast. The after-theater crowd heads here for late-evening snacks, desserts, and rich handmade chocolates. The creative breakfasts and weekend brunches are popular options. ⊠ *645 Howe St., Downtown,* ☎ *604/602–7788. AE, D, DC, MC, V.*

$$$–$$$$   ✕ **Five Sails.** This special-occasion restaurant at the Pan Pacific Hotel commands a sweeping view of Canada Place, Lions Gate Bridge, and the lights of the North Shore. The broad-reaching, seasonally changing menu takes its inspiration from both Europe and the Pacific Rim. Highlights have included slow-roasted B.C. salmon, date-crusted venison loin, and seared ahi tuna with foie gras and trumpet mushrooms. ⊠ *Pan Pacific Hotel, 300–999 Canada Pl., Downtown,* ☎ *604/891–2892. AE, DC, MC, V. No lunch.*

$$–$$$$   ✕ **Aqua Riva.** The views over the harbor and the North Shore Mountains are stunning from this lofty, lively modern room just yards from the Canada Place cruise-ship terminal. Food from the wood-fired oven, rotisserie, and grill includes thin-crust pizzas with innovative toppings, grilled salmon, and spit-roasted chicken. There's also a good selection of pastas, salads, and sandwiches and a long list of microbrewery beers and martinis. ⊠ *200 Granville St., Downtown,* ☎ *604/683–5599. AE, DC, MC, V.*

$$–$$$$   ✕ **Delilah's.** Cherubs dance on the ceiling, candles flicker on the tables, and martini glasses clink during toasts at this jovially decadent West End spot. The two velvet booths with curtains are romantic favorites. The contemporary cuisine, served in two- or four-course prix-fixe dinners, is innovative and artfully presented. Though the menu changes frequently, the Szechuan-style rack of lamb is so popular it's always available. Reservations are accepted only for groups of six or larger. ⊠ *1789 Comox St., West End,* ☎ *604/687–3424. AE, DC, MC, V. No lunch.*

**$$–$$$** ✕ **Brix.** The greenery-draped courtyard is a romantic summer dining spot. Inside, the 1912 former warehouse is fashionably comfortable, with vaulted ceilings, exposed brick, and local art exhibits. The seasonally changing fare, dubbed "progressive Pacific Northwest," presents creative treatments of local ingredients, many with Asian touches. Try the Wild B.C. caribou with a panko (Japanese bread crumb) crust or the Saltspring Island lamb stuffed with morel and wild mushrooms. An equally creative lunch menu might include an ahi tuna and salmon wrap or a duck confit salad. Tapas and more than 60 wines by the glass are available all day. ✉ *1138 Homer St., Yaletown,* ☎ *604/915–9463,* WEB *www.brixvancouver.com. AE, MC, V. Closed Sun. No lunch Sat.*

**$$–$$$** ✕ **Griffin's.** Bright yellow walls, bold black and white tiles, an open kitchen, and splashy artwork keep things lively at this high-energy bistro in the Fairmont Hotel Vancouver. The Pacific Northwest buffets—for breakfast, lunch, evening appetizers, and dessert—are the main attractions here. An à la carte menu lists salads, burgers, pizza, pasta, and seafood. ✉ *Fairmont Hotel Vancouver, 900 W. Georgia St., Downtown,* ☎ *604/662–1900. AE, D, DC, MC, V.*

**$$–$$$** ✕ **Raincity Grill.** One of the best places to try British Columbian food
★ and wine is this pretty candlelit bistro overlooking English Bay. The menu, which owner Harry Kambolis likes to call "stubbornly regional," changes seasonally and relies almost completely on local and regional products, from salmon and shellfish to game and fresh organic vegetables. At least four vegetarian selections are always on the menu, and the exclusively Pacific Northwest and Californian wine list has 100 choices by the glass. ✉ *1193 Denman St., West End,* ☎ *604/685–7337. AE, DC, MC, V. No lunch weekdays.*

**$$–$$$** ✕ **Teahouse Restaurant.** The former officers' mess in Stanley Park is perfectly poised for watching sunsets over the water. The Pacific Northwest menu includes such specialties as roasted pear salad, applewood smoked pork tenderloin, and rack of lamb. In summer you can dine on the patio, or enjoy a traditional English afternoon tea year-round. ✉ *7501 Stanley Park Dr., Ferguson Point, Stanley Park,* ☎ *604/669–3281. AE, MC, V. No afternoon tea Sun.*

**$$–$$$** ✕ **Water Street Café.** The tables at this popular Gastown café spill out onto the sidewalk for front-row views of the steam clock across the street. Inside, the slate-blue-and-white decor with tall windows overlooking bustling Water Street creates a cheerful, casual lunch or dinner atmosphere. It's tempting to pick one of the 12 varieties of pasta, but the crab chowder and the Fanny Bay oysters also are good choices. The breads are baked fresh daily. ✉ *300 Water St., Gastown,* ☎ *604/ 689–2832. AE, MC, V.*

## Continental

**$$–$$$$** ✕ **Fleuri.** Floral tablecloths, damask wall coverings, and lush garden scenes depicted in original artwork create an elegant, springlike feel at this spacious restaurant in the Sutton Place Hotel. Continental cuisine takes on Pacific Northwest influences in such seasonally changing starters as a Dungeness crab cake with apple and avocado salad, and such mains as a roulade of sole and langoustines. The dessert cart is tempting, but for the ultimate experience try the Chocoholic Bar, a 20-item all-chocolate buffet served Thursday through Sunday evenings. The Sunday brunches and Friday- and Saturday-night seafood buffets are also popular. ✉ *Sutton Place Hotel, 845 Burrard St., Downtown,* ☎ *604/642–2900. AE, D, DC, MC, V.*

**$$–$$$** ✕ **William Tell.** Silver service plates, embossed linen napkins, and a silver vase on each table set a tone of Swiss luxury at this establishment in the Georgian Court Hotel. The menu lists such Continental classics as filet mignon, steak tartare, and chateaubriand, as well as such Swiss dishes as cheese fondue and thinly sliced veal with mushrooms in a light white-wine sauce. On Sunday night is an all-you-can-eat Swiss buffet. Lunch is served only in the bar-and-bistro area, which caters to a more casual crowd than the main restaurant. ⊠ *765 Beatty St., Downtown,* ☏ *604/688–3504. AE, DC, MC, V. Main dining room closed Mon.*

## Eclectic

**$$–$$$** ✕ **Oritalia.** At this restaurant, Asian and Mediterranean traditions meet in such innovative entrées as duck breast with rye and morel strata, caramel apples, and frothed foie gras; and cashew and strawberry crusted halibut with sticky rice, rainbow chard, and roast lime sabayon. The 119-seat room, attached to the equally fashionable Sheraton Suites Le Soleil hotel, reflects the East-meets-West theme with rich golds, dark woods, and abstract Asia-inspired wall murals. The tables on the mezzanine provide vertiginous views of the open kitchen and a bird's-eye perspective of the striking handmade golden-glass and wrought-iron chandeliers. ⊠ *567 Hornby St., Downtown,* ☏ *604/689–8862. AE, DC, MC, V.*

**$$–$$$** ✕ **Zin.** Curved lines, plush banquettes, and an eye-popping color scheme of plum, raspberry, and tangerine make for a mod and trippy Pucci–meets–Austin Powers kind of room. The menu is global, sampling cuisines from around the world (mainly the tropics), but doesn't mess with fusion. Each dish, whether it's Mediterranean lamb chops, Jamaican jerk tuna, or Indonesian noodles, is true to its roots. Zin has kick-start breakfasts, too, including smoked salmon frittata and French toast with melted Brie. ⊠ *1277 Robson St., West End,* ☏ *604/408–1700,* WEB *www.zin-restaurant.com. AE, D, DC, MC, V. Closed Mon. No dinner Sun. Oct.–Apr.*

**$** ✕ **Bin 941.** Part tapas restaurant, part up-tempo bar, this bustling, sometime noisy hole in the wall serves some of the best snack-size cuisine in town. Such dishes as beef tenderloin phyllo Wellington and jumbo scallop and tiger-prawn tournedos are examples of leading-edge Pacific Northwest cuisine. Snack on a few, or have several and make a feast of it. The Bin is open until 2 AM for post-party snacks. Bin 942, a sister spot in Kitsilano, is a touch more subdued (☞ Dining, Greater Vancouver). ⊠ *941 Davie St., Downtown,* ☏ *604/683–1246,* WEB *www.bin941.com. Reservations not accepted. MC, V. No lunch.*

**$** ✕ **Tapastree.** This bistro-style restaurant near Stanley Park was among the first of Vancouver's tapas-style eateries. It's also where a number of local chefs enjoy after-work snacks. The dishes, all appetizer-size and under $11 each, run the gamut from an Asian seafood salad with papaya, scallops, and prawns to Japanese eggplant with pesto and goat cheese or lamb chops with sun-dried tomatoes and Gorgonzola. Splashy paintings and candelabra sconces shaped like human arms provide a theatrical feel. An extensive wine list rounds out the evening. ⊠ *1829 Robson St., West End,* ☏ *604/606–4680. AE, DC, MC, V. No lunch.*

## French

**$$$–$$$$** ✕ **Bacchus.** Low lighting, velvet drapes, and Venetian glass lamps, presided over by a large canvas of Bacchus, the Greek god of wine and revelry, create a decadent feel at this luxurious restaurant in the Wedgewood Hotel. The chef shines with such French-influenced delicacies as roasted loin of peppered venison, saddle of rabbit, and classic coq au vin. ⊠ *845 Hornby St., Downtown,* ☏ *604/608–5319. AE, DC, MC, V.*

**$$$–$$$$** ✕ **Le Gavroche.** Classic French cuisine receives contemporary accents at this romantic restaurant, set in a early 20th century house with mountain views. Seafood entrées range from salmon in sauce vierge to smoked sablefish with pink peppercorn sauce; meat options include a rich beef tenderloin with goat cheese and pine nuts. The chef also prepares such vegetarian options as sweet potato Napoleon and an organic vegetable cake with sweet pepper coulis. The 5,000-label wine cellar stresses Bordeaux and Californian varieties. ✉ *1616 Alberni St., West End,* ☎ *604/685–3924. AE, DC, MC, V. No lunch weekends.*

$$–$$$ ✕ **Le Crocodile.** Chef and owner Michel Jacob prepares Alsatian-influenced food at this elegant restaurant on Smithe Street off Burrard. Golden yellow walls, café curtains, and burgundy banquettes keep things cozy. Favorite dishes, many of which also appear at lower prices at lunch, include caramel-sweet onion tart, baked sea bass with lobster sauce, and venison with chanterelle sauce. ✉ *100–909 Burrard St., Downtown,* ☎ *604/669–4298. AE, DC, MC, V. Closed Sun. No lunch Sat.*

$ ✕ **Soupspoons.** You can join other guests at the long communal table, take a spot by the window, or ask for take out at this tiny café near English Bay. The look resembles a deli, but the specialty here is soup, and the French chef-owner whips up 10 fresh varieties daily. The chicken and lemongrass soup is warming, especially after a stroll around the park. Euro-sandwiches such as croque monsieurs, focaccia, and paninis fill out the menu. ✉ *990 Denman St., West End,* ☎ *604/328–7687,* WEB *www.soupspoons.com. Reservations not accepted. V.*

### Greek

$ ✕ **Stepho's Souvlaki.** Regulars swear by, and are quite prepared to wait in line for, Stepho's inexpensive and tasty roast lamb, moussaka, and souvlaki, served in a bustling taverna. The take-out menu is handy for picnics on the beach just down the street. ✉ *1124 Davie St., West End,* ☎ *604/683–2555. Reservations not accepted. AE, MC, V.*

### Hungarian

$$–$$$ ✕ **Bandi's.** Slow-roasted duck and rich veal goulash are among the Eastern European dishes served in this 1905 Victorian house. Eastern carpets on hardwood floors and antique tables set by a fireplace create a homey and romantic setting. The recipes, from the chilled sour-cherry soup to the rum-filled chocolate crepes, are made with attention to detail: herbs are plucked from the restaurant's patio, Hungarian produce is grown to order on a nearby farm, and many hard-to-find wines and liqueurs are imported from Hungary. ✉ *1427 Howe St., West End,* ☎ *604/685–3391. AE, MC, V. No lunch weekends.*

### Italian

$$–$$$$ ✕ **Cin Cin.** Gold walls, high arched windows, and terra-cotta tiles give this fashionable Italian restaurant a comfortable Tuscan air. The heated second-floor terrace, surrounded by trees, feels a long way from busy Robson Street below. The food, from the open kitchen and the wood-fired grill, oven, and rotisserie, reflects chef Romy Prasad's experience cooking in New York City, Italy, Spain, and France. Popular main dishes include pink peppercorn–crusted cod and thin-crust wood-fired pizza. The upbeat music and the social scene around the hand-carved marble bar make for a lively atmosphere. ✉ *1154 Robson St. (upstairs), West End,* ☎ *604/688–7338,* WEB *www.cincin.net. AE, DC, MC, V. No lunch weekends.*

$$–$$$$ ✕ **Circolo.** Umberto Menghi, a longtime Vancouver restaurateur, brings together the look and the cuisine of his three favorite cities—Paris, Florence, and New York—at this lofty, elegant restaurant. The menu reflects the tri-city theme: tagliata alla Fiorentina, New York steak, and filet mignon are all here. A lively oyster bar and a flower-draped patio add to the fun. ✉ *1116 Mainland St., Yaletown,* ☎ *604/687–1116. AE, DC, MC, V. Closed Sun. No lunch.*

$$–$$$ ✕ **Borgo Antico.** Terra-cotta tiles and graceful archways give this spacious room a classical feel; upstairs, tall windows look out toward the harbor. A less-expensive sister restaurant to Il Giardino di Umberto,

Borgo Antico serves such Tuscan dishes as grilled calamari salad, gnocchi with artichokes and sun-dried tomatoes, veal medallions with lemon and capers, and osso buco with risotto. The wine cellar has more than 300 selections. ⊠ *321 Water St., Gastown,* ☎ *604/683–8376. AE, DC, MC, V. Closed Sun. No lunch Sat.*

**$$–$$$**    ✕ **Caffè de Medici.** Run by the same family (with many of the same customers) since 1980, this elegant northern Italian restaurant is—despite its location on Vancouver's most fashionable street—pleasantly free of attitude. Caprese (tomato salad) made with buffalo mozzarella is a popular starter. Main courses include consistently good rack of lamb with a fresh herb crust and grilled jumbo prawns and scallops over a mascarpone risotto. The quiet atmosphere and gracious service make this a good choice for business lunches or romantic dinners. ⊠ *1025 Robson St., West End,* ☎ *604/669–9322. AE, DC, MC, V. No lunch weekends.*

**$$–$$$**    ✕ **Il Giardino di Umberto.** The beautiful vine-draped terrace with a wood-
   ★         burning oven or any of the four terra-cotta tiled rooms inside are attractive places to enjoy this long-established restaurateur's traditional Tuscan cuisine. The frequently changing menu includes grilled salmon with saffron and fennel vinaigrette and roast reindeer loin with a wine reduction. ⊠ *1380 Hornby St., Downtown,* ☎ *604/669–2422. AE, DC, MC, V. Closed Sun. No lunch Sat.*

**$$–$$$**    ✕ **Piccolo Mondo Ristorante.** Soft candlelight, bountiful flower ar-
   ★         rangements, and fine European antiques create intimacy at this northern Italian restaurant on a quiet street a block off Robson. The menu changes seasonally, but favorites have included grilled spot prawns with fennel and anise-seed vinaigrette as well as beef tenderloin with polenta and walnut and black truffle sauce. A classic osso buco is always on the menu. The wine cellar has more than 4,000 bottles (480 varieties). ⊠ *850 Thurlow St., West End,* ☎ *604/688–1633. AE, DC, MC, V. Closed Sun. No lunch Sat.*

**$$–$$$**    ✕ **Villa del Lupo.** Country-house-elegant decor sets a romantic tone at
   ★         this Victorian house on the edge of trendy Yaletown, home to one of Vancouver's most established Italian restaurants. The contemporary menu takes its inspiration from various regions of Italy. Lamb osso buco in a sauce of tomatoes, red wine, cinnamon, and lemon and sea-bass fillet roasted with white vermouth and herb butter and served with Manilla clams are favorites here. The restaurant serves lunch only to groups of 10 or more. ⊠ *869 Hamilton St., Yaletown,* ☎ *604/688– 7436,* WEB *www.villadellupo.com. AE, DC, MC, V. No lunch.*

## Japanese

**$$–$$$$**   ✕ **Misaki.** Local and visiting sushi lovers head for this elegant restaurant in the Pan Pacific Hotel. With its striking black-granite sushi bar and three intimate tatami rooms, Misaki has a relaxing ambience. The chefs here specialize in edomae-style sushi, but the menu also includes traditional Japanese dishes such as miso-broth hot pot, soba noodles, teppan yaki, and lobster and salmon tempura. ⊠ *300–999 Canada Pl., Downtown,* ☎ *604/891–2893. AE, DC, MC, V. Closed Sun. No lunch Sat.*

   **$**        ✕ **Ezogiku Noodle Cafe.** Noodles—or, more precisely, Japanese ramen noodles—are the specialty at these cheap and cheerful hole-in-the wall cafés. The two Robson Street locations fill quickly with hungry shoppers and homesick Japanese students. Some say the noodles and soups here are just like those in Tokyo. With nothing over $10, Ezogiku is one of the best values on this chic shopping strip. ⊠ *270 Robson St., at Hamilton St., West End,* ☎ *604/685–9466;* ⊠ *1329 Robson St., at Jervis St., West End,* ☎ *604/685–8606. Reservations not accepted. No credit cards.*

## Mediterranean

**$$–$$$$** ✕ **Cioppino's Mediterranean Grill.** Cioppino, a fragrant seafood stew, is the signature dish at this lofty, candlelit room. Chef Pino Posteraro impresses with homemade pastas and such light, Italian-Mediterranean dishes as casserole of sea bass and vegetables and pork tenderloin marinated in citrus and honey. Mr. Posteraro also serves more rustic Italian fare, such as char-broiled lamb chops and braised beef short ribs, at **Enoteca** (✉ 1129 Hamilton St., West End, ☎ 604/685–8462), a brick-walled sister restaurant next door. Both restaurants have street-side patios. ✉ *1133 Hamilton St., Yaletown,* ☎ *604/688–7466,* WEB *www. cioppinosyaletown.com. AE, DC, MC, V. Both closed Sun. No lunch at Cioppino's; no lunch weekends at Enoteca.*

**$$–$$$** ✕ **Allegro Café.** Cushy curved booths, low lighting, friendly staff, and a long martini menu give this downtown place near Robson Square a romantic—even flirtatious—feel. The menu is playful, too, with such rich and offbeat concoctions as pasta bundles with roasted butternut squash and Gorgonzola cream, and roast chicken breast with herbs, goat cheese, and peach-and-fig chutney. The rich daily soups and fair prices make this a good weekday lunch stop. ✉ *888 Nelson St., Downtown,* ☎ *604/683–8485. AE, DC, MC, V. No lunch weekends.*

**$$–$$$** ✕ **Provence Marinaside.** This airy modern Mediterranean-style eatery on Yaletown's waterfront presents French and Italian takes on seafood, including a delicious bouillabaisse and lush garlicky tiger prawns, though the rack of lamb and an extensive antipasti selection are also popular. A waterside patio provides marina views and makes a sunny breakfast or brunch spot. f4:*1177 Marinaside Cres., at the foot of Davie St., Yaletown,* ☎ *604/681–4144,* WEB *www.provencevancouver.com. AE, DC, MC, V.*

## Native American

**$$–$$$** ✕ **Liliget Feast House.** This intimate room looks like the interior of a
★ longhouse, with wooden walkways across pebble floors, contemporary First Nations art on the walls, and cedar-plank tables with tatami-style benches. Liliget is one of the few places in the world serving the original Northwest Coast First Nations cuisine. A feast platter lets you try most of the fare, which includes bannock bread, baked sweet potato with hazelnuts, alder-grilled salmon, buffalo smokies, venison strips, oysters, mussels, and steamed fern shoots. ✉ *1724 Davie St., West End,* ☎ *604/681–7044. AE, DC, MC, V. Closed Mon.–Tues. Dec.–Feb. No lunch.*

## Pizza

**$** ✕ **Incendio.** The hand-flipped thin-crust pizzas, with innovative toppings including Asiago cheese, prosciutto, roasted garlic, and sun-dried tomatoes, and the mix-and-match pastas and sauces (try the hot smoked-duck sausage, artichoke, and tomato combination, or the mango-basil-butter sauce) draw crowds to this Gastown eatery. The room, in a circa 1900 heritage building, with exposed brick, local artwork, and big curved windows, has plenty of atmosphere. **Incendio West** (✉ 2118 Burrard St., Kitsilano, ☎ 604/736–2220) has a similar menu in a more modern room. ✉ *103 Columbia St., Gastown,* ☎ *604/ 688–8694. AE, MC, V. No lunch weekends in Gastown; no lunch Sun. in Kitsilano.*

## Seafood

**$$$–$$$$** ✕ **C Restaurant.** Dishes such as lobster-and-crab-stuffed roasted tur-
★ bot and octopus-bacon-wrapped scallops have established C as Vancouver's most innovative seafood restaurant. Start with sashimi or shucked oysters from the raw bar, or try C's Taster Box, in which several morsels, such as quince syrup–cured wild sockeye and ahi tuna

tartare, are served dramatically on a four-tier display. An eight-course tasting menu highlights regional seafood, such as wild salmon, sablefish, and tanner crab. Both the chic, ultramodern interior (described by some as Captain Nemo meets Zen) and the waterside patio overlook the yacht and sailboat traffic on False Creek. ⊠ *2–1600 Howe St., Downtown,* ☎ *604/681–1164. AE, DC, MC, V. No lunch weekends or Oct.–Apr.*

**$$–$$$$** ✕ **Blue Water Cafe.** This fashionable restaurant shows its architectural bones with exposed timbers, beams, and brick that arrived here in the 1890s as ships' ballast. Fresh, local, well-presented seafood is the theme here, with such catch as Queen Charlotte Island halibut and B.C. sablefish, though meat, including Canadian prime beef, and vegetarian dishes are also available. The chef behind the sushi bar turns out both classic sushi and new creations using local seafood; a former loading dock makes an attractive outdoor terrace. ⊠ *1095 Hamilton St., Yaletown,* ☎ *604/688–8078,* WEB *www.bluewatercafe.net. AE, DC, MC, V. No lunch weekends in winter.*

**$$–$$$$** ✕ **Joe Fortes Seafood and Chop House.** This seafood hot spot and chop house just off Robson Street has a piano bar, a bistro, an oyster bar, and a delightful rooftop patio with a marquée, a fireplace, and an herb garden. Named for a much-loved English Bay lifeguard, Joe Fortes brings together a casual ambience, mahogany and stained-glass decor, and generous portions of fresh seafood. Try the cedar-smoked salmon, Joe's cioppino (a seafood stew), or the Lifeguard Tower on Ice—a starter of mussels, clams, scallops, prawns, shrimp, lobster, and crab that's meant to be shared. ⊠ *777 Thurlow St., Downtown,* ☎ *604/669–1940,* WEB *www.joefortes.ca. AE, D, DC, MC, V.*

**$$–$$$** ✕ **The Fish House in Stanley Park.** Tucked between Stanley Park's tennis courts and putting green, this 1930s former sports pavilion with a veranda and fireplace has a relaxed country-house ambience. The food here is hearty, flavorful, and unpretentious. Good choices are the ahi tuna steak Diane and the corn-husk-wrapped salmon with a maple glaze. Before dinner head straight for the oyster bar, or arrive between 5 and 6 to take advantage of the early-bird specials. The Fish House also serves a traditional English afternoon tea between 2 and 4 daily. ⊠ *8901 Stanley Park Dr., near Stanley Park's Beach Ave. entrance, Stanley Park,* ☎ *604/681–7275 or 877/681–7275,* WEB *www.fishhousestanleypark.com. AE, D, DC, MC, V.*

**$–$$** ✕ **Rodney's Oyster House.** This Yaletown fishing-shack look-alike has one of the widest selection of oysters in town (up to 18 varieties), from locally harvested bivalves to exotic Japanese kumamotos. You can pick your oysters individually—they're laid out on ice behind the bar and priced at $1.50 to about $3 each—or try the clams, scallops, mussels, periwinkles, and other mollusks from the steamer kettles. Chowders and other hot dishes are worth trying as well. Oyster lovers can also relax over martinis and appetizers in the attached Mermaid Lounge. ⊠ *1228 Hamilton St., Yaletown,* ☎ *604/609–0080. AE, DC, MC, V. Clo43sed Sun.*

## Steak

**$$$$** ✕ **Morton's of Chicago.** This comfortable clubby-looking room of dark woods, white linens, and plush seating is carnivore heaven. Top-of-the-line steak, whether a 14-ounce double-cut filet mignon, or a 24-ounce, or even 48-ounce, porterhouse, is the main event here. All beef served is USDA prime aged, grain fed, and shipped directly from Chicago. Atlantic lobster flown in daily, succulent prime rib, and classic steak dishes, such as steak au poivre and filet Diane, as well as rich desserts, are also specialties. The attentive service includes a pre-dinner tableside presentation of the cuts available that day. ⊠ *750 W. Cordova St., Yaletown,* ☎ *604/915–5105. AE, DC, MC, V. No lunch.*

# Greater Vancouver

### Casual

$–$$ ✕ **Earl's.** The Greater Vancouver offshoots of this local chain have all you'd expect from a popular casual restaurant: pizzas, juicy burgers, homemade desserts, comfy booths, chipper staff, and a relaxed atmosphere. Reservations are accepted only for groups of six or more. ⊠ *901 W. Broadway, Fairview,* ☎ *604/734–5995;* ⊠ *1601 W. Broadway, Kitsilano,* ☎ *604/736–5663. AE, MC, V.*

### Chinese

$$–$$$$ ✕ **Sun Sui Wah.** Sails in the ceiling add a lofty elegance to this big, bright,
★ and bustling East Side Cantonese restaurant. An offshoot of a popular Hong Kong establishment, Sun Sui Wah is best known for its dim sum (served 10:30–3 weekdays, 10–3 on weekends), which ranges from traditional handmade dumplings to some highly adventurous fare with Japanese touches. Dinner specialties include roasted squab and enormous king crab from the live tanks. There's another location in Richmond, the suburban heart of Vancouver's Chinese community. ⊠ *3888 Main St., East Vancouver,* ☎ *604/872–8822;* ⊠ *4940 No. 3 Rd., Richmond,* ☎ *604/273–8208. AE, DC, MC, V.*

$$–$$$ ✕ **Kirin Seafood Restaurant.** The south Vancouver and suburban outposts of this upscale operation focus on seafood and Cantonese creations, which are milder than the northern Chinese cuisine served at Kirin Mandarin Restaurant. Dim sum is served daily at lunchtime. ⊠ *555 W. 12th Ave., 2nd floor, Fairview,* ☎ *604/879–8038;* ⊠ *2nd floor, 3 West Centre, 7900 Westminster Hwy., Richmond,* ☎ *604/303–8833;* ⊠ *1163 Pinetree Way, Coquitlam,* ☎ *604/944–8833. AE, DC, MC, V.*

### Contemporary

$$$–$$$$ ✕ **Bishop's.** This highly regarded room serves West Coast cuisine with
★ an emphasis on organic, regional produce. The menu changes weekly, but highlights have included such starters as tea-smoked duck breast, and such mains as steamed smoked black cod and Dungeness crab cakes. All are beautifully presented and impeccably served with suggestions from Bishop's extensive local wine list. The split-level room displays elaborate flower arrangements and selections from owner John Bishop's extensive art collection. ⊠ *2183 W. 4th Ave., Kitsilano,* ☎ *604/738– 2025. AE, DC, MC, V. Closed 1st wk in Jan. No lunch.*

$$–$$$ ✕ **The Beach House.** It's worth the drive over the Lions Gate Bridge to West Vancouver for an evening at this 1912 seaside house. Whether inside the lofty room or outside on the heated beachside patio, most every table has expansive views over Burrard Inlet and Stanley Park. The Pacific Northwest menu has a Mediterranean influence, with dishes such as halibut on artichoke and tomato watercress compote, and beef tenderloin on Dungeness crab mashed potatoes. After dinner, you can take a stroll along the pier or the seaside walkway. ⊠ *150– 25th St., West Vancouver,* ☎ *604/922–1414. AE, DC, MC, V.*

$$–$$$ ✕ **Seasons Restaurant.** Tiered seating and tall windows allow virtually every table here a commanding view over the gardens in Queen Elizabeth Park, to the city and mountains beyond. Rich wood paneling and wrought-iron work make for an elegant atmosphere that is mirrored in the contemporary Pacific Northwest fare. Menu highlights include such innovative items as sake-marinated sea bass, as well as such standards as rack of lamb. Weekend brunch is popular, and three fireplaces on the patio allow for year-round outdoor dining. ⊠ *Queen Elizabeth Park, W. 33rd Ave. and Cambie St., South Vancouver,* ☎ *604/ 874–8008 or 800/632–9422. AE, MC, V.*

# Greater Vancouver Dining

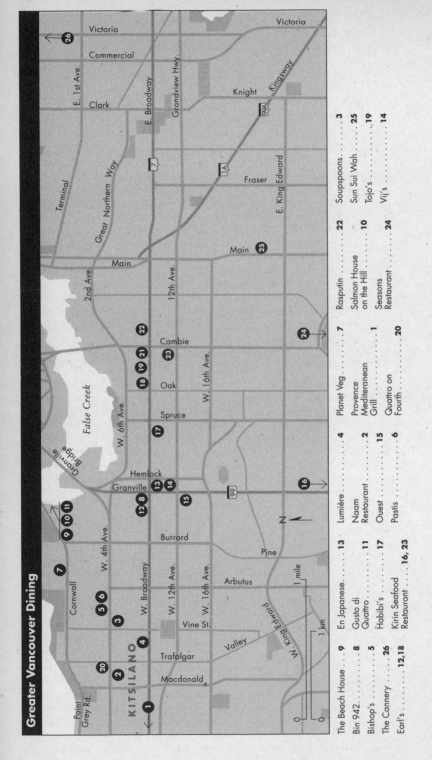

The Beach House . . . . . . . **9**
Bin 942 . . . . . . . . . . **8**
Bishop's . . . . . . . . . . **5**
The Cannery . . . . . . . . **26**
Earl's . . . . . . . . **12,18**

En Japanese . . . . . . **13**
Gusto di
Quattro . . . . . . . . **11**
Habibi's . . . . . . . . **17**
Kirin Seafood
Restaurant . . . . **16, 23**

Lumière . . . . . . . . . **4**
Naam
Restaurant . . . . . . . **2**
Ouest . . . . . . . . . **15**
Pastis . . . . . . . . . **6**

Planet Veg . . . . . . . . **7**
Provence
Mediteranean
Grill . . . . . . . . . **1**
Quattro on
Fourth . . . . . . . . **20**

Rasputin . . . . . . . . **22**
Salmon House
on the Hill . . . . . . **10**
Seasons
Restaurant . . . . . . **24**

Soupspoons . . . . . . **3**
Sun Sui Wah . . . . **25**
Tojo's . . . . . . **19**
Vij's . . . . . . **14**

## Eclectic

$ ✕ **Bin 942.** High-energy murals, low lights, and an up-tempo atmosphere draw crowds to this tapas bar. The real star here, though, is the food. From the scallop and tiger-prawn tournedos to the Chinese pepper–crusted venison or the cedar-wrapped, tamari-marinated coho salmon to the albacore tuna loin in tempura, the chef creates some of the best small plates in town. Fun is also part of the deal: the chocolate fruit fondue, for example, comes with a paintbrush. Food is served until 1:30 am, and the excellent, affordable, wine choices are all available by the glass. ⊠ *1521 W. Broadway, Kitsilano,* ☎ *604/734–9421,* WEB *www.bin941.com. Reservations not accepted. MC, V. No lunch.*

## French

$$$$ ✕ **Lumière.** The contemporary French cuisine at this light and airy restaurant isn't so much served as it's orchestrated, arranged in one of chef
★ Robert Feenie's frequently changing 8- to 12-course set menus. The menus, whether seafood, vegetarian, or the elaborate 12-course signature menu, present creative takes on French cuisine, using regionally sourced organic produce. For quick bites, a tasting bar serves individual plates of snack-size comfort food for $12 each. ⊠ *2551 W. Broadway, Kitsilano,* ☎ *604/739–8185,* WEB *www.lumiere.ca. Reservations not accepted at tasting bar. AE, DC, MC, V. Closed Mon. No lunch.*

$$$–$$$$ ✕ **Ouest.** Regional cuisine with a classically French twist is this restaurant's theme. Some highlights on the seasonally changing menu include skate with capers and parsley as well as rump of lamb crusted with aromatic couscous. Marble floors, high ceilings, and warm caramel leather set into the walls make for a sleek, urban look. The kitchen is visible, but a glass partition keeps the dining room peaceful. The wine selection includes French and New World varieties with a good choice of half bottles. ⊠ *2881 Granville St., South Granville,* ☎ *604/738–8938,* WEB *www.ouestrestaurant.com. AE, DC, MC, V. No lunch.*

$$–$$$ ✕ **Pastis.** This contemporary French bistro sticks to its roots with a signature steak tartare and great frites but has some innovative dishes, too: try the fig and Belgian endive salad with Roquefort and hazelnut vinaigrette, or the roasted duck breast and Québec foie gras. The five-course taster menus are good value, and this intimate 15-table bistro has one of the largest selections of wines by the glass in the city. The decor is simple and homey, with brown wicker chairs, a fireplace, and French doors opening onto the sidewalk. ⊠ *2153 W. 4th Ave., Kitsilano,* ☎ *604/731–5020,* WEB *www.pastisvancouver.com. AE, DC, MC, V. No lunch.*

$ ✕ **Soupspoons.** The Joinville family from Paris runs this simple soup bar, serving about 10 homemade varieties along with the other essential food groups: cheese, wine, and bread (made daily in house). Pastries and sandwiches are available, too. You can order takeout or linger at the long communal table. A second location in the West End is near English Bay (☞ Dining, Downtown Vancouver). ⊠ *2278 W. 4th Ave., Kitsilano,* ☎ *604/328–7687,* WEB *www.soupspoons.com. Reservations not accepted. V.*

## Indian

$$–$$$ ✕ **Vij's.** Vikram Vij, the genial proprietor of Vancouver's most inno-
★ vative Indian restaurant, uses local ingredients and Western ideas to create exciting takes on the cuisines of the subcontinent. The dishes, such as rack of lamb in fenugreek cream curry, or jackfruit in cayenne and black cardamom, are far from traditional but are spiced beautifully, allowing exotic flavors such as mango, tamarind, and cardamom to shine through. The simple room, with bare walls, Indian antiques, and warm lighting from lanterns, doesn't detract from the art on the

plate. You can enjoy snacks and drinks in the lounge while you wait for your table. ⊠ *1480 W. 11th Ave., South Granville,* ☏ *604/736–6664,* WEB *www.vijs.ca. Reservations not accepted. AE, DC, MC, V. No lunch.*

### Italian

$$–$$$$    ✕ **Quattro on Fourth.** Central Italian cuisine shines at this family-run neighborhood favorite. The signature Spaghetti Quattro comes with hot chilies, minced chicken, black beans, olive oil, and generous lashings of garlic. Mains, many of which are also available at the North Shore location, include deboned Cornish hen, rack of lamb with a fig and Dijon demi-glace, and pistachio-crusted sea bass. Mahogany tables, chandeliers, candlelight, and a hand-painted floor glow indoors; a patio beckons in summer. The cellar has 400 wine varieties and an extensive grappa selection. ⊠ *2611 W. 4th Ave., Kitsilano,* ☏ *604/734–4444,* WEB *www.quattrorestaurants.com. AE, DC, MC, V. No lunch.*

$$–$$$    ✕ **Gusto di Quattro.** The North Shore off-shoot of this family-run Italian spot is a quick SeaBus ride across the harbor. The cuisine draws on the best of both northern and southern traditions. Meals here include antipasti platters, bread and pasta made in-house, and such lush mains as pistachio-crusted sea bass with roasted sweet pepper sauce and deboned Cornish hen grilled with herbs, garlic, and peperoncini. This small candlelit room, with a long rosewood bar and whimsical cherubs on the wall, is also home to an impressive grappa selection. ⊠ *1 Lonsdale Ave. (next to Lonsdale Quay), North Vancouver,* ☏ *604/924–4444,* WEB *www.quattrorestaurants.com. AE, DC, MC, V. No lunch weekends.*

### Japanese

$$–$$$    ✕ **Tojo's.** Hidekazu Tojo is a sushi-making legend in Vancouver, with
★          more than 2,000 special preparations stored in his creative mind. His handsome tatami rooms on the second floor of a modern green-glass tower provide the proper ambience for intimate dining, but Tojo's 10-seat sushi bar is a convivial ringside seat for watching the creation of edible art. Reserve the spot at the end for the best view. ⊠ *202–777 W. Broadway, Fairview,* ☏ *604/872–8050. AE, DC, MC, V. Closed Sun. No lunch.*

$–$$    ✕ **En Japanese.** Modern West Coast takes on Japanese food are served in geometrically arranged, snack-size portions (order several and experiment) at this simple space. Scallops and Dungeness crab come with tamari sauce and risotto, and the Japanese-style salmon carpaccio is flash grilled and seasoned with wasabi, lemon, sea salt, and capers. The sushi, tempura, noodle dishes, and miso soup all come with surprising twists—croutons in the miso soup, or lightly deep-fried tempura-style sushi, for example. The taupe-and-white candlelit room is almost austere, though watching the elaborate creations come from the kitchen is half the fun. ⊠ *2686 Granville St., South Granville,* ☏ *604/730–0330. AE, DC, MC, V. Closed Mon. No lunch.*

### Mediterranean

$$–$$$    ✕ **Provence Mediterranean Grill.** This West Side bistro, decorated in sunny shades of gold, is run by a French-Italian husband-wife team of chefs. Together they bring the tastes of the Mediterranean—garlic, parsley, mussels, goat cheese, olive oil, tapenade, bouillabaisse, and fish flown in from Marseilles—to grateful Vancouverites. You can have a full meal, with wine skillfully paired by the helpful staff, or graze from more than a dozen grilled and marinated choices in the antipasti bar. If you want takeout, a day's notice will get you a picnic basket worthy of an afternoon in Arles. ⊠ *4473 W. 10th Ave., Point Grey,* ☏ *604/222–1980,* WEB *www.provencevancouver.com. AE, DC, MC, V.*

## Middle Eastern

$ ✕ **Habibi's.** The Lebanese home cooking at this family-run café is one of the area's best values. All the dishes are vegetarian, and all are lovingly prepared. Most of the dishes are meze-size and eaten as dips with warm pita bread. The idea is to try several, and experiment with such specialties as *lebneh* (a yogurt cheese with spices), *balila* (warm chickpeas with garlic and olive oil), and *warak anab* (rice-stuffed grape leaves marinated in lemon juice). Wooden booths, soft blues music, and family photos from the old country make a welcome change from most eateries in this price range. ⊠ *1128 W. Broadway, Fairview,* ☎ *604/ 732–7487. Reservations not accepted. V. Closed Sun.*

## Russian

$$–$$$ ✕ **Rasputin.** Don't let the glowering portrait of Rasputin on the wall put you off—this place is fun, and meals here are long and joyous occasions. The borscht is rich and flavorful. The towering appetizer arrangements—including salmon caviar with crepes, smoked salmon, and chopped egg—are meant for sharing; the main dishes, including kebabs, cabbage rolls, handmade pierogi, and trout stuffed with couscous pilaf, are consistently top-notch. The bar stocks 40 kinds of vodka, and musicians playing balalaikas or Gypsy violins (often backed up by the regulars in good voice), perform six nights a week. ⊠ *457 W. Broadway, Fairview,* ☎ *604/879–6675. AE, DC, MC, V. No lunch.*

## Seafood

$$–$$$$ ✕ **The Cannery.** This long-established East Side favorite has striking views over the harbor and the mountains beyond. Though the tables are set with white linen and china, the rustic nautical decor, including a retired fishing boat out front, gives a pretty clear indication of the specialty here. Vegetarian and meat options are available, but most diners come for the seafood classics: bouillabaisse, Dungeness crab, Nova Scotia lobster, treats from the daily fresh sheet, or the Cannery's signature salmon Wellington with a pinot noir sauce. ⊠ *2205 Commissioner St. (north foot of Victoria Dr., then right on Commissioner), East Vancouver,* ☎ *604/254–9606 or 877/254–9606,* WEB *www.canneryseafood.com. AE, D, DC, MC, V. No lunch weekends.*

$$–$$$ ✕ **Salmon House on the Hill.** Perched halfway up a mountain, this restaurant has stunning water and city views by day and expansive vistas of city lights by night. The Salmon House is best known for its alder-grilled salmon, though the grilled oysters, British Columbia prawns, and treats from the daily fresh sheet are also tempting. The Northwest Coast First Nations–theme decor is tastefully done, though it can hardly compete with what's outside the windows. The Salmon House is about 15 to 30 minutes from Vancouver by car (depending on traffic). Go over the Lions Gate Bridge and take the Folkestone Way exit off Highway 1 west. ⊠ *2229 Folkestone Way, West Vancouver,* ☎ *604/926– 3212. AE, DC, MC, V.*

## Vegetarian

$ ✕ **Naam Restaurant.** Vancouver's oldest natural-foods eatery is open 24 hours, so if you need to satisfy a late-night craving for a veggie burger, rest easy. The Naam also serves vegetarian stir-fries, wicked chocolate desserts, and wine, beer, cappuccinos, and fresh juices. Wood tables, an open fireplace, and live blues, folk, and jazz every evening create a homey atmosphere. On warm summer evenings you can sit in the outdoor courtyard. Reservations are accepted only for groups of six or more and only between Monday and Thursday. ⊠ *2724 W. 4th Ave., Kitsilano,* ☎ *604/738–7151. AE, DC, MC, V.*

$ ✕ **Planet Veg.** The influences on the fare at this fast-food restaurant range as far afield as India, Mexico, and the Mediterranean. Among the most inspired cheap eats to be found in Kitsilano are the roti rolls, spicy treats in Indian flat bread that are fun, filling, and inexpensive. Eat in, or gather a picnic to take to nearby Kits Beach. ✉ *1941 Cornwall Ave., Kitsilano,* ☎ *604/734–1001. Reservations not accepted. No credit cards.*

# LODGING

Accommodations in Vancouver range from luxurious waterfront hotels to neighborhood B&Bs and basic European-style pensions. Many of the best choices are in the downtown core, either in the central business district or in the West End near Stanley Park. The chart below shows high-season prices, but from mid-October through May, rates throughout the city can drop as much as 50%.

| CATEGORY | COST* |
|----------|-------|
| $$$$ | over $250 |
| $$$ | $170–$250 |
| $$ | $90–$170 |
| $ | under $90 |

*All prices are in Canadian dollars, for a standard double room, excluding 10% room tax and 7% GST.*

$$$$ 🏨 **Delta Vancouver Suites.** Attached to the Morris J. Wosk Centre for Dialogue, this modern luxury hotel is a nice example of early millennial chic. The striking marble and cherrywood lobby soars four stories. The suites have blond Art Deco furnishings, floor-to-ceiling windows, movable work tables, high-speed Internet access, and sliding doors or Japanese screens to close off the bedroom. Slightly pricier Signature Club suites have a private lounge, Continental breakfast, evening refreshments, and turndown service. The hotel's restaurant, Manhattan, is hidden away from the madding crowd. ✉ *550 W. Hastings St., Downtown, V6B 1L6,* ☎ *604/689–8188 or 888/663–8811,* FAX *604/605–8881,* WEB *www.deltavancouversuites.ca. 226 suites. Restaurant, room service, in-room data ports, minibars, cable TV with movies and video games, indoor pool, gym, hot tub, sauna, lobby lounge, shop, baby-sitting, children's programs (0–12), dry cleaning, laundry service, concierge, concierge floor, Internet, business services, meeting rooms, parking (fee), some pets allowed; no-smoking floors. AE, D, DC, MC, V.*

$$$$ 🏨 **Fairmont Hotel Vancouver.** The copper roof of this 1939 château-
★ style hotel dominates Vancouver's skyline. Even the standard guest rooms have an air of prestige, with high ceilings and 19th-century-style mahogany furniture. Rooms on the Entrée Gold floor have extra services, including a private lounge and its own concierge. A full-service spa adds to the pampering. ✉ *900 W. Georgia St., Downtown, V6C 2W6,* ☎ *604/684–3131,* FAX *604/662–1929,* WEB *www.fairmont.com. 556 rooms, 38 suites. 2 restaurants, room service, in-room data ports, some kitchenettes, minibars, cable TV with movies and video games, indoor pool, wading pool, gym, hot tub, massage, sauna, spa, wine bar, shops, baby-sitting, dry cleaning, laundry service, concierge, concierge floor, Internet, business services, meeting rooms, parking (fee), some pets allowed (fee); no-smoking floors. AE, D, DC, MC, V.*

$$$$ 🏨 **Four Seasons.** This 30-story downtown luxury hotel is famous for
★ pampering guests. The lobby is lavish, with seemingly acres of couches and a fountain in the lounge. Standard rooms, with understated color schemes and marble bathroom fixtures, are elegantly furnished, as are the roomier corner rooms with sitting areas. The two opulent split-level suites are handy for putting up visiting royalty. Service at the Four Seasons is top-notch, and the attention to detail is outstanding. The

many amenities include free evening limousine service. The dining room, Chartwell, is one of the best in the city. ✉ *791 W. Georgia St., Downtown, V6C 2T4,* ☎ *604/689–9333,* FAX *604/684–4555,* WEB *www. fourseasons.com. 318 rooms, 67 suites. 2 restaurants, room service, in-room data ports, in-room safes, minibars, cable TV with movies and video games, in-room VCRs, indoor-outdoor pool, gym, hot tub, sauna, bar, lobby lounge, baby-sitting, children's programs (ages 0–14), dry cleaning, laundry service, concierge, Internet, business services, meeting rooms, parking (fee), some pets allowed; no-smoking floors. AE, DC, MC, V.*

$$$$ 🛏 **Listel Vancouver.** Art and jazz adorn this elegant hotel on Vancou-
★ ver's most vibrant shopping street. Gallery-floor guest rooms and suites display original or limited-edition works by artists such as Carmelo Sortino and Bernard Cathlin; rooms on the Museum floor are decorated with work from contemporary First Nations artists such as Susan Point and Eugene Alfred. Custom-made furniture in both Gallery and Museum rooms complement the art. You can also catch live jazz nightly at O'Doul's Restaurant & Bar downstairs. ✉ *1300 Robson St., Downtown V6E 1C5,* ☎ *604/684–8461 or 800/663–5491,* FAX *604/ 684–7092,* WEB *www.listel-vancouver.com. 119 rooms, 10 suites. Restaurant, room service, in-room data ports, minibars, cable TV with movies, gym, hot tub, bar, baby-sitting, dry cleaning, laundry service, business services, meeting rooms, parking (fee); no-smoking floors. AE, D, DC, MC, V.*

$$$$ 🛏 **Metropolitan Hotel.** This full-service business district hotel was built on the principles of feng shui, and those precepts have been respected in all renovations since. The spacious rooms are decorated in muted colors, and public areas with Asian art, including two lions guarding the entrance and a striking antique gold-leaf temple carving in the lobby. Standard rooms have such amenities as down comforters, bathrobes, and newspapers; business-class rooms come with printers, fax machines, and cordless phones. Service is consistently gracious. You can catch glimpses of the hotel's restaurant, Diva at the Met, through an etched-glass wall in the lobby. ✉ *645 Howe St., Downtown, V6C 2Y9,* ☎ *604/687–1122 or 800/667–2300,* FAX *604/689–7044,* WEB *www. metropolitan.com. 179 rooms, 18 suites. Restaurant, in-room data ports, some in-room faxes, in-room safes, minibars, cable TV with movies and video games, indoor pool, gym, hot tub, sauna (women only), steam room (men only), racquetball, squash, bar, concierge, Internet, business services, meeting rooms, parking (fee), some pets allowed; no-smoking floors. AE, D, DC, MC, V.*

$$$$ 🛏 **Opus Hotel.** The design team had fun with this boutique hotel. They dreamed up a group of fictitious characters, then created a room to appeal to each. The result is five unique, chic, and modern room styles. Billy's room, for example, is fun and offbeat, with pop art and lots of color. Mike's room is urban, and minimalist, while Bob and Carol's place is a little more conservative, with softer edges and muted tones. Included among the many perks here—such as a Japanese garden in the courtyard—you'll receive a bio of the rooms' fictitious roommates. The bar and restaurant are suitably chic places for characters to meet. ✉ *322 Davie St., Yaletown, V6B 5Z6,* ☎ *604/642–6787 or 866/642–6787,* FAX *604/642–6780,* WEB *www.opushotel.com. 78 rooms, 19 suites. Restaurant, coffee shop, room service, in-room data ports, in-room safes, minibars, cable TV with movies and video games, exercise equipment, bar, dry cleaning, laundry service, concierge, Internet, business services, meeting rooms, parking (fee), some pets allowed (fee); no-smoking floors. AE, DC, MC, V.*

$$$$ 🛏 **Pacific Palisades.** Bright citrus colors, abstract art, and geometric patterns create a high-energy South Beach look at this chic Robson Street

# Vancouver Lodging

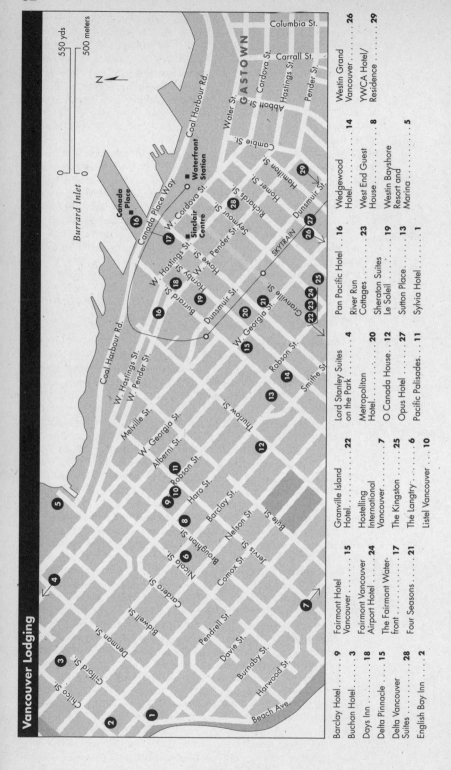

Barclay Hotel........**9**
Buchan Hotel........**3**
Days Inn............**18**
Delta Pinnacle......**15**
Delta Vancouver
Suites.............**28**
English Bay Inn.....**2**

Fairmont Hotel
Vancouver.........**15**
Fairmont Vancouver
Airport Hotel......**24**
The Fairmont Water-
front..............**17**
Four Seasons.......**21**

Granville Island
Hotel.............**22**
Hostelling
International
Vancouver.........**7**
The Kingston.......**25**
The Langtry........**6**
Listel Vancouver...**10**

Lord Stanley Suites
on the Park.......**4**
Metropolitan
Hotel.............**20**
O Canada House...**12**
Opus Hotel.........**27**
Pacific Palisades...**11**

Pan Pacific Hotel..**16**
River Run
Cottages..........**23**
Sheraton Suites
Le Soleil..........**19**
Sutton Place.......**13**
Sylvia Hotel........**1**

Wedgewood
Hotel.............**14**
West End Guest
House.............**8**
Westin Bayshore
Resort and
Marina............**5**

Westin Grand
Vancouver........**26**
YWCA Hotel/
Residence.........**29**

hotel. The cheerful decor extends to the roomy guest rooms and suites, where big balconies and wall-to-wall windows keep things light and airy and, on the higher floors, bring in sweeping water and mountain views. Fun is the idea here, from the playful decor to the minibars stocked with toys and animal crackers. The Palisades is handy to the shops and cafés of Robson Street and walking distance to downtown and Stanley Park. ⊠ *1277 Robson St. (entrance at Jervis St.), West End, V6E 1C4,* ☎ *604/688–0461 or 800/663–1815,* FAX *604/688–4374,* WEB *www.pacificpalisades.com. 50 rooms, 183 suites. Restaurant, room service, in-room data ports, some in-room faxes, some kitchens, some kitchenettes, minibars, cable TV with movies and video games, indoor pool, gym, hot tub, massage, sauna, spa, bar, shops, dry cleaning, laundry service, concierge, Internet, business services, meeting rooms, parking (fee), some pets allowed (fee); no-smoking floors. AE, D, DC, MC, V.*

$$$$ ⚏ **Pan Pacific Hotel.** A centerpiece of the waterfront Canada Place, the
★ luxurious Pan Pacific shares a complex with the Vancouver Convention and Exhibition Centre and Vancouver's main cruise-ship terminal. The decor is muted and modern, with light woods, travertine vanities, and tall windows that provide stunning ocean, mountain, or skyline views. The restaurants and health-club facilities are among the city's finest, and the high-end suites, some with a private steam room, sauna, or baby grand piano, are popular with visiting celebrities. ⊠ *300–999 Canada Pl., Downtown, V6C 3B5,* ☎ *604/662–8111; 800/ 663–1515 in Canada; 800/937–1515 in the U.S.;* FAX *604/685–8690;* WEB *www.panpacific.com. 465 rooms, 39 suites. 3 restaurants, coffee shop, room service, in-room data ports, some in-room faxes, in-room safes, some kitchenettes, minibars, cable TV with movies and video games, pool, aerobics, health club, hair salon, hot tub, outdoor hot tub, massage, sauna, spa, steam room, racquetball, squash, lobby lounge, shops, baby-sitting, dry cleaning, laundry service, concierge, Internet, business services, meetings rooms, car rental, parking (fee), some pets allowed; no-smoking floors. AE, DC, MC, V.*

$$$$ ⚏ **Sheraton Suites Le Soleil.** Cozy and stylish, this business-district boutique hotel is popular with independent travelers and businesspeople. Neither tour groups nor conventions book here, and the staff prides itself on attentive, personal service. The golden yellow decor and intimate fireplace in the neoclassical lobby and the vibrant gold and crimson fabrics in the guest rooms—most are small suites—radiate warmth. Luxurious touches, such as 300-thread-count Egyptian cotton sheets, marble bathrooms, and custom-designed Biedermeier-style furniture, abound. Two penthouse suites have 24-ft ceilings and wraparound terraces. The hotel doesn't have a pool or fitness facilities, but guests have access to the YWCA next door for an fee. ⊠ *567 Hornby St., Downtown, V6C 2E8,* ☎ *604/632–3000 or 877/632–3030,* FAX *604/632–3001,* WEB *www.lesoleilhotel.com. 10 rooms, 112 suites. Restaurant, room service, in-room data ports, in-room safes, cable TV with movies, massage, bar, dry cleaning, laundry service, concierge, Internet, business services, meeting rooms, parking (fee), some pets allowed (fee); no-smoking floors. AE, DC, MC, V.*

$$$$ ⚏ **Sutton Place.** The feel here is more of an exclusive European guest
★ house than a large modern hotel. Guest rooms are furnished with rich, dark woods, and the service is gracious and attentive. The hotel's Fleuri restaurant is known for its Continental cuisine, Sunday brunch, afternoon tea, and weekend-evening chocoholic bar. A full European health spa (also open to nonguests) offers Le Stone therapy—a massage using river stones—as well as wraps, facials, manicures, reflexology, and massage therapy. La Grande Residence (part of Sutton Place), an apartment hotel suitable for stays of at least a week, is next door, at 855 Burrard. ⊠ *845 Burrard St., Downtown, V6Z 2K6,* ☎ *604/682–5511 or 800/*

961–7555, FAX 604/682–5513, WEB *www.suttonplace.com. 350 rooms, 47 suites, 164 apartments. Restaurant, room service, some in-room safes, minibars, cable TV with movies and video games, indoor pool, health club, sauna (women only), spa, steam room (men only), lounge, piano bar, shop, baby-sitting, children's programs (ages 0–12), dry cleaning, laundry service, concierge, Internet, business services, meeting rooms, parking (fee), some pets allowed (fee); no-smoking rooms. AE, D, DC, MC, V.*

$$$$  🏨 **Wedgewood Hotel.** The small, lavish Wedgewood is run by an
★      owner who cares fervently about her guests. The lobby and guest rooms are decorated in a traditional European style with original artwork and antiques selected by the proprietor on her European travels. Guest rooms are capacious, and each has a balcony, a bar, and a desk. The four penthouse suites have fireplaces. All the extra touches are here, too: afternoon ice delivery, dark-out drapes, robes, and a morning newspaper. The turndown service incudes homemade cookies and bottled water. The sensuous Bacchus restaurant and lounge is in the lobby. ✉ *845 Hornby St., Downtown, V6Z 1V1,* ☎ *604/689–7777 or 800/663–0666,* FAX *604/608–5348,* WEB *www.wedgewoodhotel.com. 51 rooms, 38 suites. Restaurant, room service, in-room data ports, in-room safes, cable TV with movies and video games, gym, sauna, bar, baby-sitting, dry cleaning, laundry facilities, Internet, business services, meeting rooms, parking (fee); no-smoking floors. AE, D, DC, MC, V.*

$$$$  🏨 **Westin Bayshore Resort and Marina.** Perched on the best part of the harbor, adjacent to Stanley Park, the Bayshore has truly fabulous views. The rooms in the tower have small balconies and 90-degree mountain and harbor views; those in the main building have floor-to-ceiling windows, and many of these rooms also have striking views. The only downtown resort hotel, this is the perfect place to stay in warm weather, especially for families, because of its extensive recreational facilities. Fishing charters and sightseeing cruises are available from the Bayshore, which is connected to Stanley Park and the Vancouver Convention and Exhibition Centre via seaside walkway. ✉ *1601 Bayshore Dr. (off Cardero St.), West End, V6G 2V4,* ☎ *604/682–3377,* FAX *604/ 687–3102,* WEB *www.westinbayshore.com. 510 rooms, 28 suites. 2 restaurants, coffee shop, room service, in-room data ports, some in-room faxes, some in-room safes, minibars, cable TV with movies and video games, 2 pools (1 indoor), health club, hair salon, hot tub, massage, sauna, steam room, boating, marina, fishing, bicycles, bar, lounge, shops, baby-sitting, children's programs (ages 3–12), dry cleaning, laundry service, concierge, Internet, business services, convention center, car rental, travel services, parking (fee), some pets allowed; no-smoking floors. AE, D, DC, MC, V.*

$$$$  🏨 **Westin Grand Vancouver.** With its strikingly minimalist decor, cherrywood and marble lobby, and all-suites layout, the Westin Grand, shaped like a grand piano, is one of Vancouver's more stylish hotels. Most of the compact studios and one-bedroom suites have floor-to-ceiling windows with skyline views, and all units have fully equipped kitchenettes with microwaves and dishwashers tucked into armoires. Corner suites are larger and have small balconies. Office suites come with a combination fax-photocopier-printer; all rooms have high-speed Internet access. The hotel is close to the main sports and entertainment district and to the fashionable restaurants of Yaletown. ✉ *433 Robson St., Downtown, V6B 6L9,* ☎ *604/602–1999 or 888/680– 9393,* FAX *604/647–2502,* WEB *www.westingrandvancouver.com. 23 rooms, 184 suites. Restaurant, room service, in-room data ports, in-room safes, minibars, cable TV with movies and video games, some in-room VCRs, pool, gym, outdoor hot tub, sauna, steam room, bar,*

*nightclub, shop, baby-sitting, children's programs (ages 0-12), dry cleaning, laundry service, concierge, business services, meeting rooms, parking (fee); no-smoking floors. AE, D, DC, MC, V.*

**$$$-$$$$** ▦ **Delta Pinnacle.** The soaring 50-ft-high atrium lobby makes a striking entrance to this 38-story hotel a block from the cruise-ship terminal and central business district. Decorated in modern pale woods and neutral tones, each room has almost a full wall of windows with expansive views of Burrard Inlet and the North Shore Mountains or the city skyline. The hotel's Show Case restaurant and bar serves West Coast cuisine with global influences. ⊠ *1128 W. Hastings St., Downtown, V6E 4R5,* ☎ *604/684–1128,* FAX *604/298–1128,* WEB *www.deltapinnacle.bc.ca. 424 rooms, 10 suites. Restaurant, room service, in-room data ports, in-room safes, minibars, cable TV with movies and video games, some in-room VCRs, indoor pool, gym, hot tub, massage, sauna, steam room, bar, shop, baby-sitting, children's program (ages 0–12), dry cleaning, laundry service, concierge, concierge floor, Internet, business services, meeting rooms, parking (fee), some pets allowed (fee); no-smoking floors. AE, DC, MC, V.*

**$$$-$$$$** ▦ **Fairmont Vancouver Airport Hotel.** Vancouver's most luxurious airport hotel is actually part of the terminal building. Rooms and public areas are decorated in a minimalist art deco–style, with pale woods, calming neutrals, extensive use of local cedar and slate, and artworks commissioned from local artists. All rooms have soaker tubs, shower stalls, and free high-speed Internet access; they also have floor-to-ceiling windows—the triple-pane construction provides near-perfect soundproofing. Rooms on the north side have mountain views. A health club is free for guests and is open to nonguests for $15. There's also a full-service day spa for pre- or post-flight pampering. ⊠ *Vancouver International Airport, 3311 North Service Rd. (Box 23798, Richmond V7B 1X9),* ☎ *604/207–5200,* FAX *604/248–3219,* WEB *www.fairmont.com. 392 rooms, 3 suites. Restaurant, room service, in-room data ports, in-room safes, minibars, cable TV with movies and video games, indoor pool, wading pool, gym, hot tub, massage, sauna, spa, bar, piano, baby-sitting, dry cleaning, laundry service, concierge, concierge floor, Internet, business services, meeting rooms, parking (fee), some pets allowed (fee); no-smoking floors. AE, D, DC, MC, V.*

**$$$-$$$$** ▦ **Fairmont Waterfront.** An underground walkway leads from this striking 23-story glass hotel to Vancouver's Convention and Exhibition Centre and cruise-ship terminal. Views from the lobby and from 60% of the guest rooms are of Burrard Inlet, Stanley Park, and the North Shore Mountains. Other rooms look onto the city skyline and a terraced herb garden. The spacious rooms have big picture windows and are attractively furnished with blond wood furniture and contemporary Canadian artwork. Large corner rooms have the best views. Rooms on the Entrée Gold floor have extra amenities, including in-room safes, a private lounge, and a concierge. ⊠ *900 Canada Pl. Way, Downtown, V6C 3L5,* ☎ *604/691–1991,* FAX *604/691–1828,* WEB *www.fairmont.com. 489 rooms, 29 suites. Restaurant, room service, in-room data ports, some in-room safes, minibars, cable TV with movies and video games, pool, gym, hot tub, massage, steam room, lobby lounge, shops, baby-sitting, dry cleaning, laundry service, concierge, concierge floor, Internet, business services, meeting rooms, parking (fee), some pets allowed (fee); no-smoking floors. AE, D, DC, MC, V.*

**$$$-$$$$** ▦ **Lord Stanley Suites on the Park.** These small, attractive, fully equipped suites are right of the edge of Stanley Park. Each has an office nook, a a sitting room, and one or two bedrooms. Each suite overlooking busy Georgia Street has an enclosed sun room; those backing onto quieter Alberni Street have balconies. You're also close to many restaurants on Denman Street, a block away. ✉ *1889 Alberni St., West End,* ☎ *604/688–9299 or 888/767–7829,* FAX *604/688–9297,* WEB *www.lordstanley.com. 100 suites. In-room data ports, cable TV, in-room VCRs, gym, sauna, dry cleaning, laundry service, meeting rooms, parking (fee); no-smoking floors. AE, DC, MC, V. CP.*

**$$$–$$$$**     🏨 **O Canada House.** This beautifully restored 1897 Victorian, within
★     walking distance of downtown, is where the first version of "O Canada," the national anthem, was written in 1909. Each bedroom is appointed in late-Victorian antiques; modern comforts such as bathrobes help make things homey. The top-floor room is enormous, with two king beds and a private sitting area. A separate one-room coach house in the garden is a romantic option. Breakfast, served in the dining room, is a lavish affair. Guests here have free access to the pool and health club at the Sutton Place hotel. ✉ *1114 Barclay St., West End, V6E 1H1,* ☎ *604/688–0555 or 877/688–1114,* FAX *604/488–0556,* WEB *www.ocanadahouse.com. 7 rooms. Fans, refrigerators, cable TV, in-room VCRs, concierge, Internet, free parking; no a/c, no kids under 12, no smoking. MC, V. BP.*

**$$$**     🏨 **English Bay Inn.** Antiques furnish this immaculately decorated 1930s
★     Tudor-style house near Stanley Park. The inn has a Chippendale dining table in the breakfast room, sleigh beds in three of the guest rooms, and a tiny Italianate garden out back. The Honeymoon suite winds up two levels and has its own fireplace. A garden-level suite has an antique four-poster bed and its own dining area. Port and sherry are served by the fire in the living room each evening. ✉ *1968 Comox St., West End, V6G 1R4,* ☎ *604/683–8002 or 866/683–8002,* FAX *604/683–8089,* WEB *www.englishbayinn.com. 4 rooms, 2 suites. Cable TV, some in-room VCRs, Internet, free parking; no a/c, no TV in some rooms, no smoking. AE, DC, MC, V. BP.*

**$$$**     🏨 **Granville Island Hotel.** Granville Island is one of Vancouver's more entertaining neighborhoods, but unless you've moored up in a houseboat, the only overnight option is the Granville Island Hotel. The exterior of this modern water's-edge hotel looks like it's made of Lego toy blocks; inside, the decor is more refined, with marble floors and Persian rugs in the lobby and in many of the guest rooms. Most rooms also have water views, and those on the top floor (the third) have small balconies. The corridor overlooks vats brewing away for the fashionable brewpub and restaurant downstairs. ✉ *1253 Johnston St., Granville Island, V6H 3R9,* ☎ *604/683–7373 or 800/663–1840,* FAX *604/683–3061,* WEB *www.granvilleislandhotel.com. 74 rooms, 8 suites. Restaurant, room service, in-room data ports, minibars, cable TV with movies, exercise equipment, hot tub, sauna, pub, baby-sitting, dry cleaning, laundry service, Internet, meeting rooms, business services, parking (fee), some pets allowed (fee); no-smoking floors. AE, D, DC, MC, V.*

**$$–$$$**     🏨 **Days Inn.** Opened as the Abbotsford in 1920, this six-story hotel is one of the few moderately priced hotels in the business district, and it's conveniently close to the convention center, the cruise-ship terminal, and the U.S. consulate. Rooms are bright, clean, and utilitarian, with modern pine furniture and floral bedspreads. The two-bedroom, one-bathroom units are a good value for groups and families. ✉ *921 W. Pender St., Downtown, V6C 1M2,* ☎ *604/681–4335 or 877/681–4335,* FAX *604/681–7808,* WEB *www.daysinnvancouver.com. 80 rooms, 5 suites. Restaurant, in-room data ports, in-room safes, some microwaves, refrigerators, cable TV with movies, bar, dry cleaning, laundry facilities, laundry service, parking (fee); no-smoking floors. AE, D, DC, MC, V.*

**$$–$$$**     🏨 **The Langtry.** Inside this 1939 former apartment building near Robson Street and Stanley Park are six apartment-size suites furnished with antiques (including a Jacobean sofa and chair in one suite) and equipped with complete kitchens and dining areas and feather beds. Host Haike Kingma can also book sightseeing and outdoor adventures around town. ⊠ *968 Nicola St., West End, V6G 2C8,* ☎ *604/687–7798 or 888/587–7798,* FAX *604/687–7892,* WEB *www.thelangtry.com. 6 suites. Fans, kitchens, microwaves, cable TV, in-room VCRs, laundry facilities, Internet, free parking; no a/c, no smoking. MC, V.*

**$$–$$$**
**★** 🏨 **River Run Cottages.** This delightful riverside B&B is part of a historic floating-home community in the village of Ladner, 30 minutes south of downtown on the way to the ferry terminal or the U.S. border. Choose from a little gem of a floating house with a loft bed and an antique claw-foot tub; a two-level suite (once a net loft) with a Japanese soaking tub on the deck and a cozy captain's bed; or two river's-edge rooms, each with a woodstove and a deck over the water. Breakfasts, including homemade baked goods, are delivered to your room at this romantic, couples-oriented B&B; TVs and VCRs are available on request. ⊠ *4551 River Rd. W, Ladner V4K 1R9,* ☎ *604/946–7778,* FAX *604/940–1970,* WEB *www.riverruncottages.com. 2 rooms, 2 suites. Microwaves, refrigerators, boating, mountain bikes, laundry facilities, Internet, free parking, some pets allowed (fee); no a/c, no smoking, no room TVs. MC, V. BP.*

**$$–$$$**
**★** 🏨 **West End Guest House.** This Victorian house, built in 1906, is a true "painted lady," from its gracious front parlor, cozy fireplace, and early 1900s furniture to its bright pink exterior. Most of the handsome rooms have high brass beds, antiques, and gorgeous linens; two larger rooms have gas fireplaces. The inn is in a residential neighborhood, a two-minute walk from Robson Street. Book by March for summer. ⊠ *1362 Haro St., West End, V6E 1G2,* ☎ *604/681–2889 or 888/546–3327,* FAX *604/688–8812,* WEB *www.westendguesthouse.com. 8 rooms. Fans, cable TV, some in-room VCRs, bicycles, Internet, free parking; no smoking. AE, D, DC, MC, V. BP.*

**$$** 🏨 **Barclay Hotel.** A great location and low rates make this three-story former apartment building one of the city's best-value pension-style hotels. The guest rooms, with rosewood furniture and blue bedspreads, are clean if basic, but the 1930s building, with its wide corridors, skylights, and mahogany staircase, has a certain old-world charm. The Barclay is steps from the shops and restaurants of Robson Street and a 15-minute walk to either the business district or Stanley Park. Most of the front rooms overlooking Robson Street have mountain views, but the back rooms are quieter. ⊠ *1348 Robson St., West End, V6E 1C5,* ☎ *604/688–8850,* FAX *604/688–2534,* WEB *www.barclayhotel.com. 75 rooms, 10 suites. Some refrigerators, cable TV, dry cleaning, laundry service, concierge, parking (fee); no-smoking floors. AE, D, DC, MC, V.*

**$–$$** 🏨 **The Kingston Hotel Bed &Breakfast.** Convenient to shopping, the Kingston is an old-style four-story building, the type of establishment you'd find in Europe. Small and immaculate, the spartan rooms are decorated in a contemporary style, with flower-pattern bedspreads and pastel colors. The twin rooms have private bathrooms; the sleeping rooms have a sink in the room and share a bath down the hall. ⊠ *757 Richards St., Downtown, V6B 3A6,* ☎ *604/684–9024 or 888/713–3304,* FAX *604/684–9917,* WEB *www.kingstonhotelvancouver.com. 55 rooms, 9 with bath. Restaurant, room service, some fans, in-room data ports, cable TV, sauna, pub, laundry facilities, no-smoking floors; no a/c, no TV in some rooms. AE, MC, V. CP.*

**$–$$** 🏨 **Sylvia Hotel.** To stay at the Sylvia June through August, you need to book six months to a year ahead. This ivy-covered 1912 building is popular because of its low rates and near-perfect location: about 25 ft from the beach on scenic English Bay, 200 ft from Stanley Park, and a 20-minute walk from Robson Street. ⊠ *1154 Gilford St., West End, V6G*

2P6, ☎ 604/681–9321, FAX 604/682–3551, WEB *www.sylviahotel.com.*
*97 rooms, 22 suites. Restaurant, room service, in-room data ports,*
*kitchens, cable TV, lounge, dry cleaning, laundry service, parking (fee),*
*some pets allowed; no a/c, no-smoking floors. AE, DC, MC, V.*

**$–$$**   ⊡ **YWCA Hotel/Residence.** A secure, 12-story building in the heart of
★   the entertainment district, the YWCA has bright, comfortable rooms—
some big enough to sleep five. Some share a bath down the hall, some
share a bath between two rooms, and others have private baths. Shared
kitchens are available for all guests, and rates include use of the YWCA
adults-only pool and fitness facility, a 15-minute walk away at 535 Hornby
Street. ⊠ *733 Beatty St., Downtown, V6B 2M4,* ☎ *604/895–5830 or*
*800/663–1424,* FAX *604/681–2550,* WEB *www.ywcahotel.com. 155 rooms,*
*40 with bath. Coffee shop, refrigerators, cable TV, laundry facilities,*
*Internet, meeting rooms, parking (fee); no TV in some rooms, no-*
*smoking floors. AE, MC, V.*

**$**   ⊡ **Hostelling International Vancouver.** Vancouver has two Hostelling
★   International locations: a big hostel set in parkland at Jericho Beach
in Kitsilano and a smaller, downtown hostel near English Bay and Stanley Park. Each has private rooms for two to four people; bunks in men's,
women's, and coed dorms; a shared kitchen and dining room; a TV
lounge, luggage and bike storage, lockers, and a range of low-cost tours
and activities. The downtown hostel also has a rooftop patio and is
accessible to people who use wheelchairs. A free shuttle bus runs between the hostels and the bus and train station. *Downtown:* ⊠ *1114*
*Burnaby St., West End, V6E 1P1,* ☎ *604/684–4565 or 888/203–*
*4302,* FAX *604/684–4540,* WEB *www.hihostels.ca. 23 rooms, 44 4-bed*
*dorms. Mountain bikes, library, recreation room, laundry facilities, In-*
*ternet, meeting room, travel services, free parking; no a/c, no room*
*phones, no room TVs, no smoking. Jericho Beach:* ⊠ *1515 Discov-*
*ery St., Kitsilano, V6R 4K5,* ☎ *604/224–3208 or 888/203–4303,* FAX
*604/224–4852,* WEB *www.hihostels.ca. 10 rooms, 9 14-bed dorms.*
*Café, mountain bikes, recreation room, laundry facilities, Internet, travel*
*services, parking (fee); no a/c, no room phones, no room TVs, no*
*smoking. MC, V.*

# NIGHTLIFE AND THE ARTS

For **events information,** pick up a copy of the free *Georgia Straight*
(available at cafés and bookstores around town) or look in the entertainment section of the *Vancouver Sun* (Thursday's paper has listings
in the "Queue" section). The **Arts Hotline** (☎ 604/684–2787) has the
latest entertainment information. Tickets for many venues can be
booked through **Ticketmaster** (☎ 604/280–4444).

**Tickets Tonight,** at the Vancouver Tourist Info Centre (⊠ 200 Burrard
St., Downtown, ☎ 604/684–2787, WEB www.ticketstonight.ca), sells
half price day-of-the-event tickets to theater, concerts, festivals, and other
performing arts events in Vancouver.

## Nightlife

Vancouver's nightlife is increasingly vibrant, thanks to gradually relaxing liquor laws. Bars, pubs, and lounges are usually open seven nights
a week until 1 AM. Dance clubs get lively at about 10 PM and stay open
until 2 AM; many close on Sunday and Monday. Most dance clubs levy
a cover charge of about $5. Smart casual dress will do for most Van-
couver nightspots. No jeans or sports shoes is the standard dress code
in dance clubs, though patrons like to dress up for some of the smarter
places. The legal drinking age in British Columbia is 19, although some
upscale clubs ask that patrons be at least 23.

## Bars, Pubs, and Lounges

Unpretentious is the word at the **Atlantic Trap & Gill** (✉ 612 Davie St., Downtown, ☎ 604/806–6393), a downtown pub designed to help folks from Atlantic Canada (and everyone else) feel at home, with beer kegs for tables, old couches topped with afghans, Atlantic folk music, and goodies such as clam strips on the menu.

The **Bacchus Lounge** (✉ 845 Hornby St., Downtown, ☎ 604/608–5319), in the Wedgewood Hotel, is a relaxing place with plush couches, a fireplace, and a pianist.

**Bridges** (✉ 1696 Duranleau St., Granville Island, ☎ 604/687–4400), near the Public Market, has the city's biggest marina-side deck and a cozy, nautical-theme pub.

A fountain, greenery, and wicker chairs make the atrium-like **Garden Terrace** (✉ 791 W. Georgia St., Downtown, ☎ 604/689–9333) in the Four Seasons a peaceful place to relax over cocktails or a meal. The adjacent Terrace Bar is an elegant space with a copper-topped circular bar and Murano glass light fixtures.

A fireplace, wing chairs, and dark wood paneling create a clubby feel at the **Gerard Lounge** (✉ Sutton Place hotel, 845 Burrard St., Downtown, ☎ 604/682–5511).

A martini-drinking crowd fills the multiroom, '60s-theme **Ginger Sixty-Two** (✉ 1219 Granville St., Downtown, ☎ 604/688–5494); weekend performance artists and elaborate cocktails and snacks add to the fun.

For a pint of properly poured Guinness and live Irish music, try the **Irish Heather** (✉ 217 Carrall St., Gastown, ☎ 604/688–9779, 🖥 www.irishheather.com). There's also a restaurant upstairs and, out back in an atmospheric carriage house, a **Shebeen,** or whiskey house, where you can try any of about 100 whiskies.

Near Stanley Park and attached to Cardero's restaurant, the **Live Bait Yacht Club** (✉ 1583 Coal Harbour Quay, West End, ☎ 604/669–7666) has deep leather couches, marina views, and recycled ship timbers and other nautical touches. The pub grub is top-notch.

The **900 West** (✉ 900 W. Georgia St., Downtown, ☎ 604/669–9378) wine bar at the Fairmont Hotel Vancouver has 75 wines available by the glass.

You could spend a whole evening at the **Sand Bar** (✉ 1535 Johnson St., Granville Island, ☎ 604/669–9030). It's part seafood restaurant—with a sushi bar, crab and lobster from live tanks, and dancing on weekend evenings. It's also a pub, with an all-day tapas menu, deep leather chairs, and a rooftop patio with striking views over False Creek.

## Brewpubs

**Dix Barbecue and Brewery** (✉ 871 Beatty St., Downtown, ☎ 604/682–2739), near Yaletown and B.C. Place Stadium, is a relaxed and good-looking place, with exposed brick and beams, a fireplace, a long mahogany bar, and vats brewing up a variety of lagers. Dix also serves a fine southern-style barbecue, slow-smoked in-house in an apple- or cherry-wood smoker.

A seaside patio and house-brewed German-style beer make the **Dockside Brewing Company** (✉ Granville Island Hotel, 1253 Johnston St., Granville Island, ☎ 604/685–7070) a popular hangout.

Harbor views, good food, and traditionally brewed beer are the draws at woodsy, paneled **Steamworks** (✉ 375 Water St., Gastown, ☎ 604/689–2739).

The **Yaletown Brewing Company** (✉ 1111 Mainland St., Yaletown, ☎ 604/681–2739) is based in a renovated warehouse with a glassed-in brewery turning out eight tasty beers. It also has a lively singles'-scene pub, a patio, and a restaurant with an open-grill kitchen.

## Casinos

Vancouver has a few casinos; proceeds go to local charities and arts groups. No alcohol is served, and guests must be at least 19 years old. The **Great Canadian Casino** (⊠ 1133 W. Hastings St., Downtown, ☎ 604/682–8415, WEB www.gcgaming.com) is in the Renaissance Hotel. The **Royal City Star Riverboat Casino** (⊠ Westminster Quay, New Westminster, ☎ 604/878–9999, WEB www.royalcitystar.bc.ca) is a Mississippi riverboat moored on the Fraser River. Its five decks include 30 gaming tables, 300 slot machines, two lounges, and a restaurant. It's open 10 AM–3 AM daily (until 4 AM on Friday and Saturday nights) and takes cruises on the river Friday, Saturday, and Sunday afternoons between May and October. Admission is free.

## Coffeehouses

Coffeehouses play a big role in Vancouver's social life. The Starbucks invasion is nearly complete—there are blocks in town with two branches—but there are other, more colorful places to have a cappuccino, write that novel, or watch the world go by.

Granville Island has several coffee places, but only the **Blue Parrot Café** (⊠ Granville Island Public Market, 1689 Johnston St., Granville Island, ☎ 604/688–5127) provides such sweeping views of the boats on False Creek. Like the public market, the Blue Parrot is madly crowded on weekends. Cushy couches and wholesome goodies make **Bojangles Café** (⊠ 785 Denman St., West End, ☎ 604/687–3622) a good place to rest after a walk around Stanley Park. The closest thing in Vancouver to a *La Dolce Vita* set is the **Calabria Café** (⊠ 1745 Commercial Dr., Commercial Drive, ☎ 604/253–7017), with its marble tables, plaster statues, and posters of Italian movie stars. **Delaney's on Denman** (⊠ 1105 Denman St., West End, ☎ 604/662–3344) is a friendly and often crowded coffee bar near English Bay, in the heart of Vancouver's gay community. One cannot live by coffee alone, as proven by the vast selection of teas and related paraphernalia at **Tearoom T** (⊠ 1568 W. Broadway, South Granville, ☎ 604/730–8390).

## Comedy Clubs

The **TheatreSports League** (☎ 604/738–7013, WEB www.vtsl.com), a hilarious improv troupe, performs at the New Revue Stage on Granville Island. The **Vancouver International Comedy Festival** (☎ 604/683–0883, WEB www.comedyfest.com), held in late July and early August, brings an international collection of improv, stand-up, circus, and other acts to Granville Island. **Yuk Yuks Comedy Club** (⊠ 750 Pacific Blvd. S, in the Plaza of Nations Expo site, Downtown, ☎ 604/687–5233) is a popular stand-up venue.

## Gay Nightlife

A popular dance club, **Numbers** (⊠ 1042 Davie St., West End, ☎ 604/685–4077) features drag and theme nights. The **Oasis** (⊠ 1240 Thurlow, West End, ☎ 604/685–1724) is a relaxed martini lounge with a tapas-style menu and a patio. The **Odyssey** (⊠ 1251 Howe St., Downtown, ☎ 604/689–5256, WEB www.theodysseynightclub.com) is a dance club with drag shows, go-go boys, and theme nights. Anything from pool tournaments to leather and latex nights features at the **PumpJack Pub** (⊠ 1167 Davie St., West End, ☎ 604/685–3417, WEB www.pumpjackpub.com).

## Music

DANCE CLUBS

A smartly dressed crowd flocks to dance and celebrity-spot at upscale **Au Bar** (⊠ 674 Seymour St., Downtown, ☎ 604/648–2227, WEB www.aubarnightclub.com).

The funky, brick-lined **Bar None** (✉ 1222 Hamilton St., Yaletown, ☎ 604/689–7000) has R&B, hip-hop, and Top 40 dance tunes most of the week. On Monday and Tuesday, the 10-piece house band plays jazz, funk, and soul; on Friday nights, a rock-and-roll band hits the stage. The **Commodore Ballroom** (✉ 868 Granville St., Downtown, ☎ 604/739–7469, WEB www.commodoreballroom.com), a 1929 dance hall, has been restored to its Art Deco glory, complete with its massive dance floor. Live bands play here six nights a week; Tuesday is DJ night.

Jazz, soul, funk, R&B, and 44 kinds of bubbly appeal to a casually dressed over-25 crowd at **Crush Champagne Lounge** (✉ 1180 Granville St., Downtown, ☎ 604/684–0355).

DJs at the cozy, subterranean **Element Sound Lounge** (✉ 801 W. Georgia St., Downtown, ☎ 604/669–0806, WEB www.elementmusic.ca), in the basement of the Crowne Plaza Hotel Georgia, spin hip-hop, house, soul, and funk for a laid-back crowd.

R&B, house, hip-hop, and a little Top 40 draw a fashionable, over-25 crowd to chic and intimate **Luce** (✉ 686 W. Hastings St., Downtown, ☎ 604/633–3988).

The **Purple Onion Cabaret** (✉ 15 Water St., Gastown, ☎ 604/602–9442, WEB www.purpleonion.com) has both a lounge featuring live jazz, funk, reggae, and hip-hop and a dance club with DJs.

**Richard's on Richards** (✉ 1036 Richards St., Downtown, ☎ 604/687–6794, WEB www.richardsonrichards.com) is one of Vancouver's most established dance clubs, with live bands on weekdays.

**Sonar** (✉ 66 Water St., Gastown, ☎ 604/683–6695, WEB www.sonar.bc.ca) has international dance sounds and frequent touring guest DJs. The fashionable **Voda** (✉ 783 Homer St., Downtown, ☎ 604/684–3003), in the Westin Grand Hotel, is one of the few places that Vancouverites dress up for. The intimate club is popular with a thirtysomething professional crowd, who come for the Latin, funk, and R&B tunes.

### FOLK

The **Vancouver Folk Music Festival** (☎ 604/602–9798 or 800/985–8363, WEB www.thefestival.bc.ca), one of the world's leading folk- and world-music events, takes place at Jericho Beach Park in mid-July. For folk and traditional Celtic concerts year-round, call the **Rogue Folk Club** (☎ 604/736–3022).

### JAZZ AND SOUL

The hot line of the **Coastal Jazz and Blues Society** (☎ 604/872–5200) has information about concerts and clubs. The society also runs the Vancouver International Jazz Festival, which lights up 40 venues around town every June.

You can hear live jazz at the **Cellar Restaurant and Jazz Club** (✉ 3611 W. Broadway, Kitsilano, ☎ 604/738–1959). Local jazz musicians play nightly at **O'Doul's Restaurant & Bar** (✉ 1300 Robson St., West End, ☎ 604/661–1400) in the Listel hotel.

### ROCK AND BLUES

The **Backstage Lounge** (✉ 1585 Johnston St., Granville Island, ☎ 604/687–1354) stages local bands Wednesday through Saturday nights. **Rage** (✉ 750 Pacific Blvd. S, Downtown, ☎ 604/685–5585) is a rock disco most nights but also hosts occasional touring bands. In the early evening, the **Railway Club** (✉ 579 Dunsmuir St., Downtown, ☎ 604/681–1625) attracts film and media types to its pub-style rooms; after 8 it becomes a venue for local bands. Technically it's a private social club, so patrons must sign in, but everyone of age is welcome. The **Vogue Theatre** (✉ 918 Granville St., Downtown, ☎ 604/331–7909), a former movie palace, hosts a variety of concerts by visiting performers.

Vancouver's most established rhythm-and-blues bar, the **Yale** (⊠ 1300 Granville St., Downtown, ☏ 604/681–9253), has live bands most nights.

# The Arts

## Dance

A few of the many modern-dance companies in town are Karen Jamieson, DanceArts Vancouver, and JumpStart; besides the Scotia Bank Dance Centre, the Firehall Arts Centre and the Vancouver East Cultural Centre are among their performance venues.

The **Scotiabank Dance Centre** (⊠ 677 Davie St., Downtown, ☏ 604/606–6400, WEB www.thedancecentre.ca) is the hub of dance in British Columbia. The striking building, with an Art Deco facade, has performance and rehearsal space and provides information about dance in the province. **Ballet British Columbia** (☏ 604/732–5003, WEB www.balletbc.com) mounts productions and hosts out-of-town companies from November through May. Most of their performances are at the Queen Elizabeth Theatre.

## Film

Tickets are half price Tuesday at most chain-owned Vancouver movie theaters. The **Blinding Light** (⊠ 36 Powell St., Gastown, ☏ 604/684–8288) showcases short and experimental films. Occasionally audience members are invited to bring their own films, or you may catch a live band improvising scores to silent movies. The **Fifth Avenue Cinemas** (⊠ 2110 Burrard St., Kitsilano, ☏ 604/734–7469) is a small multiplex featuring foreign and independent films. The **Pacific Cinémateque** (⊠ 1131 Howe St., Downtown, ☏ 604/688–8202) shows esoteric, foreign, and art films. The **Ridge Theatre** (⊠ 3131 Arbutus St., Kitsilano, ☏ 604/738–6311) is a long-established art house cinema.

The **Vancouver International Film Festival** (☏ 604/685–0260, WEB www.viff.org) is held in late September and early October in several theaters around town.

## Music

### CHAMBER MUSIC AND SMALL ENSEMBLES

**Early Music Vancouver** (☏ 604/732–1610, WEB www.earlymusic.bc.ca) performs medieval, Renaissance, Baroque, and early classical music year-round and hosts the Vancouver Early Music Programme and Festival from mid-July to mid-August at the University of British Columbia. Concerts by the **Friends of Chamber Music** (☏ 604/437–5747, WEB www.friendsofchambermusic.ca) are worth watching for in the local-newspaper entertainment listings. The **Vancouver Recital Society** (☏ 604/602–0363, WEB www.vanrecital.com) presents both emerging and well-known classical musicians in recital September–May at the Chan Centre for the Performing Arts and the Vancouver Playhouse. In summer the society produces the Vancouver Chamber Music Festival, on the grounds of **Crofton House School** (⊠ 3200 W. 41st Ave., South Vancouver).

### CHORAL GROUPS

The **Vancouver Bach Choir** (☏ 604/921–8012, WEB www.vancouverbachchoir.com) performs a five-concert series at the Orpheum Theatre between September and June. The **Vancouver Cantata Singers** (☏ 604/921–8588, WEB www.cantata.org) present choral performances at various venues around town. The **Vancouver Chamber Choir** (☏ 604/738–6822, WEB www.vancouverchamberchoir.com) performs at several venues, including the Orpheum and the Chan Centre.

**Festival Vancouver** (✉ ☎ 604/688–1152, WEB www.festivalvancouver. bc.ca) is Vancouver's biggest music event, with up to 60 performances of orchestral, chamber, choral, world music, early music, opera, and jazz in venues around the city in early August.

The **Vancouver Symphony Orchestra** (☎ 604/876–3434) is the resident company at the Orpheum Theatre (✉ 601 Smithe St., Downtown).

## Opera

**Vancouver Opera** (☎ 604/682–2871, WEB www.vanopera.bc.ca) stages four productions a year from October through May at the Queen Elizabeth Theatre.

## Theater

The **Arts Club Theatre** (✉ 1585 Johnston St., Granville Island, ☎ 604/ 687–1644) operates two stages on Granville Island (the **Arts Club Theatre** and the **New Revue Stage**) as well as the **Stanley Theatre** at 2750 Granville Street. All three stages present theatrical performances year-round.

**Carousel Theatre** (☎ 604/685–6217) performs for children and young people at the **Waterfront Theatre** (✉ 1410 Cartwright St., Granville Island). Big international shows, from Broadway musicals to Chinese dance productions, play at the **Centre in Vancouver for Performing Arts** (✉ 777 Homer St., Downtown, ☎ 604/602–0616, WEB www. centreinvancouver.com). The **Chan Centre for the Performing Arts** (✉ 6265 Crescent Rd., University of British Columbia Campus, Point Grey, ☎ 604/822–2697) contains a 1,200-seat concert hall, a theater, and a cinema.

The **Firehall Arts Centre** (✉ 280 E. Cordova St., Downtown East Side, ☎ 604/689–0926) showcases innovative works in an intimate Downtown Eastside space. The **Queen Elizabeth Theatre** (✉ 600 Hamilton St., Downtown, ☎ 604/665–3050) is a major venue for ballet, opera, and other events. **Vancouver East Cultural Centre** (✉ 1895 Venables St., East Vancouver, ☎ 604/254–9578) is a multipurpose performance space. In the same complex as the Queen Elizabeth Theatre, the **Vancouver Playhouse** (✉ 649 Cambie St., Downtown, ☎ 604/665–3050) is the leading venue in Vancouver for mainstream theater. The **Vogue Theatre** (✉ 918 Granville St., Downtown, ☎ 604/331–7909), a former movie palace, hosts theater and live music events.

**Bard on the Beach** (☎ 604/739–0559) is a summer series of Shakespeare's plays performed in tents on the beach at Vanier Park. **Theatre Under the Stars** (☎ 604/687–0174) performs musicals at Malkin Bowl, an outdoor amphitheater in Stanley Park, during July and August. The **Vancouver Fringe Festival** (☎ 604/257–0350, WEB www.vancouverfringe.com), an annual theater festival, is staged in September at various venues on and around Granville Island.

# OUTDOOR ACTIVITIES AND SPORTS

## Beaches

An almost continuous string of beaches runs from Stanley Park to the University of British Columbia. The water is cool, but the beaches are sandy, edged by grass. All have lifeguards, washrooms, concession stands, and limited parking, unless otherwise noted. Liquor is prohibited in parks and on beaches. For information, call the **Vancouver Board of Parks and Recreation** (☎ 604/738–8535 summer only).

**Kitsilano Beach,** over the Burrard Bridge from downtown, has a lifeguard and is the city's busiest beach—in-line skaters, volleyball games, and sleek young people are ever present. The part of the beach nearest the Vancouver Maritime Museum is the quietest. Facilities include a playground, tennis courts, a heated pool, and concession stands.

The **Point Grey beaches**—Jericho, Locarno, and Spanish Banks—begin at the end of Point Grey Road and offer huge expanses of sand. The shallow water, warmed slightly by sun and sand, is good for swimming. Farther out, toward Spanish Banks, the beach becomes less crowded. Past Point Grey is Wreck Beach, Vancouver's nude beach.

Among the **West End beaches,** Second Beach and Third Beach, along Stanley Park Drive in Stanley Park, draw families. Second Beach has a guarded pool. A water slide, kayak rentals, street performers, and artists keep things interesting all summer at English Bay Beach, at the foot of Denman Street. Farther along Beach Drive, Sunset Beach is a little too close to the downtown core for clean, safe swimming.

## Participant Sports

### Biking

One of the best ways to see the city is to cycle along at least part of the **Seaside Bicycle Route.** This 39-km (23-mi), flat, car-free route starts at Canada Place downtown, follows the waterfront around Stanley Park, and continues, with a few detours, all the way around False Creek to Spanish Banks Beach.

Most bike rental outlets also rent Rollerblades and jogging strollers. Cycling helmets, a legal requirement in Vancouver, come with the rentals. If you're cycling from Canada Place, you can rent bikes and Rollerblades from **Harbour Air Adventure Centre** (✉ 1081 Coal Harbour Rd., Downtown, ☏ 604/688–9436) to the west of Canada Place where the floatplanes dock. If you're starting your bike ride near Stanley Park, try **Bayshore Bicycles** (✉ 745 Denman St., West End, ☏ 604/688–2453). They have a range of bikes and Rollerblades as well as baby joggers and bike trailers. **Spokes Bicycle Rentals** (✉ 1798 W. Georgia St., West End, ☏ 604/688–5141), at Denman and Georgia, has a wide selection of bikes, including kids' bikes, tandems, and mountain bikes, though no Rollerblades. Helmets, locks and maps are included, and group bike tours are available. **Reckless, the Bike Store** (✉ 110 Davie St., Yaletown, ☏ 604/648–2600) rents bikes on the Yaletown section of the bike path. To explore the Granville Island and Kitsilano area, stop at the Kitsilano store (✉ 1810 Fir St., at 2nd Ave., Kitsilano, ☏ 604/731–2420).

### Boating

You can charter motorboats and sailboats from Granville Island through **Blue Pacific Yacht Charters** (✉ 1519 Foreshore Walk, Granville Island, ☏ 604/682–2161 or 800/237–2392, WEB www.bluepacificcharters.ca). **Cooper Boating** (✉ 1620 Duranleau St., Granville Island, ☏ 604/687–4110 or 888/999–6419, WEB www.cooperboating.com) charters sailboats and cabin cruisers, with or without skippers. It also provides sailing and power-boating lessons.

### Fishing

You can fish for salmon all year in coastal British Columbia. **Sewell's Marina Horseshoe Bay** (✉ 6695 Nelson Ave., Horseshoe Bay, ☏ 604/921–3474, WEB www.sewellsmarina.com) leads guided and self-drive salmon-fishing charters on Howe Sound. **Westin Bayshore Yacht Charters** (✉ 1601 Bayshore Dr., off W. Georgia St., West End, ☏ 604/691–6936, WEB www.westinbayshoreyachts.com) operates fishing and yacht charters.

## Golf

For advance tee-time bookings at any of 60 British Columbia courses, or for a spur-of-the-moment game, call **Last Minute Golf** (☎ 604/878–1833 or 800/684–6344, WEB www.lastminutegolf.net). The company matches golfers and courses, sometimes at substantial greens-fee discounts. The packages at **West Coast Golf Shuttle** (☎ 604/351–6833 or 888/599–6800, WEB www.golf-shuttle.com) include the greens fee, power cart, and hotel pickup; rental clubs are available.

The challenging 18-hole, par-72 course at **Furry Creek Golf and Country Club** (✉ Hwy. 99, Furry Creek, ☎ 604/922–9576 or 888/922–9462, WEB www.furrycreekgolf.ca), a 45-minute drive north of Vancouver, has a $99 peak-season greens fee that includes a mandatory cart. The course is closed late October to early March. The facilities of the 18-hole, par-71 public **McCleery Golf Course** (✉ 7188 McDonald St., South Vancouver, ☎ 604/257–8191; 604/280–1818 advance bookings) include a driving range. The greens fee is $42–$45; an optional cart costs $28. **Northview Golf and Country Club** (✉ 6857 168th St., Surrey, ☎ 604/576–4653 or 888/574–2211, WEB www.northviewgolf.com) has two Arnold Palmer–designed 18-hole courses (both par 72) and is home of the Air Canada Championship (a Professional Golfers' Association, or PGA, tour event). The greens fee for the Ridge course (open March through October), where the PGA tour plays, is $85–$95; the fee for the Canal course (open all year) is $60–$70. An optional cart at either course costs $30. At the 18-hole, par-72 course (closed November through March) at the **Westwood Plateau Golf and Country Club** (✉ 3251 Plateau Blvd., Coquitlam, ☎ 604/552–0777 or 800/580–0785, WEB www.westwoodplateaugolf.bc.ca), the greens fee, which includes a cart, is $99–$149. The club also has a restaurant and a 9-hole course that's open year-round.

## Health and Fitness Clubs

The **Bentall Centre Athletic Club** (✉ 1055 Dunsmuir St., lower plaza, Downtown, ☎ 604/689–4424, WEB www.bentallcentreathleticclub.com) specializes in squash and also has racquetball courts and weight and cardio gyms; aerobics classes are given as well. The **YMCA** (✉ 955 Burrard St., Downtown, ☎ 604/689–9622, WEB www.vanymca.org), downtown, has daily rates. Facilities include a pool, a men's steam room and women's sauna, two cardio gyms and a weight room, as well as basketball, a boxing room, and racquetball, squash, and handball courts. The **YWCA** (✉ 535 Hornby St., Downtown, ☎ 604/895–5777, WEB www.ywcahealthandwellness.com) has an ozone pool, a cardio room, coed and women-only weight rooms, fitness classes, a whirlpool, and steam rooms.

## Hiking

The weather can change quickly in the mountains, so go prepared and leave word with someone in the city as to your route and when you expect to be back. For **weather forecasts,** call ☎ 604/664–9021.

The seaside **Lighthouse Park** (✉ Beacon La., off Marine Dr., West Vancouver) has fairly flat forested trails leading to the rocky shoreline. The rugged **Pacific Spirit Regional Park** (✉ 4915 W. 16th Ave., Point Grey, ☎ 604/224–5739), near the University of British Columbia, has fairly level forested trails and is popular with mountain bikers and hikers. **Stanley Park** (☎ 604/257–8400) has miles of trails to explore.

In the mountains of North Vancouver, **Capilano River Regional Park** (☎ 604/224–5739) has trails along the edge of a dramatic gorge. **Cypress Provincial Park** (✉ Cypress Bowl Rd., West Vancouver, ☎ 604/924–2200) is a good choice for serious hikers. North Vancouver's

**Lower Seymour Conservation Reserve** (✉ end of Lillooet Rd., North Vancouver, ☎ 604/432–6286) has some easy rain-forest walks. **Mount Seymour Provincial Park** (✉ Mount Seymour Rd. off Seymour Pkwy., North Vancouver, ☎ 604/924–2200) offers challenging mountain trails for experienced, well-equipped hikers.

The **Grouse Grind** is a steep (rising 2,800 ft in less than 2 mi), grueling trail from the Grouse Mountain parking lot to the top of the mountain; the path is packed with fit Vancouverites most summer afternoons. There are also hiking trails at the top of the mountain, accessed via the Grouse Mountain Skyride.

A number of companies conduct guided walks and hikes in nearby parks and wilderness areas (☞ Vancouver A to Z, Tours).

## Jogging

The **Running Room** (✉ 679 Denman St., West End, ☎ 604/684–9771) is a good source for information about fun runs in the area. The seawall around **Stanley Park** (☎ 604/257–8400) is 9 km (5½ mi) long; running it provides an excellent minitour of the city. You can take a shorter run of 4 km (2½ mi) in the park around Lost Lagoon.

## Skiing

### CROSS-COUNTRY

The best cross-country skiing, with 19 km (11½ mi) of groomed trails, some of it lit for night skiing, is at **Cypress Mountain** (✉ Cypress Bowl Rd., West Vancouver, Exit 8 off Hwy. 1 westbound, ☎ 604/922–0825). **Grouse Mountain** has cross-country trails as well as downhill skiing.

### DOWNHILL SKIING AND SNOWBOARDING

Whistler/Blackcomb, a top-ranked ski destination, is a two-hour drive from Vancouver. The North Shore Mountains hold three ski and snowboard areas. All have rentals, lessons, night skiing, and a variety of runs suitable for all skill levels. The season runs December to April.

**Cypress Mountain** (✉ Cypress Bowl Rd., West Vancouver, Exit 8 off Hwy. 1 westbound, ☎ 604/926–5612; 604/419–7669 snow report; WEB www.cypressmountain.com) has 34 runs on two mountains, five chairlifts, and a vertical drop of 1,750 ft. The mountain also has a tobogganing and snow-tubing area. **Grouse Mountain** (✉ 6400 Nancy Greene Way, North Vancouver, ☎ 604/980–9311; 604/986–6262 snow report; WEB www.grousemountain.com) has 24 runs, a vertical drop of 1,210 ft, extensive night skiing, restaurants, bars, ice-skating, a snowshoeing park, and great city views from the runs. **Mount Seymour** (✉ 1700 Mt. Seymour Rd., North Vancouver, ☎ 604/986–2261; 604/718–7771 snow report; WEB www.mountseymour.com) has three chairlifts and a vertical drop of 1,042 ft. With a a half-pipe and two terrain parks, it's popular with snowboarders. You can also take a snowshoeing tour or play in the tobogganing and snow-tubing areas.

## Tennis

There are 180 free public courts around town. Contact the **Vancouver Board of Parks and Recreation** (☎ 604/257–8400, WEB www.parks.vancouver.bc.ca) for locations. **Stanley Park** (☎ 604/605–8224 summer only) has 18 outdoor courts near English Bay Beach. Some courts charge a fee and can be booked in advance.

## Water Sports

### KAYAKING

Kayaks are a fun way to explore the waters of False Creek and the shoreline of English Bay. **Ecomarine Ocean Kayak Centre** offers lessons and rentals year-round from Granville Island (✉ 1668 Duranleau St.,

# When you pack your MCI Calling Card, it's like packing your loved ones along too.

Your MCI Calling Card is the easy way to stay in touch when you travel. Use it to call to and from over 125 countries. Plus, every time you call, you can earn frequent flier miles. So wherever your travels take you, call home with your MCI Calling Card. It's even easy to get one. Just visit **www.mci.com/worldphone** or **www.mci.com/partners**.

## EASY TO CALL WORLDWIDE

**1.** Just enter the WorldPhone® access number of the country you're calling from.

**2.** Enter or give the operator your MCI Calling Card number.

**3.** Enter or give the number you're calling.

| | |
|---|---|
| Aruba ⁘ | 800-888-8 |
| Bahamas ⁘ | 1-800-888-8000 |

| | |
|---|---|
| Barbados ⁘ | 1-800-888-8000 |
| Bermuda ⁘ | 1-800-888-8000 |
| British Virgin Islands ⁘ | 1-800-888-8000 |
| Canada | 1-800-888-8000 |
| Mexico | 01-800-021-8000 |
| Puerto Rico | 1-800-888-8000 |
| United States | 1-800-888-8000 |
| U.S. Virgin Islands | 1-800-888-8000 |

⁘ Limited availability.

## EARN FREQUENT FLIER MILES

# Find America *with a Compass*

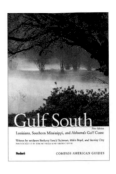

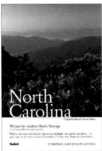

Written by local authors and illustrated throughout
with spectacular color images, Compass American
Guides reveal the character and culture of more than
40 of America's most fascinating destinations. Perfect
for residents who want to explore their own backyards
and for visitors who want an insider's perspective
on the history, heritage, and all there is to see and do.

**Fodor's** COMPASS AMERICAN GUIDES

*At bookstores everywhere.*

Granville Island, ☎ 604/689–7575, WEB www.ecomarine.com) and from early May to early September at Jericho Beach (☎ 604/222–3565). Between early April and the end of October **Ocean West Expeditions** (☎ 800/660–0051; 604/688–5770 summer only; WEB www.ocean-west. com) rents kayaks and offers lessons and tours from English Bay Beach.

### RAFTING

The **Canadian Outback Adventure Company** (☎ 604/921–7250 or 800/ 565–8735, WEB www.canadianoutback.com) runs white-water rafting and scenic (not white-water) floats on day trips from Vancouver.

### WINDSURFING

The winds aren't heavy on English Bay, making it a perfect locale for learning the sport. You have to travel north to Squamish for more-challenging high-wind conditions. Sailboard rentals and lessons are available between May and September at **Windsure Windsurfing School** (✉ Jericho Beach, Kitsilano, ☎ 604/224–0615, WEB www.windsure.com).

## Spectator Sports

**Ticketmaster** (☎ 604/280–4400) sells tickets to many local sports events.

### Football

The **B.C. Lions** (☎ 604/930–5466) Canadian Football League team plays home games at **B.C. Place Stadium** (✉ 777 Pacific Blvd. S, Downtown, ☎ 604/669–2300).

### Hockey

The **Vancouver Canucks** (☎ 604/899–7400) of the National Hockey League play at **General Motors Place** (✉ 800 Griffiths Way, Downtown, ☎ 604/899–7400.

# SHOPPING

Unlike many cities where suburban malls have taken over, Vancouver is full of individual boutiques and specialty shops. Antiques stores, ethnic markets, art galleries, and high-fashion outlets abound. Store hours are generally 9:30–6 Monday, Tuesday, Wednesday, and Saturday; 9:30–9 Thursday and Friday; and 10–5 Sunday.

## Shopping Districts and Malls

About two dozen high-end art galleries, antiques shops, and Oriental-rug emporiums are packed end to end between 5th and 15th avenues on Granville Street, in an area known as **Gallery Row. Oakridge Shopping Centre** (✉ 650 W. 41st Ave., at Cambie St., South Vancouver, ☎ 604/261–2511) has chic, expensive stores that are fun to browse in. **Metrotown Centre** (✉ 4800 Kingsway, Burnaby, ☎ 604/438–3610 or 604/438–2444), one of the largest malls in the area, is 20 minutes from downtown by SkyTrain. The **Pacific Centre Mall** (✉ 700 W. Georgia St., Downtown, ☎ 604/688–7236), on two levels and mostly underground, takes up three city blocks in the heart of downtown. **Robson Street** stretching from Burrard to Bute streets is full of boutiques and cafés. A commercial center has developed around **Sinclair Centre** (✉ 757 W. Hastings St., Downtown), catering to sophisticated and pricey tastes.

Bustling **Chinatown**—centered on Pender and Main streets—is full of restaurants and markets. Guatemalan crafts, Spanish tapas, Italian shoes, and espresso bars with soccer matches broadcast live from Italy come together on **Commercial Drive,** between East 1st Avenue and Venables Street, Vancouver's world-beat melting pot. **Granville Island** (☞ Exploring Vancouver) is home to a lively public market and a wealth of galleries, crafts shops, and artisans' studios. In **Little India,** on Main Street around 50th Avenue, curry houses, sweets shops, grocery stores, discount jewelers, and silk shops abound. Treasure hunters like the 300 block of **West Cordova Street** near Gastown, where offbeat shops sell curios, vintage clothing, and local designer goods.

## Department Stores

The **Bay** (✉ 674 Granville St., at Georgia St., Downtown, ☎ 604/681–6211), founded as part of the fur trade in the 17th century, is now a mid-price department store downtown. Modeled on Paris's Colette store, **Bruce** (✉ 1038 Alberni St., Downtown, ☎ 604/688–8802) is Vancouver's first "lifestyle" department store, offering the latest in designer fashion, home decor, and eyewear as well as CDs, books, and magazines. **Sears** (✉ 701 Granville St., Downtown, ☎ 604/685–7112) is a mid-price department store with a wide range of goods. **Holt Renfrew** (✉ 633 Granville St., Downtown, ☎ 604/681–3121) focuses on high fashion for men and women.

## Specialty Stores

### Antiques
Three key antiques hunting grounds are Gallery Row on Granville Street, the stretch of antiques stores along Main Street from 16th to 30th Avenue, and along Front Street, between 6th and Begbie streets (near New Westminster Quay) in New Westminster. **Love's Auctioneers** (✉ 1635 W. Broadway, Kitsilano, ☎ 604/733–1157) auctions antiques on the last Wednesday and Thursday of each month at 6 PM. **Vancouver Antique Centre** (✉ 422 Richards St., Downtown, ☎ 604/669–7444) has 15 antiques and collectibles dealers under one roof.

### Art Galleries
**Gallery Row** along Granville Street between 5th and 15th avenues is home to about a dozen high-end contemporary-art galleries. The **Diane Farris Gallery** (✉ 1565 W. 7th Ave., South Granville, ☎ 604/737–2629) often showcases hot new artists. The **Douglas Reynolds Gallery** (✉ 2335 Granville St., South Granville, ☎ 604/731–9292) has one of the city's finest collections of Northwest Coast First Nations art.

A number of notable galleries are also on the downtown peninsula. **Buschlen Mowatt** (✉ 1445 W. Georgia St., Downtown, ☎ 604/682–1234) and the **Buschlen Mowatt Annex** (✉ 647 Howe St., Downtown, ☎ 604/682–7777) exhibit the works of contemporary Canadian and international artists. **Coastal Peoples Fine Arts Gallery** (✉ 1024 Mainland St., Yaletown, ☎ 604/685–9298) has an impressive collection of First Nations jewelry, ceremonial masks, prints, and carvings. The **Inuit Gallery of Vancouver** (✉ 206 Cambie St., Gastown, ☎ 888/615–8399 or 604/688–7323) exhibits Northwest Coast and Inuit art. The **Marion Scott Gallery** (✉ 481 Howe St., Downtown, ☎ 604/685–1934) specializes in Inuit art.

### Books
Vancouver's two **Chapters** stores (✉ 788 Robson St., Downtown, ☎ 604/682–4066; ✉ 2505 Granville St., at Broadway, South Granville, ☎ 604/731–7822) are enormous, with a café in each and a series of author readings and other performances. **Duthie Books** (✉ 2239 W. 4th Ave., Kitsilano, ☎ 604/732–5344) is a long-established homegrown favorite. **MacLeod's Books** (✉ 455 W. Pender St., Downtown, ☎ 604/

681–7654) is one of the city's best antiquarian and used-book stores. **Sophia Books** (⊠ 492 West Hastings, Downtown, ☎ 604/684–0484) specializes in French and other foreign-language titles. **Wanderlust** (⊠ 1929 W. 4th Ave., Kitsilano, ☎ 604/739–2182) carries thousands of travel books and maps, as well as luggage and travel accessories.

## Clothes

**Dream** (⊠ 311 W. Cordova St., Gastown, ☎ 604/683–7326) is where up-and-coming local designers sell their wares. Men's and women's fashions by Versace, Yves Saint Laurent Rive Gauche, Dior, Prada, and others are available at **Leone** (⊠ 757 W. Hastings St., Downtown, ☎ 604/683–1133), in Sinclair Centre. You'll find upscale menswear at **Madison Men's Wear** (⊠ 1050 W. Pender St., Downtown, ☎ 604/683–2122). **Wear Else?** (⊠ 2372 W. 4th Ave., Kitsilano, ☎ 604/732–3521; ⊠ 4401 W. 10th Ave., Point Grey, ☎ 604/221–7755; ⊠ Oakridge Shopping Centre, 650 W. 41st Ave., at Cambie St., South Vancouver, ☎ 604/266–3613) is a popular women's wear shop selling both business and casual clothes, including shoes and accessories.

## Gifts

Museum and gallery gift shops are among the best places to buy high-quality souvenirs—West Coast native art, books, music, jewelry, and other items. The **Clamshell Gift Shop** (⊠ Vancouver Aquarium Marine Science Centre, Stanley Park, ☎ 604/659–3413), in Stanley Park, features souvenir clothing and aquatic-theme toys and gifts. The **Gallery Shop** (⊠ 750 Hornby St., Downtown, ☎ 604/662–4706), in the Vancouver Art Gallery, has a good selection of prints and cards. The **Museum of Anthropology Gift Shop** (⊠ 6393 N.W. Marine Dr., University of British Columbia Campus, Point Grey, ☎ 604/822–3825), on the University of British Columbia campus, features Northwest Coast jewelry, carvings, and prints, as well as a good collection of books on First Nations history and culture.

**Hill's Native Art** (⊠ 165 Water St., Gastown, ☎ 604/685–4249) in Gastown has Vancouver's largest selection of First Nations art. **Lattimer Gallery** (⊠ 1590 W. 2nd Ave., False Creek, ☎ 604/732–4556), near Granville Island, is full of native arts and crafts in all price ranges. At the **Salmon Shop** (⊠ 1689 Johnston St., Granville Island, ☎ 604/669–3474), in the Granville Island Public Market, you can pick up fresh or smoked salmon wrapped for travel. One of Vancouver's most extensive, but least known, native-art collections is hidden in the back room at the **Three Vets** (⊠ 2200 Yukon St., Fairview, ☎ 604/872–5475), a camping-equipment store. Ask any staff member to show you.

## Jewelry

Vancouver's leading jewelry shops are clustered along Hastings Street. **Birks** (⊠ 698 W. Hastings St., Downtown, ☎ 604/669–3333) takes up the grand lower floor of a neoclassical building that was the former headquarters of the Canadian Imperial Bank of Commerce. **Cartier Jewellers** (⊠ 408 Howe St., Downtown, ☎ 604/683–6878) is the Vancouver outlet of the famous jewelry chain. **Palladio** (⊠ 855 W. Hastings St., Downtown, ☎ 604/685–3885) carries modern, high-fashion jewelry in gold and platinum.

## Outdoor Equipment

Outdoor-oriented Vancouver is a great place to pick up camping and hiking gear. **Coast Mountain Sports** (⊠ 2201 W. 4th Ave., Kitsilano, ☎ 604/731–6181; ⊠ Park Royal Shopping Centre, Marine Dr., West Vancouver, ☎ 604/922–3336; ⊠ Metrotown Shopping Centre, Burnaby, ☎ 604/434–9397; ⊠ Coquitlam Shopping Centre, Coquitlam, ☎ 945–9511) has high-performance (and high-fashion) gear.

The massive **Mountain Equipment Co-op** (⊠ 130 W. Broadway, Fairview, ☎ 604/872–7858) is a local institution with a good selection of high-performance and mid-price clothing and equipment. A onetime $5 membership is required. The **Three Vets** (⊠ 2200 Yukon St., Fairview, ☎ 604/872–5475), near Cambie Street and Broadway, is an army-surplus–style store with budget-price family camping equipment. Ask to see the native art collections.

# VANCOUVER A TO Z

*To research prices, get advice from other travelers, and book travel arrangements, visit www.fodors.com.*

### AIR TRAVEL TO AND FROM VANCOUVER
Air Canada's regional service, Air Canada Jazz, and WestJet Airlines serve destinations around Western Canada. West Coast Air and Harbour Air Seaplanes operate 35-minute harbor-to-harbor service (downtown Vancouver to downtown Victoria) several times a day. Planes leave from near the Pan Pacific Hotel at 300–999 Canada Place. Helijet International has helicopter service from downtown Vancouver and the Vancouver airport to Seattle and Victoria. The heliport is near Vancouver's Pan Pacific Hotel.
➤ AIRLINES AND CONTACTS: **Air Canada Jazz** (☎ 888/247–2262, WEB www.aircanada.ca). **Harbour Air** (☎ 604/688–1277 or 800/665–0212, WEB www.harbour-air.com). **Helijet International** (☎ 800/665–4354 or 604/273–1414, WEB www.helijet.com). **West Coast Air** (☎ 604/606–6888 or 800/347–2222, WEB www.westcoastair.com). **WestJet Airlines** (☎ 800/538–5696, WEB www.westjet.com).

### AIRPORTS AND TRANSFERS
Vancouver International Airport is on Sea Island, about 23 km (14 mi) south of downtown off Highway 99. An airport-improvement fee is assessed on all flight departures: $5 for flights within British Columbia or the Yukon; $10 for other flights within North America; $15 for overseas flights. Major credit cards and Canadian and United States currencies are accepted. Alaska, American, British Airways, Continental, Northwest, Qantas, and United serve the airport. The two major domestic carriers are Air Canada and Canadian Airlines.
➤ AIRPORT INFORMATION: **Vancouver International Airport** (⊠ Grant McConachie Way, Richmond, ☎ 604/207–7077, WEB www.yvr.ca).

AIRPORT TRANSFER
The drive from the airport to downtown takes 20 to 45 minutes, depending on the time of day. Airport hotels provide shuttle service to and from the airport. If you're driving, go over the Arthur Laing Bridge and north on Granville Street (also signposted as Highway 99). Signs direct you to Vancouver City Centre.

The Vancouver Airporter Service bus leaves the international- and domestic-arrivals levels of the terminal building approximately every half hour, stopping at major downtown hotels. It operates from 8:55 AM until 11:30 PM. The fare is $12 one-way and $18 round-trip.

Taxi stands are in front of the terminal building on domestic- and international-arrivals levels. The taxi fare to downtown is about $25. Area cab companies include Black Top and Yellow.

Limousine service from LimoJet Gold costs about $34 one-way.
➤ TAXIS AND SHUTTLES: **Black Top** (☎ 604/681–2181). **LimoJet Gold** (☎ 604/273–1331). **Vancouver Airporter Service** (☎ 604/946–8866 or 800/668–3141). **Yellow** (☎ 604/681–1111).

## BOAT AND FERRY TRAVEL

BC Ferries operates two major ferry terminals outside Vancouver. From Tsawwassen to the south (an hour's drive from downtown), ferries sail to Victoria and Nanaimo on Vancouver Island and to the Gulf Islands (the small islands between the mainland and Vancouver Island). From Horseshoe Bay (45 minutes north of downtown), ferries sail to the Sunshine Coast and to Nanaimo on Vancouver Island.

The SeaBus is a 400-passenger commuter ferry that crosses Burrard Inlet from Waterfront Station downtown to the foot of Lonsdale Avenue in North Vancouver. Leaving every 15 to 30 minutes, the ride takes 13 minutes and costs the same as the TransLink bus. With a transfer, connection can be made to any TransLink bus or SkyTrain.

Aquabus Ferries connect several stations on False Creek, including Science World, Granville Island, Stamp's Landing, Yaletown, and the Hornby Street dock. Some Aquabus ferries take bicycles, and the company also operates two historic wooden boats on some runs.

False Creek Ferries provides foot passenger service between the Aquatic Centre on Beach Avenue, Granville Island, Science World, Stamp's Landing, and Vanier Park.

False Creek and Aquabus Ferries are not part of the TransLink system, so bus transfers aren't accepted.

### FARES AND SCHEDULES

Vehicle reservations on Vancouver to Victoria and Nanaimo routes are optional and cost $15 in addition to the fare. There's no extra charge for reservations on Gulf Island routes.

➤ BOAT AND FERRY INFORMATION: **Aquabus Ferries** (☎ 604/689–5858, WEB www.aquabus.bc.ca). **BC Ferries** (☎ 250/386–3431; 888/223–3779 in British Columbia; WEB www.bcferries.com). **False Creek Ferries** (☎ 604/684–7781, WEB www.granvilleislandferries.bc.ca). **SeaBus** (☎ 604/953–3333, WEB www.translink.bc.ca).

## BUS TRAVEL TO AND FROM VANCOUVER

Pacific Coach Lines provides service from Vancouver to Victoria every two hours. Greyhound Lines serves most other towns in the province, including Whistler and Nanaimo on Vancouver Island. Pacific Central Station is the depot for both bus companies. Quick Shuttle buses run service from downtown Vancouver and Vancouver Airport to Seattle (SeaTac) Airport and downtown Seattle. They leave five times a day in winter and up to eight times a day in summer. The downtown Vancouver depot is at the Holiday Inn, though the shuttle picks up at most downtown Vancouver hotels by prior arrangement.

➤ BUS INFORMATION: **Greyhound Lines** (☎ 604/482–8747; 800/661–8747 in Canada; 800/231–2222 in the U.S.). **Pacific Central Station** (✉ 1150 Station St., Downtown, ☎ no phone). **Pacific Coach Lines** (☎ 604/662–8074 or 800/661–1725, WEB www.pacificcoach.com). **Quick Shuttle** (☎ 604/940–4428 or 800/665–2122, WEB www.quickcoach.com). **Vancouver depot** (✉ 1110 Howe St., Downtown, ☎ no phone).

## BUS TRAVEL WITHIN VANCOUVER

TransLink buses provide regular service throughout Vancouver and its suburbs (except West Vancouver). Buses to West Vancouver (on the North Shore) are operated by West Vancouver Transit.

Exact change is needed to ride TransLink buses: $2 for regular adult fares or $3–$4 for weekday trips to the suburbs, including the SeaBus to the North Shore. Books of 10 tickets (FareSavers) are sold at convenience stores and newsstands; look for a red, white, and blue FARE

DEALER sign. Day passes, good for unlimited travel all day, cost $8. They are available from fare dealers and at any SeaBus or SkyTrain station. Transfers (ask for one when you board) are valid for 90 minutes, allow travel in any direction, and are good on buses, SkyTrain, and SeaBus.

➤ BUS INFORMATION: **TransLink** (☎ 604/953–3333, WEB www. translink.bc.ca). **West Vancouver Transit** (☎ 604/985–7777).

### CAR RENTAL

➤ MAJOR AGENCIES: **Avis** (☎ 604/606–2847 or 800/331–1212). **Budget** (☎ 604/668–7000 or 800/268–8900). **Thrifty Car Rental** (☎ 604/606–1666 or 800/847–4389).

### CAR TRAVEL

Interstate 5 in Washington State becomes Highway 99 at the U.S.–Canada border. Vancouver is a three-hour drive (226 km [140 mi]) from Seattle.

A car can be handy for touring areas outside the city center, but it isn't essential. On the compact downtown peninsula, however, it's generally easier to get around on foot or by public transport, especially in light of the congestion, limited parking, and many one-way streets.

EMERGENCY SERVICES

The British Columbia Automobile Association provides 24-hour emergency road service for members of the American and the Canadian automobile associations.

➤ CONTACT: **British Columbia Automobile Association** (☎ 604/293–2222 or 800/222–4357, WEB www.bcaa.com).

PARKING

Parking downtown is expensive and tricky to find. Two large underground pay parking garages that usually have space are the Library Square lot and the Pacific Centre lot. Parking fees run about $2 an hour or $8–$13 a day. Don't leave anything in your car, even in the trunk; break-ins are quite common downtown (hotel parking tends to be more secure, though more expensive, than public lots). Parking outside the downtown core is an easier proposition.

➤ PARKING INFORMATION: **Library Square lot** (✉ 775 Hamilton St., off Robson St., Downtown, ☎ 604/669–4183). **Pacific Centre lot** (✉ 700 block of Howe St., east side, Downtown, ☎ 604/684–9715).

TRAFFIC

It's best to avoid border crossings during peak times such as holidays and weekends. Highway 1, the Trans-Canada Highway, enters Vancouver from the east. To avoid traffic, arrive after rush hour (9 AM).

Vancouver's rush-hour traffic, about 7–9 weekday mornings and starting at 3 PM weekday afternoons, can be horrendous. The worst bottlenecks outside the city center are the North Shore bridges (especially Lions Gate Bridge), the George Massey Tunnel on Highway 99 south of Vancouver, and Highway 1 through Coquitlam and Surrey.

Right turns are allowed at most red lights after you've come to a full stop.

### EMERGENCIES

➤ EMERGENCY SERVICES: **Ambulance, fire, police** (☎ 911).

➤ HOSPITALS: **Medicentre** (✉ 1055 Dunsmuir St., lower level, Downtown, ☎ 604/683–8138), a drop-in clinic in Bentall Centre, is open weekdays 8 AM–4:30 PM. The emergency ward at **St. Paul's Hospital** (✉ 1081 Burrard St., Downtown, ☎ 604/682–2344) is open 24 hours.

➤ 24-Hour Pharmacy: **Shopper's Drug Mart** (✉ 1125 Davie St., West End, ☎ 604/669–2424).

## LODGING

Hello BC, operated by the provincial Ministry of Tourism, can book accommodations anywhere in British Columbia. Town & Country Bed and Breakfast Reservation Service specializes in B&Bs.

➤ Reservation Services: **Super, Natural BC** (☎ 604/663–6000 or 800/435–5622, WEB www.hellobc.com). **Town & Country Bed and Breakfast Reservation Service** (✉ 2803 W. 4th Ave., Kitsilano [Box 74542, V6K 1K2], ☎ FAX 604/731–5942, WEB www. townandcountrybedandbreakfast.com).

## MAIL AND INTERNET

Vancouver's main post office is open weekdays 8–5:30. There are also postal outlets in many stores, particularly Shopper's Drug Mart and Pharmasave branches, throughout the city. These outlets usually keep the same hours as the store they are in. Internet access is available at the central branch of the Vancouver Public Library. Some terminals have free access; others can be used for $2.50 for 30 minutes. Internet cafés can be found throughout the city; they charge about $3 per hour.

➤ Post Office: **Canada Post** (✉ 349 W. Georgia St., Downtown, ☎ 800/267–1177).

➤ Internet Cafés: **Cyber Madness** (✉ 779 Denman St., West End, ☎ 604/633–9389). **Vancouver Public Library** (✉ 350 W. Georgia St., Downtown, ☎ 604/331–3600).

## RAPID-TRANSIT TRAVEL

A 46-km (27-mi) rapid-transit system called SkyTrain travels underground downtown and is elevated for the rest of its route to Coquitlam and Surrey. Trains leave about every five minutes. Tickets, sold at each station from machines (correct change is not necessary), must be carried with you as proof of payment. You may use transfers from SkyTrain to SeaBus and TransLink buses and vice versa. SkyTrain is convenient for transit between downtown, B.C. Place Stadium, Pacific Central Station, and Science World.

➤ Subway Information: **SkyTrain** (☎ 604/953–3333, WEB www. translink.bc.ca).

## TAXIS

It's difficult to hail a cab in Vancouver. Unless you're near a hotel, you'll have better luck calling a taxi service. Try Black Top or Yellow.

➤ Taxi Companies: **Black Top** (☎ 604/681–2181). **Yellow** (☎ 604/ 681–1111).

## TOURS

Tour prices fluctuate, so inquire about rates when booking.

### AIRPLANE TOURS

Baxter Aviation conducts tours to the mountains, glaciers, and islands around the city from $119 per person. You can see Vancouver from the air for about $80 for 20 minutes, or take a one-hour flight ($167–$190) over nearby mountains and glaciers with Harbour Air Seaplanes. Both services leave from beside the Pan Pacific Hotel.

➤ Fees and Schedules: **Baxter Aviation** (✉ ☎ 604/683–6525 or 800/ 661–5599, WEB www.baxterair.com). **Harbour Air Seaplanes** (☎ 604/ 688–1277 or 800/665–0212, WEB www.harbour-air.com).

### BIKE TOURS

Between May and October, Velo-City Cycle Tours leads daily trips around the Stanley Park seawall, including a "peddle and paddle" option that includes kayaking in English Bay. The rides through the North Shore rain forest finish at a local pub. The pace is easy, and all equipment is supplied.

➤ FEES AND SCHEDULES: **Velo-City Cycle Tours** (☎ 604/924–0288, WEB www.velo-city.com).

BOAT TOURS

Aquabus Ferries operates tours of False Creek on small covered boats and vintage wooden ferries. Twenty-five-minute tours cost $6 and run year-round; 45-minute minicruises are offered May through October and cost $8. The tours leave every 30 minutes from the Aquabus dock on Granville Island. The company also runs full-day catered tours into Howe Sound on a historic fishing boat.

False Creek Ferries has a 40-minute tour for $8. It leaves from Granville Island daily, about four times an hour, in summer. In winter, tours run hourly on weekends only.

Harbour Cruises, at the north foot of Denman Street on Coal Harbour, operates a 1¼-hour narrated tour of Burrard Inlet aboard the paddle wheeler MPV *Constitution*. Tours are given from April through October and cost less than $20. Harbour Cruises also offers sunset dinner cruises, four-hour lunch cruises up scenic Indian Arm, and full-day trips to Bowen Island.

Paddlewheeler Riverboat Tours, at the New Westminster Quay, can take you out on the Fraser River in an 1800s-style paddle wheeler. Tours run daily, year-round, and include a variety of sightseeing and evening entertainment options, including cruises to historic Fort Langley.

➤ FEES AND SCHEDULES: **Aquabus Ferries** (☎ 604/689–5858, WEB www.aquabus.bc.ca). **False Creek Ferries** (☎ 604/684–7781, WEB www.granvilleislandferries.bc.ca). **Harbour Cruises** (✉ 1 North foot of Denman St., at W. Georgia St., West End, ☎ 604/688–7246 or 800/663–1500, WEB www.boatcruises.com). **Paddlewheeler Riverboat Tours** (✉ Unit 139, 810 Quayside Dr., New Westminster, ☎ 604/525–4465 or 877/825–1302, WEB www.vancouverpaddlewheeler.com).

BUS TOURS

Gray Line conducts a 3½-hour Grand City bus tour year-round. The tour picks up at all major downtown hotels and includes Stanley Park, Chinatown, Gastown, English Bay, and Queen Elizabeth Park. The fee is about $46. From May through October, Gray Line also has a narrated city tour aboard double-decker buses; passengers can get on and off as they choose and can travel free the next day. Adult fare is about $27.

➤ FEES AND SCHEDULES: **Gray Line** (☎ 604/879–3363 or 800/667–0882, WEB www.grayline.ca).

ECOLOGICAL TOURS

Between mid-November and mid-February, thousands of bald eagles gather at Brackendale, about an hour north of Vancouver. With Canadian Outback Adventure Company, you can watch and photograph the eagles from a slow-moving raft on the river. Vancouver All Terrain Adventures runs four-wheel-drive trips into the mountains near Vancouver, including an eagle-viewing trip.

Lotus Land Tours can take you out in a Zodiac to watch whales in the Strait of Georgia. From May through October, the company leads a four-hour sea-kayak trip—including a salmon barbecue lunch—to Twin Island (an uninhabited provincial marine park), as well as kayaking day trips to the Gulf Islands, including a floatplane flight back to Vancouver. Experience is not required; the kayaks are easy for beginners to handle.

Ocean West Expeditions, on English Bay beach at the foot of Denman Street, offers guided half-day sea-kayaking trips around English Bay and Stanley Park, as well as kayak·rentals and lessons, and multiday trips·out of Vancouver.

➤ FEES AND SCHEDULES: **Canadian Outback Adventure Company** (☎ 604/921–7250 or 800/565–8735, WEB www.canadianoutback.com). **Lotus Land Tours** (☎ 604/684–4922 or 800/528–3531, WEB www. VancouverNatureAdventures.com). **Ocean West Expeditions** (☎ 604/ 688–5770 summer only; 800/660–0051; WEB www.ocean-west.com). **Vancouver All-Terrain Adventures** (☎ 604/984–2374 or 888/754– 5601, WEB www.all-terrain.com).

### HELICOPTER TOURS

Tour Vancouver, the harbor, or the mountains of the North Shore by helicopter for $140 to $275 per person (minimum of three people). Most tours leave from the Harbour Heliport next to the Pan Pacific Hotel downtown. Shorter tours are also available from the top of Grouse Mountain.

➤ FEES AND SCHEDULES: **Helijet Charters** (✉ 455 Waterfront Rd., Downtown, ☎ 604/270–1484 or 800/987–4354, WEB www.helijet.com).

### HIKING TOURS

Hike BC conducts guided hikes to the North Shore Mountains between May and October. North Shore Hiking Services offers half-day hikes, from easy strolls to tough mountain hikes, on the North Shore. The trips include lunch and hotel pickup. Guided walks through the rain forests and canyons surrounding the city, including a popular day trip to Bowen Island in Howe Sound, are run by Rockwood Adventures.

➤ FEES AND SCHEDULES: **Hike BC** (☎ 604/540–2499). **North Shore Hiking Services** (✉ ☎ 604/929–5751, WEB www.northshorehikingservices. com). **Rockwood Adventures** (☎ 604/980–7749 or 888/236–6606, WEB www.rockwoodadventures.com).

### ORIENTATION TOURS

The one-hour Stanley Park Horse Drawn Tours operate March 15 to the end of October and cost $18.65 per person. The tours leave every 20 to 30 minutes from near the information booth on Stanley Park Drive. The Vancouver Trolley Company runs old-style trolleys through Vancouver on a two-hour narrated tour of Stanley Park, Gastown, English Bay, Granville Island, and Chinatown, among other sights. A day pass allows you to complete one full circuit, getting off and on as often as you like. Start the trip at any of the 23 stops and buy a ticket ($25) on board. The four-hour City Highlights tour run by West Coast City and Nature Sightseeing is about $47. A longer tour includes a visit to the Capilano Suspension Bridge. Pickup is available from all major hotels downtown.

North Shore tours usually include a gondola ride up Grouse Mountain, a walk across the Capilano Suspension Bridge, a stop at a salmon hatchery, a visit to the Lonsdale Quay Market, and a ride back to town on the SeaBus. North Shore tours are offered early March through late October by Landsea Tours and all year by West Coast City and Nature Sightseeing. The half-day tours are about $75.

➤ FEES AND SCHEDULES: **Landsea Tours** (☎ 604/255–7272 or 877/669– 2277, WEB www.vancouvertours.com). **Stanley Park Horse Drawn Tours** (☎ 604/681–5115, WEB www.stanleyparktours.com). **Vancouver Trolley Company** (☎ 604/801–5515 or 888/451–5581, WEB www. vancouvertrolley.com). **West Coast City and Nature Sightseeing** (☎ 604/ 451–1600 or 877/451–1777, WEB www.vancouversightseeing.com).

### PRIVATE GUIDES

Early Motion Tours picks you up at your hotel for a spin through Vancouver in a 1930 Model-A Ford convertible. Vancouver All-Terrain Adventures offers customized city tours in a luxury four-wheel-drive Suburban at $75 an hour for up to seven passengers. Individual and group tours in eight European languages are available from VIP Tourguide Services.

➤ FEES AND SCHEDULES: **Early Motion Tours** (☎ 604/687–5088). **Vancouver All Terrain Adventures** (☎ 604/984–2374 or 888/754–5601, WEB www.all-terrain.com). **VIP Tourguide Services** (☎ 604/214–4677, WEB www3.telus.net/tourguides).

### SPECIAL-INTEREST TOURS

If Vancouver looks familiar, chances are you've already seen it on screen, posing as an American city in any of the hundreds of U.S. movies and TV shows filmed here. X-Tours will take you behind the scenes to locations made famous in film and video, including the apartment used by Agent Scully in *The X-Files*. Three-hour tours run daily, year-round, and cost $49.

➤ FEES AND SCHEDULES: **X-Tours** (✉ ☎ 604/609–2770 or 888/250–7211, WEB www.x-tour.com)

### TRAIN TOURS

You can sample West Coast cuisine in the vintage rail coaches of the Pacific Starlight Dinner Train, which leaves the North Vancouver B.C. Rail station at 6:15 PM, stops at scenic Porteau Cove on Howe Sound, and returns to the station at 10 PM. The train runs Friday through Sunday, May through October, with additional Wednesday trips between late June and early September. Fares, including a three-course meal, are $89.95 for salon seating, $112.95 for the dome car. Reservations are essential.

➤ FEES AND SCHEDULES: **Pacific Starlight Dinner Train** (✉ B.C. Rail Station, 1311 W. 1st St., North Vancouver, ☎ 604/984–5246 or 800/363–3733, WEB www.bcrail.com).

### WALKING TOURS

Students from the Architectural Institute of British Columbia lead free 90-minute walking tours of the city's top heritage sites June through September. The Gastown Business Improvement Society sponsors free 90-minute historical and architectural walking tours daily June through August. Meet the guide at 2 PM at the statue of "Gassy" Jack in Maple Tree Square. Rockwood Adventures has guided walks around Vancouver neighborhoods, including Gastown, Granville Island, and Chinatown, and a special walk for art lovers.Guides with Walkabout Historic Vancouver dress in 19th-century costume for their two-hour historical walking tours around downtown and Gastown or Granville Island. Tours run mid-February to mid-November and cost $18.

➤ FEES AND SCHEDULES: **Architectural Institute of British Columbia** (☎ 604/683–8588, WEB www.aibc.bc.ca). **Gastown Business Improvement Society** (☎ 604/683–5650, WEB www.gastown.org). **Rockwood Adventures** (☎ 604/980–7749 or 888/236–6606, WEB www. rockwoodadventures.com). **Walkabout Historic Vancouver** (☎ 604/720–0006, WEB www.walkabouthistoricvancouver.com).

## TRAIN TRAVEL

The Pacific Central Station, at Main Street and Terminal Avenue, near the Main Street SkyTrain station, is the hub for rail service. Amtrak operates its *Cascades* train service between Vancouver and Eugene, Oregon. VIA Rail provides transcontinental service through Jasper to Toronto three times a week.

Rail buffs take note: trains are becoming an increasingly convenient way to get around Vancouver. Part of an effort to revive streetcar service around False Creek, the volunteer-run Downtown Historic Railway operates two restored electric trams (built in 1905 and 1913) along a 5-km (3-mi) track between Science World and Granville Island. The trams, which also stop at 1st Avenue and Ontario Street and at Legin-Boot Square, near 6th Avenue and Moberly Street, operate 12:30 to 5 PM weekends and holidays from late May to early October. The adult fare is $2.

➤ TRAIN INFORMATION: **Amtrak** (☎ 800/872–7245, WEB www. amtrak.com). **Downtown Historic Railway** (☎ 604/665–3903, WEB www.trams.bc.ca). **Pacific Central Station** (✉ 1150 Station St., Downtown, ☎ no phone). **VIA Rail** (☎ 800/561–8630 in Canada; 800/561–3949 in the U.S.; WEB www.viarail.ca).

## VISITOR INFORMATION

➤ TOURIST INFORMATION: **Granville Island Information Centre** (✉ 1398 Cartwright St., Granville Island, ☎ 604/666–5784, WEB www.granvilleisland.com). **Hello B.C.** (☎ 800/435–5622, WEB www.hellobc.com). **Vancouver Tourist Info Centre** (✉ 200 Burrard St., Downtown, ☎ 604/683–2000, WEB www.tourismvancouver.com).

# 3 VICTORIA AND VANCOUVER ISLAND

Islands have long held a fascination for travelers, and Vancouver Island, the largest island off North America's west coast, is no exception. At 483 km (300 mi) tip to tip, it holds an immense variety of landscapes—from the rolling farmland and protected beaches of the southeast to the sparsely inhabited forests of the north and the crashing surf on the west. On the southern tip, Victoria, the capital of British Columbia, has shed its tea-cozy image and reemerged as a Pacific Rim metropolis that celebrates its native, Asian, and European roots.

By Sue
Kernaghan

BEACHES, WILDERNESS PARKS, mountains, deep temperate rain forests, and a wealth of wildlife have long drawn adventurous visitors to the West Coast's largest island. These days, however, a slew of excellent restaurants, country inns, spas, and ecologically sensitive resorts means you can enjoy all that beauty in comfort—though roughing it is still an option.

Despite its growing popularity, the island rarely feels crowded. Fewer than a million people live here, and virtually all of them cluster on the island's sheltered eastern side, between Victoria and Campbell River; half live in Victoria itself. The island's west coast, facing the open ocean, is wild and often inhospitable, with few roads and only a handful of small settlements. Nevertheless, the old-growth forests, magnificent stretch of beach, and challenging trails of the Pacific Rim National Park Reserve, as well as the chance to see whales offshore, are major draws for campers, hikers, kayakers, and even surfers.

As rich as Vancouver Island's natural bounty is the cultural heritage of the Pacific Coast First Nations peoples—the Kwakiutl, Nootka, and others—who had occupied the land for more than 12,000 years before the first Europeans arrived en masse in the late 19th century. Their art and culture are on display throughout the island, in totems and petroglyphs, in city art galleries, and in the striking collections at the Royal British Columbia Museum in Victoria and the Quw'utsun Cultural and Conference Centre in Duncan.

# Pleasures and Pastimes

## Dining
"Fresh, local, organic" has become a mantra for many Vancouver Island chefs: some have even joined forces with local farmers to ensure supply of the freshest items. Wild salmon, locally made cheeses, pacific oysters, forest foraged mushrooms, organic vegetables in season, local microbrews, and even wines from the island's few family-run wineries can all be sampled here. Restaurants in the region generally are casual. Smoking is banned in all public places, including restaurants and bars, in Greater Victoria and on the Southern Gulf Islands.

| CATEGORY | COST* |
| --- | --- |
| $$$$ | over $32 |
| $$$ | $22–$32 |
| $$ | $13–$21 |
| $ | under $13 |

*per person, in Canadian dollars, for a main course at dinner

## Lodging
Accommodations on Vancouver Island range from bed-and-breakfasts and country inns to rustic cabins to deluxe ecotourism lodges. Victoria in particular has a great selection of English-style B&Bs. Most small inns and B&Bs on the island ban smoking indoors, and virtually all hotels in the area have no-smoking rooms. Most accommodations in the region lack air-conditioning, as it rarely gets hot enough to need it. Advance reservations are always a good idea, especially in July and August, and in some of the more isolated towns.

| CATEGORY | COST* |
| --- | --- |
| $$$$ | over $250 |
| $$$ | $170–$250 |
| $$ | $90–$170 |
| $ | under $90 |

*\*All prices are for a standard double room, excluding 10% provincial accommodation tax, service charge, and 7% GST, in Canadian dollars.*

## Outdoor Activities and Sports

### CANOEING AND KAYAKING

The island-dotted Strait of Georgia, on the east side of Vancouver Island, provides fairly protected seagoing, stunning scenery, and plenty of opportunities to spot orcas, eagles, and other local fauna. The Broken Group Islands, off the island's west coast, draw kayakers from around the world to their protected, wildlife-rich waters. The mountainous Strathcona Provincial Park provides scenic lake and river paddling.

### FISHING

Miles of coastline and numerous lakes, rivers, and streams lure anglers to Vancouver Island. Though salmon doesn't run as thickly as it once did, both coasts of the island still have excellent salmon fishing, and many operators run fishing charters.

### HIKING

The West Coast Trail, one of the world's most famous trails, runs along the western side of Vancouver Island. Other trails include the Juan de Fuca Marine Trail and those in Strathcona Provincial Park. But you can find fine hiking-trail networks in almost all of the island's many parks.

### WHALE-WATCHING

Three resident and several transient pods of orcas (killer whales) travel the island's eastern coastal waters. These, and the gray whales that migrate along the west coast, are the primary focus of the many whale-watching boat tours leaving Victoria, Campbell River, Telegraph Cove, Ucluelet, Bamfield, and Tofino in spring and summer months. July, August, and September are the best months to see orcas; in March and April, thousands of migrating gray whales pass close to the west coast of Vancouver Island on their way from Baja California to Alaska. Harbor seals, sea lions, porpoises, and marine-bird sightings are a safe bet anytime.

# Exploring Vancouver Island

Vancouver Island, touched by Pacific currents, has the mildest climate in Canada. Temperatures are usually above 32°F in winter and below 80°F in summer, although winter brings frequent rains (especially on the west coast). When traveling by car, keep in mind that Vancouver Island's west coast has very few roads and is accessible mainly by sea or air.

*Numbers in the text correspond to numbers in the margin and on the Vancouver Island map.*

## Great Itineraries

### IF YOU HAVE 1 TO 3 DAYS

For a short trip, ⛴ **Victoria** ①–⑯ is a fine place to begin. There's plenty to explore, from the flower-fringed Inner Harbour and the museums and attractions nearby to Market Square and the red gates of Chinatown. World-famous Butchart Gardens is only half an hour away by

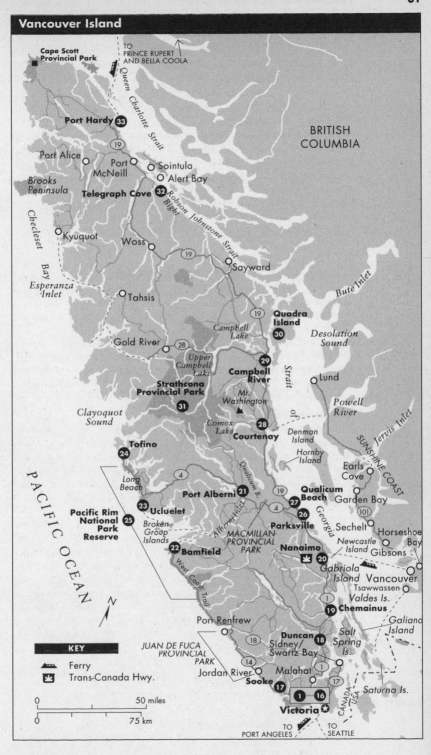

# Vancouver Island

TO PRINCE RUPERT
AND BELLA COOLA

Cape Scott
Provincial Park

BRITISH
COLUMBIA

Port Hardy **33**

Port Alice

Port
McNeill
Sointula
Alert Bay

Brooks
Peninsula

Telegraph Cove **32**

Queen Charlotte Strait

Robson Johnstone Strait

Checleset
Bay

Kyuquot

Woss

Sayward

Esperanza
Inlet

Tahsis

Bute Inlet

Gold River

Campbell
Lake

Upper
Campbell
Lake

Quadra
Island **30**

Desolation
Sound

Campbell
River **29**

Lund

Strathcona
Provincial Park **31**

Mt.
Washington

Strait

Powell
River

Clayoquot
Sound

Comox
Lake

Courtenay **28**

Denman
Island

SUNSHINE COAST

Jervis Inlet

Tofino **24**

Hornby
Island

Earls
Cove

Long
Beach

Port Alberni **21**

Qualicum R.

Qualicum
Beach **27**

Garden Bay

**101**

Georgia

Ucluelet **23**

**4**

**19**

**4**

**26**

Parksville

Sechelt

Horseshoe
Bay

Pacific Rim
National
Park
Reserve **25**

Broken
Group
Islands

Alberni Inlet

MACMILLAN
PROVINCIAL
PARK

Nanaimo **20**

Newcastle
Island

Gibsons

Bamfield **22**

Gabriola
Island  Vancouver

PACIFIC OCEAN

West Coast Trail

Tsawwassen

Valdes Is.

**1**

Chemainus **19**

Galiana
Island

Port Renfrew

**18**

Duncan **18**

Salt
Spring
Is.

JUAN DE FUCA
PROVINCIAL
PARK

**14**

Sidney/
Swartz Bay

**1**

Jordan River

Malahat

**17**

Saturna Is.

Sooke **17**

**1**  **16**

Victoria

CANADA
USA

## KEY

🛳 Ferry
🍁 Trans-Canada Hwy.

0 _____ 50 miles

0 _____ 75 km

TO
PORT ANGELES

TO
SEATTLE

car, and you might take a full day to explore the beautiful grounds. On Day 3, head west to 🖼 **Sooke** ⑰ or north, over the scenic Malahat region, to **Duncan** ⑱, **Chemainus** ⑲, or **Nanaimo** ⑳, which has ferry service to the mainland.

IF YOU HAVE 4 TO 6 DAYS
A brief stay in 🖼 **Victoria** ①–⑯ can be followed by a tour of Vancouver Island. Follow the itinerary above, heading to **Sooke** ⑰ on Day 3. Day 4 allows time to see the Quw'utsun Cultural and Conference Centre in **Duncan** ⑱ and the murals and restored Victorian buildings of 🖼 **Chemainus** ⑲. On Day 5, one alternative is to trek across the island to the scenic west coast to visit 🖼 **Ucluelet** ㉓ and 🖼 **Tofino** ㉔ (pick one for your overnight) and spend some time whale-watching or hiking around **Pacific Rim National Park Reserve** ㉕. Another choice is to continue up the east coast to visit **Strathcona Provincial Park** ㉛ or to do some salmon fishing from 🖼 **Campbell River** ㉙. Spend Day 6 retracing your steps to Victoria or Nanaimo, for ferry service to the mainland.

IF YOU HAVE 7 TO 10 DAYS
A longer trip allows more time to explore the area in and around the **Pacific Rim National Park Reserve** ㉕ or to visit **Bamfield** ㉒ or the **Broken Group Islands** on the *Lady Rose,* a coastal freighter that sails from **Port Alberni** ㉑. If you're exploring the east coast, you could visit one of the rustic islands; **Quadra** ㉚, **Denman,** and **Hornby** islands as well as the Southern Gulf Islands of Salt Spring, Mayne, and Galiano (☞ Chapter 4) are all easily reached by ferry. Otherwise, head north toward **Port Hardy** ㉝ to see the resident whale pods near Telegraph Cove. From Port Hardy, you can continue a tour of British Columbia on an Inside Passage cruise.

### When to Tour Vancouver Island

Though summer is the most popular time to visit, in winter the island has skiing at Mt. Washington, near Courtenay, and, off the west coast, dramatic storms that can be fun to watch from a cozy inn. March and April are the best time to see migrating whales off the west coast.

# VICTORIA

Originally Fort Victoria, Victoria was the first European settlement on Vancouver Island. It was chosen to be the westernmost trading outpost of the British-owned Hudson's Bay Company in 1843 and became the capital of British Columbia in 1868. Victoria has since evolved into a walkable, livable seaside town of gardens, waterfront pathways, and restored 19th-century architecture. Often described as the country's most British city, Victoria is these days—except for the odd red phone box, good beer, and well-mannered drivers—working to change that image, preferring to celebrate its combined native, Asian, and European heritage.

The city is 71 km (44 mi), or 1½ hours by ferry plus 1½ hours by car, south of Vancouver, or a 2½-hour ferry ride from Seattle.

## Downtown Victoria

*Numbers in the text correspond to numbers in the margin and on the Downtown Victoria map.*

### A Good Walk

Begin on the waterfront at the **Visitors Information Centre,** at 812 Wharf Street. Across the way on Government Street is the **Fairmont Empress** ①, a majestic hotel that opened in 1908. A short walk around the harbor along the Inner Harbour Walk (take any of the staircases from Government Street down to the water level) takes you to the **Royal London Wax Museum** ②. Across Belleville Street is the **Parliament Buildings** ③ complex, seat of the provincial government. Cross Government Street to reach the **Royal British Columbia Museum** ④, one of Canada's most impressive museums. Behind the museum and bordering Douglas Street are the totem poles and ceremonial longhouse of Thunderbird Park; **Helmcken House** ⑤, the oldest house in Victoria; and the tiny 19th-century St. Ann's Schoolhouse. A walk south on Douglas Street leads to the beautiful **Beacon Hill Park** ⑥. A few blocks west of the park on Government Street is **Emily Carr House** ⑦, the birthplace of one of British Columbia's best-known artists. Walk back to Beacon Hill Park, and then proceed north on Douglas Street until you reach Blanshard Street, on your right. Take Blanshard, where just past Academy Close (on the right) you can see the entrance to **St. Ann's Academy** ⑧, a former convent school with parklike grounds. (There's also a footpath to the academy from Southgate Street.) From St. Ann's, follow Belleville Street west. The next stop, at the corner of Douglas and Belleville streets, is the glass-roofed **Crystal Garden Conservation Centre** ⑨.

From Crystal Garden, take Belleville Street west one block to Government Street, Victoria's liveliest shopping street. Head north about five blocks to Government and View streets, where you can see the entrance to the cobblestone **Bastion Square** ⑩, the original site of Fort Victoria and the Hudson's Bay Company trading post, which now houses restaurants and offices. Just north of Government and View, on the right-hand side of Government Street, is the entrance to Trounce Alley, a pretty pedestrian-only shopping arcade.

At Bastion Square, you can stop in the **Maritime Museum of British Columbia** ⑪ to learn about an important part of the province's history. Around the corner (to the south) on Wharf Street is the **Victoria Bug Zoo** ⑫, a creepy-crawly attraction popular with kids. North of Bastion Square a few blocks, on Store Street between Johnson Street and Pandora Avenue, is **Market Square** ⑬, one of the city's most picturesque shopping districts. Across Pandora Avenue is the entrance to the narrow, shop-lined Fan Tan Alley, which leads to Fisgard Street, the heart of **Chinatown** ⑭.

You can head back south on Government Street until you hit Fort Street. From here, a 25-minute walk or a short drive east takes you to Joan Crescent and lavish **Craigdarroch Castle** ⑮. Down the hill on Moss Street is the **Art Gallery of Greater Victoria** ⑯.

In summer, a ride on Harbour Ferries from the Inner Harbour takes you to **Point Ellice House,** a historic waterside home and garden.

TIMING

Many of the attractions in downtown Victoria are within easy walking distance of one another. You can walk this tour in a day, but there's so much to see at the Royal British Columbia Museum and the other museums that you could easily fill two days. This will also allow time for some shopping and visiting Craigdarroch Castle.

## Sights to See

**⑯ Art Gallery of Greater Victoria.** Attached to an 1889 mansion, this modern building houses one of the largest collections of Chinese and Japanese artifacts in western Canada. The Japanese garden between the buildings is home to the only authentic Shinto shrine in North America. The gallery, which is a few blocks west of Craigdarroch Castle, off Fort Street, displays a permanent exhibition of works by well-known Canadian artist Emily Carr and regularly changing exhibits of

# Downtown Victoria

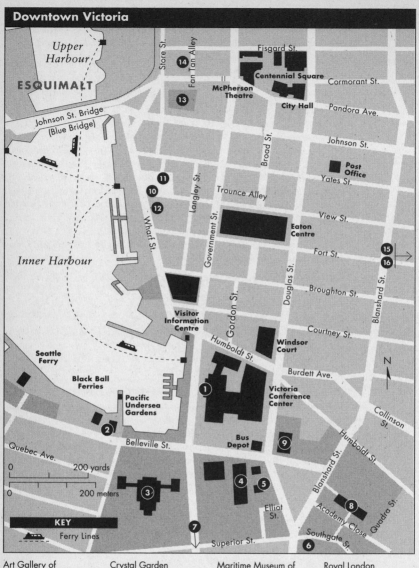

Upper Harbour

ESQUIMALT

Johnson St. Bridge (Blue Bridge)

Inner Harbour

Store St.

Fan Tan Alley

14

13

Fisgard St.

Centennial Square

McPherson Theatre

City Hall

Cormorant St.

Pandora Ave.

Johnson St.

Broad St.

Post Office

Yates St.

11

10

12

Langley St.

Trounce Alley

Government St.

View St.

Eaton Centre

Fort St.

15

16

Wharf St.

Broughton St.

Blanshard St.

Gordon St.

Visitor Information Centre

Humboldt St.

Windsor Court

Courtney St.

Douglas St.

Seattle Ferry

Black Ball Ferries

Pacific Undersea Gardens

1

Victoria Conference Center

Burdett Ave.

Collinson St.

2

Belleville St.

Bus Depot

9

Humboldt St.

Quebec Ave.

0     200 yards

0     200 meters

3

4

5

Blanshard St.

8

Quadra St.

KEY

Ferry Lines

Elliot St.

7

Superior St.

Academy Close

Southgate St.

6

N

Art Gallery of
Greater Victoria . . . **16**

Bastion Square . . . . **10**

Beacon Hill Park . . . . **6**

Chinatown . . . . . . . **14**

Craigdarroch
Castle . . . . . . . . . **15**

Crystal Garden
Conservation
Centre . . . . . . . . . . . **9**

Emily Carr House . . . **7**

Fairmont
Empress . . . . . . . . . . **1**

Helmcken House . . . . **5**

Maritime Museum of
British Columbia . . . **11**

Market Square . . . . **13**

Parliament
Buildings . . . . . . . . . **3**

Royal British
Columbia
Museum . . . . . . . . . **4**

Royal London
Wax Museum . . . . . . **2**

St. Ann's
Academy . . . . . . . . . **8**

Victoria Bug Zoo . . . **12**

Asian and historical and contemporary Western art. ✉ *1040 Moss St., Rockland,* ☎ *250/384–4101,* WEB *www.aggv.bc.ca.* ✐ *$5, Mon. by donation.* ☉ *Mon.–Wed. and Fri.–Sat. 10–5, Thurs. 10–9, Sun. 1–5.*

**❿ Bastion Square.** James Douglas, the former colonial governor for whom Douglas Street was named, chose this spot for the original Fort Victoria and Hudson's Bay Company trading post. Offices and restaurants occupy the old brick buildings. ✉ *Off Wharf St. at end of View St., Old Town.*

★ ☙ ❻ **Beacon Hill Park.** The southern lawns and ocean-side path of this spacious park have great views of the Olympic Mountains and the Strait of Juan de Fuca. Also here are ponds, jogging and walking paths, abundant flowers and gardens, a petting zoo, and a cricket pitch. The park is also home to Mile Zero of the Trans-Canada Highway. ✉ *East of Douglas St., south of Southgate St., Downtown,* ☎ *250/361–0600 City of Victoria Parks Division; 250/381–2532 petting zoo.*

OFF THE
BEATEN PATH

**BUTCHART GARDENS –** Originally a private estate and still family-run, this stunning 50-acre garden about 21 km (13 mi) north of downtown Victoria has been drawing visitors since it was planted in a limestone quarry in 1904. The site's Japanese, Italian, rose, and sunken gardens grow 700 varieties of flowers in a setting that's beautiful year-round. From mid-June to mid-September, the gardens are illuminated at night, and musicians and other entertainers perform in the afternoons and evenings. In July and August, fireworks light the sky over the gardens on Saturday nights. Also on the premises are a seed and gift shop, two restaurants, and a café. Traditional English afternoon tea is served daily in the dining room. To get to the gardens by public transit, take bus No. 75 from downtown. ✉ *800 Benvenuto Ave., Brentwood Bay,* ☎ *250/ 652–5256 or 866/652–4422,* WEB *www.butchartgardens.com.* ✐ *Mid-June–late Sept. $20; discounted rates rest of yr.* ☉ *Mid-June–Aug., daily 9 AM–10:30 PM; Sept.–mid-June, daily 9 AM–dusk (call for precise times).*

**⓮ Chinatown.** Chinese immigrants built much of the Canadian Pacific Railway in the 19th century, and their influence still marks the region. Victoria's Chinatown, founded in 1858, is the oldest and most intact such district in Canada. If you enter Chinatown from Government Street, you'll pass under the elaborate **Gate of Harmonious Interest,** made of Taiwanese ceramic tiles and decorative panels. Along Fisgard Street, merchants display paper lanterns, wicker baskets, and exotic produce. Mah-jongg, fan-tan, and dominoes were among the games of chance played on narrow **Fan Tan Alley.** Once the gambling and opium center of Chinatown, it's now lined with offbeat shops. Look for the alley on the south side of Fisgard Street between Nos. 545½ and 549½. ✉ *Fisgard St. between Government and Store Sts., Chinatown.*

**⓯ Craigdarroch Castle.** This resplendent mansion was built as the home of one of British Columbia's wealthiest men, coal baron Robert Dunsmuir, who died in 1889, just a few months before the castle's completion. Converted into a museum depicting life in the late 1800s, the castle has ornate Victorian furnishings, stained-glass windows, carved woodwork (precut in Chicago for Dunsmuir and sent by rail), and a beautifully restored painted ceiling in the drawing room. A winding staircase climbs four floors to a ballroom and a tower overlooking Victoria. ✉ *1050 Joan Crescent, Rockland,* ☎ *250/592–5323,* WEB *www. craigdarrochcastle.com.* ✐ *$10.* ☉ *Mid-June–Labor Day, daily 9–7; Labor Day–mid-June, daily 10–4:30.*

☙ ❾ **Crystal Garden Conservation Centre.** Opened in 1925 as the largest saltwater swimming pool in the British Empire, this glass-roof building today houses exotic flora and a variety of endangered tropical fauna, including flamingos, tortoises, macaws, lemurs, bats, and butterflies. ⊠ *713 Douglas St., Downtown,* ☎ *250/381–1213,* WEB *www.bcpcc. com/crystal.* ⊠ *$8.* ◷ *July–Aug., daily 9–8; Sept.–Oct. and Apr.–June, daily 9–6; Nov.–Mar., daily 10–4:30.*

**❼ Emily Carr House.** One of Canada's most celebrated artists and a respected writer, Emily Carr (1871–1945) was born and raised in this very proper wooden Victorian house before abandoning her middle-class life to live in, and paint, the wilds of British Columbia. Carr's own descriptions, from her autobiography *Book of Small,* were used to restore the house. Displays of Carr's work alternate with shows by modern-day B.C. artists. ⊠ *207 Government St., James Bay,* ☎ *250/ 383–5843,* WEB *www.emilycarr.com.* ⊠ *$5.35.* ◷ *Mid-May–mid-Oct., daily 10–5; mid-Oct.–mid-May by arrangement or during special events.*

**❶ Fairmont Empress.** Opened in 1908 by the Canadian Pacific Railway, the Empress is one of the grand château-style hotels that grace many Canadian cities. Designed by Francis Rattenbury, who also designed the Parliament Buildings across the way, the Empress, with its solid Edwardian grandeur, has become a symbol of the city. The elements that made the hotel an attraction for travelers in the past—old-world architecture, ornate decor, and a commanding view of the Inner Harbour—are still here. The archives, a historical photo display, are open to the public anytime. Nonguests can stop by the Empress for a traditional afternoon tea (reservations are recommended, and the dress code calls for smart casual wear), meet for a curry under the tiger skin in the Bengal Room, enjoy a treatment at the hotel's Willow Stream spa, or sample the superb regional cuisine in the Empress Room restaurant. **Miniature World** (☎ 250/385–9731), a display of doll-size dioramas, is on the Humboldt Street side of the complex; admission is $9. ⊠ *721 Government St., Downtown,* ☎ *250/384–8111,* WEB *www.fairmont.com.* ⊠ *Free; afternoon tea $46 June–Sept., $25 Oct.–May.*

OFF THE
BEATEN PATH

**FORT RODD HILL AND FISGARD LIGHTHOUSE NATIONAL HISTORIC SITES –** This 1895 coast artillery fort and the oldest (and still functioning) lighthouse on Canada's west coast are about 15 km (9 mi) west of Victoria, off Highway 1A on the way to Sooke. ⊠ *603 Fort Rodd Hill Rd., off Ocean Blvd., Colwood,* ☎ *250/478–5849,* WEB *parkscan.harbour.com/frh.* ⊠ *$4.* ◷ *Mar.–Oct., daily 10–5:30; Nov.– Feb., daily 9–4:30.*

Next door to Fort Rodd is **Hatley Castle,** the former estate of coal and railway baron James Dunsmuir and now part of the Royal Roads University campus. The 1908 castle is on 650 acres of beautifully landscaped grounds (including Italian, Japanese, and English rose gardens) that are open daily until dusk all year. Castle tours are given daily in summer (call for times). A small museum in the castle is open daily 1–4 PM. ⊠ *2005 Sooke Rd., Colwood,* ☎ *250/391–2600 ext. 4456,* WEB *www. royalroads.ca.* ⊠ *Grounds free, museum by donation, castle $3 (by tour only).*

**❺ Helmcken House.** The oldest house in British Columbia was erected in 1852 for pioneer doctor and statesman John Sebastian Helmcken. Audio tours of the house, whose holdings include the family's original Victorian furnishings and the doctor's 19th-century medical tools, last 20 minutes. Next door are St. Ann's Schoolhouse, one of the first schools in British Columbia (you can view the interior through the door), and Thunderbird Park, with totem poles and a ceremonial longhouse constructed by Kwakwaka'wakw chief Mungo Martin. ✉ *10 Elliot St., near Douglas and Belleville Sts., Downtown,* ☎ *250/361–0021,* WEB *www.heritage.gov.bc.ca/helm/helm.htm.* ⌨ *$5.* ☉ *May–Oct., daily 10–5; Nov.–Apr., Thurs.–Mon. noon–4.*

Ⓒ ⑪ **Maritime Museum of British Columbia.** The model ships, Royal Navy charts, photographs, uniforms, and ship bells at this museum, in Victoria's original courthouse, chronicle the province's seafaring history. Among the hand-built boats on display is the *Tilikum,* a dugout canoe that sailed from Victoria to England between 1901 and 1904. An 1899 hand-operated cage elevator, believed to be the oldest continuously operating lift in North America, ascends to the third floor, where the original 1888 vice-admiralty courtroom looks ready for a court-martial. ✉ *28 Bastion Sq., Old Town,* ☎ *250/385–4222,* WEB *www.mmbc.bc.ca.* ⌨ *$6.* ☉ *Daily 9:30–4:30.*

⑬ **Market Square.** During the late 19th century, this three-level square, built like an old inn courtyard, provided everything a sailor, miner, or lumberjack could want. Restored to its original architectural, if not commercial, character, it's a pedestrian-only, café- and boutique-lined hangout—now, as then, a great spot for people-watching. ✉ *560 Johnson St., Old Town,* ☎ *250/386–2441.*

★ ❸ **Parliament Buildings.** These massive stone structures, designed by Francis Rattenbury and completed in 1898, dominate the Inner Harbour. Two statues flank the main entrance: one of Sir James Douglas, who chose the site where Victoria was built, and the other of Sir Matthew Baille Begbie, the man in charge of law and order during the gold-rush era. Atop the central dome is a gilded statue of Captain George Vancouver, the first European to sail around Vancouver Island. A statue of Queen Victoria reigns over the front of the complex. More than 3,000 lights outline the buildings at night. The interior is lavishly done with marble floors, stained-glass windows, and murals depicting scenes from the province's history. When the legislature is in session (usually in spring and early summer), you can sit in the public gallery and watch British Columbia's often polarized democracy at work (custom has the opposing parties sitting 2½ sword lengths apart). Free, informative half-hour tours are obligatory on summer weekends (June 1 until September 2) and optional the rest of the time. ✉ *501 Belleville St., Downtown,* ☎ *250/387–3046,* WEB *www.parl-bldgs.gov.bc.ca.* ⌨ *Free.* ☉ *June–Labor Day, daily 8:30–5; Labor Day–May, weekdays 8:30–5.*

OFF THE **POINT ELLICE HOUSE** – The O'Reilly family home, an 1860s Italianate
BEATEN PATH villa overlooking the Upper Harbour, has been restored to its original splendor, with the largest collection of Victorian furnishings in western Canada. Tea and baked goods are served on the lawn (noon–4). You can also take an audio tour of the house, stroll in the gardens, or try your hand at croquet. Point Ellice House is a few minutes' drive north of downtown, but it's much more fun to come by sea. (Harbour Ferries leave from a dock in front of the Fairmont Empress hotel.) ✉ *2616 Pleasant St., Upper Harbour,* ☎ *250/380–6506,* WEB *www.heritage. gov.bc.ca.* ⌨ *$5, $17 including tea.* ☉ *Mother's Day–Labor Day, daily noon–5.*

★ Ⓒ ❹ **Royal British Columbia Museum.** This excellent museum, one of Victoria's leading attractions, traces several thousand years of British Columbian history. Exhibits include a genuine Kwakwaka'wakw longhouse (the builders retain rights to its ceremonial use) and an extensive collection of First Nations masks and other artifacts. The Natural History Gallery re-creates the sights and sounds of a rain forest, tidal wetlands, and other B.C. natural habitats, and the Open Ocean exhibit mimics a submarine journey. A replica of Captain Vancouver's ship, the HMCS *Discovery,* creaks convincingly, and a re-created frontier town comes complete with cobbled streets, silent movies, and the smells of home baking. Century Hall reviews British Columbia's 20th-century history, and an on-site IMAX theater shows *National Geographic* films on a six-story-high screen. ⊠ *675 Belleville St., Downtown,* ☎ *250/356–7226 or 888/447–7977,* WEB *www.royalbcmuseum.bc.ca.* ☜ *$10, IMAX theater $9.75, combination ticket $17.75.* ☺ *Museum daily 9–5, theater daily 9–8 (call for show times).*

➋ **Royal London Wax Museum.** A collection of life-size wax figures resides in this elegant colonnaded building, once Victoria's steamship terminal. The 300-plus characters include members of the British royal family, famous Canadians, Hollywood stars, and some unfortunate souls in a Chamber of Horrors. ⊠ *470 Belleville St., Downtown,* ☎ *250/388–4461,* WEB *www.waxworld.com.* ☜ *$8.75.* ☺ *May–Aug., daily 9–7:30; Sept.–Apr., daily 9:30–5.*

➑ **St. Ann's Academy.** This former convent and school, founded in 1858, played a central role in British Columbia's pioneer life. The academy's little chapel—the first Roman Catholic cathedral in Victoria—has been restored to look just as it did in the 1920s. The 6 acres of grounds, with their fruit trees and herb and flower gardens, are currently being restored as historic landscapes. ⊠ *835 Humboldt St., Downtown,* ☎ *250/953–8828,* WEB *www.bcpcc.com/stanns.* ☜ *By donation.* ☺ *Mid-May–Labor Day, daily 10–4; Labor Day–mid-May, call for hrs.*

☞ ⑫ **Victoria Bug Zoo.** Kids of all ages are drawn to this offbeat, two-room minizoo. Many of the bugs—mostly large tropical varieties, such as stick insects, scorpions, and centipedes—can be held, and staff members are on hand to dispense scientific information. ⊠ *1107 Wharf St., Old Town,* ☎ *250/384–2847,* WEB *www.bugzoo.bc.ca.* ☜ *$6.* ☺ *July–Aug., daily 9–9; Sept.–June, Mon.–Sat. 9:30–5:30, Sun. 11–5:30.*

**Visitor Information Centre.** You can get the lowdown on Victoria's attractions at this facility near the Inner Harbour. The staff here can help you with maps, theater and concert tickets, accommodation reservations, and outdoor-adventure day trips. ⊠ *812 Wharf St., Downtown,* ☎ *250/953–2033,* WEB *www.tourismvictoria.com.* ☺ *Mid-May–Labor Day, daily 8:30–6:30; Labor Day–mid-May, daily 9–5.*

# Dining

## Cafés

$    ✕ **Willie's Bakery.** Four generations of the Wille family ran a bakery in this handsome Victorian building near Market Square before closing shop in the 1970s. The site was reborn as a bakery-café, serving wholesome breakfasts, rich soups, delicious sandwiches made with house-baked bread, and tasty muffins, cookies, and bagels. The brick patio with an outdoor fireplace and little fountain is a great place to watch the world go by. ⊠ *537 Johnson St., Old Town,* ☎ *250/381–8414. Reservations not accepted. AE, DC, MC, V. No dinner.*

## Chinese

$–$$   ✕ **Don Mee's.** A large neon sign invites you inside this traditional Chinese restaurant, which has been in business since 1923. The entrées served in the expansive dining room include sweet-and-sour chicken, Peking duck, and ginger fried beef. Dim sum is served at lunchtime. ⊠ *538 Fisgard St., Chinatown,* ☎ *250/383–1032. Reservations not accepted for dim sum. AE, DC, MC, V.*

## Contemporary

**$$$-$$$$** ✕ **Empress Room.** Beautifully presented Pacific Northwest cuisine vies
★ for attention with the elegant setting, where candlelight dances on
tapestried walls beneath a carved mahogany ceiling. Fresh local in-
gredients go into imaginative seasonally changing dishes such as rock
fish on smashed banana and ginger polenta, and pine nut–crusted
lamb rack with mint hummus. The more than 500-label wine list is
excellent, as are the table d'hôte menus. ✉ *Fairmont Empress, 721 Gov-
ernment St., Downtown,* ☏ *250/389–2727. AE, D, DC, MC, V. No
lunch.*

**$$-$$$$** ✕ **The Victorian Restaurant.** This 45-seat candlelight restaurant in the
★ Delta Victoria Ocean Pointe Resort and Spa has striking views over
the Inner Harbour. The chef creates elegantly presented regional dishes
such as house cured salmon, crab, and fennel salad; grilled beef tenderloin with wild mushrooms and foie gras butter; and cranberry-vanilla-
balsamic glazed pork chop. The three-, four-, and five-course table d'hôte
menus are good choices; a top-flight wine list and impeccable service
round out the evening. ✉ *Delta Victoria Ocean Pointe Resort and Spa,
45 Songhees Rd., Vic West (across Johnson Street Bridge from downtown Victoria),* ☏ *250/360–5800 or 800/667–4677. AE, DC, MC, V.
Closed Jan.; closed Mon.–Wed. Nov.–Dec. and Feb.; closed Mon.–Tues.
Oct. and Mar.–Apr.*

**$$$** ✕ **Cassis.** John Hall, the chef-owner of this intimate restaurant in Cook
Street Village, a few minutes' drive from the Inner Harbour, seeks out
local organic ingredients to create a menu that reads like a map of the
surrounding countryside. The menu changes seasonally but almost al-
ways includes locally foraged greens, bouillabaisse made with freshly
caught seafood, and, in season, wild mushrooms foraged by Benedic-
tine monks in the Cowichan Valley. Most of the main courses also are
available in an appetizer size, so you can sample several. ✉ *253 Cook
St., Cook Street Village,* ☏ *250/384–1932,* WEB *www.cassisbistro.ca. AE,
MC, V. Closed Sun. and Mon. No lunch.*

**$$-$$$** ✕ **Cafe Brio.** Candlelight, hardwood floors, lush Modigliani nudes, and
rich gold walls create a warm glow at this Italian villa–style building,
a little north of the Inner Harbour. The seasonally changing menu, de-
scribed by the owners as "West Coast contemporary with a Tuscan hint,"
uses a wealth of local, organic ingredients. Appetizers might include
smoked sablefish; house-made pork, fennel, and red wine sausage; or
Dungeness crab salad. Mains could be fusilli with roast mushrooms,
arugula, and goat cheese; wild sockeye salmon; or rack of lamb. Good
vegetarian options are always available, and an extensive wine list goes
easy on the markups. ✉ *944 Fort St., Downtown,* ☏ *250/383–0009.
AE, MC, V. No lunch weekends or Oct.–Apr.*

**$$-$$$** ✕ **Camille's.** The menu concentrates on fresh local products, such as
lamb and duck, and regional exotica, like game and ostrich, often ap-
pear too. Other favorites include lemon ginger and rock prawn bisque,
pork tenderloin in a Jamaican jerk marinade, and pan-seared fillet of
salmon with red wine cream. The setting, on the lower floor of a his-
toric building in Bastion Square, is candlelit and romantic, with ex-
posed brick and intimate booths. An extensive 300-item wine list is
one of the best on the island. ✉ *45 Bastion Sq., Old Town,* ☏ *250/
381–3433. AE, MC, V. No lunch, no dinner Mon. Nov.–June.*

**$$-$$$** ✕ **Herald Street Caffe.** The menu at this lively, art-filled bistro on the
edge of Chinatown changes seasonally but always includes daily fish
grills, fresh pastas made in-house, and good vegetarian selections.
Classic French dishes, such as bouillabaisse and rabbit in calvados, share
space with wild sockeye salmon, ginger prawn spinach linguine, and
crab cakes with cilantro-lime pesto. The wine list is extensive, and the
early evening (5:30–6:30) set menu is good value. ✉ *546 Herald St.,*

*Chinatown,* ☎ *250/381–1441. AE, DC, MC, V. No lunch Mon.–Tues.*

$$ ✕ **Malahat Mountain Inn.** If you're heading up Highway 1, consider a stop at this roadhouse on the top of the Malahat hill about 30 minutes north of Victoria. It doesn't look like much from the highway, but inside, the eagle's-eye view over Finlayson Arm and the Gulf Islands is magnificent. The scenery is especially striking from the big outdoor deck. The lunch and dinner menus list such casual fare as burgers, quesadillas, and salads, as well as heartier pasta, seafood, and meat dishes. A jazz quartet plays on Saturday nights. ✉ *265 Trans-Canada Hwy., Malahat,* ☎ *250/478–1944. AE, MC, V.*

### Eclectic

$ ✕ **Süze Lounge and Restaurant.** Red velveteen drapes, exposed brick, a vintage mahogany bar, and a long martini and exotic tea list give this friendly lounge and restaurant a stylish air. The menu changes often but includes pizzas, fish, lamb, and some creative Asia-influenced dishes, including a bento box (a Japanese appetizer sampler) and pad Thai (a spicy dish of vegetables with peanut sauce and cilantro). You can order many of the mains and sides separately, enabling you to mix and match your meal. The patio is a popular summer hangout, and Süze is open until midnight for late-night snacks. ✉ *515 Yates St., Old Town,* ☎ *250/383–2829. AE, DC, MC, V. No lunch.*

### French

$$ ✕ **Brasserie L'école.** French country cooking shines at this informal Chinatown bistro. The historic room—once a schoolhouse for the Chinese community—evokes a timeless brasserie, from its white linens and patina-rich fir floors to the chalkboards above the slate bar listing the day's wines-by-the-glass. Sean Brennan, one of the city's better-known chefs, works with local farmers and fishers to source the best seasonal, local, and organic ingredients. The menu changes daily but lists such classic bistro fare as duck confit, steak frites, and mountain trout with brown butter, sage, and lemon. ✉ *1715 Government St., Chinatown,* ☎ *250/475–6260,* Ⓦ *www.lecole.ca. MC, V. Closed Sun.–Mon. No lunch.*

### Italian

$$–$$$$ ✕ **Il Terrazzo.** A charming redbrick terrace edged with potted green-
★ ery and warmed by fireplaces and overhead heaters makes Il Terrazzo—tucked away off Waddington Alley near Market Square and not visible from the street—the locals' choice for romantic alfresco dining. Starters include mussels steamed with banana peppers, sun-dried tomatoes, cilantro, garlic, Asiago cheese, and cream. Main courses, such as the Dijon-encrusted rack of lamb and osso buco with porcini mushrooms, come piping hot from the restaurant's wood oven. ✉ *555 Johnson St., off Waddington Alley, Old Town (call for directions),* ☎ *250/361–0028. AE, DC, MC, V. No lunch Sun., or Sat. Oct.–Apr.*

$–$$ ✕ **Pagliacci's.** Long lines attest to the popularity of this lively New York–meets–Victoria–style trattoria. Opened by the Siegel brothers from Brooklyn in 1979, Pagliacci's is all show biz, from the signed photos of the owners' movie-star friends plastering the walls to the live jazz playing several nights a week. The multipage menu runs from the Mae West (finally a "veal" woman) to the Prawns Al Capone and includes dozens of fresh, made-in-house pastas. "Pag's" is busy, crowded, and buckets of fun. ✉ *1011 Broad St., Downtown,* ☎ *250/386–1662. Reservations not accepted. AE, MC, V.*

$–$$ ✕ **Zambri's.** The setting is a downtown strip mall, but inside is a lively
★ trattoria worthy of a neighborhood in Rome. Lunch is casual. You order at the counter from a daily-changing roster of pastas, soups, and hot

hearty sandwiches (such as the hot meatball or Italian sausage). Dinner brings table service and a weekly changing menu of such hearty fare as tagliolini with veal, tomato, and artichoke and roasted pork loin with quince butter sauce and polenta. On Saturday nights a five-course prix-fixe menu is served to a reservation-only crowd. ⊠ *110–911 Yates St., Downtown,* ☎ *250/360–1171. Reservations not accepted, AE, MC, V. Closed Sun.*

### Seafood

$$$ ✕ **Blue Crab Bar and Grill.** Fresh daily seafood and expansive harbor views make this modern and airy restaurant a popular lunch and dinner spot. Signature dishes include Dungeness crab and shrimp cakes and a sauté of scallops and jumbo prawns. Still, something tempting is usually on the long list of daily blackboard specials. Breads and desserts, made in-house, and a wine list that highlights British Columbia and California wines round out the menu. The attached lounge area, open until 1 AM nightly, serves less-expensive meals and equally impressive views. ⊠ *Coast Harbourside Hotel and Marina, 146 Kingston St., James Bay,* ☎ *250/480–1999. AE, D, DC, MC, V.*

$$–$$$ ✕ **The Marina Restaurant.** A prime spot for Sunday brunch, the Marina has a 180-degree view over Oak Bay. The extensive menu usually lists a variety of pastas, grills, and seafood entrées, such as grilled rare ahi tuna and slow-roasted B.C. spring salmon. There's also a sushi bar. Downstairs is a more casual café-deli with seating on the patio overlooking the marina. ⊠ *1327 Beach Dr., Oak Bay,* ☎ *250/598–8555. AE, MC, V.*

$ ✕ **Barb's Place.** Funky Barb's, a blue-painted take-out shack, floats on the quay where the fishing boats dock, west of the Inner Harbour off Erie Street. Cod, halibut, oysters, seafood burgers, chowder, and carrot cake are all prepared fresh on the premises. The picnic tables on the wharf provide a front-row view of interesting vessels, including a paddle-wheeler, houseboats, and some vintage fishing boats. There's also a grassy park nearby. Ferries sail to Fisherman's Wharf from the Inner Harbour. ⊠ *Fisherman's Wharf, Erie St., James Bay,* ☎ *250/384–6515. MC, V. Closed Nov.–Feb.*

### Vegetarian

$ ✕ **Re-Bar Modern Food.** Bright and casual, this kid-friendly café in Bastion Square is *the* place for vegetarians in Victoria; the almond burgers, enchiladas, decadent home-baked goodies, and big breakfasts keep omnivores happy, too. An extensive tea and fresh-juice selection shares space on the drinks list with espresso, microbrews, and local wines. ⊠ *50 Bastion Sq., Old Town,* ☎ *250/361–9223. AE, MC, V. No dinner Sun., or Mon. Oct.–Mar.*

## Lodging

$$$$ ⊡ **The Aerie.** The million-dollar view of Finlayson Arm and the Gulf
★ Islands persuaded owner Maria Schuster to build her Mediterranean-style villa on this hilltop, north of Victoria. Most of the big, plush rooms have a patio and a fireplace. Chocolate truffles and fresh flowers are part of the pampering treatment, which includes a full-service spa. In the view-blessed dining room, the top-notch Pacific Northwest cuisine relies almost exclusively on local ingredients and incorporates organic products and heritage produce varieties into its à la carte, vegetarian, and multicourse tasting menus. ⊠ *600 Ebedora La. (Box 108, Malahat V0R 2L0),* ☎ *250/743–7115 or 800/518–1933,* ℻ *250/743–4766,* WEB *www.aerie.bc.ca. 27 rooms, 2 suites. Restaurant, room service, in-room data ports, minibars, cable TV, tennis court, indoor pool, exercise equipment, hot tubs (indoor and outdoor), sauna, spa, bar, piano,*

*laundry service, Internet, business services, meeting rooms, helipad, free
parking; no kids under 12, no smoking. AE, DC, MC, V. BP.*

**$$$$** 🏨 **Coast Harbourside Hotel and Marina.** West of the Inner Harbour
and on the water, the Coast Harbourside is handy to downtown but
removed from the traffic on Government Street. The ambience is
friendly, the decor modern but soothing. The rooms, in peach or blue
with rosewood furniture, all have balconies, and some have striking
harbor views. Fishing and whale-watching charters and the harbor ferries stop at the hotel's marina, and there's a free downtown shuttle.
The Blue Crab Bar and Grill is a popular dining spot. ⊠ *146 Kingston
St., James Bay, V8V 1V4,* ☎ *250/360–1211 or 800/663–1144,* ℻ *250/
360–1418,* WEB *www.coasthotels.com. 126 rooms, 6 suites. Restaurant,
room service, in-room data ports, minibars, cable TV with movies and
video games, indoor-outdoor pool, gym, hot tub, sauna, marina, bar,
baby-sitting, dry cleaning, laundry service, Internet, business services,
meeting rooms, free parking, some pets allowed (fee); no-smoking
floors. AE, D, DC, MC, V.*

**$$$$**
**★** 🏨 **Delta Victoria Ocean Pointe Resort and Spa.** Across the "blue
bridge" (Johnson Street Bridge) from downtown Victoria, this property has a resort's worth of facilities, including a full spa. The hotel's
two-story lobby and half of its guest rooms provide romantic views of
the Inner Harbour and the lights of the Parliament Buildings across
the water. Rooms are spacious and airy, with tall windows, rosewood
furniture, and sage green fabrics; the apartment-size suites have separate living and dining areas. The Victorian Restaurant serves fine Pacific Northwest cuisine in a scenic setting. An on-site adventure center
can arrange fishing, kayaking, sailing, whale-watching, and more. ⊠
*45 Songhees Rd., Vic West, V9A 6T3,* ☎ *250/360–2999 or 800/667–
4677,* ℻ *250/360–1041,* WEB *www.deltahotels.com. 240 rooms, 6
suites. 2 restaurants, room service, in-room data ports, minibars, cable
TV with movies and video games, 2 tennis courts, indoor pool, health
club, hot tub, sauna, bicycles, racquetball, squash, lounge, wine shop,
shop, baby-sitting, dry cleaning, laundry service, concierge, Internet,
business services, meeting rooms, travel services, parking (fee), some
pets allowed; no-smoking floors. AE, DC, MC, V.*

**$$$$**
**★** 🏨 **The Fairmont Empress.** For empire builders, movie stars, and a great
many others, the Empress is the only place to stay in Victoria. Opened
in 1908, this harborside château has aged gracefully, with sympathet-
ically restored Edwardian decor, discreet modern amenities, and service standards that recall a more gracious age. Rooms vary in size and
layout, but higher-end rooms are spacious, and all have conservative
decor, muted colors, and high ceilings. Many of those facing Government Street have front-row views of the Inner Harbour. ⊠ *721 Government St., Downtown, V8W 1W5,* ☎ *250/384–8111 or 800/441–
1414,* ℻ *250/389–2747,* WEB *www.fairmont.com. 457 rooms, 19 suites.
3 restaurants, room service, some fans, in-room data ports, some in-
room safes, minibars, cable TV with movies and video games, indoor
pool, gym, hot tub, sauna, spa, lounge, shops, baby-sitting, dry cleaning, laundry service, concierge, concierge floor, Internet, business services, convention center, parking (fee), some pets allowed (fee); no a/c
in some rooms, no-smoking floors. AE, D, DC, MC, V.*

**$$$$** 🏨 **Humboldt House.** Sparkling wine and chocolate truffles greet you
at this unabashedly romantic hideaway on a quiet side street. The pret-
tily restored Victorian has five rooms, each with elaborate boudoir decor,
a wood-burning fireplace, down duvets, a CD player, fresh flowers, candles, and a whirlpool tub (in the bedroom). (A suite with a detached
bath and a two-bedroom cottage, about 1 km [½ mi] south of the house,
are also available.) You can sip sherry in the red velvet parlor in the
evening; in the morning a picnic basket loaded with breakfast good-

ies is delivered to your room through a butler's pantry. ✉ *867 Humboldt St., Downtown, V8V 2Z6,* ☎ *250/383–0152 or 888/383–0327,* FAX *250/383–6402,* WEB *www.humboldthouse.com. 5 rooms, 1 suite, 1 cottage. Fans, refrigerators, dry cleaning, laundry service, free parking; no a/c, no room phones, no room TVs, no smoking. MC, V. BP.*

$$$–$$$$ 🖼 **Abigail's Hotel.** A Tudor-style inn built in 1930, Abigail's is within
★ walking distance of downtown. The guest rooms are attractively furnished in an English Arts and Crafts style. Down comforters, together with whirlpool tubs and fireplaces in many rooms, add to the pampering atmosphere. Six large rooms in the Coach House building are especially lavish, with whirlpool tubs, four-poster king beds, and wood-burning fireplaces. ✉ *906 McClure St., Downtown, V8V 3E7,* ☎ *250/388–5363 or 800/561–6565,* FAX *250/388–7787,* WEB *www.abigailshotel.com. 22 rooms. Fans, in-room data ports, some refrigerators, some in-room VCRs, library, shop, dry cleaning, laundry service, Internet, free parking; no a/c, no TV in some rooms, no kids under 10, no smoking. AE, MC, V. BP.*

$$$–$$$$ 🖼 **Beaconsfield Inn.** This 1905 registered historic building four blocks
★ from the Inner Harbour is one of Victoria's most faithfully restored Edwardian mansions. Though the rooms and suites all have antique furniture, mahogany floors, stained-glass windows, Ralph Lauren fabrics, and period details, each has a unique look; one room even includes an Edwardian wooden canopied tub. Lavish breakfasts and afternoon tea and sherry in the conservatory or around the library fire complete the English country-manor ambience. ✉ *998 Humboldt St., Downtown, V8V 2Z8,* ☎ *250/384–4044 or 888/884–4044,* FAX *250/384–4052,* WEB *www.beaconsfieldinn.com. 5 rooms, 4 suites. Library, dry cleaning, laundry service, Internet, free parking; no a/c, no room phones, no room TVs, no kids, no smoking. MC, V. BP.*

$$$–$$$$ 🖼 **A Haterleigh Heritage Inn.** Lead- and stained-glass windows and or-
★ nate plasterwork on 11-ft ceilings transport you to a more gracious time at this 1901 mansion two blocks from the Inner Harbour. The Victorian-theme guest rooms have whirlpool tubs or the original claw-foot tubs, high ceilings, and goose-down duvets. The Secret Garden room, with its a mountain-view balcony and oval whirlpool tub, is a romantic option, as is the Day Dreams suite, with its private sitting room. Breakfasts include homemade breads, fresh fruit, and elaborate entrées; sherry is served in the guest lounge each afternoon. ✉ *243 Kingston St., James Bay, V8V 1V5,* ☎ *250/384–9995 or 866/234–2244,* FAX *250/384–1935,* WEB *www.haterleigh.com. 4 rooms, 3 suites. Fans, Internet, free parking; no a/c, no room phones, no room TVs, no kids under 12, no smoking. MC, V. BP.*

$$$–$$$$ 🖼 **Laurel Point Inn.** Every room has water views at this modern resort hotel on a 6-acre peninsula in the Inner Harbour. The decor, especially in the Arthur Erickson–designed suites, is light and airy, with a strong Asian influence. Chinese art adorns many public areas, and the summer-only Terrace Room restaurant overlooks a Japanese garden. All rooms have balconies. ✉ *680 Montreal St., James Bay, V8V 1Z8,* ☎ *250/386–8721 or 800/663–7667,* FAX *250/386–9547,* WEB *www.laurelpoint.com. 135 rooms, 65 suites. 2 restaurants, room service, in-room data ports, some refrigerators, cable TV with movies, indoor pool, hot tub, sauna, lounge, shop, baby-sitting, dry cleaning, laundry service, Internet, business services, meeting rooms, free parking, some pets allowed (fee); no smoking. AE, D, DC, MC, V.*

$$$–$$$$ 🖼 **Oak Bay Beach Hotel & Marine Resort.** At this Tudor-style, seaside inn, guest rooms are decorated with sumptuous antiques. Many of the rooms have balconies and striking views over the inn's gardens and outlying islands; some have gas fireplaces and big soaking tubs. An on-site adventure center can arrange whale watching, kayaking, dinner

cruises, and more. The restaurant, Bentley's on the Bay, serves Pacific Northwest cuisine and, in summer, an elaborate high tea; the pub has a cozy British ambience and a sea-view patio, where you can dine. In the off-season, you can enjoy musical dinner theater at the hotel. ⊠ *1175 Beach Dr., Oak Bay, V8S 2N2,* ☎ *250/598–4556 or 800/668–7758,* FAX *250/598–6180,* WEB *www.oakbaybeachhotel.com. 45 rooms, 5 suites. Restaurant, room service, fans, minibars, some refrigerators, cable TV, dock, boating, mountain bikes, pub, baby-sitting, dry cleaning, laundry service, concierge, business services, meeting rooms, free parking; no a/c, no smoking. AE, D, DC, MC, V. CP.*

$$$–$$$$  ⊡ **Prior House Bed & Breakfast Inn.** In a beautifully restored 1912 manor
★        home on a quiet street near Craigdarroch Castle, this B&B has a pretty garden, a guest library, two parlors, antique furniture, lead-glass windows, and oak paneling. All guest rooms have fireplaces; some have whirlpool tubs and private balconies. The Garden Suite, with a private entrance and two bedrooms, is an especially good value. A chef prepares the lavish breakfasts and afternoon teas, which are included in the rates. ⊠ *620 St. Charles St., Rockland, V8S 3N7,* ☎ *250/592–8847 or 877/924–3300,* FAX *250/592–8223,* WEB *www.priorhouse.com. 3 rooms, 3 suites. Fans, refrigerators, cable TV, in-room VCRs, library, laundry service, meeting room, free parking; no a/c, no room phones, no kids under 10, no smoking. MC, V. BP.*

$$$–$$$$  ⊡ **Victoria Regent.** Originally an apartment building, this nearly all-suites hotel has an excellent waterfront location, a few minutes' walk from the Inner Harbour. The outside is plain, with a glass facade, but the large apartment-size suites are attractively decorated with rosewood furniture and contemporary art (the regular rooms have a similar look). Each suite has a kitchen, living room, dining room, balcony, and one or two bedrooms with bath, making the Victoria Regent a good choice for families. Many suites have water views, and the pricier executive suites each include a fireplace, den, and jet tub. Room rates include passes to the YWCA fitness center nearby. ⊠ *1234 Wharf St., Old Town, V8W 3H9,* ☎ *250/386–2211 or 800/663–7472,* FAX *250/386–2622,* WEB *www.victoriaregent.com. 11 rooms, 35 suites. Room service, fans, in-room data ports, minibars, cable TV, in-room VCRs, baby-sitting, dry cleaning, laundry facilities, laundry service, Internet, business services, meeting rooms, free parking; no a/c, no-smoking floors. AE, D, DC, MC, V. CP.*

$$–$$$  ⊡ **Admiral Inn.** This small, friendly blue-and-white gabled hotel along a quiet part of the Inner Harbour is a good choice for families. Blue carpet, pink and blue print bedspreads, and oak furniture adorn the rooms, and all have private entrances and a balcony or patio. There's a guest lounge with a fireplace. ⊠ *257 Belleville St., James Bay, V8V 1X1,* ☎ *888/823–6472,* ☎ FAX *250/388–6267,* WEB *www.admiral.bc.ca. 22 rooms, 10 suites. In-room data ports, some kitchens, some kitchenettes, microwaves, refrigerators, cable TV, mountain bikes, baby-sitting, dry cleaning, laundry facilities, Internet, free parking; no smoking. AE, D, MC, V. CP.*

$$–$$$  ⊡ **Château Victoria.** Wonderful views from the upper-floor suites and rooftop restaurant are a plus at this friendly, centrally located 19-story hotel. The guest rooms are modern and airy, with rose and blue fabrics and either rosewood or pine furniture. The apartment-size suites are a good choice for families: all have balconies and sitting areas, and some have kitchenettes. Standard rooms are spacious, too. ⊠ *740 Burdett Ave., Downtown, V8W 1B2,* ☎ *250/382–4221 or 800/663–5891,* FAX *250/380–1950,* WEB *www.chateauvictoria.com. 59 rooms, 118 suites. 2 restaurants, room service, fans, in-room data ports, some kitchenettes, refrigerators, cable TV with movies and video games, indoor pool, gym, hot tub, 2 lounges, baby-sitting, dry cleaning, laundry ser-*

vice, Internet, concierge, business services, meeting rooms, free parking; no a/c in some rooms, no-smoking floors. AE, D, DC, MC, V.

$$–$$$ ★ ⊞ **Spinnakers Guest House.** Three delightful houses make up the accommodations at this B&B—run by the owner of the popular Spinnakers Brew Pub. A Italian villa–style house has four suites that surround an ivy-draped courtyard. Suites have private entrances and are decorated with Asian antiques, Balinese teak butlers, and other objects gathered during the owner's world travels. Two other houses are beautifully renovated Victorian homes, decorated with original local art and English and Welsh antiques. Most rooms have fireplaces and whirlpool tubs. ⊠ *308 Catherine St., Vic West (across Johnson Street Bridge from downtown Victoria), V9A 3S8,* ☎ *250/384–2739 or 877/838–2739,* WEB *www.spinnakers.com. 5 rooms, 5 suites. Restaurant, some fans, some kitchens, some cable TV, pub, Internet, free parking; no a/c, no TV in some rooms, no kids under 10, no smoking. AE, D, DC, MC, V. BP.*

$$–$$$ ⊞ **Swans.** Near the waterfront in Victoria's Old Town and within walking distance of most of the major sights, this 1913 former warehouse is one of the city's most attractive boutique hotels. The first floor has a brewery, a restaurant, and a brewpub, and there's a nightclub in the cellar. Large, apartment-like suites with kitchens, high ceilings, and Pacific Northwest art fill the upper floors. The two-level penthouse suite has a hot tub on its private rooftop patio. ⊠ *506 Pandora Ave., Old Town, V8W 1N6,* ☎ *250/361–3310 or 800/668–7926,* FAX *250/361–3491,* WEB *www.swanshotel.com. 30 suites. Room service, fans, in-room data ports, microwaves, cable TV with movies, some in-room VCRs, wine shop, baby-sitting, dry cleaning, laundry facilities, laundry service, meeting rooms, parking (fee); no a/c, no smoking. AE, DC, MC, V.*

$ ⊞ **Hostelling International Victoria.** This hostel, in a restored historic building, is in the thick of things near the waterfront and Market Square. The accommodations include private rooms with shared baths as well as beds in men's, women's, and coed dorms. Among the amenities are a game room, TV lounge, private lockers, two shared kitchens, and loads of travel information for your trip. The reception is staffed 24 hours a day. ⊠ *516 Yates St., Old Town, V8W 1K8,* ☎ *250/385–4511 or 888/883–0099,* FAX *250/385–3232,* WEB *www.hihostels.bc.ca. 110 beds in 10 single-sex and coed dorms; 5 private rooms (2–8 people) without bath. Internet, laundry facilities; no a/c, no room phones, no room TVs, no smoking. MC, V.*

# Nightlife and the Arts

For entertainment listings, pick up a free copy of *Monday Magazine* (it comes out every Thursday), or call the **Talking Super Pages** (☎ 250/953–9000).

### The Arts

MUSIC

The **TerrifVic Jazz Party** (☎ 250/953–2011) showcases internationally acclaimed musicians every April at seven venues around Victoria. The **Victoria Jazz Society** (☎ 250/388–4423) organizes the annual JazzFest International in late June and the Vancouver Island Blues Bash in Victoria every Labor Day weekend.

The **Victoria Symphony** (☎ 250/385–6515) plays in the Royal Theatre (⊠ 805 Broughton St., Downtown, ☎ 250/386–6121) and at the University Centre Auditorium (⊠ Finnerty Rd., University of Victoria Campus, ☎ 250/721–8480).

OPERA

**Pacific Opera Victoria** (☎ 250/385–0222) performs three productions a year at the Royal Theatre.

An old church houses the **Belfry Theatre** (✉ 1291 Gladstone Ave., Fernwood, ☎ 250/385–6815), where a resident company specializes in contemporary Canadian dramas. The **Langham Court Theatre** (✉ 805 Langham Ct., Rockland, ☎ 250/384–2142), one of Canada's oldest community theaters, stages the works of internationally known playwrights between September and June. **McPherson Playhouse** (✉ 3 Centennial Sq., ☎ 250/386–6121) hosts touring theater and dance companies. Musical dinner theater runs between October and May at the **Oak Bay Beach Hotel & Marine Resort Dinner Theatre** (✉ 1175 Beach Dr., Oak Bay, ☎ 250/598–4556 or 800/668–7758, WEB www.oakbaybeachhotel.com). University of Victoria students stage productions on campus at the **Phoenix Theatre** (✉ off the Ring Rd., ☎ 250/721–8000).

## Nightlife

Deep leather sofas and a Bengal tiger skin help to re-create the days of British Raj at the **Bengal Lounge** in the Fairmont Empress Hotel. Martinis and a curry buffet are the draws through the week. On Friday and Saturday nights a jazz trio takes the stage. High-energy dance music draws a young crowd to the **Boom Boom Room** (✉ 1208 Wharf St., Old Town, ☎ 250/381–2331), on the waterfront. You can catch stand-up acts Friday and Saturday nights at the **Comedy Cellar** (✉ 759 Yates St., in the Dominion Hotel, Downtown, ☎ 250/412–1020).

The DJs at **Liquid** (✉ 15 Bastion Sq., Old Town, ☎ 250/385–2626) play Top 40, dance, R&B, and hip-hop tunes. With its cozy Tudor ambience and a waterside deck, the **Snug Pub** (✉ 1175 Beach Dr., Oak Bay, ☎ 250/598–4556), about 10 minutes from downtown in the Oak Bay Beach Hotel & Marine Resort, is the nearest thing to a traditional English pub in Victoria. **Steamers Public House** (✉ 570 Yates St., Downtown, ☎ 250/381–4340) has four pool tables and live music every night. The **Strathcona Hotel** (✉ 919 Douglas St., Downtown, ☎ 250/383–7137) is something of an entertainment complex, with a restaurant, a nightclub, and seven different bars, including a sports bar, and a hillbilly-theme bar—not to mention beach volleyball played on the roof in summer. The DJs at the dance club **Sweetwater's** (✉ Market Square, 27–560 Johnson St., Old Town, ☎ 250/383–7844) appeal to a wide age group with Top 40 dance and old-time rock-and-roll tunes.

The deck at the **Harbour Canoe Club** (✉ 450 Swift St., Upper Harbour, ☎ 250/361–1940), a marine brewpub, looks over the Gorge and is a delightful place to spend a summer afternoon; you can even rent canoes and kayaks here. Inside, the former power station has been stylishly redone, with high ceilings, exposed brick and beams, a wide range of in-house brews, top-notch bar snacks, and a restaurant. Chic and arty **Hugo's Brewhouse** (✉ 625 Courtney St., Downtown, ☎ 250/920–4844) serves lunch, dinner, and four of its own brews. This multipurpose nightspot is a pub by day, a lounge in the early evening, and a dance club at night. **Spinnakers Brew Pub** (✉ 308 Catherine St., Vic West, ☎ 250/386–2739) pours Victoria's most extensive menu of microbrews in an atmospheric setting, with a waterfront deck, a double-sided fireplace, and a multitude of cozy rooms filled with pub paraphernalia. The excellent pub grub and the in-house restaurant make this a popular eatery, too. **Swan's Pub** (✉ 1601 Store St., Old Town, ☎ 250/361–3310) serves its own microbrews in a room decorated with Pacific Northwest art; musicians play Sunday through Thursday nights.

# Outdoor Activities and Sports

## Boating

The quiet upper section of Victoria's harbor, called the Gorge, is a popular boating spot. You can rent a kayak, canoe, motorboat, or rowboat at **Harbour Rentals** (⊠ Heritage Quay, 450 Swift St., ☎ 250/386–2277). Guided trips and bicycles are also available.

To rent a powerboat or to book almost any kind of guided marine activity, including seaplane tours, fishing, and kayaking expeditions, contact the **Victoria Marine Adventure Centre** (⊠ 950 Wharf St., ☎ 250/995–2211 or 800/575–6700), on the Inner Harbour near the Visitor Information Centre. You can also rent scooters and bicycles here.

## Golf

Several companies in Victoria provide advance tee-time bookings and golf packages.

The **Cordova Bay Golf Course** (⊠ 5333 Cordova Bay Rd., ☎ 250/658–4444 or 866/380–4653) is an 18-hole, par-72 course with views of Cordova Bay and the San Juan Islands. The greens fee is $54. An optional cart costs $34.

## Hiking

The **Galloping Goose Regional Trail** (☎ 250/478–3344, WEB www.crd.bc.ca/parks), an old railroad track that's been reclaimed for walkers, cyclists, and equestrians, runs from downtown Victoria to just north of Sooke. It links with the Lochside Regional Trail to Sidney to create a continuous 100-km (62-mi) car-free route. **Goldstream Provincial Park** (☎ 250/478–9414), 19 km (12 mi) northwest of Victoria on Highway 1 at Finlayson Arm Road, has an extensive trail system, old-growth forest, waterfalls, a salt marsh, and a river. Goldstream is a prime site for viewing bald eagles in December and January. **Swan Lake Christmas Hill Nature Sanctuary** (⊠ 3873 Swan Lake Rd., ☎ 250/479–0211), a few miles from downtown, has a 23-acre lake set in 143 acres of fields and wetlands. From the 2½-km (1½-mi) trail and floating boardwalk, birders can spot a variety of waterfowl even in winter, as well as nesting birds in the tall grass. The sanctuary's Nature House is open weekdays 8:30–4 and weekends noon–4.

## Whale-Watching

To see the pods of orcas and other species that travel in the waters around Vancouver Island, you can take charter boat tours from Victoria.

**Great Pacific Adventures** (☎ 250/386–2277 or 877/733–6722) operates Zodiac (motor-powered inflatable-boat) tours year-round. A three-hour tour costs $75. **Ocean Explorations** (☎ 250/383–6722 or 888/442–6722) conducts two-hour marine tours in winter and three-hour whale-watching trips in summer—all on Zodiacs. Tours cost $69 in summer and $55 in winter. **Seacoast Expeditions** (☎ 250/383–2254 or 800/386–1525) has whale-watching and marine wildlife tours. A three-hour tour (April through October) in either a Zodiac or on a high-speed covered vessel, with two naturalists on board, is $79. Two-hour wildlife-watching trips are $59 and are run during the rest of the year.

The **Oak Bay Beach Hotel & Marine Resort Adventure Centre** (☎ 250/592–3474 or 800/668–7758, WEB www.oakbaybeachhotel.com) operates whale-watching trips, with a naturalist and lunch, on a 45-ft catamaran. It also leads other wildlife-spotting and outdoor-adventure trips, including a cycling winery tour in the Cowichan Bay area, guided kayak and hiking tours, and sunset dinner cruises.

The **Victoria Marine Adventure Centre** (✉ 950 Wharf St., ☎ 250/
995–2211 or 800/575–6700) can arrange whale-watching trips. Prices
start at $79 per person for a three-hour trip in either a covered boat
or on a Zodiac (both with naturalists on board).

# Shopping

## Shopping Districts and Malls

For a wide selection, head to the larger shopping centers downtown.
**Victoria Eaton Centre** (✉ 1 Victoria Eaton Centre, at Government and
Fort Sts., Downtown, ☎ 250/381–4012), a department store and mall,
has about 100 boutiques and restaurants. **Antique Row,** on Fort Street
between Blanshard and Cook streets, is home to more than 60 antiques,
curio, and collectibles shops. **Market Square** (✉ 560 Johnson St., Old
Town, ☎ 250/386–2441) has everything from fudge, music, and comic
books to jewelry, local arts, and new-age accoutrements. High-end fashion boutiques, craft shops, and galleries line **Trounce Alley,** a pedestrian-
only lane north of View Street between Broad and Government streets.

## Specialty Stores

Shopping in Victoria is easy: virtually everything can be found in the
downtown area on or near Government Street stretching north from
the Fairmont Empress hotel.

At **Artina's** (✉ 1002 Government St., Downtown, ☎ 250/386–7000
or 877/386–7700) you can find unusual Canadian art jewelry—mostly
handmade, one-of-a-kind pieces. The **Cowichan Trading Co., Ltd.** (✉
1328 Government St., Downtown, ☎ 250/383–0321) sells First Nations jewelry, art, moccasins, and Cowichan Indian sweaters. The **Fran
Willis Gallery** (✉ 1619 Store St., upstairs, Old Town, ☎ 250/381–3422)
shows contemporary Canadian paintings and sculpture. **Hill's Native
Art** (✉ 1008 Government St., Downtown, ☎ 250/385–3911) sells souvenirs and original West Coast First Nations art. As the name would
suggest, **Irish Linen Stores** (✉ 1019 Government St., Downtown, ☎
250/383–6812) stocks fine linen, lace, and hand-embroidered items—
hankies, napkins, tablecloths, and place mats. Local history and fic-
tion are the highlights at **Munro's Books** (✉ 1108 Government St.,
Downtown, ☎ 250/382–2464), housed in a restored 1909 building.
If the British spirit of Victoria has you searching for fine teas, head to
**Murchie's** (✉ 1110 Government St., Downtown, ☎ 250/383–3112)
for a choice of 40 varieties, plus blended coffees, tarts, and cakes. At
**Starfish Glassworks** (✉ 630 Yates St., Downtown, ☎ 250/388–7827)
you can watch glassblowers create original works.

# Victoria A to Z

*To research prices, get advice from other travelers, and book travel ar-
rangements, visit www.fodors.com.*

### AIR TRAVEL TO AND FROM VICTORIA

Victoria International Airport is served by Horizon, Pacific Coastal,
and WestJet airlines. Air Canada Jazz (Air Canada's regional service)
provides frequent airport-to-airport service from Vancouver to Victoria. Flights take about 35 minutes.

West Coast Air and Harbour Air provide 35-minute harbor-to-harbor
service (between downtown Vancouver and downtown Victoria) several times a day. Kenmore Air Harbour operates direct daily floatplane
service from Seattle to Victoria's Inner Harbour. Helijet International
helicopter service is available from downtown Vancouver, the Vancouver
airport, and downtown Seattle to downtown Victoria.

➤ CONTACTS: **Air Canada Jazz** (☎ 888/247–2262, WEB www.aircanada.ca). **Harbour Air** (☎ 604/688–1277 or 800/665–0212, WEB www.harbour-air.com). **Helijet International** (☎ 800/665–4354, 604/273–1414, or 250/382–6222, WEB www.helijet.com). **Kenmore Air Harbor** (☎ 425/486–1257 or 800/543–9595, WEB www.kenmoreair.com). **West Coast Air** (☎ 604/606–6888 or 800/347–2222, WEB www.westcoastair.com). **WestJet Airlines** (☎ 800/538–5696, WEB www.westjet.com).

## AIRPORTS AND TRANSFERS

Victoria International Airport is 25 km (15 mi) north of downtown Victoria, off Highway 17.

➤ AIRPORT INFORMATION: **Victoria International Airport** (✉ 1640 Electra Blvd., off Hwy. 17, Sidney, ☎ 250/953–7500, WEB www.victoriaairport.com).

AIRPORT TRANSFER

To drive from the airport to downtown, take Highway 17 south. A taxi ride costs between $35 and $40, plus tip. The Airporter bus service drops off passengers at most major hotels. The fare is $13 one-way, $23 round-trip.

➤ SHUTTLE: **Airporter** (☎ 250/386–2525, WEB www.airporter.travel.bc.ca).

## BOAT AND FERRY TRAVEL

BC Ferries operates daily service between Vancouver and Victoria. Ferries arrive at and depart from the Swartz Bay Terminal at the end of Highway 17 (the Patricia Bay Highway), 32 km (20 mi) north of downtown Victoria. Sailing time is about 1½ hours. Peak-season weekend fares are $9.50 per adult passenger and $33.50 per vehicle each way; lower rates apply midweek and in the off-season. Vehicle reservations on Vancouver–Victoria and Nanaimo routes are optional and cost $15 in addition to the fare.

Black Ball Transport operates car ferries daily year-round between Victoria and Port Angeles, Washington. The Oak Bay Beach Hotel & Marine Resort operates a daily, summer-only foot-passenger and bicycle ferry to Roche Harbor on San Juan Island, Washington.

The *Victoria Clipper* runs daily year-round passenger-only service between Victoria and Seattle. The round-trip fare from mid-May to late September is US$109 to US$125, depending on the time of day; the rest of the year the round-trip is US$99. You receive a discount if you order 14-day advance tickets, which have some restrictions. Washington State Ferries travel daily between Sidney, about 30 km (18 mi) north of Victoria, and Anacortes, Washington.

Within Victoria, Victoria Harbour Ferries serve the Inner Harbour, with stops that include the Fairmont Empress, Chinatown, Point Ellice House, the Delta Victoria Ocean Pointe Resort, and Fisherman's Wharf. Fares start at $3. Boats make the rounds every 12 to 20 minutes daily March through October and on sunny weekends the rest of the year. If you're by the Inner Harbour at 9:45 on a Sunday morning in summer, you can catch the little ferries performing a water ballet—they gather together and do maneuvers set to classical music that's blasted over loudspeakers.

➤ BOAT AND FERRY INFORMATION: **BC Ferries** (☎ 250/386–3431; 888/223–3779 in B.C.; 604/444–2890; 888/724–5223 in B.C. for vehicle reservations; WEB www.bcferries.com). **Black Ball Transport** (☎ 250/386–2202 or 360/457–4491, WEB www.northolympic.com/coho). **Oak Bay Beach Hotel & Marine Resort** (☎ 250/592–3474 or 800/668–7758, WEB www.oakbaybeachhotel.com). *Victoria Clipper* (☎ 206/448–5000 in Seattle; 800/888–2535 elsewhere; WEB www.victoriaclipper.com). **Victoria Harbour Ferries** (☎ 250/708–0201, WEB www.harbourferry. com). **Washington State Ferries** (☎ 206/464–6400, 888/808–7977, WEB www.wsdot.wa.gov/ferries).

## BUS TRAVEL TO AND FROM VICTORIA
Pacific Coach Lines operates daily, connecting service between Victoria and Vancouver using BC Ferries.
➤ Bus Information: **Pacific Coach Lines** (☎ 250/385–4411 or 800/661–1725, WEB www.pacificcoach.com).

## BUS TRAVEL WITHIN VICTORIA
BC Transit serves Victoria and the surrounding areas. An all-day pass costs $5.50.
➤ Bus Information: **BC Transit** (☎ 250/382–6161, WEB www.bctransit.com).

## CAR RENTAL
➤ Major Agencies: **Avis** (☎ 250/386–8468). **Budget** (☎ 250/953–5300). **Enterprise** (☎ 250/475–6900). **National** (☎ 250/386–1213).
➤ Local Agency: **Island Rent-A-Car** (☎ 250/384–4881).

## EMERGENCIES
➤ Emergency Services: **Ambulance, fire, police** (☎ 911).
➤ Hospital: **Victoria General Hospital** (✉ 1 Hospital Way, off Helmcken Rd., ☎ 250/727–4212).
➤ Late-Night Pharmacy: **London Drugs** (✉ 911 Yates St., ☎ 250/381–1113), open Monday–Saturday until 10 PM.

## LODGING
Reservations for lodging can be made through Hello B.C.
➤ Reservation Services: **Hello B.C.** (☎ 800/435–5622, WEB www.hellobc.com).

## TAXIS
➤ Taxi Company: **Empress Taxi** (☎ 250/381–2222).

## TOURS
### BOAT TOURS
The best way to see the sights of the Inner Harbour is by Victoria Harbour Ferries; harbor tours are $12 to $14.
➤ Fees and Schedules: **Victoria Harbour Ferries** (☎ 250/708–0201, WEB www.harbourferry.com).

### BUS TOURS
Gray Line double-decker bus tours visit the city center, Chinatown, Antique Row, Oak Bay, and Beacon Hill Park; a combination tour includes Butchart Gardens.
➤ Fees and Schedules: **Gray Line** (☎ 250/388–5248 or 800/663–8390, WEB www.grayline.ca/victoria).

### CARRIAGE TOURS
Tally-Ho Sightseeing and Victoria Carriage Tours operate horse-drawn tours of the city. Both tours leave from the corner of Belleville and Menzies streets, near the Parliament buildings.
➤ Fees and Schedules: **Tally-Ho Sightseeing** (☎ 250/383–5067, WEB www.tallyhotours.com). **Victoria Carriage Tours** (☎ 877/663–2207 or 250/383–2207, WEB victoriacarriage.com).

### WALKING TOURS
The Architectural Institute of British Columbia offers free walking tours of Victoria's historic neighborhoods during July and August.

> FEES AND SCHEDULES: **Architectural Institute of British Columbia** (☎ 800/667–0753; 604/683–8588 Vancouver office).

**VISITOR INFORMATION**
> TOURIST INFORMATION: **Hello B.C.** (☎ 800/435–5622, WEB www. hellobc.com). **Tourism Victoria** (✉ 812 Wharf St., ☎ 250/953–2033, WEB www.tourismvictoria.com).

# VANCOUVER ISLAND

The largest island on Canada's west coast, Vancouver Island stretches 564 km (350 mi) from Victoria in the south to Cape Scott in the north. A ridge of mountains, blanketed in spruce, cedar, and Douglas fir, crowns the island's center, providing opportunities for skiing, climbing, and hiking. Outside Victoria and Nanaimo, most towns on the island are so small as to be dwarfed by the surrounding wilderness. However, many have a unique charm, from pretty Victorian Chemainus to such isolated fishing villages as Bamfield and growing ecotourism centers, including Tofino.

## Sooke

**⑰** *42 km (26 mi) west of Victoria on Hwy. 14.*

The village of Sooke provides a peaceful seaside escape, with rugged beaches, hiking trails through the surrounding rain forest, and views of Washington's Olympic Mountains across the Strait of Juan de Fuca. **East Sooke Regional Park,** 7 km (4 mi) east of Sooke on the south side of Sooke Harbour, has more than 3,500 acres of beaches, hiking trails, and wildflower-dotted meadows. A popular hiking and biking route, the **Galloping Goose Regional Trail** (☎ 250/478–3344) is a former railway line that runs all the way to Victoria. The **Sooke Potholes Provincial Park** (✉ end of Sooke River Rd., off Hwy. 14) has a series of swimming holes by the Sooke River. **Whiffen Spit,** a natural breakwater about a mile long, makes a scenic walk with great bird-watching. It's at the end of Whiffen Spit Road, west of the village.

The **Sooke Region Museum and Visitor Information Centre** (✉ 2070 Phillips Rd., off Hwy. 14, ☎ 250/642–6351) displays First Nations crafts and artifacts from 19th-century Sooke. It's open daily 9–6 in July and August, daily 9–5 in September, and Tuesday through Sunday 9–5 the rest of the year. Donations are accepted.

OFF THE BEATEN PATH | **JUAN DE FUCA PROVINCIAL PARK –** This park between Jordan River and Port Renfrew has campsites and a long series of beaches, including Botanical Beach, which has amazing tidal pools. The **Juan de Fuca Marine Trail** is a tough 47-km (30-mi) hike set up as an alternative to the overly popular West Coast Trail that begins at China Beach, west of the Jordan River. There are three other trailheads, each with a parking lot: Sombrio Beach, Parkinson Creek, and Botanical Beach (which is 5 km [3 mi] southeast of Port Renfrew). ✉ *Off Hwy. 14, between Jordan River (southeast end) and Port Renfrew (at the northwest end),* ☎ *800/689–9025 camping reservations,* WEB *www.bcparks.ca.*

### Dining and Lodging

**$$** ✕ **Seventeen Mile House.** Originally built as a hotel, this 1894 house is a study in island architecture at the end of the 19th century. It's a good place for pub fare, a beer, or fresh local seafood on the road between Sooke and Victoria. Low-cost rooms, with a do-it-yourself breakfast, are also available here. ✉ *5126 Sooke Rd.,* ☎ *250/642–5942. MC, V.*

$$$$    ✕▥ **Sooke Harbour House.** People who are discerning about their R&R
★       are drawn to this 1929 oceanfront inn, home to one of Canada's finest
        dining rooms. The cuisine is organic, seasonal, and makes the most of
        the local bounty. The menu ($$–$$$$) changes daily, the seafood is
        just-caught fresh, and much of the produce is grown on the property.
        The wine cellar is among the country's best. The guest rooms, each with
        a sitting area and fireplace, are individually decorated (some with bird
        or seaside themes) and photo-shoot perfect; all but one have ocean views
        and private decks or patios. In summer and on weekends throughout
        the year rates include a picnic lunch. ✉ *1528 Whiffen Spit Rd., V0S
        1N0,* ☎ *250/642–3421 or 800/889–9688,* ℻ *250/642–6988,* 🌐
        *www.sookeharbourhouse.com. 28 rooms. Restaurant, room service,
        in-room data ports, some in-room hot tubs, refrigerators, massage, cro-
        quet, piano, shop, laundry service, Internet, business services, meet-
        ing rooms, some pets allowed (fee); no a/c, no room TVs, no smoking.
        DC, MC, V. BP.*

$$–$$$   ▥ **Markham House Bed & Breakfast.** The owners make you feel wel-
        come in this Tudor-style house set amid extensive grounds that include
        a trout pond, a stream, a putting green, and walking trails. The bed-
        rooms are decorated with family pieces and feather beds. The Garden
        Suite, which has a double Jacuzzi, and the Country Room are spacious;
        the Green Room is cozy but small, and its bathroom is down the hall.
        Tucked away in the woods is the Honeysuckle Cottage. Its private deck
        has a barbecue and a hot tub, and a kitchenette is inside—but break-
        fast (which is delicious) can be delivered to the door. ✉ *1853 Connie
        Rd., off Hwy. 14 (8 km [5 mi] east of Sooke), Victoria V9C 4C2,* ☎
        *250/642–7542 or 888/256–6888,* ℻ *250/642–7538,* 🌐 *www.
        markhamhouse.com. 2 rooms, 1 suite, 1 cabin. In-room VCRs, boc-
        cie, croquet, some pets allowed; no a/c, no smoking. AE, D, DC, MC,
        V. BP.*

$$–$$$   ▥ **Point No Point.** Here's a place for your inner Robinson Crusoe.
        Twenty-four cabins sit on the edge of a cliff overlooking a mile of pri-
        vate beach and the open Pacific. The one- and two-bedroom cabins,
        in single, duplex, and quad units, range from rustic to romantic. Every
        unit has a kitchen, a fireplace or woodstove, and a deck. The lodge
        restaurant ($$–$$$) serves lunch, afternoon tea, and dinner from a
        seafood-oriented menu. Each table has a pair of binoculars for spot-
        ting whales and ships on the open sea. ✉ *1505 West Coast Rd., 24
        km (15 mi) west of Sooke, V0S 1N0,* ☎ *250/646–2020,* ℻ *250/646–
        2294,* 🌐 *www.pointnopointresort.com. 24 cabins, 1 3-bedroom
        house. Restaurant, some in-room hot tubs, hiking, some pets allowed
        (fee); no a/c, no room phones, no room TVs, no smoking. AE, MC, V.
        Restaurant closed for dinner Mon.–Tues. and Jan.*

### Shopping

At the **Blue Raven Gallery** (✉ 1971 Kaltasin Rd., ☎ 250/881–0528),
Victor, Carey, and Edith Newman, a family team of Kwakiutl and Salish artists, display traditional and modern prints, masks, jewelry, and
clothing. January through March the shop is open only by appoint-
ment.

## Duncan

⑱  *60 km (37 mi) north of Victoria on the Trans-Canada Hwy., or
    Hwy. 1.*

★☃  Duncan is nicknamed the City of Totems for the many totem poles that
    dot the small community. The **Quw'utsun' Cultural and Conference Cen-
    tre,** covering 6 acres on the banks of the tree-lined Cowichan River, is
    one of Canada's leading First Nations cultural and educational facil-

ities. You can see the work of some of the Northwest's most renowned artists in a lofty longhouse-style gallery, learn about the history of the Cowichan people from a multimedia show, and sample traditional foods at the Riverwalk Café. You can also watch artisans at work in the world's largest carving house and even try your hand at carving on a visitors' pole. Crafts demonstrations and performances take place in summer. ⊠ *200 Cowichan Way,* ☎ *250/746–8119 or 877/746–8119,* ⟨WEB⟩ *www. quwutsun.ca.* ⊠ *$11.* ⊙ *May–Sept., daily 9–6; Oct.–Apr., daily 10–5; café closed Nov.–Apr.*

The **British Columbia Forest Discovery Centre** spans some 100 acres, combining indoor and outdoor forestry-related exhibits, including a 1930s-era logging camp, and hands-on displays in the *Forest Renewal B.C.* exhibition. In July and August you can ride an original 1910 steam locomotive around the property. Trails through the old-growth forest take you to trees as much as 600 years old. ⊠ *2892 Drinkwater Rd. (Trans-Canada Hwy.),* ☎ *250/715–1113,* ⟨WEB⟩ *www.bcforestmuseum.com.* ⊠ *$9.* ⊙ *Easter–May, daily 10–5; June–Aug., daily, 10–6; Sept.–mid-Oct., daily 10–5.*

### Lodging

**$$** ⊞ **Fairburn Farm Country Manor.** This 1884 manor on 130 pastoral acres is the centerpiece family farm, where hosts Anthea and Darrel Archer raise sheep, cows, and hens. Two sitting rooms, a wide verandah, meadows, and trails through the surrounding woods provide plenty of space to unwind. The rooms are country comfortable, with original woodwork, local art, and historic photos; all have private baths, though three are across the hall. Breakfasts are homegrown and organic. A two-bedroom cottage on the property, furnished with an eclectic mix of old-but-not-antique furniture, is a good choice for families. ⊠ *3310 Jackson Rd., V9L 6N7,* ☎ ⟨FAX⟩ *250/746–4637,* ⟨WEB⟩ *www. fairburnfarm.bc.ca. 6 rooms, 1 cottage. Boating, library, piano, meeting room; no a/c, no room phones, no room TVs, no smoking. Closed mid-Oct.–Easter. BP.*

### Shopping

**Quw'utsun Cultural and Conference Centre** (⊠ 200 Cowichan Way, ☎ 250/746–8119 or 877/746–8119) sells Cowichan wool sweaters, hand-knit by the Cowichan people. **Hill's Native Art** (☎ 250/746–6731), on the main Highway 1, about 1½ km (1 mi) south of Duncan, sells hand-knit Cowichan sweaters along with other crafts.

# Chemainus

★ ⑲ *25 km (16 mi) north of Duncan.*

Chemainus is known for the bold epic murals that decorate its townscape, as well as for its beautifully restored Victorian homes. Once dependent on the lumber industry, the small community began to revitalize itself in the early 1980s when its mill closed down. Since then, the town has brought in international artists to paint more than 30 murals depicting local historical events around town. Footprints on the sidewalk lead you on a self-guided tour of the murals. Restaurants, shops, tearooms, coffee bars, art galleries, horse-and-carriage tours, several B&Bs, and antiques dealers have helped to create one of the prettiest little towns on Vancouver Island. The **Chemainus Dinner Theatre** (⊠ 9737 Chemainus Rd., ☎ 250/246–9820 or 800/565–7738) presents family-oriented performances along with dinner.

### Dining and Lodging

**$$** ✕ **Hummingbird Restaurant.** A husband-and-wife team runs this little two-room café, which serves soup, salad, and sandwich lunches as well as more-elaborate dinners, including a popular warm goat-cheese salad starter and a variety of seafood and pasta entrées. Personal touches, such as the organic flowers decorating each plate, make this a popular stop. ⊠ *9893 Maple St.,* ☎ *250/246–2290. AE, V. Closed Tues. No dinner Wed.*

**$–$$** ✕ **The Waterford Restaurant.** French-trained chef Dwayne Maslen and his wife, Linda, run this tiny restaurant tucked into a historic house near the center of town. Some highlights on the French-influenced menu are chicken Cleopatra (chicken breast stuffed with crab and shrimp and topped with Hollandaise sauce) and rack of lamb with a rosemary mint demi-glace. ⊠ *9875 Maple St.,* ☎ *250/246–1046. AE, MC, V. Closed Mon.; Oct.–Mar., call for hrs.*

**$$$$** ⚑ **Castlebury Cottage.** From the royal-purple velveteen duvet to the 18th-century church window and suit of armor, this medieval-theme, single-suite cottage is a good place to act out your Camelot fantasies. A double soaking tub, CD player, and a kitchen are nods to the modern world, and stairs climb to a little Juliette balcony with views over the town and sea. The proprietors can arrange packages including horse-and-carriage rides, theater evenings, and even medieval-theme dinners with a harpist, with advance notice. A two-night minimum stay is required on weekends. ⊠ *9910 Croft St. (Box 1432, V0R 1K0),* ☎ *250/246–9228,* FAX *250/246–2909,* WEB *www.castleburycottage.com. 1 suite. Kitchen, microwave, cable TV, in-room VCRs, laundry service; no kids, no smoking. AE, MC, V. BP.*

**$$** ⚑ **Bird Song Cottage.** The whimsical white-and-lavender Victorian
★ cottage, an easy walk from the beach and town, has been playfully decorated with antiques and collectibles, including a grand piano, a Celtic harp, and Victorian hats. A full breakfast (often with piano accompaniment) is served in a glassed-in sunporch. The Nightingale room has a private garden and a claw-foot tub, and the other two rooms have baths with showers; every room has a window seat. ⊠ *9909 Maple St. (Box 1432, V0R 1K0),* ☎ *250/246–9910,* FAX *250/246–2909,* WEB *www.romanticBB.com. 3 rooms. Cable TV, in-room VCRs, piano, laundry service; no a/c, no room phones, no TV in some rooms, no kids under 8, no smoking. AE, MC, V. BP.*

# Nanaimo

**㉔** *25 km (16 mi) north of Chemainus, 110 km (68 mi) northwest of Victoria.*

Nanaimo, Vancouver Island's largest city after Victoria, is the primary commercial and transport link for the mid-island, with direct ferry service to the mainland. Though Nanaimo's many malls sprawl untidily to the north, the landscape to the south, in the regions of Cedar and Yellow Point and around the village of Ladysmith, remains pretty and rural.

Downtown Nanaimo's **Harbourside Walkway,** which starts at the foot of Bastion Street, is a pleasant shop- and café-lined stroll past visiting yachts and fishing boats. The round building overlooking the waterfront at the foot of Bastion Street is the **Bastion** (☎ 250/753–1821), an 1853 Hudson's Bay Company arsenal, one of the last of its kind in North America. The restored interior is open 10–4 daily, June 1 to Labor Day. Admission is $1.

Re-created streets from Nanaimo's Old Town and Chinatown highlight the **Nanaimo District Museum** (⊠ 100 Cameron Rd., ☎ 250/753–1821, WEB nanaimo.museum.bc.ca), which also has exhibits on the local First Nations' culture and the region's coal-mining history, and a variety of interesting temporary exhibits. May through September the museum is open 9–5 daily; the rest of the year it's open Tuesday–Saturday 9–5. Admission is $2.

From Maffeo-Sutton Park downtown, you can take a 10-minute ferry ride ($5) in summer to **Newcastle Island** (☎ 250/753–5141, WEB www.scenicferries.com ferry information), a car-free provincial park where you can camp, picnic, bike, walk trails leading past old mines and quarries, and catch glimpses of deer, rabbits, and eagles.

## Dining and Lodging

$$–$$$ ✕ **The Dar.** Curved archways and Eastern fabrics create a suitably exotic background for the Indian and Mediterranean food served at this 1892 house in Nanaimo's Old Town. Try the starter of tiger prawns in mustard, orange, cilantro, and garlic sauce; the tandoori chicken; or the Dar Mix: a skewer of chicken, lamb and prawns. An Indian buffet is laid out at weekday lunchtime, and the patio is a popular spot any time. ⊠ 347 Wesley St., ☎ 250/755–9150. MC, V. No lunch Sun.

$$–$$$ ✕ **Mahle House.** Much of the innovative Pacific Northwest cuisine served
★ at this cozy 1904 farmhouse is raised in the restaurant's organic garden or in the neighborhood. The menu changes frequently, but highlights have included different versions of lamb, rabbit, venison, mussels, and salmon, as well as good vegetarian options. On Wednesday night, you can try the Adventure Dining Experience: for $29 you get five courses chosen by the chef, and your dinner companions (up to a party of four) each get something different. Mahle House is about 12 km (7 mi) south of Nanaimo. ⊠ 2104 Hemer Rd., at Cedar Rd. (call for directions), ☎ 250/722–3621, WEB www.mahlehouse.com. AE, MC, V. Closed Mon.–Tues. and first 2 wks in Jan. No lunch.

$$–$$$ ✕ **Milano Café and Grill.** Botticelli prints, cherubs, arias on the CD player, and a flower-draped patio bring a little bit of Italy to this 1892 downtown house. The menu lists plenty of pasta options, but the seafood medley with Digby scallops and tiger prawns is a popular choice. ⊠ 247 Milton St., ☎ 250/740–1000. AE, DC, MC, V. Call for Sun. hrs.

$ ✕ **Crow and Gate Neighbourhood Pub.** Set among lawns on a country road south of Nanaimo, this weathered building is probably the most authentic British-style pub in the province. Potpies, ploughmen's lunches, and roast beef with Yorkshire pudding appear on the menu, as do local oysters and both British and British Columbian brews. From Highway 1 between Ladysmith and Nanaimo, follow the signs for Yellow Point Lodge, then the signs for the pub. ⊠ 2313 Yellow Point Rd., Ladysmith, ☎ 250/722–3731. Reservations not accepted. MC, V.

$ ✕ **Gina's.** From the surfboard on the roof to the sequinned sombreros gracing the walls, this bright and cheerful, kid-friendly cantina looks like a beach shack, even if it is on a hill in the center of town. The nachos, burritos, tacos, and quesadillas are fresh, tasty, and on the mild side—they'll spice them up if you like. Reservations are accepted only for groups of six or more. ⊠ 47 Skinner St., ☎ 250/753–5411 AE, DC, MC, V.

$$–$$$ 🛏 **Yellow Point Lodge.** Since the 1930s, this lodge, on 165 waterfront
★ acres south of Nanaimo, has been a kind of adults-only summer camp. Everything's included, from the use of kayaks, bicycles, and tennis courts to the meals and snacks served communally in the dining room (rates are for two people). Accommodations range from comfortable lodge rooms to cozy cottages with bed frames made with logs. In addition, some summer-only cabins share a bathhouse and don't have running water. ⊠ 3700 Yellow Point Rd., Ladysmith V9G 1E8, ☎ 250/245–7422, FAX 250/245–7411, WEB www.yellowpointlodge.com. 9 lodge rooms, 25 rooms, 9 units in shared cabins, 12 private cabins. Dining room, some refrigerators, 2 tennis courts, saltwater pool, outdoor hot tub, massage, sauna, beach, dock, boating, mountain bikes, bad-

minton, boccie, croquet, hiking, horseshoes, Ping-Pong, volleyball, piano, meeting room; no a/c, no room phones, no room TVs, no kids under 14, no smoking. AE, MC, V. AP.

**$$** 🏨 **Best Western Dorchester.** Once Nanaimo's opera house, this nicely restored 1889 downtown hotel overlooks the harbor. Public areas, including a clubby library with wing chairs, retain their original brass fixtures and wood trim. Guest rooms vary in size but are all freshly decorated with rich colors and rosewood furniture. ✉ 70 Church St., V9R 5H4, ☎ 250/754–6835 or 800/661–2449, FAX 250/754–2638, WEB www.dorchesternanaimo.com. 54 rooms, 9 suites. Restaurant, in-room data ports, some refrigerators, cable TV with movies, exercise equipment, lobby lounge, library, shops, dry cleaning, laundry service, business services, meeting rooms, some pets allowed (fee); no a/c in some rooms, no-smoking floors. AE, DC, MC, V.

### Outdoor Activities and Sports
KAYAKING

Kayak rentals and one- to six-day guided sea-kayak expeditions are operated by **Wild Heart Adventure Tours** (✉ 1560 Brebber Rd., ☎ 250/722–3683, WEB www.kayakbc.com). All trips are suitable for beginners.

## Gabriola Island

*3½ nautical mi (20-minute ferry ride) east of Nanaimo.*

You can stay overnight on rustic, rural Gabriola Island, about a 20-minute ferry ride from Nanaimo. The small island, where about 4,000 people live full time, has beaches, parks, campgrounds, several B&Bs, two marinas, three pubs, and a small shopping area near the ferry terminal. A number of artists' studios are open to the public. The island is also known for its prehistoric petroglyphs and delightful coastal rock formations. **BC Ferries** (☎ 250/386–3431; 888/223–3779 in B.C.) runs car and passenger service from Nanaimo.

## Port Alberni

**㉑** *80 km (50 mi) northwest of Nanaimo, 195 km (121 mi) northwest of Victoria.*

Port Alberni, a forest industry town, is a stopover on the way to Ucluelet and Tofino on Vancouver Island's west coast. The salmon-rich waters here attract anglers. The town's old industrial waterfront, at the foot of Argyle Street, has been revitalized into **Alberni Harbour Quay,** an attractive waterfront shopping area, which is also home to the town's train station and the pier for Lady Rose Marine Services. Here you can see the maritime-related exhibits at the **Maritime Discovery Centre** (☎ 250/723–6164), a lighthouse-style building on a pier in the inlet. It's open Friday to Monday noon to 5 in June, and daily 10 to 5 in July and August; admission is by donation. The **Alberni Valley Museum** (✉ 4255 Wallace St., ☎ 250/723–2181, WEB www.alberniheritage.com) displays First Nations cultural exhibits as well as local industrial history and a folk-art collection. It's open daily 10–5, with late hours (until 8) on Thursday. It's closed Sunday from October through April; admission is by donation.

A 1929 Baldwin Steam Locomotive leaves several times a day Thursday through Monday from June 15 to September 2 from the railway station at the foot of Argyle Street for a scenic 35-minute ride to the **McLean Mill National Historic Site** (✉ 5633 Smith Rd., off Beaver Creek Rd., ☎ 250/723–1376, WEB www.alberniheritage.com). The restored 1925 lumber camp and operating steam sawmill includes bunkhouses, a cookhouse, a blacksmith's forge, and much of the original steam-driven sawmill equipment. A theater troupe performs a daily stage show and leads tours through the forested site. There's also a café and gift shop. The mill is open 10–5 daily from June 15 to Labor Day (though with no stage show or mill demonstrations on Tuesday and Wednesday). Admission is $6.50, or $22 including the train trip.

From Port Alberni, you can take a breathtaking 4½-hour trip aboard the *Lady Rose,* a Scottish ship built in 1937, to Bamfield. It's run by **Lady Rose Marine Services** (☎ 250/723–8313; 800/663–7192 reservations Apr.–Sept.; WEB www.ladyrosemarine.com). The boat leaves Argyle Pier at the foot of Argyle St. (⊠ 5425 Argyle St.) at 8 AM Tuesday, Thursday, and Saturday year-round, with additional Friday and Sunday sailings in July and August. The round-trip fare is $45. Or you can take the M. V. *Francis Barkley,* which sails to the Broken Group Islands ($45 round-trip) and Ucluelet ($50). It leaves Argyle Pier at 8 AM Monday, Wednesday, and Friday between early June and late September. The company also operates the rustic **Sechart Whaling Station Lodge** ($135 a night including meals), a kayaking base adjacent to the Broken Group Islands.

About 13 km (8 mi) west of town on Highway 4 is **Sproat Lake Provincial Park,** (☎ 800/689–9025 camping reservations), with swimming, camping, and trails leading to ancient petroglyphs. Sproat Lake is also home to the only two Martin Mars water bombers still in existence. Originally World War II troop carriers, they are now used to fight forest fires.

## Lodging

**$$** ⊞ **Cedar Wood Lodge.** This modern cedar-sided lodge is on 2 acres of gardens on the road to Tofino. The rooms, most of which can sleep four, are decorated in rich greens and burgundies, with attractive art-deco furniture, gas fireplaces, and air-massage tubs. The comfortable lounge has a pool table and leather couches set around a fireplace and French doors opening onto the garden. ⊠ *5895 River Rd. (Hwy. 4), V9Y 6Z5,* ☎ *250/724–6800 or 877/314–6800,* FAX *250/724–6887,* WEB *www.cedarwood.bc.ca. 8 rooms. Fans, in-room data ports, cable TV, billiards, Internet, business services, meeting rooms; no a/c, no smoking. AE, MC, V. CP.*

## Outdoor Activities and Sports

KAYAKING AND CANOEING

**Alberni Outpost** (⊠ 5161 River Rd. [Hwy. 4], ☎ 250/723–2212 or 800/ 325–3921, WEB www.albernioutpost.com) rents kayaks and runs guided day paddles on Sproat Lake and Alberni Inlet.

# Bamfield

㉒ *100 km (62 mi) southwest of Port Alberni by gravel road.*

Bamfield, a remote community of about 300, is one of the last of British Columbia's boardwalk fishing villages. As a base for salmon fishing, boating trips to the Broken Group Islands, and hikes along the West Coast Trail of the Pacific Rim National Park Reserve, the town is well equipped to handle overnight visitors. You can take a boat here from Port Alberni to avoid the logging trucks on the unpaved road.

## Dining and Lodging

**$$$$** ✕⊞ **Eagle Nook Ocean Wilderness Resort.** Accessible only by water
★ taxi, private boat, or floatplane, this luxurious adult-oriented wilderness lodge sits on a narrow strip of land in Barkley Sound. Choose from spacious rooms with balconies and views or self-contained cabins, each with a fireplace and kitchenette. Fine Pacific Northwest cuisine

($$–$$$) is served by the grand stone fireplace in the dining room, or alfresco. Hiking trails lace the woods, and many activities, including fishing, kayaking, and nature cruises, can be prebooked. A two-night minimum stay is required; prices are per person and include meals, the water taxi from Port Alberni, a marine nature tour, and all nonguided activities. ⊠ *120 W. Dayton, Suite B6, Edmonds, WA 98020,* ☎ *425/ 672–7735, 250/723–1000, or 800/760–2777,* FAX *425/771–4518,* WEB *www.wildernessgetaway.com. 23 rooms, 2 cabins. Restaurant, exercise equipment, outdoor hot tub, massage, sauna, dock, boating, fishing, billiards, lounge, library, meeting room, helipad; no a/c, no room phones, no room TVs, no smoking. AE, MC, V. Closed Oct.–May. AP.*

# Ucluelet

**㉓**   *100 km (62 mi) west of Port Alberni, 295 km (183 mi) northwest of Victoria.*

Ucluelet, which in the Nuu-chah-nulth First Nations language means "people with a safe landing place," is, along with Bamfield and Tofino, one of the towns serving the Pacific Rim National Park Reserve. Whale-watching is another main draw, though visitors also come in the off-season to watch the dramatic winter storms that pound the coast here.

Various charter companies take boats to greet the 20,000 gray whales that pass close to Ucluelet on their migration to the Bering Sea every March and April. Some gray whales remain in the area year-round. The **Pacific Rim Whale Festival,** a two-week event (here and in Tofino), welcomes the whales each spring. The Ucluelet Chamber of Commerce (⊠ 100 Main St. [Box 428, V0R 3A0], ☎ 250/726–4641, WEB www. island.net/whalefest) has information.

Ucluelet is the starting point for the **Wild Pacific Trail,** a path that winds along the coast and through the rain forest. Eventually it will link Ucluelet to Long Beach in Pacific Rim National Park Reserve, making it possible to hike, via path and beach, all the way from Ucluelet to Tofino. At press time 13 km (8 mi) of trail in two sections had been completed. A 3-km (2-mi) loop starts at **He-Tin-Kis Park** off Peninsula Road and can also be reached from the **Amphitrite Point Lighthouse** at the end of Coast Guard Road. A 10-km (6-mi) stretch starts at **Big Beach** at the end of Matterson Road.

## Dining and Lodging

$–$$   ✕ **Matterson House.** In a tiny 1931 cottage with seven tables and an outdoor deck in summer, husband-and-wife team Sandy and Jennifer Clark serve up generous portions of seafood, burgers, pasta, and filling standards such as prime rib and veal cutlets. It's simple food, prepared well with fresh local ingredients; everything, including soups, desserts, and the wonderful bread, is homemade. The wine list has local island wines unavailable elsewhere and worth trying. Matterson House is also a good breakfast stop. ⊠ *1682 Peninsula Rd.,* ☎ *250/726–2200. MC, V.*

$$$–$$$$   ☷ **Roots Lodge at Reef Point.** The cabins at this resort on the edge of Ucluelet are set along a boardwalk in the woods overlooking the sea. They are beautifully decorated with leather furniture and rich woodsy colors and have mezzanine bedrooms and fireplaces. Twelve lodge suites are also nicely done, though they lack views. Hiking trails through a nearby park start at the resort's edge. ⊠ *310 Seabridge Way (Box 730, V0R 3A0),* ☎ *250/726–2700 or 888/594–7333,* FAX *250/726– 2701,* WEB *www.livehotels.net. 12 suites, 20 cabins (for 2–6). Some in-room hot tubs, kitchenettes, mountain bikes, some pets allowed (fee); no a/c, no room TVs, no smoking. AE, MC, V. CP in winter.*

**$$$–$$$$**   ⊞ **A Snug Harbour Inn.** Set on a cliff above the Pacific, this couples-oriented B&B have some of the most dramatic views anywhere. The rooms, all with fireplaces, private balconies or decks, whirlpool baths, and ocean views, are decorated in a highly individual style. The Lighthouse room winds up three levels for great views, the Valhalla has a nautical theme, and the Atlantis room is dramatic, with a black Jacuzzi tub for two. Eagles nest nearby, and a staircase leads down to a rocky beach. Two rooms in a separate cottage have forest views, one of which is wheelchair accessible. ✉ *460 Marine Dr. (Box 318, V0R 3A0),* ☎ *250/726–2686 or 888/936–5222,* FAX *250/726–2685,* WEB *www.awesomeview.com. 6 rooms. Outdoor hot tub, some pets allowed; no a/c, no room phones, no room TVs, no kids, no smoking. MC, V. BP.*

**$$$–$$$$**   ⊞ **Tauca Lea by the Sea.** This all-suites family-friendly resort of blue-
★     stained cedar lodges combines a host of facilities with a respect for the natural surroundings. The marina-view Boat Basin restaurant serves excellent Pacific Northwest fare based on fresh, local ingredients—some of it straight from the fishing boats. Handcrafted furniture and terra-cotta tiles decorate the spacious suites, which also have fireplaces and ocean-view decks. A boardwalk around the property leads to a sheltered viewpoint for spotting wildlife across the inlet. A rain forest–theme spa, with yoga and cooking classes, is planned for 2003; kayaking and surfing packages are available. ✉ *1971 Harbour Crescent (Box 1171, V0R 3A0),* ☎ *250/726–4625 or 800/979–9303,* FAX *250/726–4663,* WEB *www.taucalearesort.com. 65 suites. Room service, kitchens, in-room data ports, some in-room hot tubs, cable TV, some in-room VCRs, dock, lounge, shop, baby-sitting, laundry facilities, laundry service, business services, meeting rooms, some pets allowed (fee); no a/c, no smoking. AE, DC, MC, V.*

**$–$$$**   ⊞ **Canadian Princess Fishing Resort.** You can book a cabin in this 230-ft, steam-powered survey ship from 1932. Though hardly opulent, the staterooms are comfortable; each has one to four berths, and all but one share bathrooms. The original captain's cabin has a living room, bedroom, and a private bath with a claw-foot tub. Larger than the ship cabins, shoreside rooms in the resort have private entrances, more-contemporary furnishings, and balconies; a few have fireplaces, and some are large enough to sleep six. Fishing charters and whale-watching can be arranged. The Stewart Dining Room and Lounge is open to nonguests; the specialty is (no surprise) seafood. ✉ *Boat Basin, 1943 Peninsula Rd. (Box 939, V0R 3A0),* ☎ *250/726–7771 or 800/663–7090,* FAX *250/726–7121,* WEB *www.obmg.com. 40 shoreside rooms, 35 shipboard cabins without bath, 1 suite. Restaurant, dock, pub, shop, Internet, meeting rooms; no a/c, no phones in some rooms, no TV in some rooms, no smoking. AE, DC, MC, V. Closed mid-Sept.–mid-Mar.*

## Outdoor Activities and Sports

The **Canadian Princess Fishing Resort** (✉ Boat Basin, 1943 Peninsula Rd., ☎ 250/726–7771 or 800/663–7090) has 10 comfortable fishing and whale-watching boats with heated cabins and bathrooms. The relatively inexpensive charters appeal to groups and families. **Island West Fishing Resort** (✉ foot of Bay St., ☎ 250/726–7515, WEB www. islandwestresort.com) specializes in fishing charters and also has accommodations, an RV park, boat moorage, and floatplane sightseeing tours in the Ucluelet area. **Jamie's Whaling Station** (✉ 168 Fraser La., on waterfront promenade, ☎ 250/726–7444 or 888/470–7444, WEB www.jamies.com) is one of the longest-established whale-watching operators in the area, with offices in Ucluelet and Tofino. A great way to learn about the area's natural history and ecosystems is on a guided walk or hike with **Long Beach Nature** (☎ 250/726–7099, WEB www. oceansedge.bc.ca). Led by a biologist and former chief naturalist at Pacific Rim National Park, half- or full-day outings range from easy to challenging and include hikes through old-growth rain forest, beach and headland hiking, and storm watching during fall and winter. Experienced guides with **Majestic Ocean Kayaking** (☎ 250/726–2868 or 800/889–7644, WEB www.oceankayaking.com) can take you out to explore the clear waters of the Broken Group Islands. **Subtidal Adventures** (☎ 250/726–7336 or 877/444–1134, WEB www.subtidaladventures.com) specializes in whale-watching in spring and nature tours to the Broken Group Islands in summer; there's a choice of a Zodiac (a motorized inflatable boat) or a 36-ft former coast-guard rescue boat.

# Tofino

★ ㉔ *42 km (26 mi) northwest of Ucluelet, 337 km (209 mi) northwest of Victoria.*

The end of the road makes a great stage—and Tofino is certainly that. On a narrow peninsula just beyond the north end of the Pacific Rim National Park Reserve, this is as far west as you can go on Vancouver Island by paved road. One look at the pounding Pacific surf at Chesterman Beach and the old-growth forest along the shoreline convinces many people that they've reached not just the end of the road but the end of the earth.

Tofino's 1,400 or so permanent residents host about a million visitors every year, but they have made what could have been a tourist trap into a funky little town with several art galleries, good restaurants, and plenty of opportunity to get out to the surrounding wilds.

At the **Tofino Botanical Gardens** (☎ 250/725–1220, WEB www.tofinobotanicalgardens.com), trails wind through displays of indigenous plant life. The 12-acre waterfront site about 2 km (1 mi) south of the village on the Pacific Rim Highway is open 9 to dusk daily, and the $10 admission is good for three days. The on-site **Café Pamplona** (open 8 AM–11 PM daily) serves organic produce grown in the gardens.

Boats and floatplanes provide access to the surrounding roadless wilderness. The most popular day trip is to **Hot Spring Cove,** where you can soak in natural rock pools. On **Meares Island,** an easy 20-minute boardwalk trail leads to trees up to 1,600 years old. On **Flores Island,** a challenging five-hour hike called Walk on the Wild Side leads through the old growth. Tofino is a popular destination, and reservations are highly recommended any time of year.

## Dining and Lodging

$$–$$$ ✕ **Café Pamplona.** Herbs and vegetables from the surrounding gardens appear on the menu of this little café, which doubles as the Tofino Botanical Gardens Visitors Centre. Local artwork and lush garden views are the background to a brief menu of well-executed dishes using local, seasonal, organic fare. The chef-owners' philosophy of "convincing simplicity" leads to such creations as wild Pacific salmon with yam and bok choy sauté, roasted chicken breast with handmade gnocchi, and desserts using such local berries as salal. ⊠ *1084 Pacific Rim Hwy. (Hwy. 4)*, ☎ *250/725–1237. AE, MC, V.*

$$–$$$ ✕ **RainCoast Café.** The draws at this intimate central Tofino restaurant include a good selection of vegetarian dishes as well as local seafood creatively prepared using Asian techniques. For starters, consider the salad of baby greens, smoked wild salmon, and goat cheese or the Indonesian sweet potato, peanut, and coconut cream soup. Main courses include sake-roasted halibut with Thai red-curry coconut cream and wild black rice cakes with roasted cashew–ginger sauce. The

decor is minimalist and candlelit, with peekaboo sea views. ✉ *101–120 4th St.,* ☎ *250/725–2215. AE, MC, V. No lunch.*

**$$-$$$** ✕ **The Schooner on Second.** You can't miss this 1940s red-clapboard building in central Tofino—it's the one with the schooner sticking out the back; the bow of the boat takes up a chunk of the cozy rooms. The seafood-oriented menu changes frequently, but try, if it's available, the halibut Bawden Bay, which is a halibut fillet stuffed with Brie, crab, and shrimp in an apple-brandy sauce. The Schooner is also popular with locals and tourists alike for its hearty breakfasts and its lunchtime sandwiches, burgers, and pastas. ✉ *331 Campbell St.,* ☎ *250/725–3444. AE, MC, V.*

**$$$$** ✕⊞ **The Wickaninnish Inn.** Set on a rocky promontory above Chesterman Beach with open ocean on three sides and old-growth forest as a
★ backdrop, this three-story weathered-cedar building is a comfortable place to enjoy the area's dramatic scenery. Every room has an ocean view, balcony, fireplace, and soaking tub; the Ancient Cedars Spa (also open to nonguests) adds to the pampering. The glass-enclosed Pointe Restaurant ($$$$) has views of the crashing surf and is renowned for its Pacific Northwest cuisine; the kitchen makes the most of such local delicacies as oysters, gooseneck barnacles, wild mushrooms, Dungeness crab, and Pacific salmon. ✉ *Osprey La., at Chesterman Beach (Box 250, V0R 2Z0),* ☎ *250/725–3100 or 800/333–4604,* ℻ *250/725–3110,* ⎘ *www.wickinn.com. 46 rooms. Restaurant, room service, in-room data ports, minibars, microwaves, cable TV, steam room, beach, lounge, dry cleaning, laundry service, Internet, business services, meeting rooms, some pets allowed (fee); no a/c, no smoking. AE, DC, MC, V.*

**$$$-$$$$** ✕⊞ **Long Beach Lodge.** Dramatic First Nations art, a tall granite fire-
★ place, and expansive views of the crashing surf define the striking great room at Tofino's newest luxury lodge, which overlooks the long stretch of sand at Cox Beach. Throughout the lodge are handcrafted furniture, exposed fir beams, soothing earth tones, and such artful details as handwoven-kelp amenities baskets. The chef seeks out fresh, local, organic ingredients for her daily multicourse menus ($$–$$$), for the shared plates served in the great room, and even in the picnic lunches. A spa and self-contained cabins are planned for 2003. ✉ *1441 Pacific Rim Hwy. (Box 897, V0R 2Z0),* ☎ *250/725–2442 or 877/844–7873,* ℻ *250/725–2402,* ⎘ *www.LongBeachLodgeResort.com. 43 rooms. Restaurant, in-room data ports, refrigerators, cable TV, some in-room VCRs, lounge, shop, Internet, meeting room, some pets allowed (fee); no a/c, no smoking. AE, MC, V. CP.*

**$$-$$$** ✕⊞ **Inn at Tough City.** Vintage advertising paraphernalia and First Nations art create a fun and funky look at this harborside inn. The name is derived from Tofino's old nickname, from the days before roads, when life was rough here. It certainly isn't anymore: the guest rooms have bold colors, stained-glass windows, hardwood floors, antiques, covered decks or balconies, and down duvets. Several have striking views over Tofino Harbour and Clayoquot Sound; others have fireplaces and soaking tubs. The hotel's Japanese restaurant, Tough City Sushi ($–$$$), uses fresh seafood from local waters. ✉ *350 Main St. (Box 8, V0R 2Z0),* ☎ *250/725–2021 or 877/725–2021,* ℻ *250/725–2088,* ⎘ *www.toughcity.com. 8 rooms. Restaurant, cable TV, shop, some pets allowed (fee); no a/c, no smoking. AE, MC, V.*

**$$$$** ⊞ **Clayoquot Wilderness Resorts.** This two-part wilderness retreat includes a floating lodge moored next to old-growth forest and high-style camping at the Wilderness Outpost, fashioned after the Rockefellers' summer camp. Lodge rooms have water views, and the restaurant serves Pacific Northwest cuisine. The outpost has a hot tub and a sauna, cuisine served on china and crystal, luxurious tents with Persian-style carpets, Adirondack furniture, gas stoves, and water-view porches. Activities, including canoeing, kayaking, horseback riding, mountain biking, hiking, and fishing, are all included at the Outpost; some are extra at the lodge. A two-night minimum stay applies for both. ⊠ *Box 130, V0R 2Z0,* ☎ *250/726–8235 or 888/333–5405,* FAX *250/726– 8558,* WEB *www.wildretreat.com. 16 rooms, 10 tents. Lodge: restaurant, room service, fans, gym, outdoor hot tub, sauna, spa, dock, boating, fishing, mountain bikes, hiking, horseback riding, lounge. library, shop, children's program (ages 3–18), Internet, business services, meeting rooms; no a/c, no room phones, no room TVs, no smoking. AE, MC, V. Closed Nov.–Apr. AP.*

$$–$$$$   🏨 **Middle Beach Lodge.** This longtime favorite, set on a bluff over a
★    mile of private beach, has several options: serene, adults-only phone- and TV-free rooms in the Lodge at the Beach; ocean-view rooms and suites, most with kitchenettes, at the Headlands; and self-contained cabins suitable for families. The decor throughout defines West Coast rustic elegance, with recycled timbers, woodsy colors, and a smattering of antiques. Each lodge has an expansive common room with a floor-to-ceiling stone fireplace and far-reaching ocean views. In July and August dinner is available every night; the rest of the year it's served only on Saturday. ⊠ *400 MacKenzie Beach Rd. (Box 100, V0R 2Z0),* ☎ *250/725–2900,* FAX *250/725–2901,* WEB *www.middlebeach.com. 64 rooms, 10 suites, 19 cabins. Dining room, some in-room data ports, some in-room hot tubs, some kitchenettes, cable TV, some in-room VCRs, gym, Ping-Pong, baby-sitting, laundry facilities, laundry service, Internet, business services, meeting rooms; no a/c, no phones in some rooms, no TV in some rooms, no smoking. AE, MC, V. CP.*

$$$   🏨 **Chesterman Beach Bed and Breakfast.** The front yard of this rustic cedar and driftwood B&B is the wide beach and rolling ocean surf. The self-contained two-bedroom suite in the main house and the Lookout room are both romantic and cozy; the former has a sauna, gas fireplace, and a kitchen, and the latter has a gas fireplace and a private ocean-view balcony. The self-sufficient one-bedroom Garden Cottage has a secluded garden, a large deck, a kitchen, and a fireplace and is a good option for families. ⊠ *1345 Chesterman Beach Rd. (Box 72, V0R 2Z0),* ☎ *250/ 725–3726,* FAX *250/725–3706,* WEB *www.chestermanbeach.net. 1 room, 1 suite, 1 cottage. Some kitchens, microwaves, refrigerators, Internet; no a/c, no room phones, no room TVs, no smoking. MC, V. CP.*

$$   🏨 **Red Crow Guest House.** On the sheltered side of the Tofino peninsula, just south of the village, this Cape Cod–style house sits amid 17 acres of forest. Two rooms beneath the main part of the house open onto a covered veranda and a private pebble beach, providing stunning views over island-dotted Clayoquot Sound. Decorated with family heirlooms and First Nations art, each of the large, comfortable rooms has a king bed and a fireplace. A lavish breakfast can be delivered to your door for an extra $15. A cedar cottage in the woods has a full kitchen and sleeps six. ⊠ *1084 Pacific Rim Hwy. (Box 37, V0R 2Z0),* ☎ FAX *250/725–2275,* WEB *www.tofinoredcrow.com. 2 rooms, 1 cottage. Refrigerators, boating, laundry facilities; no a/c, no room phones, no room TVs, no smoking. MC, V.*

$   🏨 **Whalers on the Point Guesthouse.** With its hardwood floors, har-
★    bor-view picture windows, and big stone fireplace, this modern seaside hostel looks more like an upscale lodge than a backpackers' haven. It also has pretty much everything a budget traveler could want: a game room and TV lounge; a shared kitchen, living room, dining room, and deck overlooking the bay; even surfboard storage. Accommodation is available in private rooms with shared bathrooms, family rooms (for four) with private bathrooms, and four-bed dorms. Advance reservations are highly recommended. ⊠ *81 West St. (Box 296, V0R 2Z0),* ☎ *250/725–3443,* FAX *250/725–3463,* WEB *www.tofinohostel.com. 7*

*rooms, 11 dorms. Sauna, billiards, recreation room, laundry facilities, Internet; no a/c, no room phones, no room TVs, no smoking. MC, V.*

## Outdoor Activities and Sports

### FISHING

**Chinook Charters** (✉ 450 Campbell St., ☎ 250/725–3431) leads fishing charters into Clayoquot Sound and to nearby lakes and streams; they catch salmon, halibut and trout. **Weigh West Marine Resort** (☎ 250/725–3277 or 800/665–8922, WEB www.weighwest.com) conducts fishing charters, including saltwater fly-fishing. The outfitter can arrange complete packages including accommodations, meals, and guides.

### FLIGHTSEEING

**Tofino Air** (✉ ☎ 250/725–4454 or 866/486–3247) runs 20-minute flightseeing tours over outlying forests and beaches, flights to Hot Springs Cove, and trips to the lakes and glaciers of Strathcona Provincial Park.

### KAYAKING

**Remote Passages** (✉ 71 Wharf St., ☎ 250/725–3330 or 800/666–9833, WEB www.remotepassages.com) has easy guided paddles in sheltered waters; no experience is necessary. **Tofino Sea-Kayaking Company** (✉ 320 Main St., ☎ 250/725–4222 or 800/863–4664, WEB www.tofino-kayaking.com) rents kayaks and runs a kayaking school and multiday wilderness kayaking trips.

### SURFING

Tofino, despite the chilling waters, is a popular place to surf. **Inner Rhythm Surf Camp** (✉ ☎ 250/726–2211 or 877/393–7873, WEB www.innerrhythm.net) has lessons, rentals, surf camps, and surf tours to remote beaches. **Storm, the Tofino Surf Shop** (✉ ☎ 250/725–2155 or 888/777–9961, WEB www.pacificsurfschool.com) rents gear and runs the Pacific Surf School, which provides surfing lessons at all levels. **Surf Sister** (☎ 250/725–4456 or 877/724–7873, WEB www.surfsister.com) teaches women-only and coed surfing lessons.

### WHALE-WATCHING AND MARINE EXCURSIONS

In March and April, gray whales migrate along the coast here; resident grays can be seen anytime between May and November. In addition, humpback whales, sea otters, orca, bears, and other wildlife are increasingly seen in the area. Most whale-watching operators lead excursions along the coast and to the region's outlying islands, including Meares Island, Flores Island, and Hot Springs Cove. Services range from no-frills water-taxi drop-off to tours with experienced guides; prices vary accordingly.

**Jamie's Whaling Station** (✉ 606 Campbell St., ☎ 250/725–3919; 800/667–9913 in Canada; WEB www.jamies.com) is one of the most established whale-watching operators on the coast. It has both Zodiacs and more comfortable 65-ft tour boats. **Remote Passages Marine Excursions** (✉ 71 Wharf St., ☎ 250/725–3330 or 800/666–9833, WEB www.remotepassages.com), a well-established operator, runs whale-watching, bear-watching, and other wildlife-viewing trips with an ecological and educational focus using both Zodiacs and covered boats. **Sea Trek Tours and Expeditions** (☎ 250/725–4412 or 800/811–9155, WEB www.seatrektours.bc.ca) operates whale- and bear-watching and harbor tours as well as day trips to Hot Springs Cove and Meares Island. The **Whale Centre** (✉ 411 Campbell St., ☎ 250/725–2132 or 888/474–2288, WEB www.tofinowhalecentre.com) has a maritime museum with a 40-ft whale skeleton you can study while waiting for your boat.

## Shopping

In a traditional longhouse, the magnificent **Eagle Aerie Gallery** (✉ 350 Campbell St., ☎ 250/725–3235) houses a collection of prints, paintings, and carvings by the renowned artist Roy Henry Vickers. **House of Himwitsa** (✉ 300 Main St., ☎ 250/725–2017 or 800/899–1947) sells First Nations crafts, jewelry, and clothing. The complex also has a seafood restaurant and lodge rooms. **Islandfolk Gallery** (✉ 120 4th St., ☎ 250/725–3130) sells the work of Tofino wildlife and landscape artist Mark Hobson and other Vancouver Island artists. Photographs, paintings, carvings, pottery, and jewelry by local artists are available at **Reflecting Spirit Gallery** (✉ 411 Campbell St., ☎ 250/725–2472). The **Village Gallery** (✉ 321 Main St., ☎ 250/725–4229) sells affordable, locally made jewelry, pottery, and other crafts items. **Wildside Booksellers** (✉ 320 Main St., ☎ 250/725–4222) has an extensive selection of books and kites and houses an espresso bar.

## Pacific Rim National Park Reserve

★ ㉕   *105 km (63 mi) west of Port Alberni, 9 km (5 mi) south of Tofino.*

This national park has some of Canada's most stunning coastal and rain-forest scenery, abundant wildlife, and a unique marine environment. It comprises three separate areas—Long Beach, the Broken Group Islands, and the West Coast Trail—for a combined area of 123,431 acres, and stretches 130 km (81 mi) along Vancouver Island's west coast. The **Park Information Centre** (✉ 2 km [1 mi] north of the Tofino–Ucluelet junction on Hwy. 4, ☎ 250/726–4212) is open daily mid-June to mid-September, 9:30–5. Park-use fees apply in all sections of the park.

The **Long Beach** unit gets its name from a 16-km (10-mi) strip of hard-packed sand strewn with driftwood, shells, and the occasional Japanese glass fishing float. Long Beach is the most accessible part of the park and can get busy in summer. People come in the off-season to watch winter storms and to see migrating whales in early spring. An $8 daily group pass, or $3 for two hours, available from dispensers in the parking lots, is required for each private vehicle and includes admission to the Wickaninnish Interpretive Centre. You can camp at Long Beach at the **Green Point Campground**; it's off Highway 4 just north of the Tofino-Ucluelet junction. Walk-in sites are issued on a first-come, first-served basis and fill quickly. Drive-in sites (with no RV hookups) can be reserved by calling 800/689–9025, or through WEB www.discovercamping.ca. A theater at the campground runs films and interpretive programs about park ecology and history; park information centers have schedules.

A first stop for many Pacific Rim National Park visitors, the **Wickaninnish Interpretive Centre** (✉ Hwy. 4, ☎ 250/726–4701 center; 250/726–7706 restaurant) is on the ocean edge about 16 km (10 mi) north of Ucluelet. It's a great place to learn about the wilderness; theater programs and exhibits provide information about the park's marine ecology and rain-forest environment. Open daily mid-March to mid-October, 10:30–6, the center is also a good lunch stop—it was originally an inn, and its restaurant still serves up hearty seafood lunches and dinners (until 9 PM). Park information is available here when the Park Information Centre is closed.

The 100-plus islands of the **Broken Group Islands** can be reached only by boat. Many commercial charter tours are available from Ucluelet, at the southern end of Long Beach, and from Tofino, Bamfield, and Port Alberni. The islands and their waters are alive with sea lions, seals, and whales. The inner waters are good for kayaking.

The third element of the park, the **West Coast Trail**, runs along the coast from Bamfield to Port Renfrew. This extremely rugged 75-km

(47-mi) trail is for experienced hikers. It can be traveled only on foot, takes an average of six days to complete, and is open May through September. The park controls the number of people allowed on the trail, and reservations are required if you plan to hike between mid-June and mid-September; it's first-come, first-served the rest of the time. A number of fees apply: $25 for a reservation, $70 in park-use fees, and $25 in ferry fares. Reservations can be made up to three months in advance via Hello B.C. (☎ 800/435–5622) from March through September. ✉ *Box 280, Ucluelet V0R 3A0,* ☎ *250/726–7721,* FAX *250/726–4720,* WEB *parkscan.harbour.com/pacrim.*

# Parksville

**㉖** *47 km (29 mi) east of Port Alberni, 38 km (24 mi) northwest of Nanaimo, 72 km (45 mi) southeast of Courtenay, 154 km (95 mi) north of Victoria.*

The resort and retirement town of Parksville marks the start of the Oceanside Route, or Highway 19A, which winds along the coast to Courtenay, past sandy beaches, fish-and-chips shops, and family holiday resorts. Travelers in a hurry can travel north on the faster, newer Inland Highway (Hwy. 19).

Forest trails lead to thundering waterfalls at **Englishman River Falls Provincial Park** (✉ Errington Rd., Exit 51 off Hwy. 19), 13 km (8 mi) southwest of Parksville. In **Rathtrevor Beach Provincial Park** (✉ off Hwy. 19A), 2 km (1 mi) south of Parksville, high tide brings ashore the warmest ocean water in British Columbia.

OFF THE BEATEN PATH **COOMBS –** If you're traveling from Parksville to Port Alberni, it's worth taking the quieter Highway 4A past this odd little village, best known for the goats grazing on the grass-covered roof of its Old Country Market. Worth a stop is **Butterfly World** (✉ 1080 Winchester Rd. [Hwy. 4A], ☎ 250/248–7026), where you can wander through an atrium filled with hundreds of free-flying butterflies. It's open March and October, daily 10–4 and April–September, daily 10–5. Admission is $6.50.

## Lodging

$$–$$$ 🏨 **Tigh-Na-Mara Resort and Conference Centre.** This resort on 22 forested seaside acres attracts families to its long, sandy beachfront. The warm water and wide tidal flats are just right for the bucket-and-spade brigade, as are the playgrounds, playhouse, and extensive summertime children's programs. A full-service spa and a Pacific Northwest restaurant make this a good romantic getaway, too. At the log-construction lodge high over the water, all units have fireplaces and decks with ocean views. There's also a more basic inland lodge and several one- and two-bedroom cabins in the woods. ✉ *1095 E. Island Hwy. (Hwy. 19A), V9P 2E5,* ☎ *250/248–2072 or 800/663–7373,* FAX *250/ 248–4140,* WEB *www.tigh-na-mara.com. 88 rooms, 72 suites, 33 cabins. In-room data ports, some kitchens, cable TV, refrigerators, tennis court, indoor pool, gym, hot tub, massage, steam room, boating, bicycles, horseshoes, Ping-Pong, volleyball, lounge, shop, baby-sitting, children's programs (ages 4–12), dry cleaning, laundry facilities, laundry service, business services, meeting rooms, some pets allowed (Sept.– June only, fee); no-smoking floors. AE, DC, MC, V.*

## Outdoor Activities and Sports

With six ocean- and mountain-view courses in the area, Parksville is a major year-round golf destination. **Fairwinds Golf & Country Club** (✉ 3730 Fairwinds Dr., Nanoose Bay, ☎ 250/468–7666 or 888/781–

2777, WEB www.fairwinds.bc.ca) is a par-71, 18-hole course. **Morningstar Golf Course** (⊠ 525 Lowry's Rd., ☎ 250/248–8161 or 800/567–1320, WEB www.morningstar.bc.ca) is a par-72, 18-hole course.

*En Route*     The peaks and watersheds inland from Qualicum Beach and Parksville create an environment so distinct the area has been declared a U.N. Biosphere Reserve (the Mount Arrowsmith Biosphere Reserve). Two provincial parks, both along Highway 4 en route to Port Alberni and the west coast, provide a taste of this unique ecosystem. At **Little Qualicum Falls Provincial Park** (☎ 800/689–9025 for camping reservations), 15 km (9 mi) west of Qualicum Beach, trails and waterfalls lace the woods. At **Cathedral Grove** in MacMillan Provincial Park, 20 km (12 mi) west of Qualicum Beach, walking trails lead past Douglas fir trees and western red cedars, some as many as 800 years old. Their remarkable height creates a spiritual effect, as though you were gazing at a cathedral ceiling.

## Qualicum Beach

㉗    *10 km (6 mi) north of Parksville.*

Qualicum Beach's long stretch of sand has attracted vacationers for more than a century. The pedestrian-friendly village, on a hill above the sea, is full of interesting independent shops and cafés. From Qualicum Beach, Highway 4 travels to the island's west coast.

The **Old School House Arts Centre** (⊠ 122 Fern Rd. W, ☎ 250/752–6133) shows and sells the work of local artists. At **Milner Gardens and Woodland** (⊠ 2179 W. Island Hwy. [Hwy. 19A], ☎ 250/752–6153, WEB milnergardens.mala.bc.ca), a 1930s tea plantation–style house and 10 acres of gardens, surrounded by woodlands, are set on a bluff above the sea. The gardens are open Thursday to Sunday, April to October; admission is $10 and reservations are recommended.

Guided and self-guided spelunking tours for all levels are conducted April through October at **Horne Lake Caves Provincial Park** (☎ 250/248–7829; 250/757–8687 tour reservations; WEB www.hornelake.com). Prices start at $15 for a 1½-hour family-oriented tour; reservations are recommended. There's also a campsite at the park. The park turnoff is about 11 km (7 mi) north of Qualicum Beach off Highway 19 or 19A. From the turnoff, the park is another 13 km (8 mi) along a gravel road.

### Dining and Lodging

$–$$    ✕ **The Beach House Restaurant.** European, Asian, and Canadian dishes highlight this casual seaside restaurant, where spaetzle and schnitzel share menu space with Thai satay and West Coast bouillabaisse. A local favorite, though, is roast duckling in blackberry sauce. Sandwiches, burgers, pasta, and pizza fill the lunch menu. Both the beachfront deck and the country-look tiered interior have ocean views. ⊠ *2775 W. Island Hwy. (Hwy. 19A),* ☎ *250/752–9626. MC, V.*

$    ✕ **The Cola Diner.** A 1953 jukebox, one of Elvis Presley's original gold records, and vintage Coke ads are just some of the 20th-century memorabilia displayed at this homage to 1950s burger bars. The food is the real thing, too: made-from-scratch burgers, home-cut fries, and shakes whipped up the old-fashioned way. The diner is open for breakfast, too. Once a month, the diner hosts a swing dance in the hall next door. ⊠ *6060 W. Island Hwy. (Hwy. 19A), Qualicum Bay (11 km [7 mi] north of Qualicum Beach),* ☎ *250/757–2029,* WEB *www.colaland.com. Reservations not accepted. MC, V. Closed Tues. and Jan.*

$$    🏠 **Hollyford Bed & Breakfast.** A sunny atrium runs the length of this 1924 Craftsman-style cottage, where hosts Jim and Marjorie Ford go

out of their way to pamper guests, from morning wake-up trays to evening sherry and homemade chocolates. Two of the rooms have pretty floral decor, and a third has Arts and Crafts furniture and a Celtic feel; all have patios, fireplaces, and private entrances. Breakfast, served on silver and crystal, includes home-baked bread and scones. ✉ *106 Hoylake Rd. E (off Hwy. 4), V9K 1L7,* ☎ *250/752–8101 or 877/224–6559,* FAX *250/752–8102,* WEB *www.hollyford.ca. 3 rooms. Fans, cable TV, in-room VCRs; no a/c, no kids under 12, no smoking. MC, V. BP.*

*En Route* Between Qualicum Beach and the twin cities of Courtenay and Comox is tiny Buckley Bay, where BC Ferries leave for **Denman Island,** with connecting service to **Hornby Island.** Both these pretty rural islands have crafts shops, cafés, walking trails, and accommodations. Hornby is best known for its long, sandy beaches.

# Courtenay

❷❽ *220 km (136 mi) northwest of Victoria, 17 nautical mi west of Powell River, 57 km (34 mi) northwest of Qualicum Beach.*

This friendly town makes a good base to enjoy the area's wealth of outdoor activities, including golf, hiking, and skiing at nearby Mount Washington Alpine Resort. Ferries to Powell River on the mainland sail from Little River, 6 km (4 mi) north of Courtenay.

Dinosaur fans should love the **Courtenay and District Museum and Paleontology Centre** (✉ 207 4th St., ☎ 250/334–0686, WEB www.courtenaymuseum.ca), one of British Columbia's leading paleontology centers. It's home to the reconstructed skeleton of a 43-ft elasmosaur—a dinosaur-era sea creature found in the Comox Valley. It also has some interesting First Nations and pioneer artifacts and arranges fossil-hunting day trips in the area. Admission is $3. The museum is open daily 10–5 June through August and, during the other months, Tuesday through Saturday 10–5.

OFF THE BEATEN PATH
**COMOX –** East of Courtenay about 6 km (4 mi) is the twin town of Comox, which also serves as a base for Mt. Washington skiers. It's best known as the home to Canadian Forces Base Comox, an air force base.

At the **Filberg Heritage Lodge and Park** (✉ 61 Filberg Rd., ☎ 250/339–2715), you can stroll around 9 acres of beautifully landscaped waterfront grounds and tour the rustic 1929 lodge. The lodge is open 11–5 daily June through August, weekends in May and September. In summer, a separate petting zoo and seaside teahouse are also open. Admission to the gardens, which are open 8 AM to dusk all year, is free; lodge admission is $2.

The **Comox Air Force Museum** (✉ ☎ 250/339–8162), at Canadian Forces Base Comox in Lazo, about 1 km (½ mi) north of Comox, has an interesting collection of air-force memorabilia and historic aircraft in the nearby airpark. The museum is open daily 10–4. The airpark is open daily 10–4 June through September only. Admission is by donation.

## Dining and Lodging

$–$$$ ✕ **Old House Restaurant.** This riverside restaurant set among gardens
★ (though also overlooking a pulp mill across the way) provides casual dining in a restored 1938 house with cedar beams, four stone fireplaces, and a patio for dining. People flock here for the West Coast home-style cuisine—sandwiches and salads at lunch; seafood, steaks, and pastas, along with fancier, more innovative dishes (prawn-and-scallop stir-fry,

Fanny Bay oysters) at dinner—and the fresh daily specials. ⊠ *1760 Riverside La.,* ☎ *250/338–5406. AE, DC, MC, V.*

**$–$$**   ✕ **The Atlas Café.** A vintage map of South America and rich pomegranate walls lend an exotic feel to this casual town-center café and local gathering place. The wholesome menu appeals to a globe-trotting clientele: nori rolls, falafel, chicken satay, Greek spinach pie, and vegan dishes appear along with herb teas, microbrews, martinis, and fresh juices. The Atlas is a popular breakfast stop, too. Reservations are accepted only for groups of six or more. ⊠ *250 6th St.,* ☎ *250/338–9838. MC, V. No dinner Mon.*

**$$–$$$$**   ⊞ **Kingfisher Oceanside Resort and Spa.** Soothing is the word to de-
★   scribe this seaside resort about 7 km (4½ mi) south of Courtenay. Thirty-six beachfront suites—all with decks or patios, kitchenettes, gas fireplaces, and expansive ocean views—are decorated in soft sea blues and greens. A full-service spa and health club, also open to nonguests, provides beauty treatments, aromatherapy, hydrotherapy, yoga, nature walks, and massage. The steam room looks like a mermaid's cave, and the gym has an ocean view. The original, lower-price rooms, set a little farther back from the water, are also modern and spacious, and some have kitchens. ⊠ *4330 Island Hwy. S, V9N 9R9,* ☎ *250/338–1323 or 800/663–7929,* FAX *250/338–0058,* WEB *www.kingfisherspa.com. 28 rooms, 36 suites. Restaurant, room service, fans, in-room data ports, some kitchens, some kitchenettes, refrigerators, cable TV, some in-room VCRs, tennis court, indoor-outdoor pool, outdoor hot tub, sauna, steam room, mountain bikes, boccie, croquet, lounge, shop, baby-sitting, dry cleaning, laundry facilities, laundry service, business services, meeting rooms, some pets allowed (fee); no a/c, no smoking. AE, D, DC, MC, V.*

**$**   ⊞ **Greystone Manor.** About 3 km (2 mi) south of Courtenay, this 1918 house has a lovingly tended 1½-acre English garden and views over Comox Bay, where seals are often visible. Inside, the original hardwood floors, period furnishings, and a woodstove make things cozy. Two of the prettily decorated rooms have baths with showers; the third has a claw-foot tub in a room across the hall. The hosts, Mike and Maureen Shipton, from Bath, England, serve a full hot breakfast, which is included in the rates. ⊠ *4014 Haas Rd., V9N 9T4,* ☎ *250/338–1422,* WEB *www.greystonemanorbb.com. 3 rooms. Piano; no a/c, no room phones, no room TVs, no kids under 12, no smoking. MC, V. BP.*

## Outdoor Activities and Sports

GOLF

The 18-hole, par-72 course at the **Crown Isle Resort & Golf Community** (⊠ 399 Clubhouse Dr., off Ryan Rd., ☎ 250/703–5050 or 888/338–8439, WEB www.crownisle.com) is, at 7,024 yards, the longest course on Vancouver Island. The resort also has on-site accommodation and a lavish clubhouse. It's one of several courses in the area.

SKIING

**Mt. Washington Alpine Resort** (☎ 250/338–1386; 888/231–1499 lodging reservations), 30 km (18 mi) from Courtenay via Strathcona Parkway, has 50 downhill runs, a 1,657-ft vertical drop, five chairlifts, three surface lifts, and an elevation of 5,200 ft; it's the island's largest ski area. The resort also has 55 km (33 mi) of track-set cross-country trails, two snowboard parks, a half pipe (for snowboarding), snow-tubing chutes, and, in summer, miles of hiking and mountain-bike trails accessible by chairlift, as well as a disc golf course and horseback riding. The resort has a good selection of restaurants, shops, and hotel and B&B accommodations.

# Campbell River

**㉙** *50 km (31 mi) north of Courtenay, 155 km (96 mi) northwest of Nanaimo, 270 km (167 mi) northwest of Victoria.*

Campbell River draws people who want to fish; some of the biggest salmon ever caught on a line have been landed just off the coast here. Cutthroat trout are also plentiful in the river.

On a hill overlooking the sea, the **Museum at Campbell River** (✉ 470 Island Hwy., ☎ 250/287–3103, WEB www.crmuseum.ca) has great views, an excellent collection of First Nations artifacts, and some intriguing historical exhibits, including a re-created pioneer cabin and floathouse, and a dramatic audiovisual retelling of a First Nations legend. It's open mid-May–September, Monday–Saturday 10–5, Sunday noon–5, and October–mid-May, Tuesday–Sunday noon–5; admission for adults is $5.

The primary access to Strathcona Provincial Park is on Highway 28 west of town. Other recreational activities include kayaking, whale-watching, and diving in **Discovery Passage**, where a battleship was sunk for diving purposes. For information, contact the **Campbell River Visitor Information Centre** (✉ 1235 Shoppers Row [Box 400, V9W 5B6], ☎ 250/287 1636 or 800/463 4386).

**Haig-Brown House Education Centre** (✉ 2250 Campbell River Rd., ☎ 250/286–6646, WEB www.haig-brown.bc.ca), the preserved home of conservationist and writer Roderick Haig-Brown, is set in a riverside garden surrounded by 20 acres of trail-laced woods. The center runs seminars and workshops on topics ranging from conservation to writing and also has B&B rooms. Tours of the house are given June through August, at 1:30 daily, and by special arrangement during the rest of the year. Admission is by donation.

## Dining and Lodging

**$$-$$$$** ✕🏨 **Painter's Lodge.** Bob Hope, John Wayne, and their fishing buddies came to this waterfront lodge to catch big salmon in the 1940s and '50s. The attractive cedar complex (a newer building on the same site) still draws anglers; the resort's own fleet runs guided fishing and nature cruises. The rooms, suites, and one- to three-bedroom cabins all have balconies or patios, and some have kitchens, fireplaces, and whirlpool baths. Legends, the resort's ocean-view restaurant ($$–$$$), serves fresh seafood, and a free water taxi runs to Painters' sister property, April Point Lodge on Quadra Island, where you can dine, kayak, or explore biking and hiking trails. *✉ 1625 McDonald Rd. (Box 460, V9W 5C1), ☎ 250/286–1102 or 800/663–7090, FAX 250/598–1361, WEB www.obmg.com. 87 rooms, 3 suites, 4 cabins. Restaurant, picnic area, fans, in-room data ports, some kitchenettes, cable TV, 2 tennis courts, pool, exercise equipment, 2 outdoor hot tubs, billiards, lounge, pub, shop, baby-sitting, playground, laundry service, business services, meeting rooms, airport shuttle; no a/c. AE, D, DC, MC, V. Closed mid-Oct.–mid-Mar.*

## Outdoor Activities and Sports

**Storey Creek Golf Club** (✉ 300 McGimpsey Rd., ☎ 250/923–3673) is an 18-hole, par-72 course 15 minutes south of Campbell River.

## Shopping

Housed in a modern longhouse-style building, the **Wei Wai Kum House of Treasures** (✉ 1370 Island Hwy. [in Discovery Harbour Centre mall], ☎ 250/286–1440) has an excellent collection of local First Nations masks, jewelry, and artwork. Dance troupes perform here in the summertime.

# Quadra Island

**㉚** *10 minutes by ferry from Campbell River.*

Quadra is a thickly forested island, rich with wildlife and laced with hiking trails. The **Kwagiulth Museum and Cultural Centre** (✉ 34 Weway Rd., Cape Mudge Village, ☎ 250/285–3733) houses a collection of potlatch (ceremonial feast) regalia and historical photos. The museum was closed for renovations at press time but is expected to reopen by the summer of 2003.

## Dining and Lodging

**$$** ✕☷ **Tsa-Kwa-Luten Lodge.** Set on a bluff amid 1,100 acres of forest, this lodge, operated by the Cape Mudge First Nations band, has a foyer built in the style of a longhouse and comfortable rooms with Kwagiulth art and balconies with ocean views. Three two-bedroom beachfront cottages have gas fireplaces, whirlpool tubs, kitchenettes, and private verandas. A four-bedroom guest house is great for groups. You can visit nearby petroglyphs, kayak, bike, hike, fish, dive, snorkel, take a whale- or bear-watching cruise, and even try archery here. The restaurant ($$–$$$) serves traditional Kwagiulth cuisine—such as venison stew, clam fritters, and a breakfast dish of salmon-and-potato hash. ✉ *Lighthouse Rd. (Box 460, Quathiaski Cove V0P 1N0),* ☎ *250/285–2042 or 800/665–7745,* FAX *250/285–2532,* WEB *www.capemudgeresort.bc.ca. 30 rooms, 4 cottages. Restaurant, room service, some kitchenettes, gym, outdoor hot tub, massage, sauna, boating, mountain bikes, boccie, lounge, shop, laundry service, Internet, business services, meeting rooms; no a/c, no room TVs, no-smoking floors. AE, DC, MC, V. Closed Oct.–May.*

**$$$** ☷ **April Point Resort.** Spread across a point and surrounded by forest, this 15-acre family-oriented ecotourism resort provides whale and bear-watching, kayaking, ocean fishing, hiking, and biking. There are also scooter rentals and even a giant outdoor chess set. Pine furniture and forest green fabric enrich the roomy lodge rooms and suites. Many have rooms have fireplaces, and the three- and four-bedroom guest houses have kitchens, fireplaces, and sundecks. You have access, via free water taxi, to the tennis courts, pool, and hot tubs at Painters Lodge in Campbell River; the same water taxi makes it easy to reach April Point from Vancouver Island. ✉ *900 April Point Rd. (Box 248, Campbell River V9W 4Z9)* ☎ *250/285–2222 or 800/663–7090,* FAX *250/285–2761,* WEB *www.obmg.com. 24 rooms, 25 suites, 7 guest houses. Restaurant, picnic area, fans, some kitchenettes, some refrigerators, cable TV, boating, marina, mountain bikes, boccie, croquet, lounge, pub, shop, baby-sitting, laundry facilities, laundry service, Internet, business services, meeting rooms, helipad, some pets allowed; no room phones, no smoking. AE, DC, MC, V. Closed Oct.–Apr.*

# Strathcona Provincial Park

★ **㉛** *40 km (25 mi) west of Campbell River.*

The largest provincial park on Vancouver Island, Strathcona Provincial Park encompasses **Mt. Golden Hinde,** at 7,220 ft the island's highest mountain, and **Della Falls,** one of Canada's highest waterfalls, reaching 1,440 ft. This strikingly scenic wilderness park's lakes and 161 campsites attract summer canoeists, hikers, anglers, and campers. The main access is by Highway 28 from Campbell River; Mt. Washington ski area, next to the park, can be reached by roads out of Courtenay (☎ 800/689–9025 camping reservations).

## Lodging

**$–$$** ☷ **Strathcona Park Lodge and Outdoor Education Centre.** One of Canada's foremost outdoor education centers, this lakefront resort on the outskirts of Strathcona Provincial Park is a great place for kids and adults to try their hand at rock climbing, canoeing, kayaking, sailing, and more. Family-run and kid-friendly, the resort has comfortable cabins and lodge rooms, wholesome meals served buffet style in the rustic lodge, and striking views of the snowcapped mountains behind Upper Campbell Lake. The activities are optional but hard to resist: the guides here are renowned for their patience and skill. ⊠ *45 km (28 mi) west of Campbell River on Hwy. 28 (Box 2160, Campbell River V9W 5C5),* ☎ *250/286–3122,* FAX *250/286–6010,* WEB *www.strathcona.bc.ca. 38 rooms, 10 cabins, 1 8-bedroom guest house. Dining room, sauna, dock, basketball, hiking, volleyball, lounge (summer only), shop, children's programs (ages 6–18), laundry facilities, meeting rooms; no a/c, no rooms phones, no room TVs, no smoking. MC, V. Dining room closed Dec.–Feb.*

# Telegraph Cove

③② *182 km (109 mi) northwest of Campbell River, 56 km (34 mi) southeast of Port Hardy, 11 km (7 mi) off Hwy. 19 by gravel road.*

Fishing villages built on pilings over the water were once a common sight on Canada's west coast. Telegraph Cove, with its row of brightly painted shops and houses connected by boardwalk, is one of the last still standing. It's now home to a pub and restaurant, a general store, a marina, and several wildlife-watching and kayaking outfitters. Accommodation options include a campground and cabins run by **Telegraph Cove Resort** (☎ 250/928–3131 or 800/200–4665).

## Outdoor Activities and Sports
### KAYAKING
**North Island Kayak** (☎ 250/949–7707 or 877/949–7707, WEB www. kayakbc.ca), at the marina, rents kayaks and runs guided paddles.

### WHALE-WATCHING
Telegraph Cove overlooks Johnstone Strait, one of the best places in the province to see orca, or killer, whales especially during the salmon runs of July, August, and September. Between late May and mid-October, **Stubbs Island Whale Watching** on the boardwalk (☎ 250/928–3185 or 800/665–3066, WEB www.stubbs-island.com) runs 3½-hour whale-watching trips on its two 60-ft vessels. A naturalist accompanies the tours, and the boats are equipped with hydrophones for listening to the whales. Reservations are required.

OFF THE BEATEN PATH  **U'MISTA CULTURAL CENTRE** – From Port McNeill, 21 km (13 mi) north of Telegraph Cove, a 40-minute ferry ride takes you to Alert Bay, where you can see the First Nations artifacts housed at this centre (⊠ Front St. [Box 253, Alert Bay], ☎ 250/974–5403). You can also go to **Sointula,** a 20-minute ferry ride from Port McNeill, to visit the remains of a Finnish Utopian community.

# Port Hardy

③③ *238 km (148 mi) northwest of Campbell River, 499 km (309 mi) northwest of Victoria, 274 nautical mi southeast of Prince Rupert.*

Port Hardy is the departure and arrival point for BC Ferries' year-round trips through the scenic Inside Passage to and from Prince Rupert, the coastal port serving the Queen Charlotte Islands, and, in summer, to Bella Coola and other small communities along the mainland's midcoast. In summer Port Hardy can be crowded, so book your accommodations early. Ferry reservations for the trip between Port Hardy and Prince Rupert or Bella Coola should also be made well in advance.

North Island Transportation (☎ 250/949–6300) runs a shuttle bus between most Port Hardy hotels and the ferry terminal, which is 10 km (6 mi) from town. The fare is $5.25.

OFF THE
BEATEN PATH

**CAPE SCOTT PROVINCIAL PARK –** At the northern tip of Vancouver Island and 67 km (42 mi) north of Port Hardy by gravel road is a wilderness camping region suitable for well-equipped and experienced hikers. WEB www.bcparks.ca.

## Lodging

$$    🔲 **Glen Lyon Inn.** You can often spot eagles scouting the water for fish to prey on from this modern hotel next to the marina on Hardy Bay. All rooms have full ocean views, most have balconies, and some of the suites have whirlpool tubs and fireplaces. The inn is one of the closest to the ferry terminal, 7 km (4 mi) away. Diving, wildlife viewing, and chartered fishing can be arranged from here, and they'll even freeze your catch for you. ✉ *6435 Hardy Bay Rd. (Box 103, V0N 2P0),* ☎ *250/949–7115 or 877/949–7115,* FAX *250/949–7415,* WEB *www.glenlyoninn.com. 42 rooms, 2 suites. Restaurant, some in-room data ports, some kitchenettes, some microwaves, some refrigerators, cable TV, gym, pub, laundry facilities, business services, meeting room, some pets allowed (fee); no-smoking floor. AE, MC, V.*

$$    🔲 **Quarterdeck Inn and Marine Resort.** Most rooms have water views at this hotel on Port Hardy's waterfront. The rooms are bright and spacious with pastel decor. Two rooms have fireplaces and whirlpool tubs. A variety of outdoor activities, wildlife viewing, and First Nations cultural tours can be arranged from the hotel, which is a 10-minute drive from the ferry terminal. ✉ *6555 Hardy Bay Rd. (Box 910, V0N 2P0),* ☎ *250/902–0455 or 877/902–0459,* FAX *250/902–0454,* WEB *www.quarterdeckresort.net. 39 rooms, 1 suite. Restaurant, some kitchenettes, some in-room data ports, refrigerators, cable TV, exercise equipment, hot tub, marina, pub, laundry facilities, Internet, business services, meeting rooms, some pets allowed (fee); no-smoking floor. AE, D, DC, MC, V. CP.*

## Outdoor Activities and Sports

The **Adventure Center** (✉ 8635 Granville St., ☎ 250/902–2232 or 866/902–2232, WEB www.adventurecenter.ca) leads a wide range of ecotours, including kayaking, walking tours, whale watching, fishing, and caving, and has bike and kayak rentals.

# Vancouver Island A to Z

*To research prices, get advice from other travelers, and book travel arrangements, visit www.fodors.com.*

### AIR TRAVEL

Air Canada Jazz serves the larger towns on Vancouver Island. Baxter Aviation links Vancouver to Nanaimo by seaplane. Kenmore Air Seaplanes runs daily direct flights from Seattle to Victoria year-round and has summer service from Seattle to Nanaimo, Campbell River, Quadra Island, and other North Island and Inside Passage destinations. North Vancouver Air links Tofino with Vancouver and Seattle. Northwest Seaplanes operates summer floatplane service between Seattle and Tofino, Campbell River, Port Hardy, and other North Island destinations.

➤ AIRLINES AND CONTACTS: **Air Canada Jazz** (☎ 888/247–2262, WEB www.aircanada.ca). **Baxter Aviation** (✉ ☎ 250/754–1066 or 800/661–5599, WEB www.baxterair.com). **Kenmore Air Seaplanes** (☎ 425/486–1257 or 800/543–9595, WEB www.kenmoreair.com). **North Vancouver Air** (☎ 604/278–1608 or 800/228–6608, WEB www.northvanair.com).

Northwest Seaplanes (☎ 425/277–1590 or 800/690–0086, WEB www.
nwseaplanes.com).

## AIRPORTS

Vancouver Island is served by Victoria International Airport. Otherwise, there are domestic airports in or near many towns on the island,
including Campbell River, Comox, and Nanaimo. Tofino and Port Hardy
have airports that don't have phones. Smaller communities without airports are served by floatplanes.

➤ AIRPORT INFORMATION: **Campbell River Airport** (✉ 2000 Jubilee
Pkwy., Campbell River, ☎ 250/923–5012). **Comox airport** (✉ Cana-
dian Forces Base Comox, ☎ 250/897–3123). **Nanaimo airport** (✉ 3350
Spitfire Rd., Cassidy, ☎ 250/245–2157).

## BOAT AND FERRY TRAVEL

BC Ferries has frequent, year-round passenger and vehicle service to
Vancouver Island: a 1½-hour crossing from Tsawwassen (about an hour's
drive south of Vancouver) to Swartz Bay (a 30-minute drive north of
Victoria); a two-hour crossing from Tsawwassen to Duke Point, 15 km
(9 mi) south of Nanaimo; and a 1½-hour crossing from Horseshoe Bay
(a 30-minute drive north of Vancouver) to Departure Bay, 3 km (2 mi)
north of Nanaimo. Vehicle reservations can be made for any of these
routes; a $15 reservation fee applies.

BC Ferries also has year-round passenger and vehicle service to most
of the inhabited islands off Vancouver Island's east coast and links
Comox with Powell River on the Sunshine Coast, though reservations
cannot be made for this route.

Lady Rose Marine Services takes passengers on packet freighters from
Port Alberni to Vancouver Island's west coast. The M. V. *Lady Rose*
makes the 4½-hour trip to Bamfield on Tuesday, Thursday, and Saturday year-round, with additional Friday and Sunday sailings in July
and August. The round-trip fare is $45. The M. V. *Francis Barkley* sails
from Port Alberni to the Broken Group Islands and Ucluelet on Monday, Wednesday, and Friday between early June and late September.
The round-trip fare is $50 to Ucluelet, $45 to the Broken Group Islands.

The M. V. *Uchuck*, a 100-passenger coastal packet freighter, sails from
Gold River, 100 km (62 mi) west of Campbell River at the end of Highway 28, to a number of isolated west-coast settlements. Day trips
($40–$45 per person) and overnight trips ($265 to $310 per couple,
including one night's bed and breakfast) are available all year. Reservations (and good sea legs) are essential.

At press time, Harbour Link planned to start direct, high-speed, foot-
passenger-only service between downtown Nanaimo and downtown
Vancouver. The trip will take about an hour and cost $18.

➤ BOAT AND FERRY INFORMATION: **BC Ferries** (☎ 250/386–3431; 888/
223–3779 in B.C.; 604/444–2890 vehicle reservations; 888/724–5223
in B.C.; WEB www.bcferries.com). **Harbour Link** (WEB www.nhlc.ca). **Lady
Rose Marine Services** (☎ 250/723–8313; 800/663–7192 reservations
Apr.–Sept.; WEB www.ladyrosemarine.com). **M. V.** *Uchuck* (☎ 250/
283–2515 or 250/283–2325, WEB www.mvuchuck.com).

## BUS TRAVEL

Laidlaw Coach Lines serves most towns on Vancouver Island. Long
Beach Link runs a scheduled shuttle-bus service along the island's west
coast, serving Ucluelet, Tofino, Tofino Airport, and the Pacific Rim National Park Reserve between May and September. From Vancouver, Greyhound serves Nanaimo and Pacific Coach Lines serves Victoria.

➤ Bus Information: **Greyhound** (☎ 604/482–8747 or 800/661–8747, WEB www.greyhound.ca). **Laidlaw Coach Lines** (☎ 250/385–4411; 800/318–0818 in B.C.; 800/663–8390 from the U.S.). **Long Beach Link** (☎ 250/726–7790 or 866/726–7790, WEB www.longbeachlink.com). **Pacific Coach Lines** (☎ 250/385–4411 or 800/661–1725, WEB www. pacificcoach.com).

### CAR RENTAL
Most major agencies, including Avis, Budget, Hertz, and National Tilden, serve towns throughout Vancouver Island.

### CAR TRAVEL
Major roads on Vancouver Island, and most secondary roads, are paved and well engineered. Many wilderness and park-access roads are unpaved. Inquire locally about logging activity before using logging or forestry service roads. B.C. Highways has 24-hour highway reports; the toll call is 75¢ a minute.

Highway 17 connects the Swartz Bay ferry terminal on the Saanich Peninsula with downtown Victoria. The Trans-Canada Highway (Hwy. 1) runs from Victoria to Nanaimo. The Island Highway (Hwy. 19) connects Nanaimo to Port Hardy. (Highway 19A, the old road, runs parallel as far as Campbell River. It's a slower, seaside option.) Highway 14 connects Victoria to Sooke and Port Renfrew on the west coast. Highway 4 crosses the island from Parksville to Tofino and Pacific Rim National Park Reserve.
➤ Contact: **B.C. Highways** (☎ 900/565–4997, 75¢ a minute).

### EMERGENCIES
➤ Contacts: **Ambulance, fire, poison control, police** (☎ 911).

### LODGING
Reservations for lodging anywhere in the province can be made through Hello B.C.'s reservation service. From March through October, the provincial government also runs a toll-free Campground Reservation Line. Best Canadian Bed and Breakfast Network and Garden City B&B Reservation Service can book B&B accommodations on Vancouver Island.
➤ Reservation Services: **Best Canadian Bed and Breakfast Network** (✉ 1064 Balfour Ave., Vancouver V6H 1X1, ☎ 604/738–7207, FAX 604/732–4998, WEB www.bestcanadianbb.com). **Campground Reservation Line** (☎ 800/689–9025, WEB www.discovercamping.ca). **Garden City B&B Reservation Service** (✉ 660 Jones Terr., Victoria V8Z 2L7, ☎ 250/479–1986, WEB www.bc-bed-breakfast.com). **Hello B.C.** (☎ 800/ 435–5622, WEB www.hellobc.com).

### OUTDOORS AND SPORTS
FISHING
Separate licenses are required for saltwater and freshwater fishing in British Columbia. Both are available at sporting-goods stores, government-agency offices, and most fishing lodges and charter-boat companies in the province. A one-day license for nonresidents costs about $16 for freshwater fishing, $7.50 for saltwater fishing. Additional fees apply to salmon fishing. For information about saltwater-fishing regulations, contact Fisheries and Oceans Canada, or pick up a free *Sport Fishing Guide*, available at most tourist-information centers. Hello B.C. has brochures on freshwater and saltwater fishing.
➤ Contacts: **Fisheries and Oceans Canada** (☎ 604/666–2828, ☎ 877/ 320–3467 salmon regulations, WEB www-comm.pac.dfo-mpo.gc.ca). **Hello B.C.** (☎ 800/435–5622, WEB www.hellobc.com).

### GOLF

Vancouver Island's mild climate allows most golf courses to stay open all year. Greens fees are about $30–$60 and usually include a cart. Golf Central provides a transportation and booking service for golfers in southern Vancouver Island. For advance tee-time bookings at courses in Victoria or Parksville, you can try Last Minute Golf.

➤ CONTACTS: **Golf Central** (☎ 250/380–4653 or 866/380–4653, 🕸 golfcentraltours.com). **Last Minute Golf** (☎ 604/878–1833 or 800/684–6344, 🕸 www.lastminutegolfbc.com).

### HIKING

Ecosummer Expeditions has guided hiking trips along the West Coast trail. For parks information, contact B.C. Parks.

➤ CONTACTS: **B.C. Parks** (✉ ☎ no phone, 🕸 www.bcparks.ca). **Ecosummer Expeditions** (☎ 250/674–0102 or 800/465–8884, 🕸 www.ecosummer.com).

### KAYAKING

Several companies conduct multiday sea-kayaking trips to the coastal areas of Vancouver Island. Some of the excursions are suitable for beginners, and many trips provide an excellent chance to view orcas. Ecosummer Expeditions runs multiday paddles to Johnstone Strait and the Broken Group Islands. Gabriola Cycle and Kayak has sea-kayaking trips to the Broken Group Islands and other areas off the west coast of Vancouver Island, as well as to the Northern Gulf Islands and Johnstone Strait. Ocean West has three- to six-day paddling, camping, and orca-watching trips in Johnstone Strait. Majestic Ocean Kayaking offers guided half-day harbor tours, day trips, and multiday camping trips to the Broken Group Islands and other areas.

➤ CONTACTS: **Ecosummer Expeditions** (☎ 250/674–0102 or 800/465–8884, 🕸 www.ecosummer.com). **Gabriola Cycle and Kayak** (☎ 250/247–8277, 🕸 www.gck.ca). **Majestic Ocean Kayaking** (☎ 250/726–2868 or 800/889–7644, 🕸 www.oceankayaking.com). **Ocean West** (☎ 604/898–4979 or 800/660–0051, 🕸 www.ocean-west.com).

### TOURS

The Gourmet Trail conducts escorted tours linking three country inns on Vancouver Island and Salt Spring Island that are known for their cuisine. For a guided tour of the backcountry, including the Clayoquot Biosphere Reserve, by chauffeured four-wheel-drive, contact Rain-Coast Back Road Adventures in Ucluelet.

➤ FEES AND SCHEDULES: **Gourmet Trail** (✉ First Island Tours Ltd., 214-733 Johnson St., Victoria V8W 3C7, ☎ 250/658–5367, 🕸 www.firstislandtours.com). **RainCoast Back Road Adventures** (☎ 250/726–7625, 🕸 www.raincoastadventures.com).

### VISITOR INFORMATION

➤ TOURIST INFORMATION: **Campbell River Visitor Information Centre** (✉ 1235 Shoppers Row [Box 400, Campbell River V9W 5B6], ☎ 250/287–4636 or 866/830–1113, 🕸 www.campbellriverchamber.ca). **Comox Valley Visitor Infocentre** (✉ 2040 Cliffe Ave., Courtenay, ☎ 250/334–3234 or 888/357–4471, 🕸 www.tourism-comox-valley.bc.ca). **Hello B.C.** (☎ 800/435–5622, 🕸 www.hellobc.com). **Port Alberni Tourist Infocentre** (✉ 2533 Redford St., off Hwy. 4, Port Alberni, ☎ 250/724–6535). **Port Hardy Visitor Information Centre** (✉ 7520 Market St., Port Hardy, ☎ 250/949–7622, 🕸 www.ph-chamber.bc.ca). **Tofino Visitor Info Centre** (✉ 1426 Pacific Rim Hwy., ☎ 250/725–3414, 🕸 www.tofinobc.org) **Tourism Nanaimo** (✉ 2290 Bowen Rd., V9T 3K7, ☎ 250/756–0106 or 800/663–7337, 🕸 www.tourismnanaimo.com). **Tourism Vancouver Island** (✉ 203–335 Wesley St., Nanaimo V9R 2T5, ☎ 250/754–3500, 🕸 www.islands.bc.ca).

# 4 BRITISH COLUMBIA

From rugged mountains to lush valleys, from northern woodlands to lakeside vineyards and forested islands, this western province truly has varied natural beauty. There are plenty of opportunities for wildlife viewing, as well as for skiing, golfing, fishing, hiking, and kayaking—or you can simply relax in a peaceful country inn. Your visit may take you to First Nations villages, luxurious ski resorts, historic towns, and isolated islands.

B RITISH COLUMBIA'S MAINLAND harbors untouched forests, snowcapped peaks, powder skiing, and world-class fishing—a wealth of outdoor action and beauty. The citizens are a similarly heterogeneous mix: descendants of original Native American peoples; 19th-century British, European, and Asian settlers; and more recent immigrants from all corners of the earth.

By Sue
Kernaghan

Canada's third-largest province (only Québec and Ontario are bigger), British Columbia occupies almost 10% of Canada's total area, stretching from the Pacific Ocean eastward to the province of Alberta and from the U.S. border north to the Yukon and Northwest Territories. It spans almost 1 million square km (about 360,000 square mi), making it larger than every American state except Alaska.

With most of the population clustered in Vancouver and Victoria, those who venture farther afield have plenty of room to explore. Only two hours north of Vancouver is the popular resort town of Whistler, with North America's two biggest ski mountains. The Okanagan Valley in the east, replete with lakes and vineyards, is famous for its wines. Near Vancouver lies the Sunshine Coast, with secluded fjords and the Gulf Islands, popular vacation spots for B.C. residents. To the north are the Cariboo-Chilcotin region and northern British Columbia, vast areas of mountainous and forested terrain. Visitors to the eastern regions of the province find the foothills of the Rockies and plenty of opportunities for activities that include fishing, boating, hiking, and skiing.

## Pleasures and Pastimes

### Dining
Although Vancouver and Victoria have British Columbia's most varied and cosmopolitan cuisine, some excellent restaurants in smaller towns, particularly Whistler, and several fine country inns have helped to define a local cuisine based on the best of regional fare, including seafood, lamb, organic produce, and increasingly good wine. Attire is generally casual in the region. Almost all restaurants, and many bars and pubs, ban smoking indoors.

| CATEGORY | COST* |
| --- | --- |
| $$$$ | over $32 |
| $$$ | $22–$32 |
| $$ | $13–$21 |
| $ | under $13 |

*per person, in Canadian dollars, for a main course at dinner, not including 7% GST and 10% liquor tax

### Lodging
Accommodations range from bed-and-breakfasts and rustic cabins to deluxe chain hotels, country inns, and remote fishing lodges. In the cities you'll find an abundance of lodgings, but outside the major centers, especially in summer, it's a good idea to reserve ahead, even for campsites. In winter, many backcountry resorts close, and city hotels drop prices by as much as 50%. Most small inns and B&Bs ban smoking indoors; almost all hotels have no-smoking rooms.

| CATEGORY | COST* |
|----------|-------|
| $$$$ | over $250 |
| $$$ | $170–$250 |
| $$ | $90–$170 |
| $ | under $90 |

*All prices are in Canadian dollars, for a standard double room, excluding 10% provincial accommodation tax and 7% GST.*

## Outdoor Activities and Sports

### CANOEING AND KAYAKING

The Inside Passage, the Strait of Georgia, and the other island-dotted straits and sounds that border the mainland provide fairly protected sea-going from Washington State to the Alaskan border, with numerous marine parks to explore along the way. Two favorites for canoeing are the Powell Forest Canoe Route, an 80-km (50-mi) circuit of seven lakes, and Bowron Lake Park, in the Cariboo region.

### FISHING

Miles of coastline and thousands of lakes, rivers, and streams bring more than 750,000 anglers to British Columbia each year. The province's waters hold 74 species of fish (25 of them sport fish), including chinook salmon and rainbow trout.

### GOLF

British Columbia has more than 230 golf courses, and the number is growing. The province is an official golf destination of both the Canadian and American PGA tours. The topography tends to be mountainous and forested, and many courses have fine views as well as treacherous approaches to greens.

### HIKING

Virtually all the provincial parks have fine hiking-trail networks, and many ski resorts keep their chairlifts running throughout the summer to help hikers and mountain bikers reach trails. Heli-hiking is also very popular; helicopters deliver you to alpine meadows and verdant mountaintops.

### RAFTING

A wide range of rafting trips is available on the many beautiful rivers lacing British Columbia, including the Babine, Chilcotin, Fraser, Skeena, and Tatshenshini. You can choose between an adrenaline-rich white-water route or a scenic float suitable for photographers and families.

### SKIING AND SNOWBOARDING

With more than half the province higher than 4,200 ft above sea level, new downhill areas are constantly opening. More than 60 resorts have downhill skiing and snowboarding facilities. Most of these resorts also have groomed cross-country (Nordic) ski trails, and many of the provincial parks have cross-country trails as well. The resorts are easy to get to, as most have shuttles from the nearest airport.

## First Nations Culture

A dramatic recent development in British Columbia has been a resurgence in the culture of the province's native, or First Nations, peoples—the Kwakwaka'wakw, Haida, Nisga'a, and others—who have occupied the land for more than 12,000 years. First Nations culture is evident throughout the region in art galleries, restaurants, cultural centers, and re-created villages. The best examples are found in Northern B.C. and on the Queen Charlotte Islands, where totems and ancient villages stand, and local museums have some of the province's best collections of First Nations artifacts.

# Exploring British Columbia

Most of the population huddles in a region known as the Lower Mainland, in and around Vancouver in the province's southwest corner. In the mountains about two hours north of Vancouver is the international resort town of Whistler. Beyond the Lower Mainland, three highways climb over the Coast Mountains to the rolling high plateau that forms the central interior. To the north are the Cariboo ranch country and, beyond that, the province's vast, sparsely inhabited northern half. To the east are the Okanagan and Shuswap valleys, home to the fruit- and wine-growing region and the lake district. Farther east are the mountainous Kootenays and the foothills of the Rockies.

The southernmost stretch of coastline just north of Vancouver, called the Sunshine Coast, is popular with boaters, artists, and summer vacationers. Farther north is a roadless, fjord-cut wilderness leading to the mist-shrouded Haida Gwaii, or Queen Charlotte Islands, home to the Haida people and to old-growth forest. The gentler, more pastoral Gulf Islands, in the Strait of Georgia, just west of Vancouver, have long attracted escapists of every kind.

The North Coast and the Queen Charlotte Islands can be wet year-round. The interior is drier, with greater extremes, including hot summers and reliably snowy winters. Temperatures here drop below freezing in winter and sometimes reach 90°F in summer.

When you travel by car, keep in mind that more than three-quarters of British Columbia is mountainous terrain. Many areas, including the North Coast, have no roads at all and are accessible only by air or sea.

*Numbers in the text correspond to numbers in the margin and on the British Columbia map.*

## Great Itineraries

British Columbia is about the size of Western Europe, with as much geographical variety and substantially fewer roads. The good news is that many great sights, stunning scenery, and even wilderness lie within a few days' tour of Vancouver or the U.S. border.

### IF YOU HAVE 3 DAYS

One option is to take a ferry for a brief tour of the Sunshine Coast: **Gibsons Landing** ①, **Sechelt** ②, **Powell River** ③, and **Lund** ④. An alternative is to take a ferry out to one of the Gulf Islands—⊞ **Galiano** ⑤, ⊞ **Mayne** ⑥, or ⊞ **Salt Spring** ⑦—and stay at a romantic country inn for a night.

Another option, with stunning mountain and ocean scenery, is to take the Coast Mountain Circle tour, driving north from Vancouver along the scenic Sea to Sky Highway to ⊞ **Squamish** ⑨ and the resort town of ⊞ **Whistler** ⑩, then over the scenic Duffy Lake Road to the gold-rush town of **Lillooet** ⑪. You can then return to Vancouver through the steep gorges of the Fraser Canyon, with stops at Hell's Gate on the Fraser River near **Hope** ⑫ and at ⊞ **Harrison Hot Springs** ⑬.

### IF YOU HAVE 6 DAYS

A longer trip allows time to explore the interior. Start with a one- or two-day trip over the mountains via ⊞ **Whistler** ⑩ and **Lillooet** ⑪, through the Fraser Canyon, or by the quicker, if less scenic, Coquihalla Highway. On Days 3 through 5, loop through the High Country and the Okanagan Valley. You can make stops in ⊞ **Kamloops** ⑭ to fish or tour the Secwepemc Native Heritage Museum; in **Vernon** ⑯ to visit the mountain resort at Silver Star; or in ⊞ **Kelowna** ⑰, **Summerland and Peachland** ⑱, ⊞ **Penticton** ⑲, or ⊞ **Osoyoos** ⑳ to relax

# Exploring British Columbia

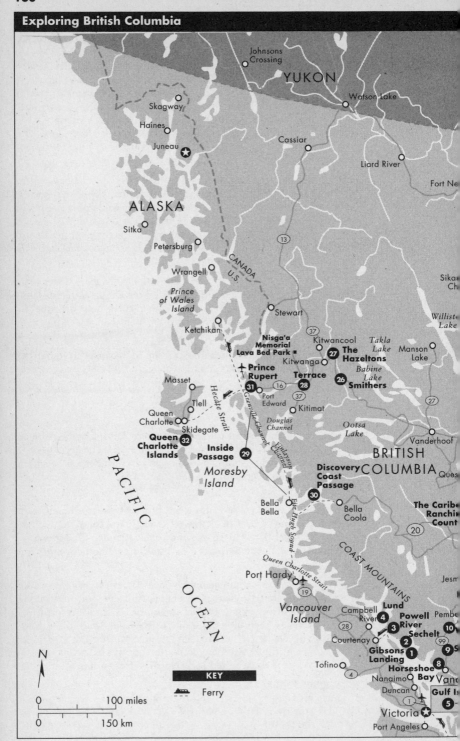

KEY

🛥 Ferry

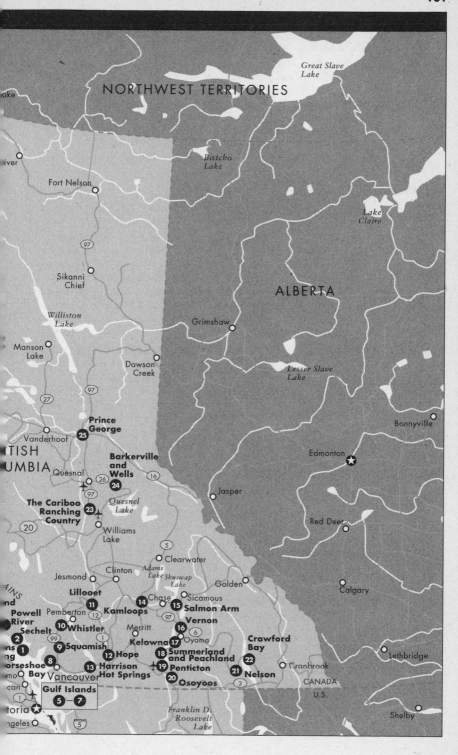

NORTHWEST TERRITORIES

*Great Slave Lake*

*Bistcho Lake*

Fort Nelson

ALBERTA

(97)

Sikanni Chief

*Lake Claire*

*Williston Lake*

Grimshaw

Manson Lake

(27)

Dawson Creek

*Lesser Slave Lake*

(97)

Bonnyville

Prince George **25**

Vanderhoof

Edmonton ★

TISH
UMBIA

Quesnal

Barkerville and Wells

**26**
(97) **24**
(16)

The Cariboo Ranching Country **23**

*Quesnel Lake*

Jasper

Red Deer

(20)

Williams Lake

(5)

Clearwater

Calgary

Jesmond

Clinton

*Adams Lake*  *Shuswap Lake*

Golden

AINS
nd

**Lillooet**

Chase

Sicamous

Powell
River

Pemberton (12)

**11**

**Kamloops**

**14**

**15** **Salmon Arm**

**Sechelt**

**10** **Whistler**

(99)

Merritt

(97)

**Vernon**

Lethbridge

**16**

(6)

Crawford Bay

ns
ng
orseshoe
**Bay**

**2**
**1**
**9** **Squamish**
**8**

(1)

**Kelowna** **17**
Oyama

**22**

Vancouver

**12** **Hope**
**13** **Harrison Hot Springs**

**18** Summerland and Peachland
**19** Penticton

**21** **Nelson**

Cranbrook

toria ★
geles

**Gulf Islands**
**5** **7**

(1)

**20** **Osoyoos**

(3)

CANADA
U.S.

*Franklin D. Roosevelt Lake*

(5)

Shelby

at a beach or tour a vineyard. Any of these towns is fine for an overnight stay.

### When to Tour British Columbia

The Gulf Islands and the Sunshine Coast are enjoyable anytime, but there are fewer ferries and more rain between September and May, and many tourist facilities close in winter. The interior—the Cariboo, High Country, Okanagan Valley, and Kootenays—can be tough to reach in winter, but more ski resorts are making it worth the effort. Spring and fall, with their blossoms and harvest and wine festivals, are attractive, peaceful travel seasons; summer is a great time for most of the interior, although the Okanagan Valley can get hot and crowded in July and August.

# SUNSHINE COAST

The stretch of mainland coast north of Vancouver, backed by mountains and accessible only by sea or air, is so deeply cut with fjords that it has the look and feel of an island—or rather, two islands. The lower Sunshine Coast to the south is popular with artists, writers, and Vancouver weekenders. The upper Sunshine Coast, a ferry ride across Jervis Inlet to the north, is wild and densely forested. Highway 101, the one paved road running the length of the coast, forms the last (or the first) 139 km (86 mi) of the Pan-American Highway, connecting the village of Lund, British Columbia, to Puerto Montt, Chile, 24,000 km (15,020 mi) away.

The coast is sunnier than the more exposed coastline to the north (hence its name), and its many provincial parks, marinas, lakes, and walking trails are popular with outdoorspeople and families, though not, as yet, with mass tourism or luxury-resort developers. The relaxed lifestyle has attracted many artists and craftspeople to the area. To visit artists in their studios, pick up a *Purple Banner Tour* map (after the banners that fly when a studio is open). It's available free from any Sunshine Coast tourist info office.

## Gibsons Landing

❶ *5 km (3 mi) plus 12 nautical mi northwest of Vancouver.*

The first stop on the Sunshine Coast, just 5 km (3 mi) north of the Langdale ferry terminal, Gibsons Landing (often just called Gibsons) is an attractive seaside town that's best known as the location of *The Beachcombers,* a long-running Canadian TV show about life on the B.C. coast. **Molly's Reach** (✉ Molly's La., ☎ 604/886–9710), a waterfront café built as a set for the show, still serves fish, chips, and TV memories.

The **Elphinstone Pioneer Museum** (✉ 716 Winn Rd., ☎ 604/886–8232, WEB www.gibsonslibrary.bc.ca) has an eclectic collection of pioneer artifacts, rare butterflies, and exhibits showcasing the region's seafaring history. It's open mid-June to Labor Day, Tuesday–Saturday 10:30–4:30, and Tuesday, Thursday, and Saturday 1:30–4:30 the rest of the year; donations are suggested.

About 15 minutes north of Gibsons on Highway 101 is the delightful village of **Roberts Creek,** where the buildings date to the 1930s and the ambience recalls the 1960s. There's a public beach a short stroll from the village and seaside camping at nearby **Roberts Creek Provincial Park.**

### Dining and Lodging

$$–$$$   ✕ **The Creekhouse.** The chef-owner at this wisteria-draped cottage in Roberts Creek serves classic French cuisine with a touch of Italian. The

menu changes seasonally, but you can always find good lamb and delectable local seafood options. Hardwood floors, white tablecloths, a fireplace, and outdoor patios create a casual, cozy ambience; many guests like to stroll down to the beach between courses. ⊠ *1041 Roberts Creek Rd., Roberts Creek,* ☎ *604/885–9321. MC, V. Closed Mon.–Thurs. No lunch.*

**$–$$** ✕ **Gumboot Garden Café.** This funky, kid-friendly, village-center café is such an area institution that the sign outside reads simply CAFÉ. The made-from-scratch soups, breads, sauces, and desserts feature, where possible, local and organic ingredients. There's a patio, woodstove, flower-stuffed gum boots (rubber boots) by the door, and a warm atmosphere that makes it tempting to just hang out. Try the eggs, sausage, and homemade granola breakfasts; the burritos, burgers, and soups at lunch; or the candlelight dinners of pizza, pasta, seafood, and vegetarian dishes. ⊠ *1057 Roberts Creek Rd., Roberts Creek,* ☎ *604/ 885–4216. MC, V. No dinner Mon.–Tues. June–Sept. or Sun.–Wed. Oct.–May.*

**$$–$$$** ✕🛏 **Bonniebrook Lodge.** For a romantic place to spend the night, consider this seaside lodge 5 km (3 mi) north of Gibsons. Rooms and suites in the original 1922 building and in the 1998 addition are attractive, with custom pine furniture, a woodsy green color scheme, fireplaces, and whirlpool tubs for two. Chez Philippe, a fine French restaurant ($$–$$$), is open to the public for dinner; the $30 four-course set menu is an excellent value. ⊠ *1532 Oceanbeach Esplanade (R.R. 5, V0N 1V5),* ☎ *604/886–2887; 877/290–9916; 604/886–2188 dinner reservations;* ℻ *604/886–8853;* ⎁ *www.bonniebrook.com. 5 rooms, 2 suites. Fans, refrigerators, cable TV, in-room VCRs; no room phones, no smoking. AE, DC, MC, V. Restaurant closed Tues.–Thurs. mid-Sept.–mid-May. No lunch. Lodge and restaurant closed Jan. BP.*

**$$** 🛏 **Country Cottage Bed & Breakfast.** Loragene and Philip Gaulin have lovingly decorated two private cottages on their 2-acre farm in the 1930s-vintage village of Roberts Creek. Tiny, romantic Rose Cottage has a woodstove and an antique sideboard. Cedar Lodge, the farm's former barn, is a feast of woodsy Canadiana—from its stone fireplace to its handmade Arts and Crafts furniture. A full breakfast, delivered to your room, and afternoon tea are included in the rates. ⊠ *1183 Roberts Creek Rd. (Box 183, Roberts Creek V0N 2W0),* ☎ *604/885–7448. 2 cottages. Kitchens, some pets allowed; no room phones, no room TVs, no kids, no smoking. No credit cards. BP.*

**$$** 🛏 **Marina House Bed & Breakfast.** From the street, this seaside home near Gibsons' town center looks like an ordinary house; from the beach side, though, it's a striking yellow three-story 1931 house. The rooms (one with a bath across the hall) are small and decorated with Victorian antiques. Molly's Room has a view over Shoal Channel and Keats Island. The lounge, the porch, and the breakfast room also overlook the sea. The town is a few minutes' stroll along the beach. ⊠ *546 Marine Dr. (Box 1696, Gibsons V0N 1V0),* ☎ *604/886–7888 or 888/ 568–6688,* ℻ *604/886–4906,* ⎁ *www.marinahouse.net. 3 rooms, 2 with bath. Beach, library; no room phones, no room TVs, no kids, no smoking. MC, V. BP.*

## Shopping
More than 100 local artists show their wares at **Gift of the Eagle Gallery** (⊠ 689 Gibsons Way, ☎ 604/886–4899).

## Outdoor Activities and Sports
**Sunshine Coast Golf & Country Club** (⊠ 3206 Hwy. 101, Roberts Creek, ☎ 604/885–9212 or 800/667–5022) is an 18-hole, par-71 course with tree-lined fairways and mountain and ocean views.

# Sechelt

**❷** *37 km (23 mi) plus 12 nautical mi northwest of Vancouver.*

Sechelt, the largest town on the lower Sunshine Coast, is home to many artists and writers as well as a strong First Nations community, the Sechelt Nation. If you're in Sechelt in mid-August, you can catch readings by internationally acclaimed Canadian writers at the **Sunshine Coast Festival of the Written Arts** (☎ 604/885–9631 or 800/565–9631, ᵂᴱᴮ www.writersfestival.ca), held at Sechelt's Rockwood Centre.

**House of Hewhiwus** (✉ 5555 Hwy. 101, ☎ 604/885–8991) includes a small First Nations museum and a gift shop–art gallery. **Porpoise Bay Provincial Park** (☎ 604/898–3678; 800/689–9025 camping reservations; ᵂᴱᴮ www.bcparks.ca), north of Sechelt on Sechelt Inlet, has camping, hiking trails, and a sandy swimming beach.

The coast's best scenery is to the north of Sechelt, around and beyond the little marinas of Madiera Park, Garden Bay, and Irvine's Landing, collectively known as Pender Harbour. Here Highway 101 winds past forests, mountains, and a confusion of freshwater lakes and ocean inlets. In summer, **Pender Harbour Ferries** (☎ 604/883–2561 Pender Harbour Info Centre) runs 1½-hour boat tours of the area.

You can experience a dramatic natural sight at **Skookumchuk Narrows Provincial Park** (✉ Egmont Rd. off Hwy. 101, ☎ 604/898–3678), 5 km (3 mi) inland from the Earls Cove ferry terminal and 45 km (28 mi) northwest of Sechelt. A 4-km (2½-mi) walk through the forest comes out at a viewpoint where, at the turn of the tide, seawater churning through the narrow channel creates thrilling tidal rapids. Tide tables are posted at the trailhead.

**Princess Louisa Inlet** is a narrow fjord at the top of Jervis Inlet; more than 60 waterfalls tumble down its steep walls. The fjord is accessible only by boat or floatplane. The *Malibu Princess* (✉ ☎ 604/883–2003, ᵂᴱᴮ www.malibuyachts.com), a 200-passenger tour boat, makes day trips to Princess Louisa Inlet from the Malibu Landing in Egmont; the fare is $69 and the ship makes about 11 sailings during its June–mid-September season; call ahead for precise dates. **Sunshine Coast Tours** (☎ 604/883–2280 or 800/870–9055) runs boat tours to Princess Louisa Inlet daily in summer.

## Dining and Lodging

**$–$$** ✕ **The Old Boot Eatery.** Upbeat jazz, mismatched furniture, and a Wild West mural create a fun atmosphere at this town-center local favorite. Twenty different pastas range from simple spaghetti with meat sauce to such elaborate creations as linguine with tiger prawns and Italian sausage. The bread, pasta sauces, and thin-crust pizza are all made from scratch. Half orders and a kids' menu make this a good choice for families. ✉ *5530 Wharf St. Plaza, Sechelt,* ☎ *604/885–2727. AE, MC, V. Closed Sun.*

**$$** ✕🏠 **Ruby Lake Resort.** The Cogrossi family from Milan chose this lake-
**★** side resort as the place to serve the area's best Italian home cooking ($–$$$$). Local seafood, house-smoked salmon, and homegrown organic produce highlight chef Aldo Cogrossi's seafood, pasta, and vegetarian dishes, served in the woodsy restaurant or on the patio. Five spacious duplex cottages, all with private entrances, pine furniture, and rich colors, are reached by a floating footbridge. They overlook a lagoon that is also a bird sanctuary. Two suites on the lake are especially romantic: each has a woodstove, soaker tub, and a lakeside deck with sunset views. ✉ *Hwy. 101 (R.R. 1, Site 20, C25, Madeira Park V0N 2H0),* ☎ *604/883–2269 or 800/717–6611,* ᶠᴬˣ *604/883–3602,* ᵂᴱᴮ

*www.rubylakeresort.com. 7 rooms, 5 suites. Restaurant, some kitchens, some kitchenettes, refrigerators, cable TV, lake, massage, dock, boating, hiking, bar, meeting room; no room phones, no TV in some rooms, no smoking. MC, V. Closed Jan.–mid-Mar. and Oct.–May. Restaurant closed Mon.–Wed and for lunch. CP.*

**$$** ⊡ **Wildflowers Bed & Breakfast.** Two serene rooms overlook a meadow at this Balinese-style cottage in the woods. Each is large and comfortable, with its own fireplace, extra-deep bathtub, and porch. The decor, from the four-poster canopy beds to the adobe mantels and touches of Balinese art, is delightfully eclectic but never cluttered. ⊠ *5813 Brooks Rd, Halfmoon Bay V0N 3A0,* ☎ *604/885–7346,* FAX *604/885–7242,* WEB *www.wildflowers-bb.com. 2 rooms. Fans, refrigerators, microwaves, cable TV, in-room VCRs, outdoor hot tub, massage, laundry service; no room phones, no kids, no smoking. MC, V. Closed 1 month in winter. BP.*

### Outdoor Activities and Sports

Pender Harbour and the Sechelt Inlet are spectacular diving spots, especially in the winter, when the water is clearest. An artificial reef has been formed by a scuttled navy ship off Kunechin Point in Sechelt Inlet. **Suncoast Diving and Water Sports** (⊠ 5643 Wharf St., ☎ 604/740–8006 or 866/740–8006, WEB www.suncoastdiving.com) is a PADI five-star dive center. A one-day dive charter with two dives is $75 per person. Based at pretty Halfmoon Bay, 15 minutes north of Sechelt, **Halfmoon Sea Kayaks** (☎ 604/885–2948, WEB www.halfmoonseakayaks.com) has rentals, tours, and lessons. **Kayak the Coast Ecotours** (⊠ 4798 Sunshine Coast Hwy., ☎ 604/885–2995, WEB www.kayakthecoast.com) conducts easy paddling day trips and lessons for beginners. For mountain-bike rentals and tours, see **On the Edge Biking** (⊠ 5642 Cowrie St., ☎ 604/ 885–4888, WEB www.ontheedgebiking.com).

# Powell River

❸ *70 km (43 mi) plus 12 nautical mi by ferry northwest of Sechelt, 121 km (75 mi) plus 12½ nautical mi northwest of Vancouver, 17 nautical mi (80-min ferry ride) east across Strait of Georgia from Comox on Vancouver Island.*

The main town on the Upper Sunshine Coast, Powell River was established around a pulp-and-paper mill in 1912, and the forestry industry remains a strong presence in the area. Renowned as a year-round salmon-fishing destination, Powell River also has 30 regional lakes with exceptional trout fishing and is a popular scuba-diving destination. The town has several B&Bs, restaurants, and parks with oceanfront camping and RV hook-ups. The Powell River Townsite, 3 km (2 mi) north of town, one of the province's oldest functioning mill towns, is a national historic site.

### Dining and Lodging

**$–$$** ✕ **Jitterbug Café.** Expansive views of Malaspina Strait, a sunny deck, and art from the neighboring gallery create a relaxed bistro air in this 1920s town-center house. The food, including local prawns and salmon, organic salads, pastas, and sandwiches made with homemade bread, is simple and seasonal. ⊠ *4643 Marine Dr.,* ☎ *604/485–7797. AE, MC, V. Closed Jan.–Mar.; Sun.–Mon. Apr.–May; and mid-Sept.–Dec.*

**$–$$** ✕ **Shingle Mill Pub.** Stunning views over Powell Lake from the big bay windows and deck are the draws at this friendly local pub just north of Powell River. Pub fare—fish-and-chips, sandwiches, and burgers—predominates, but the menu also lists steak, salmon, and halibut dishes. Kids are welcome in the bistro section, which also has water views.

✉ *6233 Powell Pl., off Hwy. 101,* ☎ *604/483–9490. Reservations not accepted. AE, MC, V.*

$  🏠 **Old Court House Inn and Hostel.** This 1939 Tudor-style building, next to the pulp mill in the historic townsite 5 km (3 mi) north of town, was Powell River's original courthouse. Private rooms are decorated in an early 20th-century style; some have antiques. There are also three dorm rooms ($20 a person) and a shared kitchen that are available. A shuttle picks you up from the bus station or the Westview (Comox) ferry terminal for $5. ✉ *6243 Walnut St., V8A 4K4,* ☎ *604/483–4000,* ⅎⅬⅩ *604/483–4089,* ⓦⒺⒷ *www.savaryonline.com/oldcourthouse. 7 rooms, 6 with bath; 1 suite; 1 four-bed dorm room; 2 two-bed dorm rooms. Kitchen, some refrigerators, cable TV, piano, Internet; no room phones, no smoking. MC, V.*

## Outdoor Activities and Sports

### HIKING AND BIKING

The Inland Lake Site and Trail System, 12 km (8 mi) inland from Powell River, is a 13-km-long (8-mi-long) hiking and biking trail around Inland Lake that's accessible to people who use wheelchairs. Hikers can also try the Sunshine Coast Trail, which runs 180 km (112 mi) from Sarah Point, north of Lund, to Saltery Bay.

### SCUBA DIVING

Sunken ships, red coral, wolf eels, enormous octopi, and—especially in winter—uncommonly clear water make Powell River one of Canada's leading scuba-diving spots. A popular attraction is the *Emerald Princess,* a 9-ft bronze mermaid statue in 60 ft of water off Saltery Bay Provincial Park. Local dive outfitters include **Don's Dive Shop** (✉ 4454 Willingdon Ave., ☎ 604/485–6969, ⓦⒺⒷ www.donsdiveshop.com), which has dive charters, gear rental, guiding services, and instruction. A one-day dive charter is $90 per person and includes two dives and tanks and weights.

# Lund

❹ *28 km (17 mi) north of Powell River.*

Founded by the Swedish Thulin brothers in 1889, the historic seaside village of Lund marks the end (or start) of the Pan-American Highway. Lund is the nearest village to **Desolation Sound,** a major draw for boaters and kayakers. You can catch a water taxi from Lund to **Savary Island** and its white-sand beaches.

## Dining and Lodging

$–$$$  ✕ **The Laughing Oyster.** All the tables and the outdoor deck at this pretty restaurant 10 minutes from Lund have stunning views over Okeover Arm. Although the menu lists vegetarian, beef, lamb, and poultry dishes, the focus here is seafood. The namesake laughing oysters are steam, shucked, and broiled with artichokes, olives, sun-dried tomatoes, hot peppers, and feta cheese. The Seafood Harvest for two has salmon, red snapper, oysters, prawns, scallops, and more. Boaters can tie up at the dock in front of the restaurant. ✉ *10052 Malaspina Rd.,* ☎ *604/483–9775. AE, MC, V. Closed Mon.–Tues. in winter.*

$$–$$$  🏠 **Desolation Resort.** Tree-house-like chalets perch high above Okeover Arm at this isolated retreat 10 minutes from Lund. The one-, two-, and three-bedroom units, handcrafted in local woods and set on stilts for the best views, have large decks and big picture windows; some have electric fireplaces, and all have showers rather than bathtubs. This is a good base to explore the scenic reaches of Desolation Sound: you can rent powerboats, kayaks, or canoes here or take a tour in the resort's 33-ft cabin cruiser. ✉ *2694 Dawson Rd. (C-36, Malaspina Rd.,*

*R.R. 2, Powell River V8A 4Z3),* ☎ *604/483–3592,* ℻ *604/483–7942,*
🌐 *www.desolationresort.com. 5 chalets, 4 suites. Kitchens, some in-room hot tubs, dock, hiking, laundry facilities; no room phones, no room TVs, no smoking. AE, MC, V.*

**$$** 🏨 **Lund Hotel.** This three-story seaside hotel with its dormer windows and wraparound veranda dates to 1912. The rooms have simple, modern decor; some have balconies, and those in a newer extension have motel-style private entrances. On-site are a post office, a sea-view restaurant and pub, a general store, and a diving and kayaking outfitter. ✉ *1436 Hwy. 101 (Box 158, Lund V0N 2G0),* ☎ *604/414–0474 or 877/569–3999,* ℻ *604/414–0476,* 🌐 *www.lundhotel.com. 27 rooms. Refrigerators in some rooms, in-room VCRs, outdoor hot tub, dive shop, boating, marina, fishing, shops, laundry facilities, Internet, business services, meeting rooms, some pets allowed; no smoking. AE, MC, V.*

### Outdoor Activities and Sports

**Rockfish Kayaks** (✉ Lund Hotel, 1436 Hwy. 101, ☎ 604/414–9355) has rentals and runs guided paddles in the area. **Powell River Sea Kayaks** (✉ 10676 Crowther Rd., off Malaspina Rd., off Hwy. 101, 5 km [3 km] south of Lund, ☎ 604/483–2160) provides lessons, rentals, and tours into Desolation Sound. A one-day kayak rental is $35; a six-hour guided kayak tour is $99, which includes lunch.

# THE GULF ISLANDS

Of the hundreds of islands sprinkled across Georgia Strait between Vancouver Island and the mainland, the most popular and accessible are Galiano, Mayne, and Salt Spring. A temperate climate (warmer than Vancouver and with half the rainfall), shell beaches, rolling pastures, and virgin forests are common to all, but each island has its unique flavor. Marine birds are numerous, and there's unusual vegetation such as arbutus trees (also known as madrones, a leafy evergreen with red peeling bark) and Garry oaks.

These islands are rustic but not undiscovered. Writers, artists, and craftspeople as well as weekend cottagers and retirees from Vancouver and Victoria take full advantage of them. Make hotel reservations for summer stays. If you're bringing a car from the B.C. mainland, ferry reservations are highly recommended; indeed, they're required on some of the busier sailings.

## Galiano Island

**⑤** *20 nautical mi (1 to 2 hrs by ferry due to interisland stops) from Swartz Bay (32 km [20 mi] north of Victoria), 13 nautical mi (a 50-min ferry ride) from Tsawwassen (39 km [24 mi] south of Vancouver).*

Galiano's long, unbroken eastern shore is perfect for leisurely walks, and the numerous coves and inlets along its western coast make it a prime area for kayaking. Biological studies show that the straits between Vancouver Island and the B.C. mainland are home to North America's greatest variety of marine life. The frigid waters have superb visibility, especially in winter. Alcala Point, Porlier Pass, and Active Pass are top scuba-diving locations.

Galiano also has miles of trails through Douglas-fir forest that beg for exploration on foot or by bike. Hikers can climb to the top of Mt. Galiano for a view of the Olympic Mountains in Washington or trek the length of Bodega Ridge. The best spots for picnics, bird-watching, and views of Active Pass and the surrounding islands are Bluffs Park and Bellhouse Park. Anglers head to the point at Bellhouse Park to spin cast for salmon from shore, or they go by boat to Porlier Pass and Trincomali Channel.

**Montague Harbour Provincial Marine Park** (⊠ Montague Park Rd. off Montague Rd., ☎ 800/689–9025 camping reservations, WEB www.bcparks.ca) has walk-in and drive-in campsites and a long shell beach famed for its sunset views. You can rent a kayak, boat, or scooter at **Montague Harbour Marina** (⊠ Montague Park Rd., just east of the park, ☎ 250/539–5733). In summer, the marina's **Deck Restaurant** serves barbecued dinners on its waterside deck.

NEED A
BREAK?

If all the outdoor activity leaves you longing for human contact, head for the **Hummingbird Inn Pub** (⊠ 47 Sturdies Bay Rd., ☎ 250/539–5472), a friendly local hangout, with live music on summer weekends. On summer evenings, the pub's free shuttle bus picks up patrons at Montague Harbour marina and park.

## Dining and Lodging

$$–$$$
★

✕🏠 **Woodstone Country Inn.** The serene inn is at the edge of a forest overlooking a meadow that's fantastic for bird-watching. Tall windows bring the pastoral setting into spacious bedrooms decorated with antiques, hand-stenciled walls, and lush designer fabrics. All guest quarters have fireplaces; most have patios and oversize tubs. A hearty gourmet breakfast and afternoon tea are included in the rates. Woodstone's elegant restaurant ($$$), the Wisteria Dining Room, serves French-influenced Pacific Northwest fare, such as sweet corn and fennel soup, or herb-crusted rack of lamb. Four-course dinners are also served here; reservations are required. ⊠ Georgeson Bay Rd. (R.R. 1, V0N 1P0), ☎ 250/539–2022 or 888/339–2022, FAX 250/539–5198, WEB www.gulfislands.com/woodstone. 12 rooms. Restaurant, lounge, library, piano, Internet, business services, meeting room; no room phones, no room TVs, no smoking. AE, MC, V. Closed Dec.–Jan. BP.

$$–$$$
★

🏠 **Bellhouse Inn.** This seaside inn, modeled on an English manor house, blends 19th-century antiques, such as the 1860 farmhouse table where breakfast is served, with modern amenities. The Kingfisher Room has a whirlpool tub and a balcony with a full water view. The Eagle Room also has a balcony, with a forest and ocean view, as well as an extra-deep tub and the original hardwood floor. You can spot whales and eagles through the picture windows in the lounge or join the owner on his 43-ft sailboat. The main house caters to adults; families can stay in one of the 1960s two-bedroom cottages, both of which have kitchens. ⊠ 29 Farmhouse Rd. (Box 16, Site 4, V0N 1P0), ☎ 250/539–5667 or 800/970–7464, FAX 250/539–5316, WEB www.bellhouseinn.com. 3 rooms, 2 cottages. Beach, croquet; no room phones, no room TVs, no smoking. MC, V. BP.

## Outdoor Activities and Sports

BIKING

Bike rentals are available from **Galiano Bicycle** (⊠ 36 Burrill Rd., ☎ 250/539–9906), within walking distance of the Sturdies Bay ferry terminal.

FISHING

**Sporades Tours** (⊠ 1289 Galiano Way, ☎ 250/539–2278, WEB www.cedarplace/sporades) runs fishing and sightseeing charters. Tours are for a minimum of three hours, at $100 an hour for up to eight people.

GOLF

The **Galiano Golf and Country Club** (⊠ 24 St. Andrew Crescent, ☎ 250/539–5533 or 877/909–7888) is a 9-hole, par-32 course in a forest clearing.

For trail riding, contact **Bodega Resort** (☎ 250/539–2677), which conducts trips for all skill levels. A ride of about 70 minutes costs $25 per person.

KAYAKING

**Gulf Islands Kayaking** (⊠ Montague Harbour Marina, Montague Harbour Rd., ☎ 250/539–2442, WEB www.seakayak.bc.ca) has equipment rentals and guided kayak tours (three hours, $38; six hours $68).

SCUBA DIVING

For dive charters, contact **Galiano Diving** (☎ 250/539–3109, WEB www.galianodiving.com).

# Mayne Island

**6** *28 nautical mi from Swartz Bay (32 km [20 mi] north of Victoria), 22 nautical mi from Tsawwassen (39 km [24 mi] south of Vancouver).*

Middens of clam and oyster shells give evidence that tiny Mayne Island—only 21 square km (8 square mi)—was inhabited as early as 5,000 years ago. It later became the stopover point for miners headed from Victoria to the gold fields of the Fraser River and Barkerville. By the mid-1800s it was the communal center of the inhabited Gulf Islands, with the first school, post office, police lockup, church, and hotel. Farm tracts and orchards, established in the 1930s and 1940s and worked by Japanese farmers until their internment in World War II, still thrive here. Mayne's mild hills and wonderful scenery make it great territory for a vigorous bike ride.

A 45-minute hike up **Mt. Parke** leads to the island's highest point and a stunning view of the mainland and other gulf islands.

The village of Miners Bay is home to **Plumper Pass Lockup** (⊠ 433 Fernhill Rd., ☎ no phone), built in 1896 as a jail but now a minuscule museum (open July 1 to Labor Day, Friday to Monday 11–3; free) chronicling the island's history. After touring the Plumper Pass Lockup, consider stopping for a drink at the seaside **Springwater Lodge** (⊠ 400 Fernhill Rd., Miners Bay, ☎ 250/539–5521), one of the province's oldest hotels. If you're in Miners Bay on a Saturday between July and mid-October, check out the **Farmers' Market** outside the Agricultural Hall. Open 10–1, it sells produce and crafts.

From Miners Bay head north on Georgina Point Road to **St. Mary Magdalene Church,** a pretty stone chapel built in 1898. Active Pass Lighthouse, at the end of Georgina Point Road, north of Miners Bay, is part of **Georgina Point Heritage Park.** It was built in 1855 and still signals ships into the busy waterway. The grassy grounds are great for picnicking. **Bennett Bay Park,** part of the new Pacific Marine Heritage Legacy National Park, has one of the island's nicest beaches. There's a pebble beach for beachcombing at shallow (and therefore warmer) **Campbell Bay.**

## Dining and Lodging

$$–$$$$  ✕🏠 **Oceanwood Country Inn.** This Tudor-style house on 10 forested
★  acres overlooking Navy Channel has English country decor throughout. Fireplaces, French doors that open onto ocean-view balconies, and whirlpool baths make several rooms deluxe. The waterfront restaurant ($$$$) serves four-course table d'hôte dinners of outstanding regional cuisine. The menu changes daily, but highlights have included roasted Pacific salmon with a ragout of Salt Spring Island mussels and seared marinated quail with golden pearl onions and bacon and sage tempura. Room rates include afternoon tea and breakfast. ⊠ 630

## Salt Spring Island

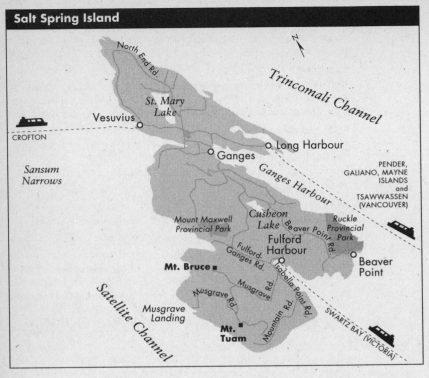

Dinner Bay Rd., Mayne Island V0N 2J0, ☎ 250/539–5074, ⒻⒶⓍ 250/539–3002, ⓌⒺⒷ www.oceanwood.com. 12 rooms. Hot tubs in some rooms, sauna, bicycles, library, meeting room; no room phones, no room TVs, no kids under 16, no smoking. MC, V. Closed Dec.–Feb. BP.

**$$–$$$** 🏠 **A Coachhouse on Oyster Bay.** Owner Brian Johnston designed this cedar waterfront house in the style of a turn-of-the-20th-century carriage house. Rooms are elegant, with bold colors, hardwood floors, private entrances, gas fireplaces, and views of Oyster Bay. The Landau Room, in a former hayloft above the barn, has a four-poster bed and a private hot tub on a deck overlooking the ocean. You can swim in the warm bay next to the property; watch seals, eagles, and whales from the gazebo on the shore; or soak in a hot tub on the ocean's edge. ✉ 511 Bayview Dr., Mayne Island V0N 2J0, ☎ 250/539–3368 or 888/629–6322, ⒻⒶⓍ 250/539–2236, ⓌⒺⒷ www.acoachhouse.com. 3 rooms. Outdoor hot tub, beach, bicycles, piano; no phones, no TVs, no smoking. MC, V. BP.

### Outdoor Activities and Sports

**Island Charters** (✉ 263 Laura Point Rd., ☎ 250/539–5040) operates half- or full-day trips on a crewed 33-ft sailboat. Half-day trips are $155 for two people, $180 for four; full-day trips are $180 and $210, respectively. At **Mayne Island Kayak and Canoe Rentals** (✉ 411 Fernhill Rd., Miners Bay, ☎ 250/539–5599, ⓌⒺⒷ www.maynekayak.com), kayak day rentals start at $45.

## Salt Spring Island

❼ 28 nautical mi from Swartz Bay (32 km [20 mi] north of Victoria), 22 nautical mi from Tsawwassen (39 km [24 mi] south of Vancouver).

Named for the saltwater springs at its north end, Salt Spring is the largest and most developed of the Gulf Islands. Among the first nonnative settlers to arrive in the 1850s were African-Americans fleeing repression in California, seafarers from Hawaii, and a small group of Australians. The agrarian tradition they and other immigrants established remains strong (a Fall Fair has been held every September since 1896), but tourism and art now support the local economy.

**Ganges,** a pedestrian-oriented seaside village about 6 km (4 mi) from the Long Harbour ferry terminal, is the main commercial center for Salt Spring Island's 10,000 residents. It has dozens of smart boutiques, galleries, and restaurants. Many of the artists' studios throughout the island are open to the public. To find them, watch for studio signs on the roadways, or pick up a studio tour map at the **visitor information center** (✉ 121 Lower Ganges Rd., ☎ 250/537–5252 or 866/216–2936, WEB www.saltspringtoday.com) in Ganges.

At the south end of Salt Spring Island, where the ferries from Victoria arrive, is the tiny village of **Fulford,** which has a café, a kayaking outlet, and several offbeat boutiques. Ferries from Crofton, on Vancouver Island, arrive on Salt Spring Island at **Vesuvius,** an even smaller village than Fulford, with a restaurant, an old-fashioned general store, a swimming beach, and crafts studios, on the west side of the island. You can catch the island's best sunset views from the deck of the **Vesuvius Inn Neighbourhood Pub** (☎ 250/537–2312) at the end of Vesuvius Bay Road.

Near the center of Salt Spring Island, the summit of **Mt. Maxwell Provincial Park** (✉ Mt. Maxwell Rd., off Fulford–Ganges Rd.) has spectacular views of south Salt Spring, Vancouver Island, and other Gulf Islands. The last portion of the drive is steep, winding, and unpaved.

**Ruckle Provincial Park** (✉ Beaver Point Rd., WEB www.bcparks.ca) is the site of an 1872 homestead and extensive fields still farmed by the Ruckle family. The park also has picnic spots and non-reservable seaside campsites, 11 km (7 mi) of coastline, a beach, and 8 km (5 mi) of trails leading to rocky headlands.

There's no public transportation on Salt Spring, so your land travel options are cabs or rental cars. Several establishments also rent bikes and scooters. The tiny *Queen of de Nile* ferry runs from Moby's Marine Pub and Ganges Marina to Ganges town center. There's also water-taxi service to Mayne and Galiano islands.

## Dining and Lodging

**$$$** ✗ **House Piccolo.** Piccolo, the Finnish-born chef-owner of this tiny nine-table restaurant, serves beautifully prepared and presented European cuisine. Piccolo, an award-winning chef, creates such Scandinavian-influenced creations as venison with a rowan and juniper-berry scented demi-glace and charbroiled fillet steak with Gorgonzola sauce. For dessert, there's homemade ice cream, vodka-moistened lingonberry crepes, and a rich chocolate terrine Finlandia. The 250-item wine list is one of the best on the islands and includes many hard-to-find vintages. The indoor tables are cozy and candlelit; the outdoor patio is a pleasant summer dining spot. ✉ *108 Hereford Ave., Ganges,* ☎ *250/537–1844. MC, V. No lunch.*

**$–$$** ✗ **The Oystercatcher.** Panfried oysters and fresh salmon share menu space with burgers, pasta, cocktail snacks, and a kids' menu at this popular spot on Ganges's waterfront. Inside, the look is casual, nautical, and up-to-date, with a river-rock fireplace, rich colors, and a scull suspended from the ceiling. On the deck and patio, harbor views steal the scene. Open for breakfast in summer, the Oystercatcher serves food all day and morphs into a Bellini bar come sundown. ✉ *104 Manson Rd., on the waterfront, Ganges,* ☎ *250/537–5041. MC, V.*

$     ✕ **Moby's Marine Pub.** Big portions of great food such as warm salmon or scallop salad and lamb burgers, a harborside deck, a cozy room with fireplaces, and Sunday evening jazz make this friendly, no-smoking pub a favorite. Be prepared to wait in line on summer weekends. Patrons must be at least 19 years of age. ⊠ *124 Upper Ganges Rd.,* ☎ *250/ 537–5559. Reservations not accepted. MC, V.*

$$$$   ✕📷 **Hastings House.** The centerpiece of this 25-acre seaside estate is a 1940 country house, built in the style of an 11th-century Sussex manor. Guest quarters in the manor, in renovated historic outbuildings, and in a newer addition overlooking Ganges Harbour are decorated in an English country style, with antiques, locally crafted woodwork, and fireplaces or woodstoves. Five-course prix-fixe dinners in the manor house are open to the public ($$$$; reservations essential, jacket required in the main dining room). The excellent cuisine includes local lamb, seafood, and herbs and produce from the inn's gardens. The spa gives facials, manicures, and massages. ⊠ *160 Upper Ganges Rd., V8K 2S2,* ☎ *250/537–2362 or 800/661–9255,* FAX *250/537–5333,* WEB *www. hastingshouse.com. 3 rooms, 14 suites, 1 guest house. Restaurant, in-room data ports, minibars, spa, bicycles, boccie, croquet, lounge, laundry service, business services, meeting rooms; no room TVs, no kids under 16, no-smoking rooms. AE, MC, V. Closed mid-Nov.–mid-Mar. BP.*

$$$   📷 **Anne's Oceanfront Hideaway.** On a steep seaside slope 6 km (4 mi) north of the Vesuvius ferry terminal, this modern home has a cozy library, a sitting room, an elevator, and two verandas. Every room has a hydromassage tub; three have balconies. The Douglas Fir and Garry Oak rooms have the best views. Luxurious amenities—morning coffee brought to your door, robes, and a welcoming bottle of wine—make this a comfortable place to unwind. One room is wheelchair accessible. ⊠ *168 Simson Rd., V8K 1E2,* ☎ *250/537–0851 or 888/474–2663,* FAX *250/537–0861,* WEB *www.annesoceanfront.com. 4 rooms. Refrigerators, outdoor hot tub, massage, boating, bicycles, library, laundry facilities, Internet; no room TVs, no kids, no smoking. AE, MC, V. BP.*

$$$   📷 **Apple Hill Farm.** Francophile Nancy France has filled this weathered hillside farmhouse with local art and whimsical treasures. The guest rooms (one with a sauna), the cozy common room with its big river-rock fireplace, and the nooks and crannies throughout are decorated in a singular European country style and have meadow and sea views. A wide deck, a rustic gazebo, and 43 acres of farmland provide plenty of opportunities for contemplation. Riding stables are just next door. Expect breakfast to include organic eggs, fruit, and vegetables from the farm. ⊠ *201 Wright Rd., V8K 2H8,* ☎ *250/537–9738,* FAX *250/ 538–0217,* WEB *www.applehillfarm.net. 3 rooms. Refrigerators, tennis court, hot tub, massage, sauna, hiking, piano; no room phones, no room TVs, no smoking. MC. BP.*

$$$   📷 **Old Farmhouse Bed and Breakfast.** A registered historic property built in 1894, this white saltbox farmhouse sits in a quiet 3-acre meadow near St. Mary Lake. The style of the main house is echoed in the four-room wing added in 1989, which has comfortable guest rooms furnished with pine bedsteads, down comforters, hardwood floors, and wicker chairs. Each has a balcony or patio. There's also a one-bedroom cottage. The breakfasts of fresh baked goods and hot entrées such as smoked-salmon soufflé are legendary. ⊠ *1077 North End Rd., V8K 1L9,* ☎ *250/537– 4113,* FAX *250/537–4969,* WEB *www.bbcanada.com/oldfarmhouse. 4 rooms, 1 cottage. Fans; no room phones, no room TVs, no kids under 6, no smoking V. Closed Nov.–Feb. BP.*

$$–$$$   📷 **Beddis House.** This 1900 waterfront farmhouse is home to a guest parlor and breakfast room. The three guest rooms, enriched with country pine and a sprinkling of antiques, are in a sympathetic modern coach house next door. All rooms have woodstoves, claw-foot tubs,

and an ocean-view deck or balcony. The Rose Bower Room takes up most of the top floor and has a king-size four-poster bed as well as sea and garden views. You can stroll in the 1¼-acre garden or step down to the inn's white clamshell beach. Local outfitters will deliver kayaks to the property, too. ⊠ *131 Miles Ave., V8K 2E1,* ☎ *250/537–1028 or 866/537–1028,* WEB *www.beddishousebandb.com. 3 rooms. Fans, beach, croquet, laundry service, Internet; no room phones, no room TVs, no kids under 14, no smoking. MC, V. Closed Dec.–Jan. BP.*

$ 📷 **Salt Spring Island Hostel.** In the 10 forested acres behind this hostel near Cusheon Lake are canvas tepees, furnished tree houses (sleeping rooms without baths) reached by a ladder or a staircase, and a Gypsy caravan for two. The main building has private guest rooms, three small dorms, a shared kitchen, and a cozy common room with a woodstove. You can rent bicycles and scooters here, and the friendly owners can arrange kayaking, sailing, and a range of other activities. ⊠ *640 Cusheon Lake Rd., V8K 2C2,* ☎ *250/537–4149,* WEB *www.beacom.com/ssihostel. 2 rooms, 1 with bath; 2 tree houses; 3 tepees; 3 dorms with 4–6 beds. Bicycles, Internet; no room phones, no room TVs, no smoking. MC. Closed mid-Oct–mid-Mar.*

## Nightlife and the Arts

To find out what's happening and who's playing, see the local weekly, the *Driftwood,* or contact the Ganges Tourist Info Centre.

You can catch a live music show or a play at **ArtSpring** (⊠ 100 Jackson Ave., ☎ 250/537–2102 or 866/537–2102), a theater and gallery complex in Ganges. If you're looking for music in Fulford, try the **Fulford Inn** (⊠ 2661 Fulford-Ganges Rd., ☎ 250/653–4432). **Moby's Marine Pub** (⊠ 124 Upper Ganges Rd., ☎ 250/537–5559) is the place to go for live jazz every Sunday night. DJs and live bands make **Talons Nightclub** (⊠ Gasoline Alley, on the waterfront, ☎ 250/537–8585) a popular hangout. The **Treehouse Café** (⊠ 106 Purvis La., ☎ 250/537–5379), next to Mouat's Trading Company, hosts local musicians throughout the summer.

## Outdoor Activities and Sports

For information about hiking trails and beach access, pick up a copy of the "Salt Spring Out-of-Doors Map," available at Salt Spring bookstores.

### BIKING

**Salt Spring Kayak and Cycle** (⊠ 2923 Fulford-Ganges Rd., Fulford, ☎ 250/653–4222), on the wharf, rents and repairs bikes.

### BOATING, KAYAKING, AND SAILING

**Island Escapades** (⊠ 163 Fulford-Ganges Rd., Ganges, ☎ 250/537–2537 or 888/529–2567, WEB www.islandescapades.com) has guided kayaking ($35–$95 for two to six hours; the longer tour includes a three-course dinner on the beach) and sailing trips ($40–$75 per person for three or four hours).

**Salt Spring Kayak and Cycle** (⊠ 2923 Fulford-Ganges Rd., Fulford, ☎ 250/653–4222) rents kayaks and provides lessons and trips. Guided day paddles are $50 ($30 for two hours at sunset).

**Salt Spring Marine Rentals** (⊠ head of Ganges Harbour next to Moby's Marine Pub, ☎ 250/537–9100, WEB www.saltspring.com/rentals) rents kayaks and powerboats. Kayaks cost $45 a day, or $12 per hour; powerboats go for $110 a day. It's also a good place to arrange fishing, sailing, and sightseeing charters; buy fishing licenses; and rent scooters ($70 a day).

**Sea Otter Kayaking** (⊠ 149 Lower Ganges Rd., on Ganges Harbour at foot of Rainbow Rd., Ganges, ☎ 250/537–5678 or 877/537–5678,

WEB www.seaotterkayaking.com) provides kayak sales, rentals, lessons, and tours. A two-hour introductory lesson is $35. The company also leads sailing charters and multiday kayaking and sailing trips around the Gulf Islands.

GOLF

**Blackburn Meadows Golf Club** (✉ 269 Blackburn Rd., ☎ 250/537–1707) borders a lake. Its 9 holes ($14; $24 for 18) provides you with a chance to play on Canada's only organic golf course.

**Salt Spring Island Golf and Country Club** (✉ 805 Lower Ganges Rd., ☎ 250/537–2121) is a pleasant 9-hole course ($20; $31 for 18 holes) with a restaurant in the clubhouse.

At **Hart Memorial Disc Golf Course** (✉ end of Seaview Ave., Ganges), players aim to hit a series of 18 targets with Frisbee-like discs. It's free (you can pick up a disc at Ganges's toy store or hardware store).

HIKING

**Island Escapades** (✉ 163 Fulford-Ganges Rd., Ganges, ☎ 250/537–2537 or 888/529–2567, WEB www.islandescapades.com) organizes hiking and climbing trips as well as easy nature tours. A three-hour hike costs about $30; outdoor rock climbing (with equipment supplied) is $65. They also run outdoor adventure programs for children and teens.

HORSEBACK RIDING

You can take small group trail rides with **Salt Spring Guided Rides** (☎ 250/537–5761). Reservations are necessary. The cost is $30 an hour.

SWIMMING

St. Mary Lake, on North End Road, and Cusheon Lake, south of Ganges, are your best bets for warm-water swimming.

## Shopping

Ganges's Mahon Hall is the site of **ArtCraft,** a summer-long sale of works by more than 200 artisans. Salt Spring's biggest arts-and-crafts gallery, **Coastal Currents Gallery** (✉ 133 Hereford Ave., Ganges, ☎ 250/537–0070) sells assorted crafts from all over British Columbia. Everything at the **Salt Spring Island Saturday Market** (☎ 250/537–4448, WEB www.saltspringmarket.com), held in Ganges's Centennial Park every Saturday April through October, has been made, baked, or grown on the island. Fresh produce, crafts, clothing, candles, toys, home-canned items, and more are for sale.

# COAST MOUNTAIN CIRCLE

A stunning sampler of mainland British Columbia, a drive into the Coast Mountains from Vancouver follows the Sea to Sky Highway (Highway 99) past fjordlike Howe Sound, the town of Squamish, and Whistler Resort, and then continues on a quiet back road to the gold-rush town of Lillooet. From Lillooet, you can continue into the High Country or return to Vancouver on Highways 12 and 1 through the gorges of the Fraser Canyon, stopping for a soak at Harrison Hot Springs on the way. This is a scenic two- to three-day drive; the roads are good but are best avoided in snow, particularly if you plan to travel past Whistler.

## Horseshoe Bay

**❽** *20 km (12 mi) north of Vancouver, 100 km (62 mi) south of Whistler.*

Tucked into a cove under the Coast Mountains, this little community is the ferry hub for boats to Nanaimo on Vancouver Island, Langdale on the Sunshine Coast, and tiny Bowen Island, a rural retreat 20 minutes across the sound that has pubs, B&Bs, crafts shops, and even a winery. Near Horseshoe Bay, off Marine Drive, is **Whytecliff Park,** with a swimming beach, picnic sites, and a rocky little island that's connected to the mainland at low tide.

From Horseshoe Bay, the Sea to Sky Highway (Highway 99) becomes one of British Columbia's most scenic roads, climbing into the mountains along the edge of Howe Sound. Most people on this road are eager to reach the resort town of Whistler, two hours to the north. A number of sights along the way are worth a stop, however.

At the **B.C. Museum of Mining,** once the British Empire's largest copper mine and now a national historic site, the knowledgeable staff offers guided tours of old mine workings and a chance to pan for gold. The museum is about an hour north of Vancouver. ⊠ *Hwy. 99, Britannia Beach,* ☎ *604/896–2233 or 800/896–4044,* ⓦⒺⒷ *www.bcmuseumofmining.org.* 🖅 *$12.95.* ☉ *May–mid-Oct., daily 9–4:30; mid-Oct.–Apr., call for times.*

About 42 km (25 mi) north of Horseshoe Bay is **Shannon Falls,** which at 1,105 ft is Canada's third-highest waterfall. You can see it from the highway or follow a short trail through the woods for a closer look.

# Squamish

🄌 *67 km (42 mi) north of Vancouver, 58 km (36 mi) south of Whistler.*

Squamish, or "mother of the winds" in the local First Nations language, has long languished in the shadow of Whistler Resort up the highway. Outdoors enthusiasts have, however, begun to discover its possibilities. The big winds that gave the area its name make it an excellent windsurfing spot. Diving in Howe Sound, kayaking on the sea and in nearby rivers, and hiking are also draws. The **Stawamus Chief,** an enormous rock face on the edge of Highway 99, is the world's second-largest granite monolith (after the Rock of Gibraltar). It attracts rock climbers from all over.

Between November and February the world's largest concentrations of bald eagles gather at the **Brackendale Eagles' Park** (⊠ Government Rd. off Hwy. 99, Brackendale, ☎ no phone), about 7 km (4 mi) north of Squamish. The park is open dawn to dusk; admission is free. You can watch the eagles from the banks of the Squamish River, off Government Road in Brackendale, or spot the birds from a raft on the Cheakamus River. The **Brackendale Eagle Festival and Count** (☎ 604/898–3333 Brackendale Art Gallery for information), with music and art events, has sprung up around the annual eagle count, held in January.

The **West Coast Railway Heritage Park,** about a 10-minute drive north of downtown Squamish, has more than 60 pieces of late-19th- and early 20th-century rolling stock. You can ride a minitrain around the site, climb on a caboose, ring the bell on a steam locomotive, and stroll through a restored 1890 first-class business car—the sort of thing railway barons rode in—as well as a 1905 colonists' car that carried settlers to the prairies in minimal comfort. It's also home to the Royal Hudson steam engine that used to run between North Vancouver and Squamish. There's a gift shop and archives in a 1915-style station house. ⊠ *39645 Government Rd.,* ☎ *604/898–9336,* ⓦⒺⒷ *www.wcra.org.* 🖅 *$8.* ☉ *Daily 10–5.*

## Dining and Lodging

**$–$$** ✕ **The Roadhouse Restaurant.** A fixture on Highway 99 since the 1970s, this wood-paneled roadhouse across from Shannon Falls serves breakfasts, lunches, and dinners of updated comfort food and Pacific

Northwest cuisine. The menu changes seasonally, but highlights have included a starter of sautéed oysters with spinach, black beans, chilies, and cream and such main dishes as baby-back ribs with honey-apple glaze, or grilled spring salmon with sun-dried cranberry cream. Most of the seats inside and on the patio have great views of the mountains and the falls. ⊠ *Klahanie, Shannon Falls, Hwy. 99 (5 km [3 mi] south of Squamish),* ☎ *604/892–5312. MC, V.*

$$ ✕⊡ **Howe Sound Inn & Brewing Company.** This cedar inn near
★ Squamish town center covers all the bases. The fireplace in the cozy post-and-beam brewpub is a great place to relax after a day of hiking or rafting. You can also watch climbers tackling Stawamus Chief from the pub's patio or take a brewery tour. The rustic yet elegant Red Heather restaurant ($–$$) serves Pacific Northwest cuisine and fresh goods from the in-house bakery (try the ale-and-cheddar bread). The rooms upstairs have furniture made of reclaimed fir; most have striking views of Stawamus Chief or the Tantalus Mountains. ⊠ *37801 Cleveland Ave. (Box 978, V0N 3G0),* ☎ *604/892–2603 or 800/919–2537,* FAX *604/892–2631,* WEB *www.howesound.com. 20 rooms. Restaurant, in-room data ports, cable TV, sauna, billiards, pub, business services, meeting rooms; no smoking. AE, MC, V.*

$$ ⊡ **Sunwolf Outdoor Centre.** A highlight of this former fishing lodge on the Cheakamus River, 10 km (6 mi) north of Squamish, is its rafting center, which specializes in Class IV (fast-moving rapids) white-water trips but also offers peaceful floats on slow-moving water. Sunwolf's cabins, tucked in the woods on the 5½-acre property, are attractive and modern, with fir floors, four-poster beds, handcrafted pine furniture, gas fireplaces, and vaulted ceilings. The cozy lodge has fireplaces and an outdoor deck. In December and January, this is a prime spot for viewing bald eagles. ⊠ *70002 Squamish Valley Rd., 4 km [2½ mi] off Hwy. 99 (Box 244, Brackendale V0N 1H0),* ☎ *604/898–1537 or 877/806–8046,* FAX *604/898–1634,* WEB *www.sunwolf.net. 10 cabins. Café, fans, some kitchenettes, outdoor hot tub, fishing, mountain bikes, badminton, croquet, horseshoes, volleyball, Internet, meeting rooms, some pets allowed (fee); no room phones, no room TVs, no smoking. MC, V.*

## Outdoor Activities and Sports

Squamish is a major rock-climbing destination and also a popular spot for hiking, diving, trail riding, sailing, rafting, and kayaking. The **Canadian Outback Adventure Company** (☎ 604/921–7250 or 800/565–8735, WEB www.canadianoutback.com) runs a variety of rafting day trips in the area, including eagle rafting trips on the Cheakamus River and an easygoing trip for families. For airplane or helicopter flightseeing tours over area glaciers, including helicopter landings on a glacier, picnics on a glacier, or other helicopter-based adventures, contact **Glacier Air Tours** (☎ 604/898–9016 or 800/265–0088, WEB www.glacierair.com). **Sea to Sky Stables** (⊠ Paradise Valley Rd., about 3 km [2 mi] off Hwy. 99, ☎ 604/898–3908 or 866/898–3934, WEB www.seatoskystables.com) leads trail rides for all levels year-round. Guided rides start at about $35 an hour. The company also has river rafting, ATV tours, kayaking, and guided hikes; you can stay overnight in chuck wagons or a teepee.

### GOLF

The challenging 18-hole, par-72 course (open early March–late October) at **Furry Creek Golf and Country Club** (⊠ Hwy. 99, Furry Creek, ☎ 604/922–9576 or 888/922–9462), south of Squamish, has striking ocean views and greens fees of about $99, including a mandatory cart. The **Squamish Valley Golf & Country Club** (⊠ 2458 Mamquam Rd., ☎ 604/898–9691 or 888/349–3688) is an 18-hole, par-72 course close to town. Greens fees are about $55.

*En Route*   Between Squamish and Whistler on Highway 99 is the 231-ft-high **Brandywine Falls.** A short trail through the woods takes you to a viewing platform.

# Whistler

★ ⑩   *120 km (74 mi) north of Vancouver, 58 km (36 mi) north of Squamish.*

Whistler and Blackcomb mountains, part of Whistler Resort, are consistently ranked among North America's top ski destinations. Between them they have the largest ski area and two longest vertical drops on the continent, as well as one of the world's most advanced lift systems. The ski-in, ski-out village has enough shops, restaurants, nightlife, and other activities that it's easy to fill a vacation without ever hitting the slopes. In winter, the resort buzzes with skiers and snowboarders from all over the world. In summer the pace is more relaxed as the focus shifts to cycling, hiking, and boating around Whistler Valley.

At the base of the mountains are Whistler Village, Village North (also called Marketplace), and Upper Village—a rapidly expanding, interconnected community of lodgings, restaurants, pubs, and boutiques. Locals refer to the entire area as Whistler Village. With dozens of hotels and condos within a five-minute walk of the mountains, the site is always bustling. Another village center, called Whistler Creek, is developing along Highway 99 a couple of miles to the south.

Whistler Village is a pedestrians-only community. Anywhere you want to go within the resort is at most five minutes away, and parking lots are just outside the village. The bases of Whistler and Blackcomb mountains are also just at the village edge; in fact, you can ski right into the lower level of the Fairmont Chateau Whistler Hotel.

## Dining

**$$$–$$$$** ✕ **Val d'Isère.** Chef-owner Roland Pfaff satisfies a skier's craving for fine French food with traditional dishes from his native Alsace and with Gallic takes on Canadian produce. Some specialties served in this elegant room overlooking the Town Plaza are Dungeness crab ravioli with smoked-salmon cream sauce, sea bass fillet baked in a potato crust with a Pinot Noir reduction, and veal tenderloin with Vancouver Island morel mushroom sauce. ⊠ *Bear Lodge, Town Plaza, 4314 Main St.,* ☎ *604/ 932–4666. AE, DC, MC, V. No lunch Nov.–May.*

**$$–$$$$** ✕ **Araxi.** Golden walls, terra-cotta tiles, and original artwork create a vibrant backdrop to the French-influenced Pacific Northwest cuisine here. Local farmers grow produce exclusively for Araxi's chef, who also make good use of cheese, game, and fish from the province. Breads and pastries are made in-house each morning. The menu changes seasonally, but dishes have included Fraser Valley rabbit and alder-smoked B.C. arctic char with saffron and oyster-mushroom sauce. Wine lovers, take note: there's a 13,000-bottle inventory and five sommeliers. A heated patio is open in summer, and the lounge, with a low-priced bar menu ($), is a popular après-ski spot. ⊠ *4222 Village Sq.,* ☎ *604/932– 4540. AE, DC, MC, V. No lunch Oct.–May.*

**$$–$$$$** ✕ **Bearfoot Bistro.** The cutesy name belies the elegance of this acclaimed bistro. The 75-seat dining room has a warm Latin feel with tall leather chairs, open kitchen, and live jazz nightly. The multicourse set menus ($85–$200) change frequently but have featured such dishes as seared Quebec foie gras, tamari-glazed black cod, blue-fin tuna tartar, and a delicious lobster in white chocolate sauce. Kobe beef and wild caribou are specialties. The adjacent wine bar serves casual French bistro fare ($$–$$$). Diners in either section can sample from the highly rated 1,600-label wine cellar. ✉ *4121 Village Green,* ☎ *604/ 932–3433. AE, D, DC, MC, V. No lunch.*

**$$–$$$$**   ✕ **Il Caminetto di Umberto.** Owner Umberto Menghi serves down-home Italian cooking in a relaxed atmosphere. Il Caminetto has an urban, Florentine style with warm gold walls and terra-cotta tiles. It's known for its grilled veal chops, osso buco, and game dishes. ✉ *4242 Village Stroll,* ☎ *604/932–4442. AE, DC, MC, V. No lunch.*

**$$–$$$$**   ✕ **La Rúa.** Reddish flagstone floors and sponge-painted walls, a wine cellar behind a wrought-iron door, modern oil paintings, and sconce lighting give La Rúa an intimate, Mediterranean ambience. Favorites from the Continental menu include charred rare tuna, loin of fallow deer, and rack of lamb. ✉ *4557 Blackcomb Way,* ☎ *604/932–5011. AE, DC, MC, V. No lunch.*

**$$–$$$$**   ✕ **Quattro at Whistler.** Vancouverites who've enjoyed the Corsi family's central Italian fare at their city restaurants flock here for warming après-ski meals. The *L'abbuffata,* a five-course Roman feast, comes on family-size platters meant for sharing; other popular mains include duck breast with blueberry and juniper-berry demi-glace, pistachio-crusted sea bass, and veal strip loin in a chardonnay butter sauce. Hand-painted Venetian chandeliers, dark woods, two fireplaces, and an open kitchen create a relaxing ambience. Nine hundred wine varieties and a impressive grappa selection fill the cellar. ✉ *4319 Main St.,* ☎ *604/ 905–4844,* WEB *www.quattrorestaurants.com. AE, DC, MC, V. No lunch.*

**$$–$$$**   ✕ **Trattoria di Umberto.** Owned by Umberto Menghi, who also owns Il Caminetto di Umberto, this relaxed restaurant specializes in such Tuscan countryside dishes as veal scallopini with marsala, and cioppino in a saffron, tomato, and fennel broth. ✉ *4417 Sundial Pl.,* ☎ *604/ 932–5858. AE, DC, MC, V.*

**$–$$**   ✕ **Pasta Lupino.** Fresh pasta at tiny prices draws hungry skiers to this little Whistler Marketplace trattoria. You can mix and match from a choice of pastas of the day with homemade alfredo, Bolognese, or fresh basil and plum tomato sauce, or dig into one of the house specialties: lasagna, ravioli, and spaghettini with meatballs are popular choices. Vegetarian pastas, decadent desserts, beer, and wine are also available. The six tables fill up quickly, but there's always takeout. ✉ *121–4368 Main St. (next to the 7-11),* ☎ *604/905–0400. Reservations not accepted. MC, V.*

## Lodging

Price categories are based on January-to-April ski-season rates; prices can be higher during Christmas and spring break and lower in summer. Many properties require minimum stays, especially during the Christmas season. Also, Whistler Village has some serious nightlife. If peace and quiet are important to you, ask for a room away from the main pedestrian thoroughfares or stay in one of the residential neighborhoods outside the village. Expect to pay C$18 to C$20 for overnight parking at hotels in the village; accommodations outside the village don't normally charge for parking.

You can book lodgings, including B&Bs, pensions, and hundreds of time-share condos, through **Whistler Central Reservations** (☎ 604/932–4222; 604/664–5625 in Vancouver; 800/944–7853 in the U.S. and Canada; WEB www.mywhistler.com).

**$$$$**   🏨 **Delta Whistler Resort.** Leather wing chairs around the lobby fireplace and a wealth of facilities highlight this family-friendly resort complex at the base of the Whistler and Blackcomb gondolas. Rooms, attractively decorated with soft greens and light pine, are so large that most can easily accommodate four people. Many have fireplaces, whirlpool baths, and balconies; some suites have saunas. An on-site spa has a variety of soothing post-ski treatments, including acupressure and stone therapy. ⊠ *4050 Whistler Way, V0N 1B4,* ☎ *604/932–1982 or 800/268–1133,* 𝔉𝔄𝔛 *604/932–7332,* 𝔚𝔈𝔅 *www.delta-whistler.com. 264 rooms, 24 suites. Restaurant, room service, in-room data ports, in-room safes, some kitchens, minibars, cable TV with movies and video games, pool, gym, hot tubs (indoor and outdoor), sauna, spa, billiards, ski shop, ski storage, bar, piano, shops, baby-sitting, children's programs (ages 4–12), dry cleaning, laundry facilities, laundry service, concierge, Internet, business services, meeting rooms, parking (fee), some pets allowed (fee); no-smoking floors. AE, DC, MC, V.*

$$$$ ⊞ **Delta Whistler Village Suites.** Gold-color walls, light pine furniture, Navajo-pattern sofas, and desert-theme art create a warm Southwest look at this family-friendly hotel near the Whistler Conference Centre. The apartment-size one- and two-bedroom suites have fully equipped kitchens, fireplaces, balconies—even an en-suite washer and dryer. The studio suites are cozy with kitchenettes. ⊠ *4308 Main St., V0N 1B4,* ☎ *604/905–3987 or 888/299–3987,* 𝔉𝔄𝔛 *604/938–6500,* 𝔚𝔈𝔅 *www.delta-whistler.com/village. 23 rooms, 184 suites. 2 restaurants, room service, in-room data ports, some kitchens, some kitchenettes, cable TV with movies and video games, indoor-outdoor pool, gym, hot tubs (indoor and outdoor), massage, sauna, steam rooms, bicycles, ski shop, ski storage, bar, nightclub, shops, baby-sitting, children's programs (ages 4–12), dry cleaning, laundry facilities, laundry service, concierge, Internet, business services, meeting rooms, parking (fee), some pets allowed (fee); no-smoking floors. AE, DC, MC, V.*

$$$$ ⊞ **Fairmont Château Whistler Resort.** This family-friendly fortress just
★ steps from the Blackcomb ski lifts is a self-contained, ski-in, ski-out resort-within-a-resort, with its own shopping arcade, golf course, and spa. The lobby is filled with rustic Canadiana, handmade Mennonite rugs, enticing overstuffed sofas, and a grand fireplace. Standard rooms are comfortably furnished and of average size, decorated in burgundies and turquoises, and most have mountain views. Rooms and suites on the Entrée Gold floors have fireplaces, whirlpool tubs, and their own concierge and private lounge. The resort's Wildflower Restaurant serves fine Pacific Northwest fare with stunning mountain views. ⊠ *4599 Château Blvd., V0N 1B4,* ☎ *604/938–8000 or 800/606–8244,* 𝔉𝔄𝔛 *604/938–2099,* 𝔚𝔈𝔅 *www.fairmont.com. 500 rooms, 56 suites. 2 restaurants, room service, in-room safes, minibars, cable TV with movies and video games, 18-hole golf course, 3 tennis courts, 2 pools (1 indoor-outdoor), gym, 4 hot tubs (1 indoor and 3 outdoor), sauna, spa, steam room, ski shop, ski storage, lobby lounge, shops, baby-sitting, dry cleaning, laundry facilities, concierge, concierge floor, Internet, business services, convention center, parking (fee), some pets allowed (fee); no-smoking floors. AE, D, DC, MC, V.*

$$$$ ⊞ **Pan Pacific Lodge.** Tucked at the base of both mountains, this eight-story lodge is steps from the Whistler and Blackcomb gondolas. Guest quarters include studios with pull-down queen beds or one- and two-bedroom suites. All units have balconies, gas fireplaces, and floor-to-ceiling windows that make the most of the mountain or valley views. The use of rich colors, cherrywood, and granite makes the rooms sleek and modern. In the evening, excellent Irish cuisine is served and you can hear traditional music in the Dubh Linn Gate Pub downstairs. ⊠ *4320 Sundial Crescent, V0N 1B4,* ☎ *604/905–2999 or 888/905–9995,* 𝔉𝔄𝔛 *604/905–2995,* 𝔚𝔈𝔅 *www.panpacific.com. 76 suites, 45 studios. Room service, kitchens, in-room data ports, in-room safes, cable TV with movies and video games, pool, gym, 2 outdoor hot tubs, massage, steam room, ski shop, ski storage, pub, shops,*

*dry cleaning, laundry facilities, laundry service, Internet, meeting rooms, parking (fee); no smoking. AE, DC, MC, V.*

**$$$$**  ⊞ **Westin Resort & Spa.** This luxury hotel has a prime location on the
★      edge of the village. Stone, slate, pine, and cedar are used throughout the two-story lobby. The studio and one- and two-bedroom suites are chic and cozy, with moss-green and rust color schemes, gas fireplaces, extra-deep tubs, and exceptionally comfortable beds. The 1,400-square-ft, split-level suites are great for families: each has a full kitchen and a loft bedroom with a whirlpool tub. The spa, with 25 treatment rooms and a mountain-view lounge, has facials, body wraps, shiatsu, hot-rock massages, and such holistic therapies as herbology and acupuncture. ⊠ *4090 Whistler Way, V0N 1B4,* ☎ *604/905–5000 or 888/634–5577,* 𝖥𝖠𝖷 *604/905–5589,* 𝖶𝖤𝖡 *www.westinwhistler.net. 204 rooms, 215 suites. Restaurant, room service, in-room data ports, in-room safes, kitchens in some rooms, cable TV with movies and video games, golf privileges, indoor-outdoor pool, health club, hot tub, outdoor hot tub, massage, sauna, spa, steam room, ski shop, ski storage, bar, shops, baby-sitting, children's programs (ages 18 months–12 years), dry cleaning, laundry facilities, laundry service, concierge, Internet, business services, meeting rooms, parking (fee); no smoking. AE, D, DC, MC, V.*

**$$–$$$$**  ⊞ **Durlacher Hof.** Custom fir woodwork and doors, exposed ceiling
★      beams, a *kachelofen* (farmhouse fireplace-oven), and antler chandeliers hung over fir benches and tables carry out the rustic Tyrolean theme of this fancy inn a few minutes' walk from the village. The bedrooms are adorned in Ralph Lauren and have custom-crafted furniture; most have balconies. Two top-floor rooms are very spacious and have such amenities as whirlpool tubs; smaller rooms have showers rather than tubs. A hearty European breakfast and afternoon tea are included, and dinner is served occasionally. ⊠ *7055 Nesters Rd., V0N 1B7,* ☎ *604/932–1924 or 877/932–1924,* 𝖥𝖠𝖷 *604/938–1980,* 𝖶𝖤𝖡 *www.durlacherhof.com. 8 rooms. Outdoor hot tub, massage, sauna, piano, ski storage, free parking; no room phones, no room TVs, no smoking. MC, V. BP.*

**$$$**  ⊞ **Chalet Luise.** This traditionally alpine, adult-oriented B&B is in a quiet residential area, a 10-minute walk to the village and ski lifts. The snug guest rooms have handcrafted pine furniture and Laura Ashley fabrics. One of the two romantic rooms with bay windows and gas fireplaces is large enough to sleep three people. Tables for two and four are set in the sunny breakfast room, and there's a hot tub in a whimsical gazebo on the patio. ⊠ *7461 Ambassador Crescent, Box 352, V0N 1B0,* ☎ *604/932–4187 or 800/665–1998,* 𝖥𝖠𝖷 *604/938–1531,* 𝖶𝖤𝖡 *www.chaletluise.com. 8 rooms. Some refrigerators, outdoor hot tub, sauna, ski storage, laundry facilities, free parking; no room phones, no room TVs, no smoking. MC, V. BP.*

**$$–$$$**  ⊞ **Summit Lodge.** Service is gracious and attentive at this friendly bou-
★      tique hotel, which is also one of Whistler's best values. Tucked in a quiet part of the village, the spacious rooms here are beautifully decorated with soft neutrals, custom-made cherrywood furnishings, original art, granite countertops, and such details as aromatherapy toiletries. All units have balconies and fireplaces. A shuttle whisks guests to the nearby slopes. ⊠ *4359 Main St., V0N 1B4,* ☎ *604/932–2778 or 888/913–8811,* 𝖥𝖠𝖷 *604/932–2716,* 𝖶𝖤𝖡 *www.summitlodge.com. 75 rooms, 6 suites. In-room data ports, kitchenettes, cable TV, in-room VCRs, pool, exercise equipment, outdoor hot tub, sauna, ski storage, dry cleaning, laundry facilities, laundry service, concierge, business services, meeting rooms, parking (fee), some pets allowed (fee), no-smoking floors. MC, V.*

**$$**  ⊞ **Edgewater Lodge.** This cedar lodge lies along glacier-fed Green Lake on 45 acres of private forested land, about 3 km (2 mi) north of the village. The rooms and suites are big, with a woodsy sage-green color scheme, private entrances, and window seats set before expansive water and mountain views. Whistler Outdoor Experience runs an activity center here, providing guests and nonguests fishing, hiking, canoeing, kayaking, and trail rides in summer and snowshoeing, sleigh rides, and cross-country skiing in winter. ⊠ *8841 Hwy. 99 (Box 369, V0N 1B0),* ☎ *604/932–0688 or 888/870–9065,* ℻ *604/932–0686,* WEB *www.edgewater-lodge.com. 6 rooms, 6 suites. Restaurant, cable TV, outdoor hot tub, meeting room, some pets allowed (fee), free parking; no smoking. AE, MC, V. CP.*

**$** ⊡ **Hostelling International Whistler.** One of the nicest hostels in Canada is also the area's cheapest sleep. Beds in men's or women's four-bunk dorms, a shared kitchen, and a game room with a pool table and woodstove make up the basic accommodations of this hostel overlooking Alta Lake. It's next to the swimming beach at Rainbow Park and is 7 km (4 mi) by road, or 4 km (2½ mi) by footpath, from the village. About five buses a day serve the hostel from Whistler Village. ⊠ *5678 Alta Lake Rd., V0N 1B5,* ☎ *604/932–5492,* ℻ *604/932–4687,* WEB *www. hihostels.ca. 28 beds in 7 dorms, 1 four-bed private room (no bath). Kitchen, lake, sauna, dock, boating, bicycles, ski storage, piano, Internet, free parking; no room phones, no room TVs, no smoking. MC, V.*

## Nightlife and the Arts

For a small mountain village, Whistler has a surprisingly good choice of nightlife, most of it in the pedestrian-oriented village and within walking distance of the hotels and ski slopes. Most of the pubs, clubs, and bars are open year-round. Dance clubs are open until 2 AM Monday–Saturday and until 1 AM on Sunday (be prepared to line up on weekends); pubs close around 1 AM, midnight on Sunday. Most nightspots serve food, which is often good value compared with Whistler's pricey restaurants, and many of them either ban smoking or have large no-smoking areas. You have to be at least 19 to enter bars or nightclubs, though many pubs have separate restaurant sections open to all. For entertainment listings, pick up a free copy of Whistler's weekly news magazine, the *Pique.*

### BARS AND PUBS

**Bearfoot Bistro.** Oenophiles will love the wine bar, which has a choice of more than 1,000 wines in an elegant setting. ⊠ *4121 Village Green,* ☎ *604/932–3433.*

**Black's Pub.** Here you'll find Whistler's largest selection of whiskeys (more than 40 varieties) and 99 beers from around the world. ⊠ *4270 Mountain Sq.,* ☎ *604/932–6945.*

**BrewHouse.** This place brews six of its own ales and lagers in a big woodsy building with fireplaces, pool tables, and a patio. The attached restaurant (open to minors) is a good place for casual meals. ⊠ *4355 Blackcomb Way,* ☎ *604/905–2739.*

**Citta'.** The village-center patio here is a great spot for people-watching and microbrew sipping. ⊠ *Whistler Village Sq.,* ☎ *604/932–4177.*

**Dubh Linn Gate Pub.** As its name implies, this place has an Irish theme. The staff pours a decent pint of Guinness and serves good Irish food. Under-19s are welcome in the restaurant section. ⊠ *Pan Pacific Hotel, 4320 Sundial Crescent,* ☎ *604/905–4047.*

**Garibaldi Lift Company.** An enormous fireplace and a big slope-side deck make this bar a popular après-ski stop. ⊠ *4165 Springs La., in the Whistler Village Gondola Building,* ☎ *604/905–2220.*

### DANCE CLUBS

**Buffalo Bill's Bar & Grill.** The DJs here play mainstream music for an older (over 25) crowd, and well-known bands jam once or twice a month. ⊠ *1–4122 Village Green,* ☎ *604/932–6613.*

**Garfinkle's.** One of Whistler's largest clubs frequently hosts live rock and roll, hip hop, funk, and jazz. ⊠ *1-4308 Main St.,* ☎ *604/932–2323.*

**Maxx Fish.** With its house, hip-hop, theme nights, and occasional live bands, Maxx Fish draws a young crowd. ⊠ *Whistler Village Sq.,* ☎ *604/932–1904.*

**Tommy Africa's.** Here, international guest DJs play alternative and progressive dance music. ⊠ *4216 Gateway Dr.,* ☎ *604/932–6090.*

FILM AND THEATER

**Maurice Young Millennium Place.** You can catch theatrical, dance, live music, and other performances here. The facility also has arts, child care, and teen centers, as well as drop-in yoga and dance classes. Ecumenical church services are held here Sunday morning. ⊠ *4335 Blackcomb Way,* ☎ *604/935–8410).*

**Rainbow Theatre.** In the Whistler Conference Centre, this theater shows first-run movies twice nightly. ⊠ *4010 Whistler Way,* ☎ *604/932–2422.*

## Outdoor Activities and Sports

Adjacent to the Whistler area is the 78,000-acre **Garibaldi Provincial Park** (⊠ off Hwy. 99, ☎ 604/898–3678), with dense mountainous forests splashed with hospitable lakes and streams.

The best first stop for any Whistler outdoor activity is the **Whistler Activity and Information Center** (⊠ 4010 Whistler Way, ☎ 604/932–2394) in the conference center at the edge of the village, where you can book activities; pick up hiking, biking, and cross-country skiing trail maps; and find out about equipment rentals.

BIKING AND HIKING

The 28-km (45-mi) paved, car-free Valley Trail links the village to lakeside beaches and scenic picnic spots. For more challenging routes, ski lifts whisk hikers and bikers up to the alpine, where marked trails are graded by difficulty.

You can rent bikes arrange for repairs or book a bike tour at **Fanatyk Co. Ski and Cycle** (⊠ 6–4433 Sundial Pl., ☎ 604/938–9452). Bike rentals are available in summer at the **Whistler Gondola Base** (⊠ 3434 Blackcomb Way, ☎ 604/905–2252). **Whistler Outdoor Experience** (⊠ Edgewater Outdoor Centre, 8841 Hwy. 99, ☎ 604/932–3389 or 877/386–1888, WEB www.whistleroutdoor.com) leads guided hikes and mountain-bike tours.

BOATING

Canoe and kayak rentals are available at Alta Lake at both Lakeside Park and Wayside Park. A spot that's perfect for canoeing is the River of Golden Dreams, which connects Alta Lake with Green Lake.

The **Canadian Outback Adventure Company** (☎ 604/921–7250 or 800/565–8735, WEB www.canadianoutback.com) leads river-rafting trips in the area, including an easygoing trip for families. For guided canoeing and kayaking trips as well as sailing, call **Whistler Outdoor Experience** (⊠ 8841 Hwy. 99, ☎ 604/932–3389 or 877/386–1888, WEB www.whistleroutdoor.com) at the Edgewater Outdoor Centre on Green Lake. **Whistler River Adventures** (☎ 604/932–3532 or 888/932–3532, WEB www.whistlerriver.com) has both river-rafting and jet-boating trips on rivers near Whistler.

CROSS-COUNTRY SKIING

The meandering trail around the Whistler Golf Course in the village is an ideal beginners' route. The 28 km (17 mi) of track-set trails that wind around scenic Lost Lake, Chateau Whistler Golf Course, the Nicklaus North Golf Course, and Green Lake include routes suitable for all levels; 4 km (2½ mi) of trails around Lost Lake are lighted for night skiing 4–10 each evening. **Whistler Outdoor Experience** (✉ Edgewater Outdoor Centre, 8841 Hwy. 99, ☎ 604/932–3389 or 877/386–1888) organizes cross-country ski treks.

### DOWNHILL SKIING AND SNOWBOARDING

**Blackcomb and Whistler mountains** (☎ 604/932–3434 or 800/766–0449, WEB www.whistlerblackcomb.com) receive an average of 360 inches of snow a year. The regular season is the longest in Canada, with lifts operating from late November to early June. If that's not enough, Blackcomb's Horstman Glacier is open June to early August for summer glacier skiing. The mountains' statistics are impressive: the resort covers 7,071 acres of skiable terrain in 12 alpine bowls and on three glaciers; it has more than 200 marked trails and is served by the continent's most advanced high-speed lift system. Blackcomb has a 5,280-ft vertical drop, North America's longest, and a top elevation of 7,494 ft. Whistler's drop comes in second at 5,020 ft, and its top elevation is 7,160 ft.

For a primer on the ski facilities, drop by the resort's free Whistler Welcome Night, held at 6:30 every Sunday evening during ski season at the base of the village gondolas. First-timers at Whistler, whether beginners or experienced skiers or snowboarders, may want to try Ski or Ride Esprit. Run by the resort, these three- to four-day programs combine ski or snowboarding lessons, après-ski activities, and an insider's guide to the mountains.

The **Mountain Adventure Centre** (✉ Pan Pacific Lodge, 4320 Sundial Crescent, ☎ 604/905–2295) rents high-performance gear and lets you swap equipment during the day. It also has two alpine locations, one in the Fairmont Chateau Whistler and another at Blackcomb Day Lodge. **Whistler/Blackcomb Ski and Snowboard School** (✉ 4545 Blackcomb Way, ☎ 604/932–3434 or 800/766–0449) has lessons for skiers of all levels. Equipment rentals are available at the **Whistler Gondola Base** (✉ 3434 Blackcomb Way, ☎ 604/905–2252) and at several outlets in the village.

### FISHING

All five of the lakes around Whistler are stocked with trout. The guides at **Cougar Mountain Adventures** (✉ 36–4314 Main St., ☎ 604/932–3474) can take you fly-fishing or spinning in the lakes and rivers around Whistler. Gear is supplied. **Whistler Fishing Guides** (✉ Whistler Village Gondola Building, 4165 Springs La., ☎ 604/932–3532 or 888/932–3532, WEB www.whistlerriver.com) conducts guided trips on rivers in the area. The staff takes care of everything: equipment, guides, transportation.

### GOLF

Golf season runs from May through October; greens fees range from $125 to $185. The **Big Sky Golf and Country Club** (✉ ☎ 604/894–6106 or 800/668–7900, WEB www.bigskygolf.com) is an 18-hole, par-72 course, in Pemberton, 30 minutes north of Whistler. **Chateau Whistler Golf Club** (✉ 4612 Blackcomb Way, ☎ 604/938–2092 or 877/938–2092) has an excellent 18-hole, par-72 course designed by Robert Trent Jones Jr. The **Nicklaus North Golf Course** (✉ 8080 Nicklaus North Blvd., ☎ 604/938–9898 or 800/386–9898) is a challenging 18-hole, par-71 course designed by Jack Nicklaus. Arnold Palmer designed the 18-hole, par-72 championship course at the **Whistler Golf Club** (✉ 4010 Whistler Way, ☎ 604/932–4544 or 800/376–1777).

### HELI-SKIING

**Whistler Heli-Skiing** (✉ 3-4241 Village Stroll, ☏ 604/932–4105 or 888/ 435–4754, WEB www.whistlerheliskiing.com) has helicopter-accessed guided day trips with three or more glacier runs for intermediate to expert skiers. The cost starts at $625 per person.

### HORSEBACK RIDING

**Whistler Outdoor Experience** (✉ Edgewater Outdoor Centre, 8841 Hwy. 99, ☏ 604/932–3389 or 877/386–1888, WEB www.whistleroutdoor.com) on Green Lake runs trail rides (starting a $35 for a one-hour ride) for kids and adults.

### SNOWMOBILING, SNOWSHOEING, AND SLEIGH OR SLED RIDES

**Blackcomb Snowmobiles** (✉ ☏ 604/932–8484, WEB www. blackcombsnowmobile.com) runs guided snowmobile trips into the backcountry. The company has outlets at the Fairmont Chateau Whistler and the Delta Whistler Resort. **Cougar Mountain Wilderness Adventures** (✉ 36–4314 Main St., ☏ 604/932–4086 or 888/297–2222, WEB www.cougarmountain.ca) has dogsled trips as well as snowmobiling and snowshoeing tours. **Outdoor Adventures@Whistler** (✉ Timberline Lodge, 4122 Village Green, ☏ 604/932–0647, WEB www. adventureswhistler.com) can take you for walks in the deep powder on snowshoes. **Whistler Outdoor Experience** (✉ Edgewater Outdoor Centre, 8841 Hwy. 99, ☏ 604/932–3389 or 877/386–1888) runs romantic horse-drawn sleigh rides, including sleigh rides with dinner at a lakefront restaurant, as well as snowshoeing trips.

### SPORTS COMPLEX

**Meadow Park Sports Centre** (✉ 8107 Camino Dr., ☏ 604/935–7529), about 6 km (4 mi) north of Whistler Village, has a six-lane indoor pool, children's wading pool, ice-skating rink, hot tub, sauna, steam room, gym, aerobics studio, and two squash courts. Day passes are $9.

## Shopping

Whistler has almost 200 shops, including chain and designer outlets, art galleries, gift shops, and, of course, outdoor-clothing and ski shops. Most are clustered in the pedestrian-only Whistler Village Centre; more can be found a short stroll away in Village North, Upper Village, and in the shopping concourses of the major hotels. Most of the goods reflect the tastes (and budgets) of the international moneyed set that vacations here, though savvy shoppers can get good deals on ski gear in spring and on summer clothing in fall.

Almost anything you buy in British Columbia is subject to a Canada-wide 7% Goods and Services Tax (GST) and a 7.5% Provincial Sales Tax (PST), and these are added at the register. If you aren't a Canadian resident, you can reclaim the GST on goods you take out of the country. **Maple Leaf GST Refund Services** (✉ 4299 B Mountain Sq., ☏ 604/905–4977) can give you an immediate refund.

### ART GALLERIES

**adele-campbell Fine Art Gallery** has paintings and sculptures by both established and up-and-coming B.C. artists (many with wildlife and wilderness themes), including many affordable pieces. ✉ *Delta Whistler Resort, 4050 Whistler Way,* ☏ *604/938–0887.*

**Black Tusk Gallery** displays Northwest Coast native art, including limited-edition silk-screen prints, and such traditional crafts as masks, paddles, bowls, jewelry, and totem poles. ✉ *101–4359 Main St.,* ☏ *604/ 905–5540.*

**Northwest Connection Gallery of Native Art** sells the works of Northwest Coast native artists, including prints, masks, and handmade gold and silver jewelry. ✉ *2–4232 Sunrise Alley,* ☏ *604/932–4646.*

**Plaza Galleries** showcases the painting efforts of Hollywood stars Tony Curtis, Anthony Quinn, and Red Skelton, as well as works by Canadian visual artists. ⊠ *Whistler Town Plaza, 22–4314 Main St.,* ☎ *604/938–6233.*

**Whistler Art Galleries** has sculpture, painting, and glassworks by Canadian and international artists. The Westin Resort & Spa branch features Inuit sculptures. ⊠ *Delta Whistler Resort, 4050 Whistler Way,* ☎ *604/938–3001;* ⊠ *Westin Resort & Spa, 4090 Whistler Way,* ☎ *604/935–3999.*

### CLOTHING

**Amos and Andes** sells handmade sweaters and dresses in offbeat designs. ⊠ *2–4321 Village Gate Blvd.,* ☎ *604/932–7202.*

**Helly Hansen** sells its own brand of Norwegian-made skiing, boarding, and other outdoor wear. ⊠ *Westin Resort & Spa, 115–4090 Whistler Way,* ☎ *604/932–0142.*

**Horstman Trading Co.** specializes in ski togs and accessories, including a good selection of Bogner, Tsunami, and other high-fashion gear. ⊠ *4555 Blackcomb Way,* ☎ *604/938–7725;* ⊠ *Westin Resort & Spa, 4090 Whistler Way,* ☎ *604/905–2203.*

**Open Country** stocks casual designs for men and women by Polo–Ralph Lauren, Tommy Hilfiger, Calvin Klein, and others. ⊠ *Fairmont Chateau Whistler Resort, 4599 Chateau Blvd.,* ☎ *604/938–9268.*

**Roots**—the Canadian-owned enterprise known for its sweatshirts and cozy casuals—is something of a fixture in Whistler, especially now that it outfits both the Canadian and American Olympic teams. ⊠ *4229 Village Stroll,* ☎ *604/938–0058.*

### SPORTS EQUIPMENT

**Can-Ski,** operated by Whistler-Blackcomb Resort, has four locations with a good selection of brand-name ski gear, clothes, and accessories. The staff also offers custom boot fitting and repairs. ⊠ *Crystal Lodge, Whistler Village,* ☎ *604/938–7755;* ⊠ *Deer Lodge, Town Plaza,* ☎ *604/938–7432;* ⊠ *Glacier Lodge, Upper Village,* ☎ *604/938–7744;* ⊠ *Creekside,* ☎ *604/905–2160.*

**Fanatyk Co. Ski and Cycle** sells skis, boots, and custom boots in winter. In summer the shop specializes in top-of-the-line mountain bikes as well as bike rentals, repairs, and tours. ⊠ *6–4433 Sundial Pl.,* ☎ *604/938–9455.*

**Showcase Snowboards** supplies gear to the growing number of snowboarders at Whistler. ⊠ *Deer Lodge, 32 Whistler Town Plaza,* ☎ *604/938–7432;* ⊠ *4340 Sundial Crescent,* ☎ *604/938–7519.*

**Snowcovers Sports** carries brand-name ski equipment and outerwear in winter; in summer, it carries high-end bikes and cycling gear. ⊠ *126–4340 Lorimer Rd.,* ☎ *604/905–4100.*

# Lillooet

⑪ *131 km (81 mi) northeast of Whistler.*

Beyond Whistler, Highway 99 is much less traveled as it passes lakes and glaciers, past the town of Pemberton, through the Mount Currie First Nations reserve, and over the mountains to Lillooet.

The arid gullies and Wild West landscape around Lillooet may come as a surprise after the greenery of the coast and mountains. During the 1850s and 1860s this was Mile Zero of the Cariboo Wagon Road, which took prospectors to the gold fields. There are several motels in Lillooet.

# Hope

**⑫** *153 km (95 mi) south of Lillooet, 150 km (93 mi) east of Vancouver.*

Hope is the only sizable town on Highway 1 between Vancouver and the province's interior; it's also the point where the scenery changes suddenly from the steep gorges of the Fraser Canyon to the wide, flat farmland of the Fraser Valley. If you're traveling into the interior from Vancouver, you have a choice of three routes here: Highway 1 through the Fraser Canyon, the Coquihalla (Highway 5), and Highway 3. Highway 1, the Trans-Canada Highway, follows the Fraser River as it cuts through the Coast Mountains to the High Country; the deepest, most dramatic cut is the 38-km (24-mi) gorge between Yale and Boston Bar, north of Hope, where the road clings to the hillside high above the water. Highway 5 is a fast, high-altitude toll road, and Highway 3 is a quiet back road through Manning Park.

You'll find plenty of facilities for overnight stays in Hope. The Fraser and Thompson rivers north of town are popular rafting centers. Several operators are based in Lytton and Yale.

At the **Coquihalla Canyon Provincial Park** 6 km (4 mi) northeast of Hope off Highway 5, you can walk through the abandoned tunnels of the old Kettle Valley Railway and catch spectacular views of the Coquihalla Canyon. The tunnels are open dawn to dusk April through mid-October, weather permitting. The Hope Visitor Info Centre (☎ 604/869–2021) has information.

At **Hell's Gate**, about 55 km (33 mi) north of Hope on Highway 1, an aerial gondola (cable car) carries you across the foaming canyon above the fishways, where millions of sockeye salmon fight their way upriver to spawning grounds. At the far side of the river, you'll find displays on the life cycle of the salmon, a fudge factory, ice cream parlor, general store, and restaurant. ⌧ *Hwy. 1, 10 km (6 mi) south of Boston Bar,* ☎ *604/867–9277,* WEB *www.hellsgateairtram.com.* 🎫 *Cable car $11.* ☉ *Apr. and Oct., daily 10–4; May–June and Sept., daily 9–5; July–Aug., daily 9–6.*

*En Route*     Following Highway 3 east to Princeton and Penticton, you pass through **Manning Provincial Park,** which has campgrounds, hiking trails, swimming, boating, and trail rides, in addition to downhill and cross-country skiing in the winter.

## Lodging

**$–$$**  🏨 **Manning Park Resort.** This lodge in Manning Park has been a family holiday spot since the 1970s and still makes a handy stopover on the long drive to the interior. Though updated with such modern treats as a hot tub and gym, the resort retains its old-fashioned summer camp feel, from the bear-shape house posts to the snowshoes dangling from the restaurant ceiling. There's biking, hiking, trail riding, and lake paddling in the summer; snowshoeing, snowboarding, and downhill and cross-country skiing in winter. Accommodations are a mix of lodge rooms with modern decor; kitchen-equipped cabins for up to 10 people; and rustic, low-priced chalets that can sleep up to 16. ⌧ *64 km (38 mi) east of Hope on Hwy. 3 (Box 1480, Hope V0X 1L0),* ☎ *250/840–8822 or 800/330–3321,* FAX *604/840–8848,* WEB *www.manningparkresort.com. 41 rooms, 35 cabins. Restaurants, café, in-room data ports, some kitchens, microwaves, refrigerators, cable TV with movies, 2 tennis courts, gym, hot tub, sauna, steam room, boating, mountain bikes, basketball, billiards, boccie, croquet, horseshoes, Ping-Pong, volleyball, ski shop, lounge, pub, piano, recreation room, shop, playground, laundry facilities, business services, meeting rooms, some pets allowed (fee). AE, MC, V.*

# Harrison Hot Springs

**13** *128 km (79 mi) northeast of Vancouver.*

The small resort community of Harrison Hot Springs lies at the southern tip of picturesque Harrison Lake, off Highway 7 in the Fraser Valley. Mountains surround the 64-km-long (40-mi-long) lake, which is ringed by pretty beaches. Besides the hot springs, boating, windsurfing, and swimming are popular here.

A striking 200-ft-high waterfall is the main attraction at **Bridal Veil Falls Provincial Park** (⊠ off Hwy. 1 about 15 km [9 mi] southeast of Harrison Hot Springs, ☎ 604/824–2300), open dawn to dusk. A short path through the forest leads to a viewing platform.

The **Harrison Public Pool,** across from the beach in Harrison Hot Springs, is an indoor hot spring–fed pool. ⊠ *224 Esplanade,* ☎ *604/796–2244.* ☞ *$7.25.* ☉ *Daily 9–9.*

**Kilby Historic Store and Farm,** a 20-minute drive west of Harrison Hot Springs, re-creates a rural B.C. store and farm of the 1920s with farm animals, some original buildings and some replicas, and 1920s-style home cooking in the Harrison River Restaurant ⊠ *215 Kilby Rd., off Hwy. 7, Harrison Mills,* ☎ *604/796–9576,* WEB *www.kilby.ca.* ☞ *$7.* ☉ *May–Sept., Thurs.–Mon. 11–5; call for off-season hrs.*

**Minter Gardens,** 8 km (5 mi) southwest of Harrison Hot Springs, is a 27-acre site with 11 beautifully presented theme gardens including rose, lake, and stream gardens, and a giant evergreen maze. ⊠ *Exit 135 off Hwy. 1, 52892 Bunker Rd., Rosedale,* ☎ *604/794–7191 or 888/646–8377,* WEB *www.mintergardens.com.* ☞ *$12.* ☉ *Apr. and Oct., daily 10–5; May and Sept., daily 9–5:30; June, daily 9–6; July–Aug., daily 8:30–7.*

## Dining and Lodging

$$$–$$$$ ✕🛏 **Harrison Hot Springs Resort & Spa.** A fixture on Harrison Lake since 1926, the hotel originally was set up to take advantage of the hot springs and the lake, and it still does. There's a full-service spa, several hot springs–fed pools, and a marina with such water sports as sturgeon-fishing charters, canoeing, kayaking, waterskiing, and lake cruises. Most of the contemporary-look rooms have patios or balconies; those on the north side have views over the lake and nearby glacier-topped mountains. The Copper Room Restaurant ($$–$$$) serves beautifully prepared, locally sourced Continental cuisine and has a dance band Tuesday through Saturday nights. ⊠ *100 Esplanade, V0M 1K0,* ☎ *604/796–2244 or 800/663–2266,* FAX *604/796–3682,* WEB *www.harrisonresort.com. 323 rooms, 11 cottages. 2 restaurants, café, room service, cable TV with movies, 2 tennis courts, 5 pools (2 indoor), wading pool, gym, 2 outdoor hot tubs, saunas, steam room, boating, bicycles, volleyball, bar, shops, playground, dry cleaning, laundry service, concierge, Internet, convention center, some pets allowed (fee); no-smoking floor. AE, D, DC, MC, V.*

## Outdoor Activities and Sports

The **Hemlock Valley Resort** (⊠ Hemlock Valley Rd., off Hwy. 7, Agassiz, ☎ 604/797–4411; 800/665–7080 snow report), 40 km (24 mi) northwest of Harrison Hot Springs, is a family-oriented ski resort with three chairlifts, 35 runs, and a vertical rise of 1,200 ft. You can also try cross-country skiing and snow tubing here.

*En Route*    From Harrison Hot Springs, two routes lead back to Vancouver. Highway 7 is a scenic back road along the north side of the Fraser River. Highway 1 is the faster, main highway. On Highway 1, you pass the turnoff to **Fort Langley National Historic Site of Canada,** a restored 1850s Hudson's Bay trading post about an hour west of Harrison Hot Springs. Costumed guides demonstrate woodworking, blacksmithing, and other fur-trade activities, and you can try your hand at gold panning. The nearby village of Fort Langley retains a 19th-century charm. ⊠ *23433 Mavis Ave., Fort Langley,* ☎ *604/513–4777,* WEB *www.parkscanada. gc.ca/langley.* ⊡ *$4.* ☉ *Mar.–Oct., daily 10–5.*

# THE HIGH COUNTRY
# AND THE OKANAGAN VALLEY

South-central British Columbia (often simply called the "interior" by Vancouverites) encompasses the high arid plateau between the Coast Mountains on the west and the Monashees on the east. The Okanagan Valley, five hours east of Vancouver by car, or one hour by air, contains the interior's largest concentration of people. The region's sandy lake beaches and hot, dry climate have long made it a family-holiday magnet for Vancouverites and Albertans, and rooms and campsites can be hard to come by in summer.

The Okanagan Valley is also the fruit-growing capital of Canada and a major wine-producing area. Many of the region's more than 45 wineries are in scenic spots, and they welcome visitors with tastings, tours, and restaurants. The Wine Museum in Kelowna and the British Columbia Wine Information Centre in Penticton can help you create a winery tour and can provide details about annual wine festivals. In addition, 25 golf course and several ski resorts in the draw sports people to the region year-round.

Throughout the Okanagan you'll see depictions of a smiling green lizard that looks a bit like the Loch Ness Monster without the tartan cap. This is Ogopogo, a harmless, shy, and probably mythical creature said to live in Okanagan Lake.

## Kamloops

🅐 *355 km (220 mi) northeast of Vancouver, 163 km (101 mi) northwest of Kelowna.*

Virtually all roads meet at Kamloops, the High Country's sprawling transport hub. From here, highways fan out to Vancouver, the Okanagan, the Cariboo, and Jasper in the Rockies. Kamloops is also the closest town to Sun Peaks, one of the province's leading ski resorts.

The **Kamloops Museum and Archives** has extensive and regularly changing displays about the area's human and natural history. ⊠ *207 Seymour St.,* ☎ *250/828–3576,* WEB *www.city.kamloops.bc.ca/parks/ index.html.* ⊡ *Free.* ☉ *Tues.–Sat. 9:30–4:30.*

You can see 70 species of local and endangered animals, including zebras, antelope, grizzly bears, and Siberian tigers, in natural settings at the **Kamloops Wildlife Park.** In summer, a miniature train runs around the property. ⊠ *Hwy. 1, 15 km (9 mi) east of Kamloops,* ☎ *250/573– 3242,* WEB *www.kamloopswildlife.com.* ⊡ *$8; lower rates in the off-season.* ☉ *Sept.–June, daily 8–4:30; July–Aug., daily 8 AM–8:30 PM.*

The **Secwepemc Museum and Heritage Park,** a reconstructed village on a traditional gathering site, interprets the culture and lifestyle of the Secwepemc (Shuswap) people, who have lived in this area for thousands of years. Displays in the 12-acre parklike setting include a replica winter pit-house village, a summer lodge, and ethnobotanical gardens showcasing plants used by the Secwepemc. There's also a wildlife marsh, and the museum holds recorded oral history, photographs, and artifacts. At the gift shop you can pick up local First Nations artwork. ⊠ *202–355 Yellowhead Hwy. (Hwy. 5),* ☎ *250/828–9801,* 〚WEB〛 *www.secwepemc.org.* 🎫 *June–Labor Day $6; rest of yr $5.* ☉ *June–Labor Day, weekdays 8:30–8, weekends 10–6; Labor Day–May, weekdays 8:30–4:30.*

<table>
<tr><td>OFF THE<br>BEATEN PATH</td><td>

**WELLS GRAY PROVINCIAL PARK –** This vast wilderness area has great canoeing, fishing, and hiking. About 120 km (74 mi) north of Kamloops on Highway 5 is Clearwater, the major access point to Wells Gray. There's a visitor information center at the junction of Highway 5 and the Clearwater Valley Road. ☎ *250/674–2646,* 〚WEB〛 *www.bcparks.ca.*

</td></tr>
</table>

## Dining and Lodging

**$–$$** ✕🏨 **Quilchena Hotel & Resort.** Movie stars and outlaws have stayed at this 1908 inn on the grounds of a working cattle ranch, 75 km (45 mi) south of Kamloops. The hotel has a Victoriana–meets–Wild West ambience, with 19th-century antiques, original woodwork, an elegant parlor, and a saloon with a lovingly preserved bullet hole behind the bar. The Ladies' Parlour Room has a private sunporch, and Jack's Room (where Jack Nicholson stayed while filming in the area) has views of the lake across the road. A two-bedroom ranch house is also available. The restaurant ($$–$$$) is worth a trip for the local venison or the filet mignon. ⊠ *Hwy. 5A, Quilchena, 20 km (12 mi) north of Merritt, V0E 2R0,* ☎ *250/378–2611,* 〚FAX〛 *250/378–6091,* 〚WEB〛 *www.quilchena.com. 16 rooms, 6 with bath. Restaurant, coffee shop, fans, 9-hole golf course, tennis court, lake, dock, billiards, boccie, hiking, horseback riding, horseshoes, pub, piano, shop, meeting rooms, airstrip; no room phones, no room TVs, no smoking. AE, MC, V. Closed mid-Oct.–mid-Apr.*

**$$–$$$** 🏨 **Plaza Heritage Hotel.** Built in 1927 as the province's premier hotel, this six-story Spanish mission–style boutique hotel in the heart of Kamloops has been restored to its original look; rooms have a period feel with reproduction pine and wicker furniture and 1930s fixtures. ⊠ *405 Victoria St., V2C 2A9,* ☎ *250/377–8075 or 877/977–5292,* 〚FAX〛 *250/377–8076,* 〚WEB〛 *www.plazaheritagehotel.com. 66 rooms. Restaurant, room service, in-room data ports, some refrigerators, cable TV, hair salon, wine shop, Internet, business services, meeting rooms; no-smoking floors. AE, DC, MC, V.*

## Outdoor Activities and Sports

GOLF

**Rivershore Golf Links** (⊠ 330 Rivershore Dr., ☎ 250/573–4622) is an 18-hole, par-72 course designed by Robert Trent Jones Sr. It's about 20 km (12 mi) east of Kamloops on Highway 1. Greens fees are $60 on weekdays, $70 on weekends.

SKIING

With a 2,891-ft vertical drop, 3,408 skiable acres on three mountains, lots of sunshine, powder snow, and a 2,500-ft-long snowboard park, **Sun Peaks Resort** (⊠ 1280 Alpine Rd., Sun Peaks, ☎ 250/578–5484 or 800/807–3257, 〚WEB〛 www.sunpeaksresort.com), 53 km (33 mi) north of Kamloops, is one of B.C.'s leading ski resorts. The compact Tyrolean-theme village has a number of ski-in, ski-out hotels; several restaurants; and a 9-hole golf course. Ski facilities include 114 downhill runs (the longest is 8 km [5 mi]), five chairlifts, and 20 km (12 mi) of groomed and tracked cross-country trails. A lift ticket goes for about $52. This family-friendly resort also offers a ski school, day care, snowshoeing, dogsledding, snowmobiling, and sleigh rides. In summer, visitors come for trail rides, canoeing, and lift-accessed hiking and mountain biking in wildflower-strewn meadows.

## Salmon Arm

**⓯** *108 km (67 mi) east of Kamloops, 106 km (66 mi) north of Kelowna.*

Salmon Arm is the commercial center of the Shuswap (named for Shuswap Lake), a greener and less-visited region than the Okanagan to the south. From Sicamous, 27 km (16 mi) northeast of Salmon Arm, you can take a two- to six-hour summer (May to October) trip on Shuswap Lake on the **Phoebe Anne** (☒ 117 Finlayson St., Sicamous, ☎ 250/836–2220), a 48-passenger paddle wheeler. Prices start at $25.

**R. J. Haney Heritage Park and Museum.** This 40-acre open-air museum re-creates an early 20th-century North Okanagan village. Most of the buildings, which include a log gas station and a fire hall, a school (where a Miss Hellpenny teaches real kids in a 1914 style), and a manor house, are originals. A 3-km (2-mi) nature trail winds around the site. A tearoom on-site serves lunches, and a theater troupe performs outdoor dinner theater three times a week in summer. ☒ *751 Hwy. 97B, off Hwy. 1, 5 km (3 mi) south of Salmon Arm,* ☎ *250/832–5243,* WEB *www. sjs.sd83.bc.ca.* ☒ *Site free, house tours $2.* ☉ *June–Sept., daily 10–5.*

**Roderick Haig-Brown Provincial Park** (☒ off Hwy. 1 at Squilax, ☎ no phone, WEB www.bcparks.ca) is where thousands of salmon come to spawn in the Adams River in late September and October. The park is about 40 km (25 mi) northwest of Salmon Arm.

### Dining and Lodging

**$$–$$$** ✗🖼 **Quaaout Lodge Resort.** This modern three-story hotel, with its 40-ft-high lobby shaped like a traditional First Nations winter home, provides the chance to experience the culture of interior native peoples. Some of the large, well-appointed rooms have log furniture, gas fireplaces, and whirlpool baths for two under windows overlooking the lake. The restaurant ($$–$$$) serves such First Nations–influenced fare as rainbow trout stuffed with blueberries. On the grounds are a ceremonial sweat lodge and a reconstructed *kekuli,* or winter shelter, as well as a sandy beach and trails through hundreds of forested acres. The hotel is 43 km (27 mi) northwest of Salmon Arm. ☒ *Little Shuswap Rd. Off Hwy. 1 (Box 1215, Chase V0E 1M0),* ☎ *250/679–3090 or 800/663–4303,* FAX *250/679–3039,* WEB *www.quaaout.com. 72 rooms. Restaurant, room service, some refrigerators, indoor pool, gym, hot tub, steam room, dock, boating, mountain bikes, bar, shop, baby-sitting, playground, laundry facilities, business services, meeting rooms, some pets allowed (fee); no-smoking floors. AE, MC, V.*

### Outdoor Activities and Sports

Sicamous on Shuswap Lake is a mecca for houseboat vacationers. **Three Buoys** (☒ 630 Riverside Ave., Sicamous, ☎ 250/836–2403 or 800/663–2333, WEB www.threebuoys.com) rents luxurious houseboats ($1,000–$4,000 a week), many with hot tubs, that sleep 10 to 12. **Twin Anchors** (☒ 101 Martin St., Sicamous, ☎ 250/836–2450 or 800/663–4026, WEB www.twinanchors.com) has a range of fully equipped houseboats that can accommodate 8 to 22 people and rent for $1,000–$6,000 per week; all have hot tubs.

## Vernon

**⓰** *117 km (73 mi) southeast of Kamloops.*

Because Vernon has no public access to Okanagan Lake, it's less of a draw than other towns in the area. Nearby are two other lakes and the all-season, gaslight era–theme village resort atop Silver Star Mountain.

The 50-acre **Historic O'Keefe Ranch** provides a window on 19th-century cattle-ranch life. Among the many original and restored ranch buildings are the O'Keefe mansion, a church, and a general store. There's also a restaurant and a gift shop on-site. ✉ *9380 Hwy. 97, 12 km (8 mi) north of Vernon,* ☎ *250/542–7868,* WEB *www.okeeferanch.bc.ca.* ✇ *$7.* ☉ *May–mid-Oct., daily 9–5; tours by appointment rest of yr.*

**Kalamalka Lake Provincial Park** (✉ Kidston Rd., ☎ 250/494–6500) has warm-water beaches and some of the most scenic viewpoints and hiking trails in the region.

## Outdoor Activities and Sports

### GOLF

**Predator Ridge Golf Resort** (✉ 301 Village Centre Pl., ☎ 250/542–3436 or 888/578–6688) is a 27-hole facility, with a par-36 on each 9. Greens fees for 18 holes are $115 with a cart, $95 without a cart. It's about 15 km (9 mi) south of Vernon on Highway 97.

### SKIING

**Silver Star Mountain Resort** (✉ Silver Star Rd., Silver Star Mountain, ☎ 250/542–0224; 800/663–4431 reservations; WEB www.skisilverstar. com), 22 km (13 mi) northeast of Vernon, has six chairlifts and two T-bars, a vertical drop of 2,500 ft, 108 runs on 2,725 skiable acres, and night skiing. A one-day lift ticket is $49. The resort also has 70 km (44 mi) of groomed, track-set cross-country trails; two halfpipes for boarders; snow tubing, snowmobile, or snowshoe tours; and sleigh rides, skating, and dogsledding. Day care and free ski tours are also available at this friendly resort, and hiking and mountain-biking trails open in summer. The Victorian-style village has several ski-in, ski-out hotels and lodges, restaurants, and shops, many of which are open all year.

# Kelowna

**⑰** *46 km (29 mi) south of Vernon, 68 km (42 mi) north of Penticton.*

The largest town in the Okanagan Valley, Kelowna (population 97,000), on the edge of Okanagan Lake, makes a good base for exploring the region's beaches, ski hills, wineries, and golf courses. Although its edges are looking untidily urban these days, the town still has an attractive, walkable core and a restful beachside park. It's also at the heart of British Columbia's wine and fruit-growing district.

The **Wine Museum** (✉ 1304 Ellis St., ☎ 250/868–0441, WEB www. kelownamuseum.ca), set in a historic packinghouse, has wine-making exhibits and daily wine tastings, as well as a wine shop and information about touring local wineries. Admission is by donation; the museum is open Monday–Saturday 10–5, Sunday noon–5. The **British Columbia Orchard Industry Museum** (✉ 1304 Ellis St., ☎ 250/763–0433), in the same building as the Wine Museum, has displays about the area's other critical industry.

On the **Okanagan Valley Wine Train** (✉ 600 Recreation Ave., ☎ 250/712–9888 or 888/674–8725, WEB www.okanaganvalleywinetrain.com), you can take a five-hour round trip to Vernon along Kalamalka Lake and taste wines on board. The 1950s vintage train leaves Saturday from early July to mid-October. The trip alone is $30; with dinner and entertainment, it's $80.

The **Father Pandosy Mission** (✉ 3685 Benvoulin Rd., ☎ 250/860–8369), the first European settlement in central British Columbia, was founded here by Oblate missionaries in 1859. The 4-acre site has three original mission buildings made of logs (including a tiny chapel) as well as a farmhouse and settler's cabin. The buildings, furnished to look as they did in the late 19th century, are open for viewing (Easter to mid-October, daily 8–8; as weather permits during the rest of the year). Admission is $2.

The **Kelowna Art Gallery** (✉ 1315 Water St., ☎ 250/762–2226) is an elegant public art gallery with a variety of local and international exhibits. It's open Tuesday–Saturday 10–5, Thursday until 9, and Sunday 1–4.

☼ For many Canadians, the Okanagan means apples, and much of the valley is still covered with orchards. One of the largest and oldest (it dates from 1904) is the **Kelowna Land & Orchard Company,** which you can tour on foot or in a tractor-drawn covered wagon. The farm animals are a hit with kids; a excellent lake-view restaurant on-site serves lunch and dinner. ✉ *3002 Dunster Rd., 8 km (5 mi) east of Kelowna,* ☎ *250/ 763–1091; 250/712–9404 restaurant reservations;* WEB *www.k-l-o.com.* ☒ *Site free, tours $5.25.* ☺ *Apr.–Dec., daily 9–5. Tours May–Oct., daily at 11, 1 and 3.*

### WINERIES

Almost all of the region's wineries offer tastings and tours throughout the summer and during the Okanagan Wine Festivals held in April and October; several have restaurants and most also have wine shops open year-round. The Wine Museum can help you create a winery tour and can provide details about annual wine festivals. Several local operators will act as guides and designated drivers.

**Cedar Creek Estate Winery** (✉ 5445 Lakeshore Rd., ☎ 250/764–8866 or 800/730–9463, WEB www.cedarcreek.bc.ca), south of Kelowna, has a scenic lakeside location with picnic areas. Free tours are given daily mid-May to mid-October; call for times.

Atop a hill overlooking Okanagan Lake, **Mission Hill Family Estate** was built to look, as the owner describes it, like "a combination of monastery, Tuscan hill village, and French winery," complete with a vaulted cellar blasted from volcanic rock and a 12-story bell tower. Tours— vineyard, cellar, or landscape and architecture—include a video presentation and tastings (prices vary). Snacks and wine by the glass are served on the terrace, which overlooks the vineyard and lake, and an outdoor amphitheater hosts music and theater events on summer evenings. ✉ *1730 Mission Hill Rd., Westbank,* ☎ *250/768–7611 or 800/957–9911,* WEB *www.missionhillwinery.com.* ☒ *Tours $5.* ☺ *July– Aug., daily 10–7, tours 11–5; Sept.–June, daily, call for tour times.*

**Quails' Gate Estate Winery** (✉ 3303 Boucherie Rd., ☎ 250/769–4451 or 800/420–9463, WEB www.quailsgate.com), on the edge of Okanagan Lake, gives tours ($5) daily from late April to the middle of October. It has a wine shop in a 19th-century log home and a patio restaurant (open for lunch and dinner late April to mid-October) with views of the vineyard and lake.

**Summerhill Estate Winery** (✉ 4870 Chute Lake Rd., ☎ 250/764– 8000 or 800/667–3538, WEB www.summerhill.bc.ca), south of Kelowna on the east side of the lake, is an organic producer best known for its sparkling and ice wines. What tends to startle visitors, though, is the four-story-high replica of the Great Pyramid at Cheops; it's used to age and store the wine. You can visit the wine shop, a preserved settler's cabin, and a re-created First Nations earth house. An on-site restaurant with a veranda overlooking Okanagan Lake serves lunch daily year-round and dinner daily in summer. Tours and tasting are free and are run year-round; call for times.

## Dining and Lodging

**$$$** ✕ **de Montreuil Restaurant.** This cozy downtown restaurant makes the most of the regional bounty, serving dishes such as duck breast with coronation grape and roast shallot confit as well as rack of lamb with rosemary, garlic, and mint, which the owner has dubbed Cascadian cuisine. The menu, priced by the number of courses rather than by the dish, encourages experimentation; the warm yellow decor encourages lingering. ⊠ *368 Bernard Ave.,* ☎ *250/860–5508. AE, DC, MC, V. No lunch weekends or May–Sept.*

**$$–$$$** ✕ **Fresco Restaurant.** Seasonally inspired, locally sourced contemporary cuisine is the theme at this downtown Kelowna restaurant. Chef-owner Rodney Butters, one of B.C.'s better-known chefs, prepares creative seafood dishes, such as his signature Dungeness crab cappuccino, and Asian, Italian, and other touches for his frequently changing menus. The decor is simple, with an open kitchen and exposed brick and beams revealing the historic building's architectural roots. ⊠ *1560 Water St.,* ☎ *250/868–8805. AE, MC, V. Closed Sun.–Mon. Oct.–May. No lunch.*

**$$–$$$** ✕ **Guisachan House Restaurant.** Once the summer home of Lord Aberdeen, a former governor general of Canada, this 1891 house on 2½ garden acres is now an attractive restaurant. White cane chairs, pink tablecloths, period furniture, and seating on the glassed-in veranda re-create a Victorian summertime ambience. Chef Georg Rieder, originally from Germany, offers a lengthy menu that features several varieties of schnitzel, risottos, pastas, and seafood, as well as bison, local venison, and such Asian-influenced dishes as Szechuan pork tenderloin. A four-course lunch for less than $9 is an especially good value. ⊠ *1060 Cameron Ave.,* ☎ *250/862–9368. AE, DC, MC, V. No dinner Mon.–Wed.*

**$$$** ✕🏠 **Manteo Resort Waterfront Hotel & Villas.** This striking Tuscan-look resort sits on a sandy swimming beach on the shores on Okanagan Lake. All the water sports are here, from windsurfing to parasailing to waterskiing and simply messing about in boats. Accommodation choices include rooms and suites, all with balconies, in the main building and two- and three-bedroom villas with full kitchens. The villas are especially attractive, with gas fireplaces, terra-cotta tiles, high ceilings, and patios. The restaurant, the Wild Apple Grill ($–$$$), serves Pacific Northwest cuisine inside and on its big lakeside patio. ⊠ *3766 Lakeshore Rd., V1W 3L4,* ☎ *250/860–1031 or 800/445–5255,* ℻ *250/ 860–1041,* 🕸 *www.manteo.com. 48 rooms, 30 suites, 24 villas. Restaurant, coffee shop, room service, in-room data ports, some kitchens, some refrigerators, cable TV, some in-room VCRs, putting green, tennis court, 3 pools (1 indoor), wading pool, gym, hot tubs (indoor and outdoor), massage, sauna, spa, steam room, dock, jet skiing, mountain bikes, billiards, lounge, cinema, baby-sitting, children's programs (ages 3–12), playground, dry cleaning, laundry service, meeting rooms; no smoking. AE, DC, MC, V.*

**$$$$** 🏠 **Grand Okanagan Resort.** On the shore of Okanagan Lake, this resort is a five-minute stroll from downtown Kelowna, though you may never have to leave the grounds because of all the amenities. Most standard rooms and suites are spacious, with balconies, sitting areas, and attractive modern decor (the north tower is newer than the south tower). About half the rooms have views over the lake and the surrounding hills. The two-bedroom waterfront condo suites are a good option for families: they have two full baths, full kitchens, washer-dryers, gas fireplaces, and whirlpool baths. ⊠ *1310 Water St., V1Y 9P3,* ☎ *250/763–4500 or 800/465–4651,* ℻ *250/763–4565,* 🕸 *www. grandokanagan.com. 261 rooms, 34 suites, 60 condominiums. 3 restaurants, café, room service, in-room data ports, some in-room hot tubs,* some kitchens, minibars, cable TV with movies, pool, indoor-outdoor pool, gym, hair salon, hot tubs (indoor and outdoor), sauna, spa, dock, boating, mountain bikes, lounge, pub, casino, shops, baby-sitting, dry cleaning, laundry service, concierge, concierge floor, Internet, business services, convention center, travel services, some pets allowed (fee); no-smoking floors. AE, D, DC, MC, V.

$$$-$$$$ 📺 **Lake Okanagan Resort.** This self-contained, kid-friendly resort 25 km (15 mi) from Kelowna spreads across a mile of waterfront and 300-acres of mountainside on the west side of Okanagan Lake. The attractive modern units, decorated with rich colors and pine furniture, range from studio and one-bedroom suites in the main hotel to three-bedroom villas. Most have lake views and balconies or decks. Activities are plentiful, including lots of supervised kids' programs in July and August, and a resort shuttle scoots you up and down the hillside. ⊠ 2751 Westside Rd., V1Z 3T1, ☎ 250/769–3511 or 800/663–3273, FAX 250/769–6665, WEB www.lakeokanagan.com. 12 rooms, 105 suites, 12 villas. Restaurant, café, some kitchens, some kitchenettes, some in-room data ports, cable TV, 9-hole golf course, 7 tennis courts, 3 outdoor pools, gym, hot tubs (2 indoor and 1 outdoor), massage, sauna, beach, boating, marina, waterskiing, badminton, basketball, billiards, hiking, horseback riding, horseshoes, Ping-Pong, volleyball, 2 bars, lounge, recreation room, video game room, shop, baby-sitting, children's programs (ages 4–16), playground, laundry facilities, business services, meeting rooms; no-smoking rooms. AE, DC, MC, V.

$$-$$$ 📺 **The Cedars.** Period furniture, stained glass, and the original fireplaces create an elegant ambience at this 1908 Tudor-style cottage a block from the beach and a short stroll to the town center. The three rooms are done in restful florals with hardwood floors and romantic canopied beds. Breakfasts, with such elaborate dishes as sautéed pears with candied ginger and cinnamon, are served in the dining room or on the terrace by the pool. ⊠ 278 Beach Ave., V1Y 5R8, ☎ 250/763–1208 or 800/951–0769, FAX 250/763–1109, WEB www.cedarsinnokanagan.com. 3 rooms. Fans, in-room data ports, cable TV, refrigerators, pool, outdoor hot tub, mountain bikes, library, Internet; no kids, no smoking. AE, MC, V. Closed Dec. BP.

## Outdoor Activities and Sports

### BIKING AND HIKING

Bikers and hikers can try the rail bed of the **Kettle Valley Railway** (☎ 250/861–1515 visitor's bureau) between Penticton and Kelowna. The visitor's bureau in Kelowna can provide maps and information.

### GOLF

With four championship golf courses close to town, Kelowna is a major golf destination. **Gallagher's Canyon Golf and Country Club** (⊠ 4320 Gallagher's Dr. W, ☎ 250/861–4240 or 800/446–5322, WEB www.golfbc.com), about 15 km (9 mi) southeast of Kelowna, has an 18-hole, par-72 championship course and a 9-hole, par-32 course; greens fees for the 18-hole course are $95 in high season. Surrounded by orchards (golfers can pick fruit as they play), **Harvest Golf Club** (⊠ 2725 KLO Rd., ☎ 250/862–3103 or 800/257–8577, WEB www.harvestgolf.com) is an 18-hole, championship par-72 course. Greens fees in high season are $90. The Harvest Dining Room, in the clubhouse, has lake views and is open to nongolfers for dinner. The **Okanagan Golf Club** (⊠ 3200 Via Centrale, ☎ 250/765–5955 or 800/446–5322, WEB www.golfbc.com) has two 18-hole, par-72 championship courses with Okanagan Valley views. The Quail Course is a challenging hillside course with tight tree-lined fairways; the newer Jack Nicklaus Group–designed Bear Course is more forgiving. High-season greens fees are $85 for either course.

One of B.C.'s leading ski destinations, **Big White Ski Resort** (⊠ Big White Rd., off Hwy. 33 about 1 hr southeast of Kelowna, ☎ 250/765–8888; 800/663–2772; 250/765–7669 snow reports; WEB www.bigwhite.com) is an affordable, family-oriented resort with excellent day care and children's programs; a ski school; a good mix of more than 100 runs; and 13 up-to-date lifts including a gondola and four high-speed quad chairs. Snow hosts take you out on the mountain for a half day at no charge. A one-day lift ticket is $55. You can ski or walk anywhere in the compact village, which has several restaurants and a total of 10,000 beds in hotels, condos, B&Bs, and hostels. There are 2,565 acres of skiable terrain, a vertical drop of 2,550 ft, average annual snowfall of more than 24 ft, and night skiing five times a week. You'll also find three snowboard parks and 25 km (15 mi) of cross-country trails, as well as snowmobiling, ice-skating, horse-drawn sleigh rides, Canada's largest snow-tubing park, and even dogsledding.

## Summerland and Peachland

🔞 *Summerland is 52 km (31 mi) south of Kelowna; Peachland is 25 km (15 mi) southwest of Kelowna.*

Between Kelowna and Penticton, Highway 97 winds along the west side of Okanagan Lake, past vineyards, orchards, fruit stands, beaches, picnic sites, and some of the region's prettiest lake and hill scenery. In Summerland, you can ride the historic **Kettle Valley Steam Railway** (⊠ 18404 Bathville Rd., 7 km [4 mi] off Hwy. 97, ☎ 250/494–8422 or 877/494–8424, WEB www.kettlevalleyrail.org), which has trips along 10 km (6 mi) of a 1915 rail line between mid-May and mid-October for $15. The train runs Saturday through Monday in May, June, September, and October, and Thursday through Monday in July and August.

**Hainle Vineyards Estate Winery** (⊠ 5355 Trepanier Bench Rd., Peachland, ☎ 250/767–2525 or 800/767–3109, WEB www.hainle.com), British Columbia's first organic winery and also the first to make ice wines, is a small producer open for tastings (though not tours). The Amphora Bistro ($) has lake views and dishes that incorporate seasonal and organic ingredients. The bistro is open for lunch and dinner, daily, year-round.

Tours are given daily from May until mid-October at **Sumac Ridge Estate Winery** (⊠ 17403 Hwy. 97 N, Summerland, ☎ 250/494–0451, WEB www.sumacridge.com), but you can taste or buy wines here all year. The $5 tour fee comes off the price of any wine you buy. The Cellar Door Bistro ($$–$$$) serves Pacific Northwest cuisine using fresh, local, organic ingredients. It's open for lunch and dinner April–December.

## Penticton

🔞 *16 km (10 mi) south of Summerland, 395 km (245 mi) east of Vancouver.*

Penticton, with its long, sandy beach backed by motels and cruising pickup trucks, is a nostalgia-inducing family-vacation spot. A growing city extends to the south, but the arid hills around town are full of orchards, vineyards, and small farms. The S.S. *Sicamous* (⊠ 1099 Lakeshore Dr. W, ☎ 250/492–0403), a paddle wheeler moored at the lakeside, is now a museum. It's open daily 9–9 from mid-June to Labor Day and daily 9–5 mid-January to mid-December. Admission is $4.

The **British Columbia Wine Information Centre** (⊠ 888 Westminster Ave. W, ☎ 250/490–2006, WEB www.bcwineinfo.com) will help you plan a self-drive winery tour and can provide details about annual wine festivals, held in spring and fall. It also stocks more than 300 local wines.

WINERY

**Lake Breeze Vineyards** (⌧ 930 Sammet Rd., Naramata, ☎ 250/496–5659) is one of the region's most attractively located wineries. Tastings are available but not tours, and the winery is open mid-May to mid-October, daily 10–5. The outdoor **Patio Restaurant** ($–$$) is open daily for lunch (weather permitting) between mid-June and mid-September.

## Dining and Lodging

$$$$ ✕ **Country Squire.** Plan to spend the evening if you book a meal at this rambling country house in Naramata, 10 km (6 mi) north of Penticton. Diners are asked to choose one of seven or eight main courses when they reserve their table; the chef then designs a five-course meal around it. The options change each evening but have included various treatments of sea bass, duck breast, ostrich, venison, and rack of lamb. There's only one sitting per evening, so lingering over the meal—even taking a stroll along the lake between courses—is very much the thing to do. The wine cellar has hundreds of local and imported labels. ⌧ *3950 1st St., Naramata,* ☎ *250/496–5416. Reservations essential. MC, V. No lunch; no dinner Sun.–Wed.*

$$–$$$$ ✕ **Historic 1912 Restaurant.** This lakeside restaurant 14 km (8 mi) south of Penticton is stocked with 20th-century memorabilia, including *a Titanic* corner, and a '50s-kitchen corner. You can also dine in the gardens or the lake-view conservatory. The Pacific Northwest menu changes frequently but has included such entrées as rack of lamb rubbed with rosemary, thyme, and Dijon mustard and such desserts as chocolate pâté with fresh-fruit coulis. The cellar has a large selection of B.C. wines. There's a lakeside B&B room and a free shuttle back to Penticton. ⌧ *100 Alder Ave., Kaleden,* ☎ *250/497–6868 or 888/633–1912. AE, MC, V. Closed Jan. No lunch.*

$$$–$$$$ ☷ **Penticton Lakeside Resort, Convention Centre and Casino** On the shore of Okanagan Lake, this modern resort is within walking distance of Penticton's beachfront and town center. It has an elegant Italianate lobby and spacious rooms with modern decor, large balconies, and lake or mountain views. The facilities include a health club, a casino, a private beach, and a lakeside café. Magnum's restaurant ($$–$$$) serves Pacific Northwest cuisine and has lakeside seating. ⌧ *21 Lakeshore Dr. W, V2A 7M5,* ☎ *250/493–8221 or 800/663–9400,* FAX *250/493–0607,* WEB *www.rpbhotels.com. 197 rooms, 7 suites. 2 restaurants, room service, in-room data ports, cable TV with movie and video games, indoor pool, health club, hair salon, hot tub, beach, dock, windsurfing, boating, jet skiing, parasailing, waterskiing, 2 bars, casino, shop, babysitting, dry cleaning, laundry service, Internet, convention center; no-smoking floors. AE, D, DC, MC, V.*

$$ ☷ **God's Mountain Crest Chalet.** This adult-oriented Mediterranean-style villa sits on 115 acres of sunny hilltop overlooking Skaha Lake, 4 km (2½ mi) south of Penticton. The three common rooms are filled with European antiques, plush cushions, and theatrical props. The patio, poolside bar and gazebo, and several suites have expansive lake views. The Rooftop Queen room is fun and romantic: it has a fireplace, private hot tub, and four-poster bed with a shake roof, but the room itself is open to the stars. There's also an elaborate two-story penthouse suite. Dinners are available here with advance notice. ⌧ *4898 Lakeside Rd., V2A 8W4,* ☎ FAX *250/490–4800,* WEB *www.godsmountain.com. 5 rooms, 7 suites. Dining room, fans, some refrigerators, pool, hiking, shop, Internet, meeting room, helipad; no room phones, no room TVs, no smoking. MC, V. Closed Nov.–Feb. BP.*

## Outdoor Activities and Sports

For downhill skiing, **Apex Mountain Resort** (⊠ Apex Mountain Rd. off Green Mountain Rd., ☎ 250/292–8222 or 877/777–2739, WEB www. apexresort.com) has 67 trails, five lifts, a vertical drop of 2,000 ft, and a peak elevation of 7,187 ft. The resort, known for its intimate ambience and soft powder snow, also has night skiing as well as a terrain park and halfpipe for boarders, a snow-tube park, an outdoor ice rink, a skating trail through the forest, and snowmobile tours. Summer brings lift-accessed hiking and mountain biking, and trail rides and helicopter tours. Apex is 33 km (21 mi) west of Penticton. A one-day lift ticket is $46. The resort village has a full-service hotel, cabins, condos, restaurants, bars, shops, ski rentals, a ski school, and children's programs.

# Osoyoos

**㉒** *58 km (36 mi) south of Penticton.*

South of Penticton between the southern tip of Lake Okanagan and the U.S. border, Highway 97 runs along a chain of lakes: Skaha, Vaseaux, and Osoyoos, and through Canada's only desert. The hot, dry climate also makes this a prime wine-producing area; several wineries run tours and tastings. For information on wine tours and tastings around B.C., contact the **British Columbia Wine Information Centre** (⊠ 888 Westminster Ave. W, ☎ 250/490–2006) in Penticton. Accommodations are available in Osoyoos and other towns in the region.

The northern tip of the Great Basin Desert is home to flora and fauna found nowhere else in the country. You can learn more about the unique local ecology at the **Desert Centre,** where you can take a guided tour along a boardwalk desert trail. ⊠ *Road 146, off Hwy. 97, 4 km (3 mi) north of Osoyoos,* ☎ *250/495–2470 or 877/899–0897,* WEB *www.desert.org.* ☜ *$6 (including tour).* ⊙ *Daily. Tours 10–3 on the hr.*

# THE KOOTENAYS

Tucked between Highways 1 and 3, along which most travelers rush to and from the Rockies, the Kootenays are an idyllic backwater of mountains, lakes, natural hot springs, ghost towns, and preserved Victorian villages. Kootenay Lake and Lower Arrow Lake define the region. A century ago this area was booming because of the discovery of silver in the hills, and with the prospectors came vestiges of European society: stately homes, an elegant paddle wheeler, and the town of Nelson—built in respectable Victorian brick. These days the Kootenays are filled with fine restaurants, historic country inns, and a wealth of opportunities for outdoor activities amid fantastic scenery.

# Nelson

★ **㉑** *321 km (199 mi) east of Penticton, 657 km (407 mi) east of Vancouver.*

Bypassed a little by history, this city of 10,000, with its Victorian architecture, lake and mountain setting, and college-town ambience, is one of British Columbia's most attractive towns. Nelson has a wealth of crafts shops and coffee bars, several B&Bs, three youth hostels, and a restored 1906 streetcar running along the lakeshore. The visitor info center offers self-guided walking or driving tours of many of the town's 355 historic buildings.

About 45 km (30 mi) north of Nelson is **Ainsworth Hot Springs Resort** (⊠ Hwy. 31, Ainsworth Hot Springs, ☎ 250/229–4212 or 800/

668–1171), where you can wade through a network of caves and plunge into hot and cold spring-fed pools.

On the west side of Kootenay Lake, as you head north from Nelson on Highway 31, is the pretty village of **Kaslo.** An 1898 stern-wheeler, the S.S. *Moyie* (☎ 250/353–2525), is moored on the lakeshore. Its cargo deck has been restored to look as it did in the 1930s; the salon deck revisits the year 1898. The *Moyie* is open 9:30–5, daily mid-May to mid-October. Admission is $5.

If you head west from Kaslo on scenic, winding Highway 31A, you'll pass a number of 19th-century silver-mining towns. Most were abandoned when the ore ran out, but **Sandon,** off Highway 31A, is enjoying a resurgence as a historic site, with several shops and a café. It's also home to Canada's oldest operating power plant; some of the equipment dates to 1890s.

## Dining and Lodging

$–$$$  ✕ **All Seasons Cafe.** Tucked into an alley between Baker and Victoria
★       streets, this former family cottage serves innovative cuisine that its owners have dubbed (because people kept asking) Left Coast Inland Cuisine. In practice, this means a seasonally changing menu that uses fresh, local, often organic produce and lists lots of vegetarian creations. Among the good choices are juniper marinated breast of duck with Saskatoon berry reduction and wild rice risotto cakes, and sesame sautéed spring salmon on potato leek rosti. The guava and ricotta cheesecake is a popular dessert. ⊠ *620 Herridge La.,* ☎ *250/352–0101. MC, V. No lunch.*

$–$$$  ✕ **Fiddler's Green.** Imaginative Northwest cuisine featuring local organic produce and an exclusively B.C. wine list is featured in this ivy-covered 1920s country house, about 10 km (6 mi) north of Nelson. Dinner is served in the main dining room, in any of three smaller rooms (two have fireplaces), or in the garden. Highlights on the seasonally changing menu have included seafood ravioli, rack of lamb, and rhubarb raspberry strudel with homemade ginger ice cream. ⊠ *2710 Lower Six Mile Rd.,* ☎ *250/825–4466. MC, V. Closed some evenings in winter. No lunch Mon.–Sat.*

$–$$   🏠 **Inn the Garden B&B.** This 1900 painted lady one block from Nelson's restaurants and shopping is adorned with plants, wicker, and antiques. You can relax in the sitting room, on the front porch or the sunny back deck, and a full hot breakfast (the inn caters to special diets if necessary) is included in the rates. A two-bedroom suite has a kitchenette and private entrance. The three-bedroom guest house next door, with a full kitchen and private backyard, is a good choice for families. Ask about golf, ski, and spa packages. ⊠ *408 Victoria St., V1L 4K5,* ☎ *250/352–3226 or 800/596–2337,* FAX *250/352–3284,* WEB *www.innthegarden.com. 5 rooms, 3 with bath; 1 suite; 1 guest house. Fans, kitchen, kitchenette; no room phones, no TVs, no kids under 12 in main house, no smoking. AE, MC, V. BP.*

$–$$   🏠 **Willow Point Lodge.** About 6 km (4 mi) north of Nelson, this three-
★       story 1920 country inn with a broad, covered veranda is perched on 3½ acres of forested hillside. Four rooms have expansive views of Kootenay Lake and the Selkirk Mountains; the others overlook an extensive garden. A favorite is the Oak Room, with its big stone fireplace, red-velvet bed canopy, and a private entrance. The Green Room has a private balcony, and the Kokanee Room has a detached bath. A lavish breakfast is included in the rate, and trails lead from the property to waterfalls nearby. ⊠ *2211 Taylor Dr., V1L 6K3,* ☎ *250/825–9411 or 800/949–2211,* FAX *250/825–3432,* WEB *www.willowpointlodge.com. 6 rooms. Outdoor hot tub, hiking, Internet; no room phones, no smoking. AE, MC, V. BP.*

## Outdoor Activities and Sports

### HIKING

**Kokanee Creek Provincial Park** (⊠ north of Nelson, off Hwy. 3A, WEB 250/422–4200; 800/689–9025 campground reservations) has lake swimming, walking trails, picnic sites, drive-in camping, and nearby boat rentals. **Kokanee Glacier Provincial Park** (⊠ north of Nelson off Hwy. 3A, ☎ 250/422–4200) is a backcountry park with hike-in campsites and extensive trail networks.

### SKIING

**Red Mountain Resorts** (⊠ 1000 Red Mountain Rd., Rossland, ☎ 250/362–7384 or 800/663–0105, WEB www.ski-red.com), about an hour southwest of Nelson, spans two mountains and has 83 marked runs, five lifts, and a vertical drop of 2,900 ft as well as cross-country ski trails and heli- and cat-skiing. Famed for its powder and tree skiing, the resort also has accommodations, ski rental, and ski lessons. A one-day lift ticket is $45. **Whitewater Ski and Winter Resort** (⊠ Whitewater Ski Rd., off Hwy. 6, ☎ 250/354–4944 or 800/666–9420, WEB www.skiwhitewater.com), about 20 minutes south of Nelson, has 43 runs, three lifts, a 1,300-ft vertical drop, and plenty of powder skiing. Ski rentals and lessons are available, though the resort doesn't offer lodging. A one-day lift pass goes for $40.

# Crawford Bay

**㉒** *40 km (25 mi) northeast of Nelson, including ferry ride.*

This peaceful backwater has pastoral scenery framed by snowcapped mountains. It's home to several artisans, including an ironworker and a glassblower, whose workshops are open to the public. On the east side of Kootenay Lake, Crawford Bay can be accessed by a scenic, 45-minute car ferry from Balfour, north of Nelson. By car, it's off Highway 3 on Route 3A.

## Lodging

**$–$$**
**★** 🖭 **Wedgwood Manor.** Built for the daughter of the famous china magnate, this 1909 country manor with a wide veranda has Edwardian beauty. Rooms are elegant: two have whirlpool baths, and several have canopy beds and fine, original woodwork. Much of the 50-acre estate is forested walking trails lead through the woods, and the Purcell Mountains form a striking backdrop to croquet games on the lawn. The house makes an atmospheric setting for the murder mystery weekends held here in the spring and fall, and the hosts can also arrange golf packages. A one-bedroom cottage with a kitchen is available year-round. ⊠ *16002 Crawford Creek Rd. (Box 135, V0B 1E0),* ☎ FAX *250/227–9233 or 800/862–0022,* WEB *www.bctravel.net/wedgwood. 6 rooms, 1 cottage. Badminton, croquet, hiking; no room phones, no room TVs, no kids under 3, no smoking. MC, V. Main house closed mid-Oct.–Easter. BP.*

## Outdoor Activities and Sports

The 18-hole, par-72 **Kokanee Springs Golf Resort** (⊠ 16082 Woolgar Rd., ☎ 250/227–9226 or 800/979–7999) has views of Kokanee Glacier, accommodations, and a restaurant. Greens fees are $52 on weekdays and $55 on weekends.

# THE CARIBOO-CHILCOTIN

This is British Columbia's wild west: a vast, thinly populated region stretching from the dense forests of the north to the rolling ranchlands of the south. The Cariboo-Chilcotin covers an area roughly bordered by Bella Coola in the west, Lillooet in the south, Wells Gray Park in the east, and Prince George in the north, though the part most visitors see is along Highway 97, which winds 640 km (397 mi) from Kamloops to Prince George.

In the 19th century, thousands followed this route, called the Cariboo Wagon Road or the Gold Rush Trail, looking for—and finding—gold. Those times are remembered throughout the region, most vividly at the re-created gold-rush town of Barkerville. You can still pan for gold here, but these days most folks come for ranch and spa getaways, horseback riding, fly-fishing, mountain biking, and cross-country skiing.

## The Cariboo Ranching Country

**②③** *73 km (44 mi) west of Kamloops.*

The Cariboo is home to some of the biggest working ranches in North America as well as a growing number of guest ranches that range from basic riding holidays to luxurious full-service spa resorts.

You can tour an 1863 roadhouse, visit a First Nations pit house, and take a stagecoach ride on the old Cariboo Wagon Road at **Historic Hat Creek Ranch** (✉ Hwy. 97, 11 km [7 mi] north of Cache Creek at junction with Hwy. 99, ☎ 250/457–9722, WEB www.hatcreekranch.com), once a major stagecoach stop on the Gold Rush Trail. There's also a restaurant, gift shop, and campsite. The ranch is open mid-May to mid-October, daily 9–5; admission is $7.

### Lodging

$$$$  🏨 **Echo Valley Ranch&Spa.** A palacelike Baan Thai ("Thai house") pre-
★     sides over a view-blessed hillside at this remote luxury resort, 48 km (30 mi) west of Clinton. The Baan Thai is home to yoga classes and a lavish Thai-style guest suite. The spruce-log construction and vaulted ceilings of the resort's main lodge, guest lodge, and cabins are equally beautiful. You can enjoy a Thai massage in the full-service spa, ride Tennessee Walking horses, hike, bike, fish, or simply enjoy the fresh mountain air. Meals, taken family-style in the main lodge, feature the ranch's own organic produce. A three-night stay (two nights in winter) is required. ✉ *Box 16, Jesmond V0K 1K0,* ☎ *250/459–2386 or 800/253–8831,* FAX *250/459–0086,* WEB *www.evranch.com. 15 rooms, 1 suite, 3 cabins. Dining room, fans, some refrigerators, indoor pool, gym, 2 outdoor hot tubs, sauna, spa, fishing, mountain bikes, billiards, hiking, horseback riding, shuffleboard, sleigh rides, recreation room, shop, laundry service, Internet, meeting room, airstrip, helipad; no kids under 13, no room phones, no room TVs, no smoking. MC, V. FAP.*

$$–$$$  🏨 **The Flying U Ranch.** Founded in 1849, Canada's oldest guest ranch oozes Wild West charm, right down to the swinging doors at the Longhorn Saloon. Rustic log cabins with a shared bathhouse and hearty, basic meals served family style in the 1880s lodge recall ranch life of a century ago. You can ride all you want here through the miles of surrounding ranchland; guides are optional—the horses know their way home. Hayrides and square dances round out the days. A two- to three-day minimum stay applies; rates include riding and most activities. ✉ *North Green Lake Rd. (Box 69, 70 Mile House V0K 2K0), 33 km (20 mi) south of 100 Mile House,* ☎ *250/456–7717,* FAX *250/ 456–7455,* WEB *www.flyingu.com. 27 cabins without baths, 2 tepees, 2 tents. Dining room, lake, massage (summer only), sauna, dock, boating, fishing, hiking, horseshoes, volleyball, sleigh rides, snowmobiling, pub, piano, shop, baby-sitting, playground, meeting rooms, airstrip; no room phones, no room TVs. MC, V. Closed Mar. and Nov.–mid-Dec; no riding in winter. AP.*

**$$** 🏨 **The Hills Health Ranch.** Hiking, riding, going on hay rides, and line dancing mix with spa treatments, wellness programs, and aerobics classes at this homey, affordable, and long-established health retreat. You can book structured wellness packages or just relax and enjoy the many activities at your own pace. Accommodations include woodsy three-bedroom A-frame chalets and lodge rooms with standard hotel decor. The spa cuisine is excellent (and calorie counted), but heartier ranch meals and continental fare are also available. ⊠ *108 Mile Ranch at Hwy. 97, 60 km (36 mi) south of Williams Lake, 180 km (108 mi) northwest of Kamloops (Box 26, V0K 2Z0),* ☎ *250/791–5225,* FAX *250/791–6384,* WEB *www.spabc.com. 26 rooms, 19 chalets. Restaurant, dining room, picnic area, tea shop, fans, some kitchens, indoor pool, health club, 2 hot tubs, sauna, spa, boating, mountain bikes, billiards, hiking, horseback riding, Ping-Pong, cross-country skiing, downhill skiing, ice skating, ski shop, sleigh rides, snowmobiling, pub, recreation room, shop, playground, laundry service, Internet, business services, meeting rooms, airstrip, some pets allowed; no phones in some rooms, no smoking. AE, MC, V.*

## Barkerville and Wells

24 *80 km (50 mi) east of Quesnel on Hwy. 26.*

In 1862, when news of a rich gold strike at this out of the way spot reached the outside world, this tiny settlement rapidly boomed into the biggest town west of Chicago and north of San Francisco.

★ **Barkerville Historic Town,** with 125 original and re-created buildings, is now the largest heritage attraction in western Canada. Actors in period costume, merchants vending 19th-century goods, stagecoach rides, and live musical revues capture the town's heyday. The site is open year-round, but most of the theatrical fun happens in summer. ⊠ *Hwy. 26, Barkerville,* ☎ *250/994–3302,* WEB *www.heritage.gov.bc.ca/bark/bark.htm.* 🎫 *Mid-May–mid-June $6 for 2-day pass; mid-June–Sept. 30, $8.50 for 2-day pass; free in winter.* ☉ *Daily 8–8.*

**Bowron Lake Provincial Park** (⊠ end of Hwy. 26, ☎ 800/435–5622 canoe trip reservations, WEB www.hellobc.com), 30 km (19 mi) east of Barkerville by gravel road, has a 116-km (72-mi) chain of rivers, lakes, and portages that make up a popular canoe route. Canoeists must reserve ahead and pay a fee of $50 per person fee, plus an $18 per boat reservation fee.

Eight kilometers (5 miles) west of Barkerville, tiny **Wells** is a fascinating stop. A thriving mining town until the 1940s, it's now an atmospheric mountain village of brightly painted false-front buildings. The village, home to a thriving arts community, has several art galleries and cafés and a summer arts school. A big draw here is the **Jack 'O Clubs Casino and Music Hall** (☎ 250/994–3222) on Highway 26, a 1930s-theme casino with musical revues three times a day between May and September. All ages are welcome at the shows; guests must be 19 to enter the casino.

## Lodging

**$–$$** 🏨 **Wells Hotel.** The faithfully refurbished 1934 Wells Hotel makes a good base for visiting nearby Barkerville and the Bowron Lake canoeing area and for accessing the 80 km (50 mi) of hiking, biking, and cross-country ski trails nearby. Comfortable rooms and suites are decorated in a 1930s style with hardwood floors, local art, and period photos. ⊠ *2341 Pooley St. (Box 39, Wells V0K 2R0),* ☎ *250/994–3427 or 800/860–2299,* FAX *250/994–3494,* WEB *www.wellshotel.com. 16 rooms, 9 with bath. Restaurant, outdoor hot tub, pub; no room phones, no room TVs, no smoking. AE, MC, V. CP.*

# NORTHERN BRITISH COLUMBIA

It's a truism that even those well traveled in B.C. rarely use the top half of their maps. The area most British Columbians refer to as "The North" comprises a full half of the province, most of it little-visited, thinly populated, stunningly beautiful, wildlife-rich wilderness. The north is home to the people of several First Nations tribes who have lived in the regions for thousands of years and compose most of the population in many areas. Insights into these ancient cultures, at 'Ksan, near Hazelton, Kitwanga and Kitwancool on the Stewart Cassiar Highway, and in towns and villages throughout the region, are, for many, the most rewarding part of a trip north.

Outdoor adventure increasingly draws those seeking out the north's untraveled hiking paths, canoe routes, white-water rivers, and freshwater lakes. Driving through the region can feel like going on an adventure. Towns are few and far between, and drivers need a good spare tire and a sharp eye on the gas gauge. The rewards, though, are many: snow peaks; hot springs; sightings of bear, moose, and bighorn sheep; long summer days; and occasional glimpses of the northern lights.

Three major highways cross the north. Highway 16, the Yellowhead Highway, runs from Jasper in Alberta via Prince George to Prince Rupert, a route that can also be traveled by train on VIA Rail's Skeena line. Highway 97 heads north from Prince George to Dawson Creek, where it becomes the Alaska Highway. Farther to the west, the little-traveled Stewart-Cassiar Highway links Highway 16 to the Alaska Highway, making it possible to take a multiday circle tour of the region.

## Prince George

**㉕** *786 km (487 mi) north of Vancouver, 412 km (247 mi) south of Dawson Creek, 440 mi (273 mi) southeast of Hazelton, 721 km (447 mi) east of Prince Rupert.*

At the crossroads of two railways and two highways, Prince George is the province's third-largest city and the commercial center of northern British Columbia.

**The Exploration Place** has lots of fun, science-related exhibits for kids, including two life-size dinosaur models and a virtual-reality theater. Other exhibits feature re-creations of historic local buildings, and First Nations' artifacts and oral histories. ⊠ *333 Becott Place (in Fort George Park at east end of 20th Ave.),* ☎ *250/562–1612,* WEB *www. theexplorationplace.com.* ⬚ *$8.95, $10.95 including virtual reality theater.* ☉ *Mid-May–mid-Oct., daily 10–5; mid-Oct.–mid-May, Wed.– Sun. 10–5.*

Century-old cabooses, locomotives, dining cars, and luxury sleeping cars are some of the dozens of restored railcars collected at the **Prince George Railway and Forestry Museum,** an outdoor museum that also displays historic logging and sawmill equipment. ⊠ *850 River Rd., next to Cottonwood Park,* ☎ *250/563–7351,* WEB *www.pgrfm.bc.ca.* ⬚ *$6.* ☉ *Mid-May–late Sept., daily 9–5.*

**Two Rivers Gallery** (⊠ 725 Civic Plaza, ☎ 250/614–7800) has a changing roster of shows by local, national, and international artists, though the focus is on Canadian works. The gift shop is a good place to pick up local crafts. It is open Tuesday, Wednesday, Friday, and Saturday 10–5; Thursday 10–9; and Sunday noon–5. Admission to the gallery is $4.50, free Thursday 3–9.

### Lodging

**$$** ⊞ **Coast Inn of the North.** This centrally located, full-service hotel has a striking rosewood lobby with a brass fireplace. All the services are here, including a gym, a pool, and a day spa in the attached retail concourse. Rooms are attractive with rosewood furniture and such added amenities as desks and coffeemakers. The standard rooms have two double beds, the premium rooms are corner units with balconies, and the suites have jetted tubs and fireplaces. The two restaurants include a clubby room serving Continental fare and a traditional Japanese steak house. ⊠ *770 Brunswick St., V2L 2C2,* ☎ *250/563–0121,* FAX *250/ 563–1948,* WEB *www.coasthotels.com. 155 rooms, 2 suites. 2 restaurants, coffee shop, room service, in-room data ports, some minibars, cable TV (movies and video games in some rooms), indoor pool, gym, hair salon, hot tub, sauna, spa, lounge, pub, shops, dry cleaning, laundry service, business services, meeting rooms, some pets allowed (fee); no-smoking floors. AE, DC, MC, V.*

### Outdoor Activities and Sports

**Strider Adventures** (⊠ 17075 E. Perry Rd., ☎ 250/963–9542 or 800/ 665–7752, WEB www.pgweb.com/strider) can take you on a trek through the local wilds with the help of friendly llamas.

### Shopping

The **Prince George Native Art Gallery and Gift Shop** (⊠ 1600 3rd Ave., ☎ 250/614–7726) sells traditional and contemporary works, including carvings, sculpture, jewelry, and literature.

OFF THE BEATEN PATH   **FORT ST. JAMES NATIONAL HISTORIC SITE –** This parklike site, 52 km (31 mi) north of Vanderhoof on Highway 27, on the south shore of Stuart Lake, is a former Hudson's Bay Company fur-trading post and the oldest continually inhabited European settlement west of the Rockies. Careful restoration of the original buildings, costumed staff, and demonstrations of aboriginal arts and food preparation help you experience life as a fur trader in 1896. ☎ 250/996–7191, WEB parkscan.harbour.com/fsj. ⊠ $4. ⊙ Mid-May–Sept., daily 9–5; off-season tours by advance reservation.

## Smithers

🙶 *371 km (222 mi) northwest of Prince George, 353 km (211 mi) northeast of Prince Rupert, 1,149 km (689 mi) northwest of Vancouver.*

The main town of the Bulkley Valley, Smithers sits under the snow-capped backdrop of 8,700-ft Hudson's Bay Mountain. The Bavarian-theme town center has hotels, restaurants, and several outdoor-equipment outfitters to help visitors explore the surrounding peaks and rivers.

## The Hazeltons

🙷 *293 km (182 mi) northeast of Prince Rupert, 439 km (272 mi) northwest of Prince George, 1,217 km (755 mi) northwest of Vancouver.*

Three villages—New, Old, and South Hazelton, each couple of miles apart—combine to form the Hazeltons, an area rich in the culture of the Gitxsan and Wet'suwet'en peoples. New Hazelton is a modern service strip along Highway 16; South Hazelton is a hamlet just off Highway 16. Old Hazelton is a delightful village of old-fashioned false-front buildings where an old paddle wheeler houses a café and art gallery. It's 4 km (2½ mi) north of New Hazelton, across the Bulkley River by suspension bridge. There are motels in New Hazelton, B&Bs in Old Hazelton, and a campsite and RV park adjacent to 'Ksan Historical Village and Museum.

At **Kispiox,** 11 km (7 mi) north of Old Hazelton on Kispiox Valley Road, you can see 15 intricately carved totems, some more than 100 years old. Guided tours and local crafts are available at the **Kispiox Cultural and Information Centre** (☎ 877/842–5911 or 250/842–7057).

★ **'Ksan Historical Village and Museum,** is a re-created Gitxsan village. The community of seven longhouses was built in 1965 as a replica of the one that stood on the site, at the confluence of the Skeena and Bulkley rivers, for thousands of years before European contact. Gitxsan guides lead informative tours through three of the longhouses. At the Frog House, artifacts and an audio presentation tell of life in the distant past; at the Wolf House, audiovisual effects re-create the experience of being an honored guest at a feast. The Fireweed House exhibits the elaborate performing regalia of the 'Ksan Performing Arts Group, who perform here, reenacting ancient songs and dances of the Gitxsan people, Friday evenings during the summer. A gift shop sells goods from First Nations groups across the province; a café serves traditional Gitxsan foods. ⊠ *High Level Rd. (Hwy. 62), Old Hazelton,* ☎ *250/842–5544 or 877/842–5518,* WEB *www.ksan.org.* ⌦ *$2, $10 with tour.* ☺ *June–Sept., daily 9–6, tours on the ½ hr; call for winter hrs.*

### Outdoor Activities and Sports

**Skeena Eco-Expeditions** (⊠ ☎ 877/842–5911 or 250/842–7057, WEB www.kispioxadventures.com) operate hiking and rafting tours.

## Terrace

**㉘** *147 km (88 mi) east of Prince Rupert on Hwy. 16, 577 km (346 mi) northwest of Prince George, 1,355 km (813 mi) northwest of Vancouver.*

Terrace is a logging town and the major commercial center for the Skeena Valley. The region is also home to the Tsimchian peoples. The Terrace Travel Info Centre on Keith Avenue (Hwy. 16) has information about area attractions.

**Ferry Island Municipal Park,** in the Skeena River on the east side of town and accessed by bridges, has a campground, picnic sites, and hiking trails. **Heritage Park** (⊠ 4113 N. Sparks St., ☎ 250/635–4546) is a re-created turn-of-the-20th-century village, with costumed guides and many original buildings. It's open Thursday–Monday 10–4:30, May–August; admission is $3. **Lakelse Lake Provincial Park** (☎ 250/798–2466; 800/689–9025 camping reservations), 15 minutes south of Terrace on Highway 37, has camping, hiking trails, and a swimming beach. At **Mt. Layton Hot Springs Resort** (⊠ ☎ 250/798–2214, on Hwy. 37 S), are pools and water slides. About 80 km (48 mi) north of Terrace, partly on gravel road, is the **Nisga'a Memorial Lava Bed Park** (☎ 250/798–2277), the site of Canada's most recent volcanic eruption (more than 250 years ago).

About 35 km (21 mi) northwest of Terrace, off Highway 16, is the ski resort at **Shames Mountain** (☎ 250/635–3773, 250/638–8754 snow report; WEB www.shamesmountain.com). It has a vertical rise of 1,608 ft, a double chairlift, and 20 trails. Anglers flock to the **Skeena River** and its tributaries for some of the province's richest sport fishing (a 99-pound salmon, said to be a world-record catch, was caught in the Skeena).

*En Route* Traveling west towards Prince Rupert, both Highway 16 and the railway line follow the wide Skeena River. The route, which passes under snowcapped mountain peaks and past waterfalls, is one of the most scenic in the province.

# The Alaska Highway

*406 km (243 mi) from Prince George to Dawson Creek, 985 km (591 mi) from Dawson Creek to Watson Lake, Yukon.*

From Prince George, Highway 97, or the Hart Highway, continues northeast to Dawson Creek, where it becomes the Alaska Highway, the most popular route north for Alaska-bound travelers. It then winds through the foothills and pine forests of the northern Rocky Mountains, past the communities of Fort St. John and Fort Nelson, before crossing the B.C.-Yukon border at Watson Lake and continuing to Delta Junction, near Fairbanks, Alaska.

The Alaska Highway skirts the edges of a Muskwa-Kechika Management Area, a vast, roadless wilderness so rich in wildlife it's been called the Serengeti of the North. Even from the highway, sightings of deer, moose, elk, mountain sheep, and bear are commonplace.

The two-lane highway is paved and open year-round. Communities along the way are small, but basic services (gas, food, lodging) are available at least every few hours en route. Pine Pass, about 200 km (132 mi) north of Prince George, marks the boundary between the Pacific and Mountain time zones. Clocks go forward an hour here.

**Dawson Creek,** a town of about 11,000, is best known as Mile Zero of the Alaska Highway. The much-photographed signpost is at Mile Zero Square (⊠ 10th St. and 102nd Ave.). Also at the square is **Alaska Highway House** (⊠ 10201 10th St., ☎ 250/782–4714), which has a small exhibit about the history of the highway. It's open weekdays 8:30–4:30. The **Station Museum** (⊠ 900 Alaska Ave., ☎ 250/782–959), in the town's old railway station, has natural history and railway history displays and shows a film several times a day about the building of the Alaska Highway. The station is also home to the Dawson Creek Tourist Information Centre.

To the north, **Stone Mountain Provincial Park,** 140 km (87 mi) west of Fort Nelson, gets its name from the dramatic rock formations and treeless tundra found in the park. At **Muncho Lake Provincial Park,** 250 km (150 mi) northwest of Fort Nelson, two campgrounds sit on the edge of pretty, blue Muncho Lake. Sheep, caribou, moose, and deer are attracted to salt licks along the highway here.

At **Liard River Hotsprings Provincial Park** (⊠ 320 km [192 mi] northwest of Fort Nelson, ☎ 800/689–9025 camping reservations) heat from the springs has generated an oasis of tropical plants, including orchids, in this remote northern spot. Two natural outdoor hot springs–fed pools are a short walk from the campground; there's no charge to use the pools. The campsite here is very popular, and reservations are recommended.

## Lodging

$$ &#x1F4FA; **Northern Rockies Lodge.** This modern log lodge on Muncho Lake, 30 minutes from Liard River Hot Springs, provides comfortable lodge rooms, rustic cabins, lakefront chalets, and a campground with RV hook-ups. A range of boating and outdoor activities is available at the lakeside, and the owner's own bush plane can take you on photo safaris, flightseeing tours, or fishing on a remote mountain lake. You can also stay overnight at one of the lodge's rustic fly-in outpost cabins. ⊠ *Mile 462, Alaska Hwy. (Box 8, Muncho Lake V0C 1Z0),* ☎ *250/776–3481 or 800/663–5269,* FAX *250/776–3482,* WEB *www.northern-rockies-lodge.com. 21 rooms, 19 cabins, 3 outpost cabins. Restaurant, some refrigerators, cable TV, sauna, boating, fish-*

*ing, mountain bikes, hiking, laundry facilities, Internet, business services, meeting rooms, airstrip, helipad, some pets allowed (fee); no room phones, no TV in some rooms, no-smoking rooms. MC, V.*

# The Stewart-Cassiar Highway

*725 km (450 mi) from Kitwanga on Hwy 16 to Upper Liard, Yukon, on the Alaska Highway.*

Linking Highway 16 to the Alaska Highway (the Yellowhead Highway), Highway 37, also called the Stewart-Cassiar Highway, is the road less traveled between B.C. and the Yukon. Though challenging to drive, it is arguably prettier than the Alaska Highway, with striking mountain views at every turn.

Most of Highway 37 is paved, though there are still some gravel sections. Watch for potholes, logging trucks, single-lane bridges, and low-flying aircraft (parts of the road double as a landing strip). As in all active logging areas, it's best to drive with your lights on during the day to stay visible to logging trucks. Settlements are small, gas stations and mechanics are few, and snow can fly at any time of year (though it's pretty rare in the summer.) The provincial **Ministry of Transportation and Highways** (WEB www.th.gov.bc.ca/roadreports.htm) has up-to-date road reports.

Just a couple of miles north of the Yellowhead junction, the village of **Kitwanga** is home to a stunning array of ancient totems. Nearby is the **Battle Hill National Historic Site**, the site of a decisive First Nations battle in about 1600. One of the largest and oldest collection of totem poles in North America stands at **Kitwancool** (also known as Gitanyow), just 15 km (9 mi) north of the Yellowhead junction.

The 1.6-million-acre **Spatsizi Plateau Wilderness Park** is one of Canada's largest and most remote parks and one of its richest wildlife reserves. Home to caribou, grizzly bears, black bears, mountain goats, and 140 species of birds, it's virtually untouched wilderness, accessible only by foot, horseback, canoe, or floatplane. **B.C. Parks** (☎ 250/847–7320) in Smithers has information about guides and outfitters.

OFF THE
BEATEN PATH

**THE GLACIER HIGHWAY –** The Glacier Highway (Highway 37A) leaves the Cassiar Highway at Meziadin Junction, about 170 km (112 mi) north of the Yellowhead Junction, and travels 65 glacier-lined km (39 mi) west to the oddly paired towns of Stewart, B.C., and Hyder, Alaska. The towns sit about 3 km (2 mi) apart on either side of the international border at the head of the Portland Canal, a 112-km-long (70-mi-long) fjord on the edge of Alaska's Misty Fjords National Monument. Stewart, with a population of about 1,000, has a bank, hotels, restaurants, and camping. Across the border, tiny Hyder, with a population of about 100, has no road links to the rest of the United States, except the highway through Canada. The few shops here accept Canadian money. It's a tradition for visitors to get "Hyderized": essentially by downing a shot of grain alcohol at the bar.

**TELEGRAPH CREEK –** From Dease Lake, a scenic 115-km (71-mi) gravel road, steep and winding in places, leads to this picturesque ghost town of gold rush–era buildings on the Stikine River, said to be the oldest community in northern B.C. The folks at Stikine Riversong (☎ 250/235–3196, WEB www.stikineriversong.com), in the original Hudson's Bay Company store, have food, accommodations, guided hikes, and river tours.

## Lodging
**$$**   🏠 **Bell II Lodge.** Fly-fishing and heli-skiing are the specialties at this river-side resort, though travelers overnighting on the long drive north will also appreciate the comforts here. The guest rooms, in attractive modern log chalets, all have separate entrances, soapstone fireplaces, pine furniture, and down duvets. There are RV and tent sites here, too. ✉ *At Bell II, 250 km (150 mi) north of Hwy. 16 junction (Box 1118, Vernon BC V1T 6N4),* ☎ *604/881–8530 or 877/617–2288,* FAX *604/881–8330,* WEB *www.bell2lodge.com. 20 rooms. Restaurant, coffee shop, exercise equipment, outdoor hot tub, sauna, fishing, billiards, Ping-Pong, lounge, recreation room, shop, laundry facilities, Internet, meeting room, some pets allowed (fee); no room TVs, no smoking. AE, MC, V.*

# NORTH COAST

Gateway to Alaska and the Yukon, this vast, rugged region is marked by soaring snowcapped mountain ranges, scenic fjords, primordial islands, and towering rain forests. Once the center of a vast trading network, the mid- and north coasts are home to First Nations peoples who have lived here for 10,000 years and to more recent immigrants drawn by the natural resources of fur, fish, and forest. The region is thin on roads, but you can travel by ferry, sailboat, cruise ship, plane, or kayak to explore the ancient villages of the coast and the Queen Charlotte Islands. The climate of this mist-shrouded region is one of the world's wettest. Winters see torrential rains, and summers are damp; rain gear is essential year-round.

## Inside Passage

★ ㉙   *507 km (314 mi), or 274 nautical mi, between Port Hardy on northern Vancouver Island and Prince Rupert.*

The Inside Passage, a sheltered marine highway, follows a series of natural channels along the green-and-blue-shaded B.C. coast. The undisturbed landscape of rising mountains and humpbacked islands has a striking, prehistoric look. You can take a ferry cruise along the Inside Passage or see it on one of the luxury liners that sails from Vancouver to Alaska.

The comfortable **Queen of the North** ferry carries up to 800 passengers and 157 vehicles and has cabins, cafeteria, buffet, a gift shop, an elevator, children's play areas, and a licensed lounge on board. Between mid-May and late September, sailings from Port Hardy on Vancouver Island to Prince Rupert (or vice versa) are direct and take 15 hours, almost entirely in daylight. Sailings are less frequent and longer the rest of the year, as the ferry makes stops along the way. Reservations are required for vehicles and recommended for foot passengers. It's also a good idea to make hotel reservations at Port Hardy and Prince Rupert. ✉ *BC Ferries, 1112 Fort St., Victoria V8V 4V2,* ☎ *250/386–3431; 888/223–3779 in B.C. and Alberta;* FAX *250/381–5452;* WEB *www.bcferries.com.* ⛴ *One-way summer passage for a car $233; each adult passenger $99; cabin $50–$60 (fares lower Oct.–May).* ☉ *Mid-May–mid-Oct. departing on alternate days from Port Hardy and Prince Rupert at 7:30 AM, arriving 10:30 PM.*

## Discovery Coast Passage

★ ㉚   *258 km (160 mi), or 138 nautical mi, between Port Hardy on northern Vancouver Island and Bella Coola.*

This BC Ferries summer-only service travels up the Inside Passage to the First Nations community of Bella Bella and then turns up Dean

Channel to the mainland town of Bella Coola. The scenery is stunning, and the route allows passengers to visit communities along the way, including Shearwater, Klemtu, and Ocean Falls. It also provides an alternative route into the Cariboo region, via the steep and winding Highway 20 from Bella Coola to Williams Lake. Lodging at ports of call varies from luxury fishing lodges to rough camping, but it is limited and must be booked in advance.

The *Queen of Chilliwack,* carrying up to 389 passengers and 115 vehicles, takes from 13 to 30 hours (depending on the number of stops) to travel from Port Hardy on Vancouver Island to Bella Coola. Reservations are required for vehicles and advised for foot passengers. There aren't any cabins. ✉ *BC Ferries, 1112 Fort St., Victoria V8V 4V2,* ☎ *250/386–3431; 888/223–3779 in B.C. only;* FAX *250/381–5452;* WEB *www.bcferries.com.* ⌑ *One-way fares between Port Hardy and Bella Coola for passengers $102, cars $205, campers $261.* ☉ *Mid-June–early-Sept., departs Port Hardy on Tues., Thurs., and Sat.; leaves Bella Coola on Mon., Wed., and Fri.*

# Prince Rupert

③ *1,502 km (931 mi) by road and 750 km (465 mi) by air northwest of Vancouver, 15 hrs by ferry northwest of Port Hardy on Vancouver Island.*

The deep sea port of Prince Rupert is the largest community on the North Coast. It's the final stop on the BC Ferries route through the Inside Passage, as well as the base for ferries to the Queen Charlotte Islands and a port of call for Alaska ferries. The terminals for both BC and Alaska ferries and the VIA Rail Station are side by side, about 2 km (1 mi) from town; in summer, a downtown shuttle bus meets each ferry. Prince Rupert is also a port of call for some Alaska-bound cruise ships. Famous for its wet weather, the town is surrounded by some of the province's most beautiful coastal wilderness.

**Cow Bay,** a 10-minute walk from downtown, is a historic waterfront area of shops, galleries, seafood restaurants, and fishing boats. Cow Bay takes its name seriously: lamp posts, benches, and anything else stationary is painted Holstein-style. While here, you can grab a coffee at **Cowpuccino's,** dine at the **Cow Bay Café,** shop for local crafts, take a kayak tour to explore the nearby wilderness, and stop in at Prince Rupert's **Visitor Info Centre.** Cow Bay will also be home to the **Atlin Cruise Ship Terminal,** a facility for Alaska-bound vessels set to open in 2004.

★ The **Museum of Northern British Columbia,** in a longhouse-style facility overlooking the waterfront, has one of the province's finest collections of coastal First Nations art, with some artifacts that date back 10,000 years. Artisans work on totem poles in the carving shed, and in summer museum staff run walking tours of the town. The museum also operates the **Kwinista Railway Museum,** a five-minute walk away on the waterfront. ✉ *100 1st Ave. W,* ☎ *250/624–3207,* WEB *www.museumofnorthernbc.com.* ⌑ *$5.* ☉ *Oct.–mid-May, Mon.–Sat. 9–5; mid-May–Aug., Mon.–Sat. 9–8, Sun. 9–5; Sept. daily, 9–5.*

In the late 19th century, hundreds of cannery villages, built on pilings on the edge of the wilderness, lined the coast between California and Alaska. Most are gone now, but B.C's oldest (it dates to 1889) and most

★ complete is the **North Pacific Historic Fishing Village** in Port Edward, 20 km (12 mi) south of Prince Rupert at the mouth of the Skeena River. Once home to more than 700 people during each canning season, the town, including managers' houses, the company store, and cannery works, is now a national historic site. Staff lead tours and demonstrations about fishing methods, the canning process, and the unique culture of cannery villages. In summer, be sure to catch the one-man play about the area's history. You can spend the night, too: the village boasts a seafood restaurant, a comfortable waterfront inn, cottages with kitchens, and a rustic (bring your own bedding) bunkhouse. ⊠ *Off Hwy. 16, Port Edward,* ☎ *250/628–3538,* WEB *www.district.portedward.bc.ca/ northpacific.* ⌨ *May 1–mid-Oct. village free, cannery building, tours, and shows $10; mid-Oct.–May by donation.* ⊙ *May 1–Sept. 30, daily 9–6; Oct.–Apr., daily 9–5.*

### Dining and Lodging

$$–$$$  ✕⌷ **Crest Hotel.** On a bluff overlooking the ocean, this full-service hotel has Prince Rupert's best views. The restaurant, lounge, most of the guest rooms, and the outdoor hot tub all command expansive vistas of the harbor and outlying forested islands. The rooms are large, comfortable, and modern; the pricier rooms, called treat suites, have double Jacuzzi tubs set before ocean-view windows. The restaurant ($$–$$$), decorated with brass rails and beam ceilings, specializes in seafood, particularly salmon. You can also book cruises and fishing charters from here. ⊠ *222 1st Ave. W., V8J 1A8,* ☎ *250/624–6771 or 800/663–8150,* FAX *250/627–7666,* WEB *www.cresthotel.bc.ca. 101 rooms, 1 suite. Restaurant, coffee shop, room service, in-room data ports, some minibars, cable TV with movies, gym, outdoor hot tub, steam room, fishing, lounge, laundry service, Internet, business services, meeting rooms, some pets allowed (fee); no-smoking floor. AE, D, DC, MC, V.*

### Outdoor Activities and Sports

**Eco-Treks Adventures** (⊠ 203 Cow Bay Rd., ☎ 250/624–8311, WEB www.citytel.net/ecotreks) has kayak rentals and kayaking as well as Zodiac tours (one- and multiday) of nearby fjords and islands. Itineraries include trips to ancient petroglyphs and pictographs, visits to the edge of the nearby Khutzeymateen grizzly-bear sanctuary, and whale-watching excursions. Many of the trips are suitable for beginners.

## Queen Charlotte Islands (Haida Gwaii)

★ ㉜  93 *nautical mi southwest of Prince Rupert, 367 nautical mi northwest of Port Hardy.*

The Queen Charlotte Islands, or Haida Gwaii (Islands of the People), have been called the Canadian Galápagos. Their long isolation off the province's North Coast has given rise to subspecies of wildlife found nowhere else in the world. The islands are also the preserve of the Haida people, who make up about half the population. Their vibrant culture is undergoing a renaissance, evident throughout the islands.

Most of the islands' 6,000 permanent residents live on Graham Island—the northernmost and largest of the group of 150 islands—where 108 km (65 mi) of paved road connects the town of Queen Charlotte in the south to Masset in the north. Moresby Island, to the south, is the second-largest of the islands and is largely taken up by the Gwaii Haanas National Park Reserve and Haida Heritage Site, a roadless ecological reserve with restricted access. The wildlife (including bears, eagles, and otters), old-growth forest, and stunning scenery are like nothing else on earth, and kayaking enthusiasts from around the world are drawn to waterways here. Towns on Graham Island have most services, including banking, grocery stores, and a range of accommodation and campsites; accommodation is also available in Sandspit, on Moresby Island. In summer it's a good idea to make hotel reservations before arriving.

The **visitor information centre** on Wharf Street in Queen Charlotte has information about area activities, including visits to Gwaii Haanas.

**Island Transit** (✉ ☎ 250/559–4461 or 877/747–4461, WEB www. qciislands.net/eagle) buses meet each ferry from Prince Rupert in the summer and run about once a day between the airport in Sandspit, Queen Charlotte, and Masset. **Eagle Cabs,** at the same phone number, also provide transportation on the islands.

The 1,470-square-km (570-square-mi) **Gwaii Haanas National Park Reserve and Haida Heritage Site,** managed jointly by the Canadian government and the Council of the Haida Nation, protects a vast tract of wilderness, unique flora and fauna, and many historic and cultural sites. These include the island of SGang Gwaay (Anthony Island) a UNESCO World Heritage Site, where SGang Gwaay 'llnagaay is one of the best examples of a traditional Northwest Coast First Nations village site. The reserve is on Moresby Island and 137 smaller islands at the archipelago's southern end. The protected area, accessible only by air or sea, is both ecologically and culturally sensitive. One way to visit—and highly recommended for those unfamiliar with wilderness travel—is with a licensed operator. Parks Canada and the Queen Charlotte Visitor Information Centre have information about operators. To visit on your own (without a licensed operator), you must make a reservation, register for each trip, and attend a mandatory orientation session. Park-use fees start at C$10 per person per day, plus a $15 per person reservation fee. ✉ *Parks Canada, Box 37, Queen Charlotte V0T 1S0,* ☎ *250/559–8818; 800/435–5622 information pack and reservations;* FAX *250/559–8366;* WEB *parkscan.harbour.com/gwaii.*

★ Just a kilometer (½ mile) north of the Skidegate ferry terminal, the **Haida Gwaii Museum at Qay'llnagaay** is set in a striking longhouse facility on a bluff overlooking the water. Six totem poles, erected in 2001, stand outside. The museum's collection of Haida masks, totem poles, works by contemporary Haida artists, carvings of silver and argillite (soft black slate), and other artifacts is expanding with the addition of works repatriated from other museums. A gift shop sells Haida art, and a natural-history exhibit gives interesting background on island wildlife. At press time, plans were in place to expand the museum, which will form part of the **Qay'llnagaay Heritage Centre,** a cultural center built in the style of a traditional Haida village. Built on a site once occupied by the old village of Qay'llnagaay, or Sea Lion Town, the center will, when complete in about 2005, include a theater and an art school. ✉ *Second Beach Rd. off Hwy. 16, Skidegate,* ☎ *250/ 559–4643,* WEB *www.haidagwaiimuseum.com.* ⊡ *$4.* ☉ *June–Aug., weekdays 10–5, weekends 1–5; May and Sept., weekdays 10–noon and 1–5, Sat. 1–5; Oct.–Apr., Mon. and Wed.–Fri. 10–noon and 1–5, Sat. 1–5.*

East Beach, an 80-km (50-mi) stretch of sand, runs the length of **Naikoon Provincial Park** (☎ 250/557–4390), in the northeast corner of Graham Island. Untouched forests, bogs, and wildlife, including some of North America's largest black bears, fill the interior of this vast wilderness preserve. At the south end of the park, in Tlell, are the Park Headquarters and Misty Meadows Campground, which has non-reservable drive-in camping. From the Tlell day-use area nearby, a 10-km (6-mi), three-hour round-trip hike leads onto East Beach and to the wreck of a 1928 logging vessel, the *Pesuta.* At the park's north end, near the town of Masset, Agate Beach has non-reservable drive-in beachfront camping. A one-hour round-trip climb up 400-ft Tow Hill gives stunning views of the wide beach at McIntyre Bay. It's possible to walk along East Beach for days, though hikers planning extended trips in the park are advised to register with B.C. Parks or the Royal Canadian Mounted Police in Masset before setting out.

## Dining and Lodging

$$ ✕ **Hummingbird Café.** This cedar-sided shack in Port Clements has a classic 1950s-diner look, right down to the vinyl booths and stools at the counter. The bistro-style chalkboard menu is a departure, though. The menu changes daily but usually includes such seafood appetizers as mussels, calamari, or Cajun oysters and big portions of such homey mains as lasagna, prime rib, fish-and-chips, or seafood curry. ⊠ *9 Cedar Ave. E, Port Clements,* ☎ *250/557–8583. AE, MC, V. Closed Mon.*

$ ✕ **Hanging by a Fibre.** The sign outside this little café-gallery promises "art, cappuccino and conversation." Heartier fare includes made-from-scratch soups, quiches, wraps, pastas, and baked goodies. The three tiny rooms are decorated with a movable feast of local art, most of it for sale. ⊠ *3207 Wharf St.,* ☎ *250/559–4463. Reservations not accepted. No credit cards. No dinner.*

$$ ⊡ **Alaska View Lodge.** On a clear day, you can see the mountains of Alaska from the large front deck of this B&B, 13 km (8 mi) east of Masset. A 10-km-long (6-mi-long) sandy beach borders the lodge on one side, and there are woods on the other. Eagles are a familiar sight, and in winter you can often catch glimpses of the northern lights. Common areas are attractively decorated with European antiques. Two rooms in the main lodge share a bathroom; rooms in the guest house each have a private deck overlooking the wide beach at this adult-oriented lodge. ⊠ *12291 Tow Hill Rd. (Box 227, Masset V0T 1M0),* ☎ *250/626–3333 or 800/661–0019,* FAX *250/626–3303,* WEB *www.alaskaviewlodge.com. 4 rooms, 2 with bath. Beach, hiking; no room TVs, no kids, no smoking. MC, V. BP.*

$ ⊡ **Dorothy and Mike's Guest House.** Folk art, batiks and other treasures from their travels decorate the pretty rooms at this view-blessed B&B on a hill overlooking the village. Hand-built of hand-milled cedar, the house feels spacious and comfortable, with high ceilings and hardwood floors. You can kick back in the book-lined common room, on either of the two water-view decks, or in the whimsical driftwood gazebo in the garden. ⊠ *3125 2nd Ave., Queen Charlotte V0T 1S0,* ☎ FAX *250/559—8439,* WEB *www.qcislands.net/doromike. 5 rooms, 2 with bath; 3 suites. Kitchenettes in some rooms, refrigerators in some rooms; no smoking. MC, V. BP.*

$ ⊡ **Spruce Point Lodge.** This cedar-sided building, encircled by a balcony, is right on the water's edge at the west end of Queen Charlotte, about 5½ km (3½ mi) from the ferry terminal at Skidegate. Rooms are bright and simple with modern pine furniture; the suite has a full kitchen. All rooms open onto the veranda, providing views of the water and passing eagles. An on-site tour company, Queen Charlotte Adventures, rents kayaks and offers a range of tours. ⊠ *609 6th St. (Box 735, Queen Charlotte V0T 1S0),* ☎ FAX *250/559–8234,* WEB *www. qcislands.net/sprpoint. 6 rooms, 1 suite. Kitchenettes in some rooms, kitchen, refrigerators, cable TV, boating; no smoking. MC, V. CP.*

## Outdoor Activities and Sports

**Queen Charlotte Adventures** (☎ 250/559–8990 or 800/668–4288, WEB www.qcislands.net/qciadven), in Queen Charlotte, rents kayaks and leads a variety of kayak, boat, and land tours around the islands.

## Shopping

The Haida carve valuable figurines from argillite, a variety of soft, black slate. Other island specialties are silk-screen prints and silver jewelry. In Queen Charlotte, the wacky-looking **Rainbows Gallery** (⊠ 3201 3rd Ave., ☎ 250/559–8420) is hard to miss, with its Tree of Lost Soles (old shocs) and tangle of fishing floats outside. Inside is an excellent selection of original Haida Art, including paintings and argillite (black slate) carvings. **Bill Ellis Books** (✉ 720 Hwy. 33, ☎ 250/559–4681) has one of the best collections of Northwest Coast First Nations books to be found anywhere. In Old Masset, at the islands' north end, **Sarah's Haida Arts and Jewelry** (✉ 387 Eagle Rd., ☎ 250/626–5560) specializes in local crafts, carvings, and jewelry.

# BRITISH COLUMBIA A TO Z

*To research prices, get advice from other travelers, and book travel arrangements, visit www.fodors.com.*

### AIR TRAVEL

Air Canada Jazz and WestJet connect Vancouver with most major towns in the province. Kenmore Air Harbour has summer floatplane service from Seattle to Pender Harbour, Desolation Sound, and Salt Spring Island. Northwest Seaplanes offers summer floatplane service between Seattle and fishing lodges in the Inside Passage.

Amigo Airways flies from Vancouver to all the southern Gulf Islands. Harbour Air Seaplanes provides regular service from Victoria, Nanaimo, and Vancouver to the Southern Gulf Islands. Harbour Air also runs scheduled floatplane service from Prince Rupert to Sandspit, Masset, and Queen Charlotte City.

Pacific Coastal Airline has scheduled and charter service from Vancouver International Airport to the Sunshine Coast, Inside Passage, and Vancouver Island. Pacific Spirit/Tofino Air has scheduled floatplane service from Vancouver International Airport to all southern Gulf Islands. Seair Seaplanes flies from Vancouver to Salt Spring Island.

➤ AIRLINES AND CONTACTS: **Air Canada Jazz** (☎ 888/247–2262, WEB www.aircanada.ca). **Amigo Airways** (☎ 250/758–7450 or 866/692–6440, WEB www.amigoairways.ca). **Harbour Air Seaplanes** (☎ southern routes: 604/274–1277 or 800/665–0212; Prince Rupert–Queen Charlotte Island routes: 250/627–1341; 800/689–4234 in B.C. only; WEB www.harbour-air.com). **Kenmore Air Harbour** (☎ 425/486–1257 or 800/543–9595, WEB www.kenmoreair.com). **Northwest Seaplanes** (☎ 800/690–0086, WEB www.nwseaplanes.com). **Pacific Coastal Airlines** (☎ 604/273–8666 or 800/663–2872; for floatplane services: 250/949–6477 or 800/343–5963, WEB www.pacificcoastal.com). **Pacific Spirit/Tofino Air** (☎ 250/247–9992 or 800/665–2359, WEB www.tofinoair.ca). **Seair Seaplanes** (☎ 604/273–8900 or 800/447–3247, WEB www.seairseaplanes.com). **WestJet Airlines** (☎ 800/538–5696, WEB www.westjet.com).

### AIRPORTS

British Columbia is served by Vancouver International Airport. There are domestic airports in most cities.

➤ AIRPORT INFORMATION: **Vancouver International Airport** (☎ 604/207–7077, WEB www.yvr.ca).

### AIRPORT TRANSFERS

LimoJet Gold runs a limousine service from Vancouver Airport to Whistler. Perimeter Whistler Express has daily service from Vancouver International Airport to Whistler (14 times a day in ski season, with slightly fewer trips in the summer). Perimeter has a ticket booth at domestic arrivals Level 2 and one at the airport's international receiving lounge. The fare is around $59 one-way; reservations are highly recommended.

➤ TAXIS AND SHUTTLES: **LimoJet Gold** (☎ 604/273–1331 or 800/278–8742, WEB www.limojetgold.com). **Perimeter Whistler Express** (☎ 604/266–5386 in Vancouver; 604/905–0041 in Whistler; WEB www.perimeterbus.com).

## BOAT AND FERRY TRAVEL

### SUNSHINE COAST

BC Ferries has passenger and vehicle service between Horseshoe Bay north of Vancouver and Langdale on the Sunshine Coast; Earls Cove to Saltery Bay (these towns are about halfway up the coast); and Powell River on the coast to Comox on Vancouver Island. The company also has service to Texada Island off the coast of Powell River. These routes cannot be reserved. If you're planning to combine travel to the Sunshine Coast and Vancouver Island, ask BC Ferries about discount packages.

### THE GULF ISLANDS

BC Ferries provides service to Galiano, Mayne, Pender, Saturna, and Salt Spring islands from Tsawwassen (vehicle reservations area recommended and are required on some sailings) and from Swartz Bay, on Vancouver Island (reservations are not accepted). Salt Spring Island can also be reached from Crofton on Vancouver Island. The northern Gulf Islands, including Gabriola, Denman, Hornby, Quadra, and Cortes, can be reached from ports on Vancouver Island.

On Salt Spring Island the *Queen of de Nile* runs from Moby's Marine Pub and Ganges Marina to Ganges town center. Gulf Islands Water Taxi runs passengers and bicycles between Salt Spring, Mayne, Pender, and Galiano islands. The boats run Wednesday and Saturday in summer, and on weekdays the rest of the year. Reservations are recommended.

### THE NORTH COAST

BC Ferries sails along the Inside Passage from Port Hardy to Prince Rupert (year-round) and from Port Hardy to Bella Coola (summer only). Reservations are required for vehicles and recommended for foot passengers.

### QUEEN CHARLOTTE ISLANDS

The *Queen of Prince Rupert,* a BC Ferries ship, sails six times a week in July and August, reducing to three times a week in the winter. The crossing from Prince Rupert to Skidegate, near Queen Charlotte on Graham Island, takes about seven hours. High-season fares are $23.50 per adult passenger and $86.50 per vehicle. Some sailings are overnight; cabins are available for an additional $40 to $45. Reservations are required for vehicles and recommended for foot passengers; it's a good idea to book as early as possible, as summer sailings fill quickly. BC Ferries also connects Skidegate Landing to Alliford Bay on Moresby Island (near the airport at Sandspit). Access to smaller islands is by boat or air; make plans in advance through a travel agent.

### THE KOOTENAYS

On the east side of Kootenay Lake, Crawford Bay can be accessed by a scenic 45-minute car ferry from Balfour, north of Nelson.
➤ BOAT AND FERRY INFORMATION: **BC Ferries** (☎ 250/386–3431; 888/223–3779 in B.C. and Alberta; WEB www.bcferries.com). **Gulf Islands Water Taxi** (☎ 250/537–2510). **Kootenay Lake Ferry** (☎ 250/229–4215). *Queen of de Nile* (☎ no phone; contact Ganges Tourist Info Centre for details: 250/537–5252).

## BUS TRAVEL

Greyhound Canada connects destinations throughout British Columbia with cities and towns all along the Pacific Northwest coast. The company has service to Whistler from the downtown Vancouver depot every few hours. West Vancouver Blue Buses provides direct service from downtown Vancouver to Horseshoe Bay.

Whistler transit operates a free public transit system that loops throughout the village, and paid public transit serves the whole valley. Malaspina Coach Lines has routes from Vancouver to towns on the Sunshine Coast. Sunshine Coast Transit serves towns between Langdale and Halfmoon Bay on the Sunshine Coast.

➤ BUS INFORMATION: **Downtown Vancouver Depot** (✉ 1150 Station St., ☎ no phone). **Greyhound Canada** (☎ 604/482–8747 or 800/661–8747, WEB www.greyhound.com). **Malaspina Coach Lines** (☎ 877/227–8287). **Sunshine Coast Transit** (☎ 604/885–3234). **West Vancouver Blue Buses** (☎ 604/985–7777). **Whistler Transit** (☎ 604/932–4020).

## CAR RENTAL
Most major agencies, including Avis, Budget, Enterprise, National Tilden, Thrifty, and Hertz, serve cities in the province. With Vancouver All-Terrain Adventures you can charter a four-wheel-drive Suburban from the Vancouver airport or downtown Vancouver to Whistler. The vehicles travel regardless of the weather and can stop for sightseeing along the way. The cost is $325 each way for up to seven passengers.

➤ LOCAL AGENCY: **Marine Drive Car Rentals** (☎ 250/537–9100 or 250/537–6409, WEB www.saltspring.com/rentals) rents cars on Salt Spring Island. **Vancouver All-Terrain Adventures** (☎ 604/984–2374 or 888/754–5601, WEB www.all-terrain.com).

## CAR TRAVEL
Driving time from Seattle to Vancouver is about three hours by I–5 and Highway 99. From other Canadian regions, three main routes lead into British Columbia: through Sparwood, in the south, Highway 3; from Jasper and Banff, in the central region, Highways 1 and 5; and through Dawson Creek, in the north, Highways 2 and 97.

Highway 99, also known as the Sea to Sky Highway, connects Vancouver to Whistler and continues to Lillooet in the interior. The Trans-Canada Highway (Highway 1) connects Vancouver with Kamloops and points east via the Fraser Canyon. Highway 3 winds along the province's southern edge, from Hope to the Rockies. The Coquihalla Highway (Highway 5), a toll road ($10 for cars and vans) linking Hope and Merritt, is the fastest route to the interior. Highway 101, the Pan-American Highway, serves the Sunshine Coast from Langdale to Lund. Highway 97, the Cariboo Highway, links Kamloops to Dawson Creek, where it becomes the Alaska Highway. Highway 16 cuts east–west across the north, linking Jasper to Prince Rupert. Highway 37, the Stewart Cassiar Highway, travels through the northwest, linking Highway 16 to the Alaska Highway. Highway 20, the Freedom Highway, is a steep, winding, partially paved route linking Williams Lake to Bella Coola on the coast.

BC Highways has recorded highway reports.
➤ CONTACTS: **BC Highways** (☎ 900/565–4997; 75¢ a minute). **Inquiry BC** (☎ 800/663–7867 in B.C.; 604/660–2421 in Vancouver and outside B.C.).

## EMERGENCIES
A few areas do not have 911 service, so if you don't get immediate response, dial "0." British Columbia has many hospitals, including Kelowna General Hospital, Lady Minto Hospital in Ganges on Salt

Spring Island, Prince George Regional Hospital, and Royal Inland Hospital in Kamloops.

➤ CONTACTS: **Ambulance, fire, police, poison control** (☎ 911 or 0).
➤ HOSPITALS: **Kelowna General Hospital** (✉ 2268 Pandosy St., ☎ 250/862–4000). **Lady Minto Hospital** (✉ 135 Crofton Rd., Ganges, Salt Spring Island, ☎ 250/538–4800). **Prince George Regional Hospital** (✉ 2000 15th Ave., ☎ 250/565–2000; 250/565–2202 emergencies). **Royal Inland Hospital** (✉ 311 Columbia St., Kamloops, ☎ 250/374–5111).

## OUTDOORS AND SPORTS

### FISHING

Separate licenses are required for saltwater and freshwater fishing. Both are available at sporting-goods stores, government-agency offices, and most fishing lodges and charter-boat companies. A one-day license for nonresidents costs $16 for freshwater fishing and $7.50 for saltwater fishing. Additional fees apply for salmon fishing. For information about saltwater-fishing regulations, contact Fisheries and Oceans Canada or pick up a free *Sport Fishing Guide,* available at most tourist-information centers, or visit www.sportfishing.bc.ca. Hello B.C. has brochures on freshwater and saltwater fishing.

➤ CONTACTS: **Fisheries and Oceans Canada** (☎ 604/666–2828; 877/320–3467 salmon regulations; WEB www-comm.pac.dfo-mpo.gc.ca). **Hello B.C.** (☎ 800/435–5622, WEB www.hellobc.com).

### GOLF

There are courses throughout the region, though Whistler and the Okanagan are the most popular golf destinations. Most courses are open April to mid-October, with greens fees ranging from about $80 to $115, including a cart. Whistler courses, usually open May to late September, are pricier, with greens fees of $125–$205.

You can arrange advance tee-time bookings at courses in Kelowna and Whistler by calling Last Minute Golf. The company matches golfers and courses, sometimes at substantial greens-fee discounts.
➤ CONTACT: **Last Minute Golf** (☎ 604/878–1833 or 800/684–6344, WEB www.lastminutegolfbc.com).

### HIKING

➤ CONTACT: **B.C. Parks** (✉ Box 9398, Station Provincial Government, Victoria V8W 9M9, ☎ no phone, WEB www.bcparks.ca).

### HELI- AND SNOW-CAT-SKIING

For a list of helicopter- and Snow-Cat-skiing operators in the province, contact the BC Helicopter and Snowcat Skiing Operators Association.
➤ CONTACT: **BC Helicopter and Snowcat Skiing Operators Association** (☎ 250/542–9020).

## TOURS

### ADVENTURE TRIPS

Bluewater Adventures has 8- to 10-day sailing and natural history tours of the Central Coast, Johnstone Strait, and the Queen Charlotte Islands. Canadian River Expeditions specializes in multiday wilderness rafting expeditions on the Chilcotin, Fraser, Babine, Skeena, and Tatshenshini. Ecosummer Expeditions has guided multiday sea-kayaking and sailing trips to the Gulf Islands, the Inside Passage, Johnstone Strait, and the Queen Charlotte Islands, including an inn-to-inn kayaking trip in the Gulf Islands. Some trips involve both sailing and kayaking.

Fraser River Raft Expeditions, with bases in Yale and Lytton in the Fraser Canyon, offers a range of day trips and longer expeditions on several rivers. Fresh Tracks Canada has dozens of outdoor-adventure trips around the province, including hiking, kayaking, river-rafting, rail journeys, and sailing adventures. Gabriola Cycle and Kayak run multiday paddles to the Queen Charlottes. Hyak Wilderness Adventures, with bases in Lytton and Chilliwack, picks up at Vancouver hotels for rafting on the Chilliwack and Thompson rivers.

Kanata Adventure Specialists, based in Clearwater, operates multiday guided hiking, riding, and canoeing trips in Wells Gray Provincial Park and canoeing and riding trips in the Bowron Lakes. Dogsledding, snowmobiling, snowshoeing, and skiing trips are run in winter.

Ocean West Expeditions conducts multiday camping and lodge-based kayaking tours to the Gulf Islands, Johnstone Strait, and Desolation Sound.

➤ FEES AND SCHEDULES: **Bluewater Adventures** (☎ 604/980–3800 or 888/877–1770). **Canadian River Expeditions** (☎ 604/938–6651 or 800/898–7238, WEB www.canriver.com). **Ecosummer Expeditions** (☎ 250/674–0102 or 800/465–8884, WEB www.ecosummer.com). **Fraser River Raft Expeditions Ltd.** (☎ 604/863–2336 or 800/363–7238, WEB www.fraserraft.com). **Fresh Tracks Canada** (☎ 604/737–8743 or 800/667–4744, WEB www.freshtracks.ca). **Gabriola Cycle and Kayak** (☎ 250/247–8277, WEB www.gck.ca). **Hyak Wilderness Adventures** (☎ 604/734–8622 or 800/663–7238, WEB www.hyak.com). **Kanata Adventure Specialists** (☎ 250/674–2774 or 866/452–6282, WEB www. canadian-adventures.com). **Ocean West Expeditions** (☎ 800/660–0051, WEB www.ocean-west.com).

### HELICOPTER TOURS

Blackcomb Helicopters flies year-round flightseeing tours over Whistler's stunning mountains and glaciers. In summer, it offers heli-hiking, -biking, -fishing, -picnics, and even heli-weddings.

➤ FEES AND SCHEDULES: **Blackcomb Helicopters** (☎ 604/938–1700 or 800/330–4354, WEB www.blackcombhelicopters.com).

### SIGHTSEEING TOURS

In summer, Glacier Transportation and Tours offer trolley tours around the Whistler area, with insights into history and ecology and tips on celebrity and wildlife spotting. In winter, it runs day trips to Vancouver for guided city tours and also offers outings to see NHL ice-hockey games in Vancouver.

Gold Safari Tours runs sightseeing van tours from Quesnel and Prince George to Barkerville and Wells; tours include gold panning and wildlife viewing. With Okanagan Limousine you can tour the wine area in chauffeur-driven style. Okanagan Wine Country Tours gives narrated wine-country tours. West Coast City and Nature Sightseeing offers a sightseeing tour to Whistler that allows you to stay over and return on your date of choice to Vancouver. The tours run year-round; the cost is about $73.

➤ FEES AND SCHEDULES: **Glacier Transportation and Tours** (☎ 604/932–7565 or 888/287–7488, WEB www.glaciercoachlines.com). **Gold Safari Tours** (☎ 250/994–3463 or 888/996–4653, WEB www.cariboojoy.com). **Okanagan Limousine** (☎ 250/717–5466 or 877/295–9373). **Okanagan Wine Country Tours** (☎ 250/868–9463 or 866/689–9463). **West Coast City and Nature Sightseeing** (☎ 877/451–1777; 604/451–1600 in Vancouver; WEB www.vancouversightseeing.com).

### TRAIN TOURS

Rocky Mountaineer RailTours is a luxury, catered train tour that travels across British Columbia from Vancouver to Jasper (in Alberta) and from Vancouver to Calgary via Banff.

BC Rail's luxurious *Whistler Northwind* train tour travels from North Vancouver to Prince George, between May and October. The train features fine Pacific Northwest cuisine, and all passenger cars are domed, providing 180-degree views of some of the province's best scenery. The *Northwind* tour can be combined with connections to VIA Rail for a circle tour.

➤ FEES AND SCHEDULES: **Rocky Mountaineer RailTours** (☎ 604/606–7200 or 800/665–7245, WEB www.rockymountaineer.com). **VIA Rail** (☎ 800/561–8630 in Canada; 800/561–3949 in the U.S.; WEB www.viarail.ca). **Whistler Northwind** (☎ 604/984–5246 or 800/663–8238, WEB www.whistlernorthwind.com).

## TRAIN TRAVEL

VIA Rail offers service between Vancouver and Jasper (in Alberta) and from Prince Rupert to Jasper with an overnight stop in Prince George.
➤ CONTACT: **VIA Rail** (☎ 800/561–8630 in Canada; 800/561–3949 in the U.S.; WEB www.viarail.ca).

## VISITOR INFORMATION

Hello B.C., run by the provincial ministry of tourism, has information about the province. The principal regional tourist offices are as follows: Cariboo, Chilcotin, Coast Tourism Association; Northern British Columbia Tourism Association, for information on the Queen Charlotte Islands and northern British Columbia; Northern Rockies, Alaska Highway Tourism Association for information on northeastern British Columbia; Thompson Okanagan Tourism Association; Vancouver, Coast & Mountains Tourism Region for information about the Coast Mountain Circle and the Sunshine Coast. Many towns in the region also have visitor information centers, though not all are open year-round.
➤ REGIONAL TOURIST INFORMATION: **Cariboo, Chilcotin, Coast Tourism Association** (✉ 118A N. 1st Ave., Williams Lake, ☎ 250/392–2226 or 800/663–5885, WEB www.landwithoutlimits.com). **Hello B.C.** (☎ 888/435–5622, WEB www.hellobc.com). **Northern British Columbia Tourism Association** (✉ 850 River Rd. [Box 2373, Prince George V2N 2S6], ☎ 250/561–0432 or 800/663–8843, WEB www.northernbctravel.com). **Northern Rockies, Alaska Highway Tourism Association** (✉ 9923 96th Ave., Fort St. John, ☎ 250/785–2544 or 888/785–2544, WEB www.hellonorth.com). **Thompson Okanagan Tourism Association** (✉ 1332 Water St., Kelowna, ☎ 250/860–5999 or 800/567–2275, WEB www.thompsonokanagan.com). **Vancouver, Coast & Mountains Tourism Region** (✉ 250–1508 W. 2nd Ave., Vancouver, ☎ 604/739–9011 or 800/667–3306, WEB www.vcmbc.com).
➤ LOCAL TOURIST INFORMATION: **Hope Visitor Info Centre** (✉ 919 Water Ave., off Hwy. 1, ☎ 604/869–2021). **Penticton Visitors Information Centre** (✉ 888 Westminster Ave. W, ☎ 250/493–4055 or 800/663–5052). **Powell River Visitors Bureau** (✉ 4690 Marine Ave., ☎ 604/485–4701 or 877/817–8669). **Prince Rupert Visitor Info Centre** (✉ 100–215 Cow Bay Rd., ☎ 250/624–5637 or 800/667–1994). **Queen Charlotte Island Visitor Information Centre** (✉ 3220 Wharf St., Queen Charlotte, ☎ 250/559–8316; ✉ 1 Airport Rd., in the airport terminal, Sandspit, ☎ 250/637–5362; ✉ Hwy. 16, Masset, ☎ 250/626–3982; WEB www.qcinfo.com). **Salt Spring Island Visitor Information Centre** (✉ 121 Lower Ganges Rd., ☎ 250/537–5252 or 866/216–2936, WEB www.saltspringtoday.com). **Terrace Visitor Information Centre** (✉ 4511 Keith Ave., Hwy. 16, ☎ 250/635–2063, WEB www.terracechamber.ca). **Tourism Kelowna** (✉ 544 Harvey Ave., ☎ 250/861–1515 or 800/663–4345, WEB www.tourismkelowna.org). **Tourism Prince George** (✉ 1198 Victoria St., ☎ 250/562–3700 or 800/668–7646, WEB www.tourismpg.bc.ca). **Tourism Whistler** (✉ 4010 Whistler Way, ☎ 604/932–4222; 604/664–5625 in Vancouver; 800/944–7853 in the U.S. and Canada; WEB www.mywhistler.com). **Whistler Activity and Information Center** (✉ 4010 Whistler Way, ☎ 604/932–2394).

# INDEX

# Fodor's Key to the Guides

America's guidebook leader publishes guides for every kind of traveler. Check out our many series and find your perfect match.

**Fodor's Gold Guides**
America's favorite travel-guide series offers the most detailed insider reviews of hotels, restaurants, and attractions in all price ranges, plus great background information, smart tips, and useful maps.

**Fodor's Road Guide USA**
Big guides for a big country—the most comprehensive guides to America's roads, packed with places to stay, eat, and play across the U.S.A. Just right for road warriors, family vacationers, and cross-country trekkers.

**COMPASS AMERICAN GUIDES**
Stunning guides from top local writers and photographers, with gorgeous photos, literary excerpts, and colorful anecdotes. A must-have for culture mavens, history buffs, and new residents.

**Fodor's CITYPACKS**
Concise city coverage with a foldout map. The right choice for urban travelers who want everything under one cover.

**Fodor's EXPLORING GUIDES**
Hundreds of color photos bring your destination to life. Lively stories lend insight into the culture, history, and people.

**Fodor's POCKET GUIDES**
For travelers who need only the essentials. The best of Fodor's in pocket-size packages for just $9.95.

**Fodor's To Go**
Credit-card–size, magnetized color microguides that fit in the palm of your hand—perfect for "stealth" travelers or as gifts.

**Fodor's FLASHMAPS**
Every resident's map guide. 60 easy-to-follow maps of public transit, parks, museums, zip codes, and more.

**Fodor's CITYGUIDES**
Sourcebooks for living in the city: Thousands of in-the-know listings for restaurants, shops, sports, nightlife, and other city resources.

**Fodor's AROUND THE CITY WITH KIDS**
68 great ideas for family days, recommended by resident parents. Perfect for exploring in your own backyard or on the road.

**Fodor's ESCAPES**
Fill your trip with once-in-a-lifetime experiences, from ballooning in Chianti to overnighting in the Moroccan desert. These full-color dream books point the way.

**Fodor's FYI**
Get tips from the pros on planning the perfect trip. Learn how to pack, fly hassle-free, plan a honeymoon or cruise, stay healthy on the road, and travel with your baby.

**Fodor's Languages for Travelers**
Practice the local language before hitting the road. Available in phrase books, cassette sets, and CD sets.

*Karen Brown's Guides*
Engaging guides to the most charming inns and B&Bs in the U.S.A. and Europe, with easy-to-follow inn-to-inn itineraries.

*Baedeker's* Guides
Comprehensive guides, trusted since 1829, packed with A–Z reviews and star ratings.

At bookstores everywhere.　　　　　www.fodors.com/books